Innovation in Health Informatics

Innovation in Health Informatics
A Smart Healthcare Primer

Edited by

Miltiadis D. Lytras
Effat College of Engineering, Effat University, Jeddah, Saudi Arabia

Akila Sarirete
Effat College of Engineering, Effat University, Jeddah, Saudi Arabia

Series Editor
Miltiadis D. Lytras
Effat College of Engineering, Effat University, Jeddah, Saudi Arabia

Anna Visvizi
Deree Cllege — The American College of Greece, Greece;
Effat College of Business, Effat University, Jeddah, Saudi Arabia

Ernesto Damiani
University of Milan, Italy; Khalifa University, UAE

ELSEVIER

ACADEMIC PRESS
An imprint of Elsevier

Academic Press is an imprint of Elsevier
125 London Wall, London EC2Y 5AS, United Kingdom
525 B Street, Suite 1650, San Diego, CA 92101, United States
50 Hampshire Street, 5th Floor, Cambridge, MA 02139, United States
The Boulevard, Langford Lane, Kidlington, Oxford OX5 1GB, United Kingdom

Notices
Knowledge and best practice in this field are constantly changing. As new research and experience broaden our
understanding, changes in research methods, professional practices, or medical treatment may become
necessary.

Practitioners and researchers must always rely on their own experience and knowledge in evaluating and using
any information, methods, compounds, or experiments described herein. In using such information or
methods they should be mindful of their own safety and the safety of others, including parties for whom they
have a professional responsibility.

To the fullest extent of the law, neither the Publisher nor the authors, contributors, or editors, assume any
liability for any injury and/or damage to persons or property as a matter of products liability, negligence or
otherwise, or from any use or operation of any methods, products, instructions, or ideas contained in the
material herein.

British Library Cataloguing-in-Publication Data
A catalogue record for this book is available from the British Library

Library of Congress Cataloging-in-Publication Data
A catalog record for this book is available from the Library of Congress

ISBN: 978-0-12-819043-2

For Information on all Academic Press publications
visit our website at https://www.elsevier.com/books-and-journals

Publisher: Stacy Masucci
Senior Acquisition Editor: Rafael E. Teixeira
Editorial Project Manager: Sara Pianavilla
Production Project Manager: Kiruthika Govindaraju
Cover Designer: Greg Harris

Typeset by MPS Limited, Chennai, India

Contents

Chapter 2: Syndromic surveillance using web data: a systematic review 39

Loukas Samaras, Elena García-Barriocanal and Miguel-Angel Sicilia

Chapter 5: Human activity recognition using machine learning methods in a smart healthcare environment *123*

Abdulhamit Subasi, Kholoud Khateeb, Tayeb Brahimi and Akila Sarirete

Chapter 6: Application of machine learning and image processing for detection of breast cancer *145*

*Muhammad Kashif, Kaleem Razzaq Malik, Sohail Jabbar
and Junaid Chaudhry*

Chapter 7: Toward information preservation in healthcare systems *163*

Omar El Zarif and Ramzi A. Haraty

Section C Emerging technologies and systems for smart healthcare 187

Chapter 8: Security and privacy solutions for smart healthcare systems 189

Yang Lu and Richard O. Sinnott

Chapter 9: Cloud-based health monitoring framework using smart sensors and smartphone 217

Abdulhamit Subasi, Lejla Bandic and Saeed Mian Qaisar

Karla Maria Carneiro Rolim, Mírian Caliópe Dantas Pinheiro,
Plácido Rogério Pinheiro, Mirna Albuquerque Frota,
José Eurico de Vasconcelos Filho, Izabela de Sousa Martins,
Maria Solange Nogueira dos Santos and
Firmina Hermelinda Saldanha Albuquerque

Michael Kouroupis, Nikolaos Korfiatis and James Cornford

Chapter 12: Virtual reality and sensors for the next generation medical systems ...279

*Félix Mata, Miguel Torres-Ruiz, Roberto Zagal-Flores and
Marco Moreno-Ibarra*

**Chapter 13: Portable smart healthcare solution to eye examination for diabetic
retinopathy detection at an earlier stage 305**

Nighat Mir, Mohammad A.U. Khan and Mome Gul Hussain

Chapter 14: Improved nodule detection in chest X-rays using principal component analysis filters

Mohammad A.U. Khan, Nighat Mir and Fahad Hameed Ahmad

Chapter 15: Characterizing internet of medical things/personal area networks landscape

Adil Rajput and Tayeb Brahimi

Section D Social Issues and policy making for smart healthcare 373

Chapter 16: Threats to patients' privacy in smart healthcare environment 375

Samara M. Ahmed and Adil Rajput

Chapter 17: Policy implications for smart healthcare: the international collaboration dimension 395

Miltiadis D. Lytras, Akila Sarirete and Vassilios Stasinopoulos

List of contributors

Fahad Hameed Ahmad College of Engineering, Effat University, Jeddah, Saudi Arabia

Samara M. Ahmed College of Medicine, King Abdulaziz University, Jeddah, Saudi Arabia

Firmina Hermelinda Saldanha Albuquerque MSc. in Nursing from the Graduate Program in Collective Health of the University of Fortaleza (PPGSC/UNIFOR), Fortaleza, Brazil

Lejla Bandic International Burch University, Faculty of Engineering and Information Technologies, Francuske Revolucije bb. Ilidza, Sarajevo, Bosnia and Herzegovina

Tayeb Brahimi Natural Sciences, Mathematics, and Technology Unit, College of Engineering, Effat University, Jeddah, Saudi Arabia

Junaid Chaudhry College of Security and Intelligence, Embry-Riddle Aeronautical University, Prescott, AZ, United States

James Cornford Norwich Business School, University of East Anglia, Norwich, United Kingdom

Izabela de Sousa Martins MSc. in Technology and Innovation in Nursing, University of Fortaleza, Brazil (MPTIE/UNIFOR), Fortaleza, Brazil

José Eurico de Vasconcelos Filho DSc in Computer Science from the Pontifical Catholic University of Rio de Janeiro (PUC/RJ). Coordinator of the Laboratory of Innovation in ICT of the University of Fortaleza (NATI/UNIFOR). Professor of Computer Engineering at UNIFOR. Professor of the Professional Master's Degree in Technology and Innovation in Nursing (MPTIE/UNIFOR). Director of Citizenship and Digital Culture of the Coordination of Science Technology and Innovation of the Municipality of Fortaleza (CITINOVA/PMF), University of Fortaleza (UNIFOR), Fortaleza, Brazil

Maria Solange Nogueira dos Santos MSc. in Technology and Innovation in Nursing, University of Fortaleza, Brazil (MPTIE/UNIFOR), Fortaleza, Brazil

Omar El Zarif Department of Computer Science and Mathematics, Lebanese American University, Beirut, Lebanon

Mirna Albuquerque Frota DSc in Nursing from the Federal University of Ceará (UFC), Brazil. Full Professor of the Undergraduate Nursing Course of the University of Fortaleza (UNIFOR). Coordinator of the Graduate Program in Collective Health (PPGSC/UNIFOR). Professor of the Professional Master's Degree in Technology and Innovation in Nursing (MPTIE/UNIFOR), University of Fortaleza (UNIFOR), Fortaleza, Brazil

Elena García-Barriocanal Computer Science Department, University of Alcalá, Ctra. De Barcelona km. 33.6, 28871 Alcalá de Henares, Spain

Ramzi A. Haraty Department of Computer Science and Mathematics, Lebanese American University, Beirut, Lebanon

Mome Gul Hussain College of Engineering, Effat University, Jeddah, Saudi Arabia

Sohail Jabbar Department of Computer Science, National Textile University, Faisalabad, Pakistan

Muhammad Kashif Department of Computer Science, Air University Multan Campus, Multan, Pakistan

Mohammad A.U. Khan College of Engineering, Effat University, Jeddah, Saudi Arabia

Kholoud Khateeb Information Systems Department, College of Engineering, Effat University, Jeddah, Saudi Arabia

Nikolaos Korfiatis Norwich Business School, University of East Anglia, Norwich, United Kingdom

Michael Kouroupis Department of Ophthalmology, The Queen Elizabeth Hospital NHS Foundation Trust, King's Lynn, United Kingdom

Yang Lu School of Computing and Information Systems, The University of Melbourne, Australia

Miltiadis D. Lytras Deree College—The American College of Greece, Athens, Greece; Effat College of Engineering, Effat University, Jeddah, Saudi Arabia

Kaleem Razzaq Malik Department of Computer Science, Air University Multan Campus, Multan, Pakistan

Félix Mata Instituto Politécnico Nacional, UPALM Zacatenco, Mexico City, Mexico

Nighat Mir College of Engineering, Effat University, Jeddah, Saudi Arabia

Marco Moreno-Ibarra Instituto Politécnico Nacional, UPALM Zacatenco, Mexico City, Mexico

Paraskevi Papadopoulou Deree College—The American College of Greece, Athens, Greece

Mírian Calíope Dantas Pinheiro DSc in Nursing from the Federal University of Rio de Janeiro (UFRJ), Brazil. Full Professor of the Undergraduate Nursing Course of the University of Fortaleza (UNIFOR). Professor of the Professional Master's Degree in Technology and Innovation in Nursing (MPTIE/UNIFOR), University of Fortaleza (UNIFOR), Fortaleza, Brazil

Plácido Rogério Pinheiro DSc in Systems Engineering and Computing from the Federal University of Rio de Janeiro (UFRJ). Coordinator of the Graduate Program in Applied Informatics of the University of Fortaleza (PPGIA/UNIFOR), Fortaleza, Brazil

Saeed Mian Qaisar Electrical and Computer Engineering Department, College of Engineering, Effat University, Jeddah, Saudi Arabia

Adil Rajput Department of Computer Science, College of Engineering, Effat University, Jeddah, Saudi Arabia; Information Systems Department, Effat University An Nazlah Al Yamaniyyah, Jeddah, Saudi Arabia

Karla Maria Carneiro Rolim DSc in Nursing from the Federal University of Ceará (UFC), Brazil. Full Professor of the Undergraduate Nursing Course of the University of Fortaleza (UNIFOR). Professor of the Graduate Program in Collective Health (PPGSC/UNIFOR). Coordinator of the Professional Master's Degree in Technology and Innovation in Nursing (MPTIE/UNIFOR), University of Fortaleza (UNIFOR), Fortaleza, Brazil

Loukas Samaras Computer Science Department, University of Alcalá, Ctra. De Barcelona km. 33.6, 28871 Alcalá de Henares, Spain

Akila Sarirete Effat College of Engineering, Effat University, Jeddah, Saudi Arabia

Miguel-Angel Sicilia Computer Science Department, University of Alcalá, Ctra. De Barcelona km. 33.6, 28871 Alcalá de Henares, Spain

Richard O. Sinnott School of Computing and Information Systems, The University of Melbourne, Australia

Marco Spruit   Utrecht University, Utrecht, The Netherlands

Vassilios Stasinopoulos   Frederick University, Limmasol, Cyprus

Abdulhamit Subasi   Information Systems Department, College of Engineering, Effat University, Jeddah, Saudi Arabia

Miguel Torres-Ruiz   Instituto Politécnico Nacional, UPALM Zacatenco, Mexico City, Mexico

Sander van der Rijnst   Utrecht University, Utrecht, The Netherlands

Roberto Zagal-Flores   Instituto Politécnico Nacional, UPALM Zacatenco, Mexico City, Mexico

Preface

Innovation in Health Informatics: A Smart Healthcare Primer explains how the most recent advances in information and communication technologies have paved the way for new breakthroughs in healthcare. The book showcases current and prospective applications in a context defined by an imperative to deliver efficient, patient-centered, and sustainable healthcare systems. Topics discussed include big data, medical data analytics, artificial intelligence, machine learning, virtual and augmented reality, 5G and sensors, Internet of Things, nanotechnologies, and biotechnologies. Additionally, there is a discussion on social issues and policy-making for the implementation of smart healthcare.

This book is a valuable resource for undergraduate and graduate students, practitioners, researchers, clinicians, and data scientists who are interested in how to explore the intersections between bioinformatics and health informatics.

- Provides a holistic discussion on the new landscape of medical technologies, including big data, analytics, artificial intelligence, machine learning, virtual and augmented reality, 5G and sensors, Internet of Things, nanotechnologies, and biotechnologies.
- Presents a case study driven approach, with references to real-world applications and systems.
- Discusses topics with a research-oriented approach that aims to promote research skills and competencies of readers.

This volume covers a wide range of emerging topics and initiates a scientific dialogue for their contribution to *Next Generation Technology Driven Personalized Medicine and Smart Healthcare*. The entire discussion is organized around 4 sections and 17 chapters covering a demanding agenda for Healthcare Informatics.

Section A: Smart Healthcare in the era of Big Data and data science

Chapter 1, Smart Healthcare: emerging technologies, best practices, and sustainable policies

Miltiadis D. Lytras, Paraskevi Papadopoulou, and Akila Sarirete

Chapter 2, Syndromic surveillance using web data: a systematic review

Loukas Samaras, Elena García-Barriocanal, and Miguel-Angel Sicilia

Chapter 13, Portable smart healthcare solution to eye examination for diabetic retinopathy detection at an earlier stage

Nighat Mir, Mohammad A.U. Khan, and Mome Gul Hussain

Chapter 14, Improved nodule detection in chest x-rays using principle component analysis filters

Mohammad A.U. Khan, Nighat Mir, and Fahad Hameed Ahmad

Chapter 15, Characterizing Internet of Medical Things/Personal Area Networks landscape

Adil Rajput and Tayeb Brahimi

Section D: Social issues and policy-making for smart healthcare

Chapter 16, Threats to patients' privacy in smart healthcare environment

Samara M. Ahmed and Adil Rajput

Chapter 17, Policy implications for smart healthcare: the international collaboration dimension

Miltiadis D. Lytras Akila Sarirete, and Vassilios Stasinopoulos

We are proud for the intellectual outcome of a collaborative and synergetic process that took more than 16 months to be delivered and for the impact of our work. We do hope that our readers will value this first volume and will join us also in the next two forthcoming editions of this series related to HealthCare Big Data Analytics and applications of Artificial Intelligence and Machine Learning for Personalized Medicine.

Innovations in healthcare informatics are about bringing social impact to the high-level interventions of technology in healthcare and for improving the quality of life and healthcare worldwide. It is a privilege for all of us that worked in this edition to promote a global vision for a better world for all.

The Editors
Miltiadis D. Lytras and Akila Sarirete

Acknowledgments

This edited volume is the first volume in our, recently launched, Elsevier book series entitled *Next Generation Technology Driven Personalized Medicine and Smart Healthcare*. It brings together the wisdom, experience, and innovative knowledge; systems and applications of scholars; practitioners and researchers; and worldwide. This edited volume serves as a reference edition for all those interested in the latest developments of emerging technologies and their implications for personalized medicine and smart healthcare. We are confident that the next decade will feature a new era in technology-driven innovation in healthcare. We are grateful to the contributing authors, who responded to our invitation to join this project, and worked with commitment and professionalism, covering a wide, and interesting agenda of topics and research areas. We would like to thank them for their hard work and inspiration for the entire team. We are grateful to the publisher and the entire team that dealt with the book production process. Miltiadis dedicates this edited volume to his son Demetrios Lytras, who enrolled in the Medical School of Athens with exceptional performance in the relevant examinations.

The Editors
Miltiadis D. Lytras
Akila Sarirete

Smart Healthcare in the Era of Bid Data and Data Science

Smart Healthcare: emerging technologies, best practices, and sustainable policies

Miltiadis D. Lytras[1,2], Paraskevi Papadopoulou[1] and Akila Sarirete[2]
[1]*Deree College—The American College of Greece, Athens, Greece,* [2]*Effat College of Engineering, Effat University, Jeddah, Saudi Arabia*

1.1 Introduction

The integration of innovation within healthcare is a key aspect of the so-called next generation medical systems. Toward this direction the contribution of this volume is multifold. First, it demystifies the new wave of emerging and streamline technologies and uncovers the added value of their components. Second, it underlines a new policy-based era of health governance, since the integration of innovation within healthcare must be understood from the key stakeholders and needs to be implemented taking into account various limitations. Last but not least, innovation in healthcare must be seen as a human-centric process where complicated and sophisticated, distributed medical services and processes are utilized.

The adoption of advanced Healthcare Information Systems and Medical Informatics requires an integrated approach sensitive to various social, economic, political, and cultural factors. The challenges that the adoption and use of sophisticated information and communication technologies (ICTs) generate need to be considered too. Smart Data and Data Analytics along with cognitive computing are the promising technologies with great value added for the domain of healthcare.

The focus of this edited volume is to examine the social, economic, political, and cultural impacts, and challenges emerging from the use of sophisticated ICTs for patient-centric systems in healthcare. By offering a detailed comprehensive and comparative insight into diverse advances in ICT and their application across issues and domains, this edited volume occupies a unique position on the market. This is because it brings together not only a discussion on the most promising technologies and their current and prospective uses, but also dwells on managerial and policymaking challenges and opportunities this process creates.

Innovation in Health Informatics.
DOI: https://doi.org/10.1016/B978-0-12-819043-2.00001-0

1.2 Bridging innovative technologies and smart solutions in medicine and healthcare

Major advances and breakthroughs in science and technology are transforming our world. More specifically, incredible developments in biology and technology have broad ramifications in the ways the world population increases and how our health and life spans will be affected. An increased world population, of currently more than 7.7 billion people, together with the expected increasing life spans, which were made possible by scientific and technological advances, create new challenges. The High-level Political Forum on Sustainable Development is the central UN platform adopted at the United Nations on September 2015 as a plan of action for people, the planet as a whole and prosperity. It is expected that their goals and targets will stimulate action up to 2030. Within the 17 Sustainable Development Goals and 169 targets, Goal 3 aims to ensure healthy lives and promote well-being for all ages (United Nations, 2019). Healthcare sciences, therefore, will be essential for interpreting the genetic variation in comparison with the gene/environment interactions which seem to be at the core of most diseases and biological phenomena. Improved sanitary conditions and hygiene, the use of vaccines and antibiotics, improved understanding of diseases, and innovative treatments have helped keep many hereditary and infectious diseases in check. Moreover, improved home and work conditions have contributed to healthy aging and longer life spans as well as provided access to better quality food and nutrients. In fact, the booming population of older adults, in mostly the developed countries, is a testament to the incredible developments in science and technology. According to the World Bank, the public expenditure on healthcare in the EU could jump from 8% of GDP in 2000 to 14% in 2030. How effectively will we be able to explore such advances and innovations in regard to health both locally and globally? How will we manage to tackle our disease burden to improve our day-to-day well-being especially if in developed countries "The global population of people over 80 will be more than triple by 2050" and in the less-developed countries the youth profile will escalate? Will Europeans, for example, find ways to balance budgets and restrain spending and come up with a sustainable survival strategy for Europe's healthcare systems? Will all the children born in less-developed countries have access to clean water, good quality food, and receive good medical care?

We have already taken the first step toward tackling genetic and infectious diseases at the root. Largely we have managed to integrate genetic, environmental, and behavioral factors in the hope to prevent and treat illnesses and diseases. Many of the techniques used are still in their early stages, but the promise is remarkable. To a point, we have managed to strengthen prevention. We have also recognized the heterogeneity that exists among patients and various populations of the world. The ultimate goal would be to successfully make healthcare and community health services predictive, preventive, and personal.

1.2.1 From genomics to proteomics to bioinformatics and health informatics

The contribution of *genomics* to our understanding of disease and health has expanded significantly the last few years especially after the publication of the reference Human Genome in 2001. Genomics as an interdisciplinary field of biology aims at the collective characterization and quantification of genes focusing on their structure and function, and also evolution and mapping.

The next field that emerged is the field of *proteomics* which through gene expression directs the production of proteins with the assistance of enzymes and various types of RNA molecules and other translational factors. In turn, proteins, generally speaking, are structural components of cells, tissues, and organs, or serve as enzymes in most chemical reactions and carry signals in and between cells. With the advent of Next Generation Sequencing and other high throughput technologies, Whole Genome Sequencing became possible including Whole Exome Sequencing as well as Genome-Wide Association Studies. Similarly, *metabolomics* emerged as the scientific systematic study of chemical processes involving metabolites with their unique chemical fingerprints and metabolite profiles more like a snapshot of the physiological state of cells and of organisms.

Then came the use of the *exposome* in the practice of epidemiology. Wild in his 2005 paper stated, "At its most complete, the exposome encompasses life-course environmental exposures (including lifestyle factors), from the prenatal period onwards." Exposome has been defined as *the totality of exposure individuals experience over their lives and how those exposures affect health* (DeBord et al., 2016). The Exposome, could conceptually and practically speaking, provide a holistic view of human health and disease. Genome sequence information needs to be linked with information about our diets and nutrition including variation in metabolism; our behaviors and lifestyles; our disease profile and medications; and our microbial, chemical, and physical exposures to understand the environmental/genetic interactions that ultimately affect human health. Measuring the exposome though is a major challenge, yet, it is obvious it plays a critical role in understanding chronic disease formation and progression. Exposure assessments require the integration of different types of exposure information, and by managing to identify stressors and their actions we could improve our understanding of various diseases and ultimately improve disease prevention. All these advances in genomics and proteomics have triggered a revolution in discovery-based research. *Pharmacogenomics* became the study of genetic material in relationship with drug targets. Currently, there is growing attention toward personalized medicine and precision medicine. Systems biology facilitates our understanding of even the most complex biological systems such as the brain.

Bioinformatics became a highly interdisciplinary field of storing, retrieving, and analyzing large amounts of biological information. Bioinformatics deals with research data and uses it for research purposes, *medical informatics* deals with data from individual patients for the purposes of clinical management (diagnosis, treatment, and prevention), and *biomedical informatics* is the bridge between the two as it leads to effective use of biomedical data. The emerging advances of bioinformatics in fact and the need to improve healthcare and the management of Medical Systems have already contributed toward the establishment of better next generation medicine and medical systems by putting emphasis on improvement of prognosis, diagnosis, therapy, and prevention of diseases (Lytras & Papadopoulou, 2018).

Health informatics is another common term used. Health informatics is also known as clinical informatics, medical informatics, and biomedical informatics with the most inclusive term being biomedical informatics. Health informatics is the field of information science concerned with mainly the management of healthcare data and information. All these terms may cause confusion but it is useful to remember that in reality, technology serves as means of transportation, not of destination.

Health informatics, nevertheless, has helped to promote research collaborations of researchers from the field of Bioinformatics and Health Informatics together with administrators, clinicians, and data scientists. Having access to high-speed computers, mobile technology, voice recognition, and more, healthcare professionals have begun to examine ways to incorporating the latest computational intelligence with Big Data Analytics as well as Data Mining and Machine Learning Methodologies.

The increased need to improve healthcare, and the welfare of patients and people, in general, requires that we fast improve prognosis, diagnosis, and therapies to advance personalized medicine and targeted drug/gene therapy (Alyass, Turcotte, & Meyre, 2015; Chen, Qian, & Yan, 2013; Tenenbaum, 2016). Since technology is advancing faster then professionals can follow there is a new need for investing on education and translation of emerging technologies and the data/information they generate into healthcare information (Greene, Giffin, Greene, & Moore, 2015). There are lots of data but less information, knowledge, and wisdom. Information is data with meaning. Again, it is always up to Humans to provide knowledge and wisdom.

We expect that the *100,000 genome project* will help bridge the gaps between these disciplines by combining genomic sequence data with medical records and that this will be a groundbreaking resource on how to best interpret the data for the benefit of patients.

The original 4−5 Big Data Vs such as data volume, data velocity, data veracity, data validity, and data value (see Fig. 1.1; Papadopoulou, Lytras, & Marouli, 2018) were expanded to 10 Big Data Vs to include in addition data variability, data vulnerability, data volatility, data variety, and data variety (Firican, 2017). Those 10 Big Data characteristics are examined in terms of usefulness and importance as to which is the most decisive criterion turning data from big to smart as a real-time assistance for the improvement of

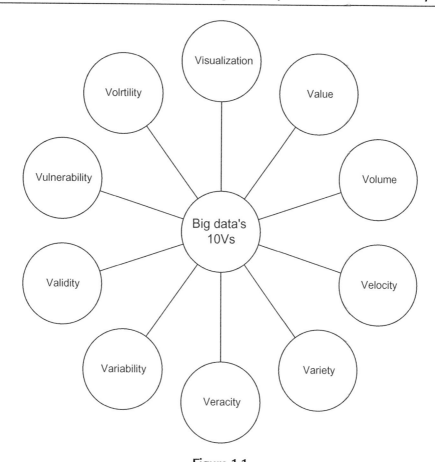

Figure 1.1
The 10 Vs of Big Data as they contribute to smart and wise data.

living conditions. Fig. 1.1 depicts the 10 Big Data Vs and main characteristics as they could apply to healthcare as well. For a more extensive coverage on the 10 Vs, see Firican (2017) and Suwinski et al. (2019). It is important to note that it is not enough to manage to filter structured or unstructured Big Data into smart data but to also use it to make wise decisions which will serve both the individual and society as a whole.

1.2.2 Ways of developing intelligent and personalized healthcare interventions

Massive amounts of Big Data both structured and unstructured have been collected in the healthcare industry. To filter Big Data and turn it into smart data is not an easy task. Even more so, to analyze it for insights that would lead to smarter operations and more efficient decision-making. Whether it is Big Data originating from smart sensors then to be sent to collection points and from there to analytic platforms within Internet of Thing (IoT) systems or Big Data that is processed waiting to be turned into actionable information is very challenging indeed.

Electronic health records (EHRs), for example, and multiple other healthcare information systems provide the ability and the need to collate and analyze large amounts of data to improve health and financial decisions.

As genetic information collection grows, datasets are huge (Big Data) and part of EHRs. Mining the Data becomes a major task. All large healthcare organizations will collect and analyze a variety of clinical, financial, and administrative data to make wise clinical and business decisions. Therefore Data Analytics is very important and it requires well-educated individuals. There is high need for Informaticians (or informaticists) who can manage to harness the power of information technology to expedite the transfer and analysis of data, leading to improved efficiencies and knowledge.

Here are some examples of top Healthcare innovations (https://getreferralmd.com/):

- Payer—Provider Analytics/Data Software
- Artificial Intelligence
- BlockChain for Healthcare
- Internet of Medical Things
- Patient Engagement
- Centralized Monitoring of Hospital Patients
- Gene Therapy for Inherited Retinal Diseases
- Hybrid Closed-Loop Insulin Delivery System
- Noninvasive Diabetes Monitoring
- 5G Mobile Technology

1.2.3 Advancing medicine and healthcare: insights and wise solutions

It is evident that the driving forces behind Health Informatics are strong. Intensive training is needed, which includes in addition to good understanding of biological systems, IT knowledge about networks and systems, usability, process reengineering, workflow analysis, and redesign. This should be followed by focusing on proper training and quality improvement, efficient project management, wise leadership, and teamwork so as to ensure medical excellence and proper implementation (see Fig. 1.2).

1.2.4 Ways of disseminating our healthcare experience

Health Informatics is a relatively new and exciting field with many new job opportunities including in the Academia world. Research in health informatics is being published at an increasing rate so hopefully new approaches and tools will be evaluated more often and more objectively.

Although technology holds great promise, it is not the solution for every problem facing medicine today. We must continue to focus on improved patient care as the single most important goal of this new field.

Table 1.1 outlines a number of ICT solutions and managerial issues pertaining to healthcare, the type of educational training, and citizen engagement.

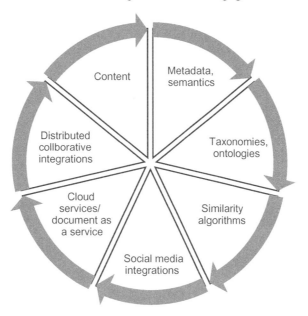

Figure 1.2
Content management resilient Smart Healthcare systems cluster.

Table 1.1: The utilization of these emerging technologies, toward healthcare services and applications.

ICT solutions	Education training	Managerial issues	Engage citizens
Invest in state-of-the-art technology which supports the provision of multidisciplinary, patient-centered services	Invest in Medical Infrastructure	Ensure wise leadership	Built in trust and also patient-centered attitude
Develop EHRs	Improve medical education	Improve healthcare quality (patient outcomes) resulting in improved patient safety	Communities to highlight and share "best HIT practices"
Patient portals	Train medical personnel	Increase ergonomics and reduce healthcare costs	Advance person-centered and self-managed health
Mobile technology	Train higher administration	Standardize medical care and focus on medical prevention and built wellness centers	Improve healthcare access with technologies such as telemedicine and online scheduling

(Continued)

Table 1.1: (Continued)

ICT solutions	Education training	Managerial issues	Engage citizens
Telemedicine	Teach health informatics	Address privacy and ethical concerns	Expanded medical care and coverage for the uninsured
Support the public health information network	Invest on expertise, as few have formal training in informatics	Expand financial resources	Develop behavioral risk factor surveillance systems
Improve interoperability between technologies	Foster research, scientific knowledge and innovation	Improve coordination and continuity of care	Improve the public services profile
Enhance nation's health IT and infrastructure	Develop Health Informatics curricula at the community college and university level	Increase healthcare efficiency and productivity	Ensure patient mobility
Share technologies	Establish International Medical and Academic Collaborations and Affiliations	Hospitals operate under the strictest international quality criteria	Inform citizens
BlockChain technologies	Train medical and healthcare personnel	Application of BlockChain technologies in the healthcare sector	Inform citizens

1.3 Visioning the future of resilient Smart Healthcare

The constitutional technological parts, of smart healthcare, including numerous emerging and streamline technologies, are summarized in the following table together with some policy implications that will be discussed further in Chapter 17, Policy implications for Smart Healthcare: the international collaboration dimension.

Technologies (ICT)	Policy and technology implications
Data warehouses	Interoperability of patients data worldwide
	Compliance of healthcare systems to GDPR
Robotics	Standardization
	Moral issues related to use of robotics in healthcare
Big Data Analytics	Decision-driven medicine regulations
	Design of KPIs and analytics for health decision-making
Cloud computing	Data protection
	Healthcare as a service
	Healthcare as an infrastructure in the cloud
	Policies for distributed healthcare services on the cloud
5G networks	On demand resilient healthcare services

(Continued)

(Continued)

Technologies (ICT)	Policy and technology implications
Anticipatory computing	Opinion mining and sentiment analysis of policy awareness for resilient Smart Healthcare
Cognitive computing and AI	Artificial intelligence for personalized medicine
	AI for healthcare budgeting and control
	AI for health recommendation services
Virtual reality	VR for medical education
	VR labs
BlockChain	Trusted healthcare networks for personalized services
	Advanced privacy and security for smart resilient healthcare
Data privacy and security	Regulation frameworks
	Interoperability of healthcare records
Interoperability	Interoperability of services, data, applications

In the next section, we elaborate on selective applications and services for smart healthcare.

1.4 Content management resilient Smart Healthcare systems cluster

Even though the content management cluster is not the most sophisticated in terms of computing complexity, it provides though a significant number of value adding services of massive use, which are critical for the realization of any Resilient Smart Healthcare Computing Vision. While there are many diverse IT vendors and provides of services, including open source cloud solutions and integrated content workflow systems, it is important to understand from the beginning the main characteristics of these applications. The following list of features is representative for the capacities of content management systems to support greater scenarios of engagement and services.

- They enable the modular integration of textual data found in policies, official documents, digital archives.
- They can be enriched with advances metadata schemas, taxonomies, ontologies, and semantics enabling complementary views of the same content based on some well-defined criteria.
- They can adopt advanced matching and similarity algorithms, challenging the exploration of content based on user preferences and needs.
- They can be integrated with collaborative platforms and social media or networks, enabling a superficial artificial meta-context of exploitation. The integration of content with social networks or human networks in general sets an amazing new context for exploitation especially for resilient Smart Healthcare applications.
- They can support different cloud computing scenarios based on document as a service, promoting a paper free, trusted resilient Smart Healthcare computing culture in different context that will be applied.

All these characteristics are significant, although they cannot be realized in value adding services without creativity in perceptions. This is to our opinion the critical challenge for resilient Smart Healthcare applications. There must be a concrete vision and a scalable approach of incremental diffused value for the establishment of simple, fully functional, and sustainable services. In the next section, we discuss some ideas for many applications or clusters of resilient Smart Healthcare applications in which the content management component is the main value integrator.

1.4.1 Resilient Smart Healthcare learning management systems cluster

This cluster is related to the developmental aspect of the Smart Healthcare ecosystem. It is critical in the context of resilient Smart Healthcare design to integrative innovative, collaborative learning infrastructures that cultivate a learning culture in the context of the Smart City, engaging citizens and visitors in a developmental process. Promoting the knowledge, the skills, the competencies, and the talents of inhabitants should be a key strategic objective in modern cities. In the next paragraphs, we are discussing seven areas of interest for resilient Smart Healthcare LMSs. Each of these areas represents a context of application as well as a context of inquiry a public dialogue for the various services and underlying philosophy of implementations. For sure there are many more application areas (Fig. 1.3).

- *Lifelong learning integrated resilient Smart Healthcare university*: The idea of establishing an Open Informal educational space accessible by the Smart Cities Inhabitants sounds as a very promising area. Different implementation scenarios could be adopted. For example, the integration of Massive Open Online Courses in a simple

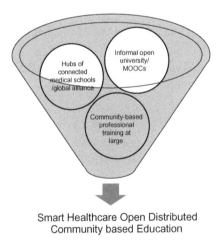

Smart Healthcare Open Distributed
Community based Education

Figure 1.3
Resilient Smart Healthcare open distributed community-based education applications (1).

access point, or a community-based open approach where stakeholders in the resilient Smart Healthcare can contribute content and lectures in such an infrastructure. This Smart Open University should serve as an open space of dialogue for the key issues of modern living in cities. It can be also used as a community platform for knowledge diffusion between the youth generation and policy makers. The lifelong learning and distributed perspective are also of great significance.

- *Community-based professional training at large scale:* Thinking about learning initiatives at a large scale, it is given that one of the main aspects should be the collaborative engagement of a great number of resilient Smart Healthcare citizens. Community-based professional training refers to the capacity of a relevant infrastructure to diffuse learning content and programs in formal or informal modes to a great number of people. Consider for example a Teachers community to use a relevant service or application for interacting and collaboration.

- *Massive open online courses (MOOCs) technologies and paradigm:* The adoption of MOOCs paradigm in the context of resilient Smart Healthcare design can be a very good approach. Implementing MOOCs integrated with social mining capabilities and analytics can enhance significantly the capacity of an urban area to learn and evolve.

- *Hubs of connected medical schools:* The integration through LMSs or other ICTS of various Schools at an urban district or at a large, it is a key movement. The scenarios can be different. For example, the development of a cloud, open accessible infrastructure with open source technologies, promoting the feeling of belonging and learning in the same resilient Smart Healthcare area. Capabilities related to advanced profiling, collaborative projects between schools, flipped classrooms can provide additional value perceptions.

- *Collaborative, exploratory, constructivist, active learning for resilient Smart Healthcare inhabitants:* One of the key value propositions of resilient Smart Healthcare learning applications should be the promotion of a collaborative, active learning approach. The use of available ICTs should be made on a creative engaging way, so that the participants in these experimental approaches should feel the impact and the added value of resilient Smart Healthcare open distributed community-based education. For example, consider an open system where active citizen organize campaigns, seminar interactions for key societal challenges such as the Climate Change, The Energy Consumption, The Public Safety, a community-based social entrepreneurship model.

- *Global integration/smart global alliance for learning:* Modern resilient Smart Healthcare areas should adopt an openness to the globe. They must build synergetic services, some applications that promote multicultural interactions, and create advanced mechanisms for social integration of diversity. Toward this direction resilient Smart Healthcare learning management systems can serve as a vehicle for learning content diffusion between smart cities, associations, social coalitions, and political ideas. This idea of Global Integration must find supporters at the policymaking level and should be a continuous improvement process rather than a per-case standalone implementation. Consider for example a resilient Smart Healthcare LMS that brings together Medical Experts from China and Saudi Arabia and delivers learning content related to the cultural understanding of doing business in these areas.

- *Inclusion, diversity, equality through smart learning:* This application domain is maybe one of the most critical for the furnishing of a multicultural, diverse, and inclusive resilient Smart Healthcare culture. There are many propositions of services and projects in this area. Consider for example an application for smartphones which will integrate citizens and will connect them on a basis of social inquiry. For example, LMSs will aggregate microcontent contributed by various inhabitants on a case of disease treatment, diversity, and equality.

The previous mentioned are only few exemplary cases of application related to resilient Smart Healthcare learning management systems. We must emphasize that even though these cases represent meaningful solutions for certain problems, the real value of this category of application can be expanded by mixing more enabling technologies. In the next section, we elaborate on another content management technology that enables the so-called Resilient Smart Healthcare Document Management applications.

1.4.2 Resilient Smart Healthcare document management systems cluster

The provision of an integrated approach that promotes the vision of Document as a Service is critical toward the resolve of many inefficiencies especially in the interactions of citizens with authorities and offices. Current Document Management Technologies, provide a variety of services and features that meet most of the requirements of value services. The development of a fully functional infrastructure for the issuing, signing, commenting, integration, collaborative authoring, annotation, extraction, merge and management of documents in different formats it is a bold initiative toward the realization of smart cities vision. Given also the fact that documents represent the so-called explicit knowledge it is more than critical to support their entire life cycle from creation, to distribution, use, store, etc., with policies and relevant tools. In the next paragraphs, very briefly we present six main ideas for applications related to resilient Smart Healthcare document management value adding services. This list is not exhaustive but rather representative of the capacities of document management systems to be problem solvers (Fig. 1.4).

- *Smart cities digital signatures integrated framework—trust and advanced encryption:* One of the most critical aspects for the provision of advanced document-based services is the design implementation and provision of digital signatures infrastructures. This will facilitate several dynamic content and document exchanges and will for sure enhance a document-based business processes automation. For example, an integrated resilient Smart Healthcare application that will manage the issuing of digital signatures

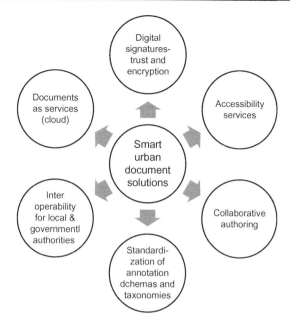

Figure 1.4
Resilient Smart Healthcare document management applications (1).

and will link human entities with different privileges and signature grants over documents could be an excellent proposition in this category.

- *Large-scale accessible archives—accessibility applications for documents:* Accessibility must be one of the key priorities in resilient Smart Healthcare design. Unfortunately, in our days at a global basis, there is rather a little concern for accessibility options. Most of city Information Technology services do not consider accessibility options or when they make it they have a very narrow perspective. Smart applications that add accessibility options over archival documents or set up mechanisms to automate accessibility options for any generated document is a key development. For example, consider an application that adds voice descriptions in documents for blind people or enables speech navigation to menus of resilient Smart Healthcare services.

- *Collaborative construction of resilient Smart Healthcare Wikis and Blogs*: The development of Open Collaborative Wikis for different topics in the context of resilient Smart Healthcare design cultivates further the community culture and builds connections between citizens. The provision of a Wiki and Blog ecosystem within a resilient Smart Healthcare area adds significant credits to knowledge management and shared vision of citizens. An application in which Open Wikis technologies can be exploited for the construction of content archives can be a good approach for this category. In addition, the use of such a central wiki hub can be the basis for opinion and social mining. Open Blogs and Wikis should be critical information flows for more advanced analytics and insights related to City Life, perceptions about quality of life, opinions and ideas for prosperity and response to critical social problems.

- *Standardization for Smart Healthcare annotation and taxonomies schemas for documents and human and social entities:* The standardization process and the agreement of various stakeholders on the metadata elements, the annotation schemas and the taxonomies to be used in the description and cataloguing of social entities, individuals, and organizations in the context of resilient Smart Healthcare design is critical. Without this level of abstractions and specification, it is hard to achieve the potential of a knowledge-based performance. Applications that permit this kind of standardization are useful for any other higher level of sophisticated services. Consider an application that will use a specific annotation schema to catalogue comments of citizens over medical organizations and authorities social networking profiles. Then another service to be able to apply social mining based on the annotations schemas can be used. In addition, consider a collaborative filtering application in which citizens of a city use and characterize medical content or other resources available in various web sites or open systems of local authorities. Alternatively, a toolbar available in a browser with the name "LoveMyCity" permitting users to add rating to local medical services or resources in an urban territory. Another example would be also a community system in which people collaboratively build the taxonomies and the annotation schemas for use in their own resilient Smart Healthcare area.

- *Interoperable clusters of distributed documents beyond local and governmental authorities*: The interoperability quest in the context of resilient Smart Healthcare design is a significant milestone. Without securing the effective, efficient, and functional distribution and interoperability of documents beyond and across medical information systems in the context of Smart Healthcare, many inefficiencies and problems will occur. To achieve a critical level of interoperability over distributed systems between local and government authorities, there are several service level agreements (SLAs) that are required and also a system of systems approach permitting an advanced level of application integration. A pilot project in this context would be a supervising system of system capable of aggregating and routing all relevant documents across distributed procedures. There are several scenarios for the necessity of such a service. Consider for example the need to use the "Citizen Record" from a local resilient Smart Healthcare application to a foreign authority as this person enjoys mobility across Europe or the world. Alternatively, consider automatic integrational of educational systems where student records are automatically transferred to institutions abroad.

- *Documents as services for resilient Smart Healthcare automation*: Dealing with documents as services is a value adding proposition for resilient Smart Healthcare design. With the premises of cloud computing and other technologies, the consideration of each document as a service that can be utilized under specific circumstances and conditions enables great flexibility and permits the design of advanced integrated services. Consider a resilient Smart Healthcare application that offers as a service the issuing of a certificate of birth. Alternatively, a similar application integrates a workflow model and delivers as a service all the payments of a specific citizen to the medical organizations authorities.

1.4.3 Resilient Smart Healthcare workflow automation

The design of interoperable workflows, capable of exchanging critical data and synchronizations is not only a step toward automation but mostly it is a proof that the technological innovations of resilient Smart Healthcare design are well fit in a strategic plan that has in its focus the key priorities of modern smart cities. We must admit though that workflow automation is a long-term objective that many times is not realized at the early stages of resilient Smart Healthcare evolution (Fig. 1.5).

- *One Stop Shop for Smart Healthcare services powered by advanced workflow automation:* The basic idea for the One Stop Shop of all resilient Smart Healthcare services in a resilient Smart Healthcare design derives from the need to have a central hub where all main smart services can be accessible from citizen. Thus an application that provides a web interface or access through any mobile device be a one-stop entrance to all the value adding services of a resilient Smart Healthcare

Figure 1.5
Resilient Smart Healthcare workflow management automation applications.

design. For such a development, it is required to design several advanced workflow automations so that different systems or services can communicate with each other and exchange critical information. For example, consider a smart One Stop Shop application that informs citizens for waiting queues in Municipality Medical Center Real time, etc.

- *Resilient Smart Healthcare business process reengineering strategy and modeling:* For the successful implementation of any resilient Smart Healthcare initiatives, it is required to conduct an extensive business process reengineering of services offered. Only a strategic vision about the resilient Smart Healthcare design we can have a sustainable implementation of smart applications rather than isolated initiatives. In this cluster, the focus of the applications is on the delivery of fresh insights about the avoidance of bureaucracy and the exploitation of human capital and social capital within resilient Smart Healthcare design. Consider for example an application that helps administrators or policy makers or computer engineers, to model workflows related to the realization of resilient Smart Healthcare services and to generate prototype systems for testing and empirical analysis of pilot data.

- *Advanced distributed applications for performance, monitoring, and control of shared process and distributed tasks*: It is critical to enable in the context of any strategic resilient Smart Healthcare design a monitoring and control level with advanced decision-making capabilities. Such services can supervise shared processes and distributed tasks and can be linked with advanced analytics allowing the support of decision-making. Consider an application and a service that will generate visual analytics related to several critical measures related to the performance of the smart healthcare. Indexes related to quality of living, happiness, fear, medical care, and psychological condition.

- *Resilient Smart Healthcare role-based access control, integrative notifications, and cloud services Integration:* The fostering of a fully functioning resilient Smart Healthcare design requires an integrative approach to role-based management, access, and control. A detailed specification of user modeling should be conducted and a strategic plan of related privileges and access modes should be granted. At the full extend a resilient Smart Healthcare design is a complex conceptual system, where applications and services bring together human entities organizations and knowledge resources. From this point of view, a sophisticated role management system permits the integration and the reliability of resources and interactions. Applications in this area include enterprise resources planning systems, enterprise application integration (EAI), as well as APIs that allow the exchange of critical microcontent notifications related to the activities of the various roles in the context of the resilient Smart Healthcare design. The availability of cloud computing allows also the development of cloud-based infrastructure where the value adding services are uses to support different roles. Consider for example a cloud-based e-marketplace of skills and competencies of subjects in the smart systems and an advanced matching algorithm that brings together potential group that can undertake a specific task.

- *Key performance indicator (KPI) management and analytics:* Advanced analysis, justification, and calculation of advanced analytics and KPI is a critical competence for the resilient Smart Healthcare design. The idea is that through the provision of an ecosystem of smart services, critical data can be exploited for the realization of critical insights or for revealing hidden patterns related to behavior, experience, user engagement. The analytical work on KPIs means that the critical dimensions of resilient Smart Healthcare related to health, quality of life, psychological status, etc., must be measured in terms of quantitative and qualitative metrics that will allow a strategic discussion for required actions and readjustment of the resilient Smart Healthcare design strategic plan. Consider an application that calculates on real-time 10 KPIs related to quality of life, and delivers this report to several key stakeholders including policy makers, social partners, educators, scientists, and citizens.
- *Resilient Smart Healthcare SLAs for quality of process automation:* This is an advanced requirement that allows a direct communication of several services. It has a great potential and the SLAs should promote a scalable, incremental approach for more complex services and interapplication communication. Consider for example a system that uses some social mining algorithms, analyzes the opinions of citizen in open dialogue forums and synthesizes these main arguments to strategic advices in the design of new smart services or adjusts the financial strategies of smart city.

1.4.4 Resilient Smart Healthcare microcontent services and systems

In our days, microcontent has a great value and a great impact in different decisions. Social Networks, Social Media applications, Sensor Networks, and IoTs enable many different microcontent data streams. Within the context of resilient Smart Healthcare design, microcontents should be analyzed and must be provided as feeds for enhanced decision-making. Resilient Smart Healthcare design should promote a microcontent exchange culture and systems should be used for the setup of relevant data flow channels as well as for the aggregation and transformation of microcontents to meaningful formats for decision-making. Several applications in this cluster reveal the great potential of microcontents and their capacity to target many human-centric services. The next list provides a very short selection of indicative applications in the area (Fig. 1.6).

- *Resilient Smart Healthcare news alerts ecosystems:* Alerts and notification applications in different context of resilient Smart Healthcare design can improve significantly the perceptions of quality of life and health. A wide variety of simple applications fall into this category. Examples include traffic notification systems, social life notifications, alerts for services operation, announcements for civil inquiry, etc. More complex

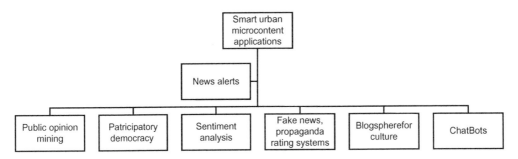

Figure 1.6
Resilient Smart Healthcare microcontent applications.

applications are related to rating systems of resilient Smart Healthcare services, microcontent matching requests for collaboration, microcontent exchanges between co-operating applications, etc.

- *Public opinion mining applications:* Social mining has a great potential to strategize the use of microcontent analysis for the delivery of critical insights on opinions shared over social networks. Many sophisticated approaches related to data mining algorithms can be used, enabling several interpretations of opinions. From simple cluster analysis services indexing similar groups of opinions to advanced link analysis and association rules analysis permitting the understanding of complex aspects of behavior. Consider for example a smart application that mines through social networks the dominant ideas of participants about health, and quality of medical services and their providers. Or an application that creates a social index of exclusion, putting together the ideas of people that feel excluded and synthesizing their shared experiences on social media. A more advanced application could for example check the consistency of opinions over time or if in the context of resilient Smart Healthcare some of the shared opinions had an evolution or change. Consider for example an environmental project for which a citizen shares an opinion during the proposal phase and he changed this opinion after couple years when he/she realizes the positive impact of the project in the quality of life.

- *Participatory democracy contributions:* One of the key pillars of resilient Smart Healthcare design is the evolution of participatory democracy. A collaborative mentality of active participation for the key issues and themes of the resilient Smart Healthcare should be embodied in the daily interactions of citizens with the social establishments and communities. Participatory democracy implies openness to archives, flexible infrastructures for sharing of ideas and dialogue, voting systems, open discussion platforms and forums. In any modern resilient Smart Healthcare design applications that promote the understanding of diversity and the collaborative filtering of ideas are more than welcome. An example application for this cluster would be a governmental platform for discussion on planned reforms and feedback management. Advanced functionalities in participatory democracy applications would be dynamic aggregations of converging opinions, groupings based on beliefs, or even monitoring of terrorist acts.

- *Public dialogue applications:* In the same context with Participatory Democracy Applications, Public Dialogue applications foster the exchange of ideas, facilitate discussions, can be used for gathering of public and individual opinions on critical social issues, can also vision future initiatives. There are several technologies that promote the objectives of this vision. For example, latest technologies on Semantic Open Wikis can be used for the semantic annotation of discussion, the visualization of ideas, the linkage of dialogue concepts with each other and its integrations. Furthermore, recommender systems can be used to link human entities with each other for integration of belief and constructive dialogue or cognitive computing application can be used over social networks to drill down to analysis of discussion. Significant is also in the context the automatic annotation of public dialogue with metadata, tags, or annotation taxonomies. One more comment related to this category of resilient Smart Healthcare applications is the push and pull side of services. Several public dialogue applications could be push, for example, one application over smartphones asking citizens their opinion on a critical urgent medical or health issue.
- *Sentiment analysis for smart cities quality of life and living evaluation:* An interesting trend of our times especially in the domain of data mining is to go beyond numerical analysis and decision-making and to focus on textual data describing opinions, beliefs, and ideas. Sentiment analysis is a rather emerging method that allows the understanding of sentiments and beliefs of human actors over social networks or information systems. A variety of resilient Smart Healthcare applications can exploit the merits of sentiment analysis. Consider an application summarizing the trending opinions and feeling of citizens related to their quality of living, or complaints they might have from local authorities. Or a continuous index for measuring happiness, sense of security, quality of transportation, etc.
- *Resilient Smart Healthcare fake news rating application*: This cluster of applications gains more importance as the evolution of social networks and other microblogging applications permits the widespread of information and news of with critical ambiguity. While the problem is more complicated it is a critical responsive action to create applications and services capable of aggregating news, analyzing their trustworthiness and rating their quality based on the profiles of their contributors the level of its consistency and truth. With increasing harm and spoofing this level will increase the security levels of the resilient Smart Healthcare design and potentially can promote the dialogue and the quality of the democracy. An example of an application at this cluster could be a supervising application frocking the distribution of news that are rated as fake or a toolbar helping member of the resilient Smart Healthcare design to tag news as fake and thus preventing others from harm. Another application could be a similar data mining smart service capable of aggregating the

main aspects of fake news including a smart network of fake identities of a summary of main trends in face news.

- *Smart cities blogosphere for healthcare:* Undoubtedly, the health domain is one of the most important for the coherence of the smart city. The integration of different technologies can promote the creativity and the impact of smart cultural applications. Technologies like Virtual Reality, Recommender Systems, Cognitive Computing, Sensors, and other provide a very challenging mix of technological capabilities. One example for sure could be a fully annotated, searchable ecosystem of healthcare blogs. Applications also related to accessibility, for example, automatic translation or voice navigation to medical context, can have great value.

- *Chatbots for public service citizens' support:* Chatbots represent a very promising technology for automatic interactions with cognitive systems. Many chatbots applications can be deployed under a strategic consideration, for various interactions of citizens with public or local services. Chatbots offering information about services, requirements, providing support in urgent inquiries can promote a level of information systems maturity in resilient Smart Healthcare design. The integration of chatbots in different citizens support modes and context could promote the feeling and the citizen support experience in the context of smart city. For example, consider a chatbot that provides support to citizens requesting the issuing of a medical certificate. Or another chatbot offering guidelines to patients interested in booking for a medical examination.

1.4.5 Resilient Smart Healthcare collaboration systems and services

Collaboration systems in resilient Smart Healthcare design can promote a synergetic culture within the context of the smart cities and also can support value connectors with international systems and infrastructures and dimensions. Advanced considerations to collaboration services integrate some of the latest technological propositions from cognitive computing, machine learning, and recommender systems. Algorithms related to matching peers and context are also new sound propositions. The facilitation of online collaboration through shared coworking spaces also stretches the need for ontology-based annotations and context awareness. These are some of the most promising aspect of collaboration systems, but we must emphasize also on issues related to trust and security. In Fig. 1.7, we present an indicative overview of main propositions for resilient Smart Healthcare collaboration systems and services.

A brief description of the main application areas is provided below with the comments that the value is maximized with the integration of these systems with other resilient Smart Healthcare design applications and capabilities.

- *Enterprise medical messaging:* The management of smart enterprise messaging or the facilitation of messaging between entities and authorities in the context of the smart

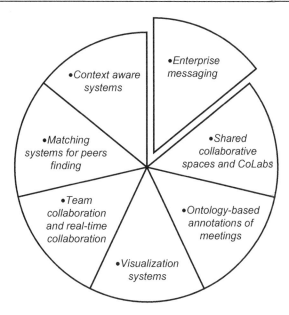

Figure 1.7
Resilient Smart Healthcare collaboration systems and services.

healthcare is a very challenging domain. Not only because of the potential volume of data or the criticality of interactions for meaningful tasks but mostly because messaging provides the basic notion of connectivity and interactions. Several services can be envisioned in this context. An example could be a smart application aggregating similar requests and responding fast to patient's inquiries. Another application could be a Question and Answering System where collaborative filtering and suggestions can provide solutions to citizen's inquiries. A more advanced service could be an automated message exchanging system between different medical authorities and institutions in the resilient Smart Healthcare context, for automating the workflow of distributed processes affecting citizen's perceptions about health services.

- *Shared collaborative spaces:* Several smart shared collaborative spaces can be provided in the resilient Smart Healthcare design. A very interesting area of implementations could be related to community-based consultation. Consider an application that doctors or medical experts collaboratively contribute their ideas and creativity toward the design of community-based problems to healthcare issues and problems. Another example could be a system where students in medical schools collaborate with peers from abroad interacting with the development of meaningful medical learning stories over open content platforms. Collaborative systems design for resilient Smart Healthcare administrators could support another critical thread of applications promoting the efficiency and the performance of resilient Smart Healthcare resources.

- *Ontology-based annotations of meetings:* The design of applications capable of adding value layers for knowledge dissemination and use over large medical data is also very important for smart solutions. The automatic annotation of meetings by electronic means can increase significantly the use of knowledge for retrieval and decision-making. Consider a smart ontology annotation system that scans the entire minutes of medical meetings. Consider also this advanced capability in video data and recorded meetings files.

- *Visualization systems:* One of the weakest aspects of modern resilient Smart Healthcare systems is related to visualizations. Poor designs in interfaces, very weak accessibility options to systems, rather strict and inflexible menus, limited customization capabilities rather make citizens life difficult. From this point of view, it is necessary to put more effort combined with creative ideas for the design of patient-centric interfaces and systems. One example could be an advanced visualization system for analytics related to medical records and medical analytics. A control panel for each citizen accompanied with nice figures and stats related to use of resources, calculation of Smart Indexes related to health, happiness, etc., could enhance the value adding perceptions of resilient Smart Healthcare to individuals as well as the feeling of belonging.

- *Team collaboration and real-time collaboration:* Team collaboration platforms are significant toward the realization of the benefits of collective collaborative work and filtering. In our days, technological capabilities offer a variety of services and different options. Semantic ontological annotations of meetings, automatic annotation of videos, distributed infrastructures for sharing of knowledge and systems of systems fetching information from different collaborative spaces make the design of sophisticated collaboration systems challenging. Consider for example an application that offers share spaces for communities of practice in the context of smart healthcare. Alternatively, a system of systems interface that integrates through APIs medical discussions in social media and constructs automatically consultation documents about critical healthcare issues. Alternatively, an intelligent matching collaboration service that brings together groups based on their expertise or capacities for promoting greater medical collaboration.

- *Matching systems for peers finding:* Matching algorithms exploit different aspects of data, and use different approaches like ontologies, semantics, neural networks, graphs, ranking and rating systems, indexes, and many other computational methods. Their capacity to reveal joint connections or hidden patterns can be sued for several sophisticated resilient Smart Healthcare applications. Consider an application in the context of smart city that puts together people that experienced the same quality of local healthcare services and they expressed similar complaints in social media or other platforms and then provides them with supports to modify the bad perception they developed.

- *Context aware systems:* There are several scenarios for resilient Smart Healthcare applications capable of delivering context aware value propositions. Consider for example, a customized healthcare system based on preferences or dynamic profiling portal that provides personalized medical information and notifications to citizens.

Another context aware smart system could be an automatic service selection system based on workflow automation.

- *Co-Labs:* Collaborative laboratories supported by distributed communication platforms are a key response to various healthcare challenges. The exploitation of human potential requires the establishment of flexible infrastructures. Several technologies can be used for the implementation of Co-Labs. Consider for example a mobile application that helps citizens to connect remotely for medical advice. Alternatively, a global resilient Smart Healthcare network connecting medical research institutions all over the world for the promotion of a humanistic vision.

In the previous section, we provided a rather analytical discussion of numerous smart content management system clusters. For the other five categories of emerging technologies that enable smart cities initiatives, we will use an alternative approach. We will discuss selective applications per category with an emphasis to the ones that we consider as the most promising for smart cities.

1.5 Networking technologies for resilient Smart Healthcare systems cluster

The convergence of computing and telecommunications in the last decade developed a brand-new era for smart applications. Especially in the last 5 years, the evolution of IoTs, and Sensors integrated with Big Data management capabilities initiated the discussion for diverse, flexible, and integrated applications and systems, capable of supporting multiple roles and different scenarios. In this section, we highlight some of the most interesting application clusters for networking.

In Fig. 1.8, we summarize the indicative list of advanced networking applications and systems for the resilient Smart Healthcare design.

Beyond the smart cities networking applications that highlighted in the previous section α number of smart systems is also recommended. We mention only few indicatives as follows.

1.5.1 Smart systems

- *Systems of systems for smart processing over distributed networks:* The idea of systems of systems in the context of resilient Smart Healthcare design provided an upper layer of cognition and advanced information processing capability. The idea of integrating information from various systems and processing it in meaningful scenarios is a high impact case. An example of such a system could be a supervising resilient Smart Healthcare system building dynamically profiles of citizens based on their interaction with several other value adding systems related to their daily life and interaction with all the types of activities and services offered in the context of smart city.

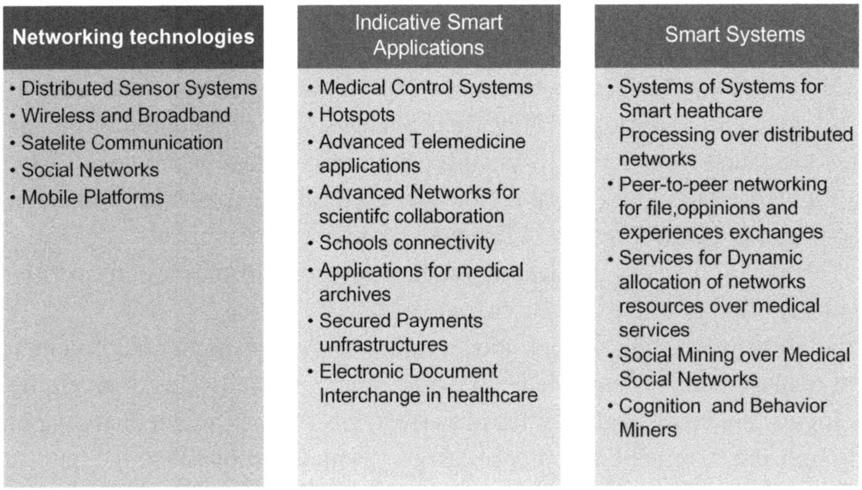

Networking technologies	Indicative Smart Applications	Smart Systems
• Distributed Sensor Systems • Wireless and Broadband • Satelite Communication • Social Networks • Mobile Platforms	• Medical Control Systems • Hotspots • Advanced Telemedicine applications • Advanced Networks for scientifc collaboration • Schools connectivity • Applications for medical archives • Secured Payments unfrastructures • Electronic Document Interchange in healthcare	• Systems of Systems for Smart heathcare Processing over distributed networks • Peer-to-peer networking for file,oppinions and experiences exchanges • Services for Dynamic allocation of networks resources over medical services • Social Mining over Medical Social Networks • Cognition and Behavior Miners

Figure 1.8

Networking technologies for resilient Smart Healthcare systems and applications.

- *Peer-to-peer networking for file, experiences exchanges:* The design and implementation of a peer-to-peer networking systems in the context of the resilient Smart Healthcare design can facilitate and support several services. A peer-to-peer application like MyCitySmartConnect can be installed in smartphones enabling the effective sharing of files, as well as opinions, ideas, etc.
- *Dynamic allocation of networks services resources:* A supervising system for the dynamic allocation of network resources to different applications run in the resilient Smart Healthcare design can secure an excellent quality of services. Such infrastructure as a system can use log files and demand requests or cookies to predict and to manage effectively the consumption of networking resources in the resilient Smart Healthcare design avoiding bottlenecks and long queues in services.
- *Social miners over social networks:* According to our opinion and due to the great diffusion of social networks, we believe that for the next 10 years one of the most significant systems would be the so-called social miners over social networks. These are systems executing a variety of social mining algorithms integrating text mining, social network analysis, and cognitive computing capabilities toward the understanding of hidden patterns of behavior.

1.6 Data warehouses and distributed systems for resilient Smart Healthcare applications

The evolution of data science in the past years has been based on a sustainable development of databases and data warehouses technologies. Several commercial vendors, as well as

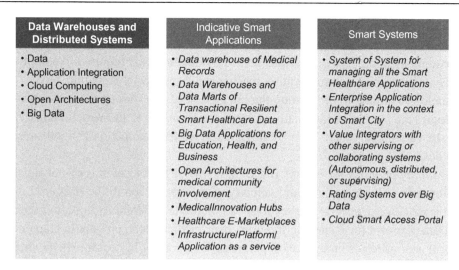

Figure 1.9
Data warehouses and distributed systems for resilient Smart Healthcare systems and applications.

various free and open source solutions and services expand significantly the availability of data warehouses. In this section, we provide a rather simplistic analysis of potential smart applications and systems powered by advanced data warehouses. The emphasis is paid on applications and systems with potential toward the sustainability of smart healthcare and the promotion of the quality of life and happiness (Fig. 1.9).

1.6.1 Indicative smart applications for data warehouses in the context of resilient Smart Healthcare design

The following is an indicative list of applications and systems powered by advanced data warehouses technologies:

- *Data warehouse of medical records:* The integration of citizen's records and their dynamic profiling in multidimensional databases will improve significantly the quality of services in the context of smart cities. The development of consistent, accurate, unique, timely, and complete data records for all the citizens will set the basis for the design of more sophisticated services and customization. In this context, several applications can be developed. An idea can be a semiautomatic annotator of citizens records with a widespread scan of all the dispersed databases as a first basis for integration. Another simple application could also allow advanced notification services for status changes related to the human activity. Additionally, an application exploiting sophisticated methods of EAI for the merge of various records is needed.
- *Data warehouses and data marts of transactional resilient Smart Healthcare data:* The efficient management of various resilient Smart Healthcare transactions, including

processes related to living, energy, finance, entertainment, health, etc., requires the design of an integral data management strategy. Within this strategy the implementation and communication between various dedicated data marts is required. An application in this context can be a communication mechanism powered by Semantic Web Technologies aiming to orchestrate the integration of the various data marts with ontologies annotation. Additionally, an application mapping the various transactions over the various data marts be a significant service for automation and advanced analytics.

- *Big Data applications for health:* Big Data is one of the buzzwords of our times. Dealing with volume, variety, and velocity of generated data in the resilient Smart Healthcare context, several applications can facilitate different exploitation scenarios. A Big Data platform for managing inquiries over medical data, automatic planning of medical appointments or services supervising cost control in health expenditures are included in this category.

- *Open Architectures for community involvement:* The exploitation of open source technologies and the openness in the design philosophy are critical for the evolution of smart cities on reasonable economics. Applications capable of mobilizing and motivating the resilient Smart Healthcare community for contributions can enhance further the capacity of the resilient Smart Healthcare to evolve and prosper. Examples in this category include Open Architectures for community-based problem solving and Open Social Networking for collaboration.

- *Innovation hubs:* Advanced data warehouses can be exploited for the design of a new generation of innovation hubs, where matching algorithms and other computational methods can bring together business and innovators toward the realization of new business models. The difficult and more challenging aspects of these hubs are the integration services. An application related to this challenge can be a resilient Smart Healthcare integral hub for businesses listing and collaboration. Or the design of an innovation hub, where innovators, individual or businesses, industrial partners, and funding organization collaborate to build joint alliances.

- *Healthcare e-marketplaces:* Advanced multidimensional data warehouses can also support new forms of electronic marketplaces in the healthcare. This successful business model can empower smart cities urban designs with flexible services. Exemplary applications include e-marketplaces of skills and competencies dedicated to promoting the human capital in the healthcare domain, or e-marketplaces dedicated to local medical services products, research artifacts, or e-marketplaces at local or global scale.

- *Infrastructure/platform/application as a service*: Resilient Smart Healthcare Design should also be a customizable infrastructure. Thus it must provide various smart services and applications as infrastructures on demand. This cloud-based data warehousing approach is significant. Any infrastructure platform or application of resilient Smart Healthcare be a potential service on demand. Applications that promote this vision will be critical for the sustainability of smart city. Consider for example an Infrastructure that powers e-marketplaces capable of exploited by any entity in the resilient Smart Healthcare interested in maintaining its own marketplace. Or a secure payment service that can be used by any member of the resilient Smart Healthcare on demand for the design of an export activity.

1.6.2 Smart systems

- *System of system for managing all the resilient Smart Healthcare applications:* The integration of all the various resilient Smart Healthcare applications in a unified accessible portal is a sustainability act. The idea of implementing such a system expands the value contribution of resilient Smart Healthcare and delivers a critical space for creativity, prosperity, and entrepreneurship. A one-stop-shop of resilient Smart Healthcare services is an essential component of the resilient Smart Healthcare design and can cultivate the resilient Smart Healthcare culture. A unique point of reference for all the resilient Smart Healthcare services also increases the feeling of belonging to the resilient Smart Healthcare, and thus, the implementation of this system must be prioritized. The only critical issue that must be considered is the openness and the scalability of it to avoid waste of resources.
- *EAI in the context of smart city:* The EAI should be a transparent methodology and as a system available in the context of resilient Smart Healthcare design. It implies an extended philosophy of building bridges and communication channels between applications and systems. The overall strategic evolution of the resilient Smart Healthcare must be a continuous integration effort of isolated and standalone systems and services. This EAI resilient Smart Healthcare primer can help resilient Smart Healthcare to move to another maturity level in terms of sophistication of services and exploitation of more advanced computational techniques.
- *Value integrators with other supervising or collaborating systems (autonomous, distributed, or supervising):* The exploitation of the EAI system within the resilient Smart Healthcare leads to the design of various value integrators with other systems. Another example is the value integration in terms of strategic long-term objectives. For example, the utilization of the resilient Smart Healthcare infrastructure for the enhancement of youth entrepreneurship or startups networks.
- *Rating systems over Big Data*: One of the significant systems component σ of the resilient Smart Healthcare design is related to sophisticated rating mechanism. The maintenance and availability of rating system over the various services of the resilient Smart Healthcare can promote a synergetic, collaborative, approach for the enhancement of the quality of life. Such rating system can be used to aggregate the collaborative wisdom, feedback, and reflection of the living and evolving resilient

Smart Healthcare community. It can also be used for understanding the convergence of beliefs, opinions, and ideas of human entities and social networks.

- *Cloud smart access portal:* The cloud ideas are not new. The availability of services on the internet is as old as the history of internet. The new insights though to cloud computing enable fresh services. The triptych of cloud vision for Infrastructure, Platform, and Application as a Service that discussed previously is a key value integrator for the resilient Smart Healthcare design. The idea of a cloud-based system for accessing the smart services, and expanding them is interesting. Additionally, a cloud-based marketplace of expandable services is also in the right direction for sustainable smart cities. More on these ideas will be provided in our second monograph on the resilient Smart Healthcare applications and case studies.

1.7 Analytics and business intelligence resilient Smart Healthcare systems cluster

The past years of computing are characterized by the dynamic diffusion of Analytics Research in different domains. Business intelligence applications are promoted by the main IT/IS vendors as key responses to modern business challenges. The main characteristic of these technologies is their capacity to reveal hidden patterns over data and to execute meaningful transformation of data to information and knowledge. In other words, Analytics and Business Intelligence applications have an increased problem-solving capability. Their exploitation in the context of resilient Smart Healthcare design can be strategized with several application and system clusters that are briefly presented in the following section (Fig. 1.10).

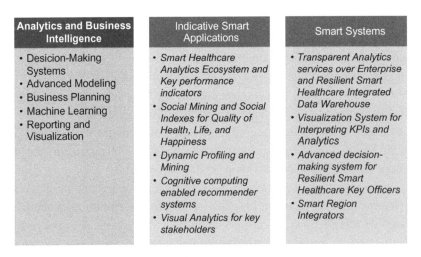

Figure 1.10
Analytics and BI, smart cities applications and systems cluster.

1.7.1 Indicative smart applications

- *Smart Healthcare analytics ecosystem and KPIs:* The development of applications aiming to set up the required ecosystem of analytics for the resilient Smart Healthcare advanced decision-making capability is necessary. In parallel the detailed justification of various KPIs, capable of providing a metrics-based efficiency and performance capability can also be seen as a continuous improvement process. Applications that provide a transparent ecosystem of open and distributed, publicly accessible analytics will gain great significance in the forthcoming years. Organizations, local authorities, or third-party partners that will build extensible learning analytics applications will gain significant role in the exploitation of win—win relations in the context of smart cities evolution. Analytics applications related to satisfaction rates or grouping and clustering of citizens based on their key characteristics are examples for further investigation.
- *Social mining and social indexes for quality of health, life, and happiness:* Advanced data mining algorithms capable of supporting metrics and calculations of social indexes and social mining are also crucial. Currently various technology intensive startup companies dealing with cognitive computing, business intelligence, and analytics provide various value adding services. To our opinion, the dynamic calculation of social indexes related to poverty, loneliness, psycho-load, and happiness will evolve as emerging resilient Smart Healthcare services.
- *Dynamic profiling and mining*: Dynamic profiling application as already mentioned will lead an integrated approach for the aggregation and annotation of personal and group features. For sure several ethical concerns arise in this context, but the evolution of resilient Smart Healthcare requires a holistic approach to the management of personal identities.
- *Cognitive computing enabled recommender systems:* Cognitive computing is related to various other aspects of emerging technologies already discussed. We do believe though that it corresponds to the new era of computing that needs still more time for the realization of its full potential. The integration of thinking and reasoning capabilities in computer-based systems will also offer a significant enabler of various resilient Smart Healthcare services. An idea of such an application is a recommender system promoting peers for potential collaboration for joint entrepreneurship. More advanced cognitive applications can capitalize on the gained wisdom from publicly shared comments of citizens over social networks to create social influencer networks within the σmart urban design context.
- *Visual analytics for key stakeholders:* This is rather a down to earth cluster of applications. The design and provision of stakeholders' centric analytics will promote advance decision-making. An application for example providing key cost metrics related to resilient Smart Healthcare can add useful insights to policy makers.

1.7.2 Smart systems

- *Transparent analytics system over enterprise and resilient Smart Healthcare integrated data warehouse:* This system is responsible for the unification and integration of all the different analytics services over the resilient Smart Healthcare data. It is a high potential system and requires a standardization process and a strategic planning. The availability of transparent analytics for businesses and individual is a bold act toward autonomous smart cities applications.
- *Visualization system for interpreting KPIs and analytics:* The design and implantation of a generic visualization system is required for the development of the resilient Smart Healthcare design vision. The different aspects of this system should be analyzed with community involvement and long-term planning.
- *Advanced decision-making system for resilient Smart Healthcare key officers:* This system should act as an EAI bridge between the various legacy systems that exist in resilient Smart Healthcare entities

   What is evident from this short presentation of various application related to analytics and business intelligent is that the data in the context of resilient Smart Healthcare is a great asset and from this perspective several competing entities will need to apply sophisticated methods for their acquisition.

1.8 Emerging technologies resilient Smart Healthcare systems cluster

Beyond the various streamline technologies, the evolution of emerging and converging technologies is moving Smart cities toward new levels of sophistication and unique value propositions. Haptics and wearables, augmented reality, IoTs, cognitive computing, and robotics are few examples of this new Immersive and Cognitive Era of computing that will have a great impact on the design of resilient Smart Healthcare applications. In this short section, we provide an introductory mapping of the most influential resilient Smart Healthcare applications and systems related to Emerging technologies (Fig. 1.11).

1.8.1 Indicative smart applications

- *Advanced navigation and mapping applications:* The integration of augmented virtual reality and cognitive computing capabilities will enable a new era of navigation and mapping systems. The enhanced of reality with digital objects based on an advanced analysis and recommendation based on machine learning algorithms will promote an unforeseen before era of navigation systems. These ideas integrated with advanced robotics and unmanned (aerial) vehicles research will also permit numerous services for fast transportation, tracking and navigation.

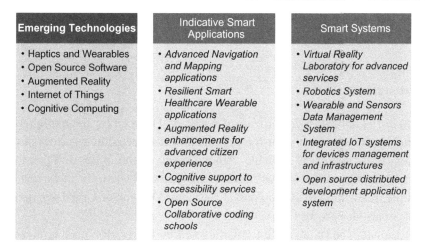

Figure 1.11
Emerging technologies for resilient Smart Healthcare applications and services.

- *Resilient Smart Healthcare wearable applications:* The capacity of portable wearables integrated with sensor technologies and Big Data Analytics allows sophisticated services for smart cities. At least a simple application is related with the provision to every citizen of a smart wearable, for example, MyCityBracelet capable of activating services and managing several citizens to local authorities' interactions. Also, the web side of such an application can populate with significant qualitative data a relevant data warehouse.

- *Augmented reality enhancements for advanced citizen experience:* At the current stage of its evolution Augmented Virtual Reality has shown its capacity to enrich several user experiences in the domains of healthcare, education, entertainment, and business. We believe it is an excellent addition to resilient Smart Healthcare applications a service related to augmented reality enhanced provision of cultural content. Consider an AR application in the historical centers of World Capitals enabling access to immersive scenarios of content explorations. Or an AR system supporting a resilient Smart Healthcare Schools Distributed Open Laboratory of Life Sciences.

- *Cognitive support to accessibility services:* The cognitive computing capabilities enhance the customization and the adaptability of services to profiles information and other dynamic variables. The use of artificial intelligence techniques can be used for better targeting of accessibility services and personalized content and support to specific groups of people. Consider an Application capable of customizing the interface of smart applications to disabled people or a smart mobile application capable or recommending news alerts to citizens based on their opinions as they are expressed in social media.

- *Open source collaborative coding schools:* Open source technologies are a dynamic pillar of resilient Smart Healthcare design. The use of Free and Open Source applications especially in schools must be an opportunity to enhance computing skills to young students and to promote a collaborative working culture. An application designed to provide a coding lab to young students is a good example in this cluster.

1.8.2 Smart systems

- *Virtual Reality Laboratory for advanced services:* The idea for the exploitation of virtual and augmented reality for the provision of a value adding system in the resilient Smart Healthcare context is valuable. Among many opportunities and possibilities one of our key suggestions is a Virtual Reality Laboratory System for advanced services, for example, realization of Prototypes of Services, Designs of User Experiences for Resilient Smart Healthcare Interaction.
- *Robotics system:* The future of Smart Cities will be full of Robotics applications. From this perspective, it is a valuable addition in the portfolio of resilient Smart Healthcare systems to have a Robotics Lab where showcases and experimentations can take place. This at an introductory level can be focused on Educational Robots and Industrial Robots covering two complementary aspects of living and
- *Wearable and sensors data management system:* One of the key technological infrastructures that must be set up in any resilient Smart Healthcare design is an integrated sensors and wearables platform capable of collecting a variety of diverse textual, audio and video data. This system can be used on demand by third parties or in a continuous basis for improving several aspects of modern living. Consider an integrated system of Audio Sensors in urban areas detecting the noise and customizing policies for its management and protection of urban areas. Or an advanced sensor system with cameras and cognitive capabilities alarming authorities for abnormal behavior.
- *Integrated IoT systems for devices management and infrastructures:* The predicted influence of IoT in business for the next years is very promising. Several ideas for deploying IoT technologies can be implemented. For example, an advanced IoT service for the fleet management of vehicles in resilient Smart Healthcare designs for cost utilization and monitoring.

1.9 Resilient Smart Healthcare innovation

1.9.1 The evolution of resilient smart

Healthcare and its internal capacity to improve its quality and services must be based on continuous innovation and research. Toward this direction many Smart Applications and Systems are recommended. This cluster in fact is about building inheriting capacity for continuous improvement and evolution (Fig. 1.12).

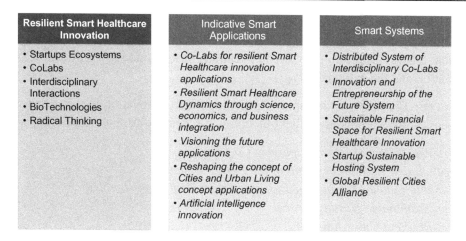

Figure 1.12
Resilient Smart Healthcare innovation applications and systems.

1.9.2 Indicative smart applications

- *Co-Labs for resilient Smart Healthcare innovation applications:* The design of Co-Labs dedicated to the design of resilient Smart Healthcare innovation applications can build a huge community of advocates of resilient Smart Healthcare innovations.
- *Resilient Smart Healthcare dynamics through science, economics, and business integration:* Innovation is a matter of putting together different perspectives. Thus applications that enhance the resilient Smart Healthcare dynamics through the integration of multidisciplinary communities is a must. Consider a dialogue platform that for the same problem aggregates the propositions of different scientific or social communities.
- *Visioning the future applications:* This cluster is about test beds of futuristic scenarios and services. Resilient Smart Healthcare should experiment new ideas, new technologies, and also should mix things in new ways. The implementations of an application where citizens and other stakeholders vision the City of 2050 or City of 2060 are good initiatives for minds and creativity. The collective wisdom should be exploited for good purposes.
- *Reshaping the concept of cities and urban living concept applications:* This is also in the same direction with the previous proposition. Resilient Smart Healthcare must challenge also its constitutional elements. There should be a constant questioning of key pillars of resilient Smart Healthcare design, continuous measurement of quality factors as well as adjusting mechanisms. Smart cities should not be seen as monolithic, slow adjusting social institutions, but rather as evolving living mechanisms adapting to a fast-changing environment and technology.

- *Artificial intelligence innovation:* Resilient Smart Healthcare design need to capitalize on the very promising technology of AI. For this reason, applications that bring into resilient Smart Healthcare daily life applications of this kind are significant for the innovation and the sustainability.

Smart systems: The following are some fascinating Smart Innovation Systems that will be on the focus of our analysis in our next monograph scheduled for publication in early 2018.

- *Distributed System of Interdisciplinary Co-Labs*
- *Innovation and Entrepreneurship of the Future System*
- *Sustainable Financial Space for Resilient Smart Healthcare Innovation*
- *Startup Sustainable Hosting System*
- *Global Resilient Cities Alliance*

1.10 Conclusion

The discussion in this chapter is content intensive. Many ideas, concepts, and services are introduced. Some discussion is provided but the most significant effort was dedicated in defining our own perception on the Smart and Cognitive pillar of Modern Cities.

All these recommended services and applications cultivate jointly a resilient Smart Healthcare vision for modern urban areas having as a prerequisite the engagement and the involvement of various local stakeholders. The promotion of participatory models in decision-making and the exploitation of personal and individual contribution in the context of resilient Smart Healthcare community is recognized as a catalyst for the quality of life and social integration. The brief discussion and the density of content in this chapter of all these great areas of applications was a challenge for us. We had to compromise the need to be analytical with the necessity to discuss as more clusters of applications as we could give the specific strategic objective of this edition.

References

Alyass, A., Turcotte, M., & Meyre, D. (2015). From Big Data analysis to personalized medicine for all: Challenges and opportunities. *BMC Medical Genomics, 8*(33). Available from 26112054.

Chen, J., Qian, F., & Yan, W. (2013). Translational biomedical informatics in the cloud: Present and future. *BioMed Research International*, Article ID 658925.

DeBord, D. G., Carreón, T., Lentz, T. J., Middendorf, P. J., Hoover, M. D., & Schulte, P. A. (2016). Use of the "Exposome" in the practice of epidemiology: A primer on -omic technologies. *American Journal of Epidemiology, 184*(4), 302−314.

Firican, G. (2017). The 10 Vs of Big Data. Available from <https://tdwi.org/articles/2017/02/08/10-vs-of-big-data.aspx?m = 1> Accessed 03.06.19.

Greene, A. C., Giffin, K. A., Greene, C. S., & Moore, J. H. (2015). Adapting bioinformatics curricula for Big Data. *Briefings in Bioinformatics, 17*(1), 43−50.

Lytras, M. D., & Papadopoulou, P. (2018). *Applying Big Data analytics in bioinformatics and medicine* (pp. 1−465). Hershey, PA: IGI Global. Available from https://doi.org/10.4018/978-1-5225-2607-0.

Papadopoulou, P., Lytras, M., & Marouli, C. (2018). Bioinformatics as applied to medicine: Challenges faced moving from Big Data to smart data to wise data. In M. Lytras, & P. Papadopoulou (Eds.), *Applying Big Data Analytics in bioinformatics and medicine* (pp. 1−25). Hershey, PA: IGI Global. Available from https://doi.org/10.4018/978-1-5225-2607-0.ch001.

Tenenbaum, J. D. (2016). Translational bioinformatics: Past, present, and future. *Genomics, Proteomics & Bioinformatics, 14*(1), 31−41. Available from https://doi.org/10.1016/j.gpb.2016.01.003. PMID:26876718.

United Nations. (2019). Sustainable development goals. 17 goals to transform the world. Retrieved March 6, 2019, from <http://www.un.org/sustainabledevelopment/sustainable-development-goals/>.

Further reading

Agyeman, A., & Ofori-Asenso, R. (2015). Perspective: Does personalized medicine hold the future for medicine? *Journal of Pharmacy & Bioallied Sciences, 7*(3), 239.

Bibri, S. E., & Krogstieb, J. (2017). Smart sustainable cities of the future: An extensive interdisciplinary literature review. *Sustainable Cities and Society, 31*, 183−212.

Chui, K., & Lytras, M. (2019). A novel MOGA-SVM multinomial classification for organ inflammation detection. *Applied Sciences, 9*(11), 2284. MDPI AG. Retrieved fromhttps://doi.org/10.3390/app9112284.

Karvonen, A., Federico, C., & Federico, C. (Eds.), (2018). *Inside smart cities: Place, politics and urban innovation.* London & New York: Routledge.

Lin, W., Dou, W., Zhou, Z., & Liu, C. (2015). A cloud-based framework for home-diagnosis service over big medical data. *Journal of Systems and Software, 102*, 192−206. Available from https://doi.org/10.1016/j.jss.2014.05.068.

Lützkendorf, T., & Balouktsi, M. (2017). Assessing a sustainable urban development: Typology of indicators and sources of information. *Procedia Environmental Sciences, 38*, 546−553.

Lytras, M., Raghavan, V., & Damiani, E. (2017). Big Data and Data Analytics research: From metaphors to value space for collective wisdom in human decision making and smart machines. *International Journal of Semantic Web and Information Systems, 13*(1), 1−10.

Lytras, M. D., Aljohani, N., Daniela, L., & Visvizi, A. (2019). *Cognitive computing in technology-enhanced learning* (pp. 1−350). Hershey, PA: IGI Global. Available from https://doi.org/10.4018/978-1-5225-9031-6.

Lytras, M. D., & Visvizi, A. (2018). Who uses smart city services and what to make of it: Toward interdisciplinary smart cities research. *Sustainability, 2018*(10), 1998. Available from https://doi.org/10.3390/su10061998.

Lytras, M. D., Visvizi, A., & Sarirete, A. (2019). Clustering smart city services: Perceptions, expectations, responses. *Sustainability, 11*(6), 1669.

Meulendijk, M., Spruit, M., Willeboordse, F., Numans, M., Brinkkemper, S., Knol, W., ... Askari, M. (2016). Efficiency of clinical decision support systems improves with experience. *Journal of Medical Systems, 40*(4), 1−7.

Ng, K., Ghoting, A., Steinhubl, S. R., Stewart, W. F., Malin, B., & Sun, J. (2014). PARAMO: A PARAllel predictive MOdeling platform for healthcare analytic research using electronic health records. *Journal of Biomedical Informatics, 48*, 160−170. Available from https://doi.org/10.1016/j.jbi.2013.12.012. Available from 24370496.

Papadopoulou, P., Daniella, L., & Lytras, M. (2019). Virtual and augmented reality in medical education and training: Innovative ways for transforming medical education in the 21st century. In M. D. Lytras, N. Aljohani, L. Daniela, & A. Visvizi (Eds.), *Cognitive computing in technology-enhanced learning* (pp. 1−350). Hershey, PA: IGI Global.

Papadopoulou, P., Marouli, C., & Misseyanni, A. (2019). *Environmental exposures and human health challenges* (pp. 1−280). Hershey, PA: IGI Global. Available from https://doi.org/10.4018/978-1-5225-7635-8.

Spruit, M., & Lytras, M. (2018). Applied data science in patient-centric healthcare: Adaptive analytic systems for empowering physicians and patients. *Telematics and Informatics*, *35*(4), 643−653. Available from https://doi.org/10.1016/j.tele.2018.04.002.

Spruit, M., Vroon, R., & Batenburg, R. (2014). Towards healthcare business intelligence in long-term care: An explorative case study in the Netherlands. *Computers in Human Behavior*, *30*, 698−707, Special Issue: ICTs for Human Capital.

The Phenotype-Genotype Integrator (PheGenI). (2019). Retrieved March 6, 2019, from https://www.ncbi.nlm.nih.gov/gap/phegeni.

The Precision Medicine Initiative® (PMI) Cohort Program. (2019). Retrieved March 6, 2019, from https://www.nih.gov/precision-medicine-initiative-cohort-program.

Visvizi, A., & Lytras, M. (2018b). Rescaling and refocusing smart cities research: From mega cities to smart villages. *Journal of Science and Technology Policy Management (JSTPM)*. Available from https://doi.org/10.1108/JSTPM-02-2018-0020.

Visvizi, A., & Lytras, M. D. (2018a). It's not a fad: Smart cities and smart villages research in European and global contexts. *Sustainability*, *2018*(10), 2727. Available from https://doi.org/10.3390/su10082727.

Visvizi, A., Lytras, M. D., & Mudri, G. (Eds.), (2019). *Smart villages in the EU and beyond*. Bingley, UK: Emerald Publishing, ISBN: 9781787698468 (forthcoming June 2019). Available from https://books.emeraldinsight.com/page/detail/Smart-Villages-in-the-EU-and-Beyond/?K = 9781787698468.

Wild, C. P. (2005). Complementing the genome with an "exposome": The outstanding challenge of environmental exposure measurement in molecular epidemiology. *Cancer Epidemiology, Biomarkers & Prevention*, *14*(8), 1847−1850.

CHAPTER 2

Syndromic surveillance using web data: a systematic review

Loukas Samaras, Elena García-Barriocanal and Miguel-Angel Sicilia

Computer Science Department, University of Alcalá, Ctra. De Barcelona km. 33.6, 28871 Alcalá de Henares, Spain

2.1 Introduction: background and scope

Smart Healthcare or *Smart Health* is a new form of healthcare. This term (Active Advice, 2017) describes the technology that contributes to better diagnostic tools and better treatment for patients, by using devices and means that improve the quality of life. Smart Healthcare technologies combine the term *Smart Technology* with health, that is smart technologies used for health purposes. Such technologies (Patient@home, 2018) can be applied to health information recording from increasingly advanced electronic devices and sensors, to storing and computing this information automatically and finally to delivering the information either for personalized advice or automated actions from the collected data. Furthermore, these new technologies concern smart home services, as well as intelligent and connected medical devices.

Under these definitions, Smart Healthcare refers to smart health, including eHealth and mHealth services. The term *mHealth* is determined by the World Health Organization (2011) as the medical and public health practice supported by mobile devices. These (electronic) devices include mobile phones, patient monitoring devices, personal digital assistants, and other wireless devices.

Syndromic surveillance, on the other hand, refers to monitoring of epidemics. According to the Centres of Disease Control and Prevention (CDC, USA, 2004) (Henning, 2004), *Syndromic surveillance has been used for early detection of outbreaks, to follow the size, spread, and tempo of outbreaks, to monitor disease trends, and to provide reassurance that an outbreak has not occurred.* Many information systems have been created based on data from the internet to fulfill this goal; the early detection of epidemics. During the last 14 years, a new approach has begun since 2004 with the famous work of Johnson et al. (2004), when the scientists tried to take advantage of the Web search queries to reveal the spread

Innovation in Health Informatics.
DOI: https://doi.org/10.1016/B978-0-12-819043-2.00002-2

and the peak of influenza in the United States. Since then, various researches have been conducted with the help of web data (social media, search engines, etc.) to establish the fundamentals of internet surveillance systems. This novel approach deals with the implementation of information systems based on data from the web to track epidemics and to create patterns and rules for an early prediction. Across all over the world, at universities, organizations, or research centers, scientists study the potential of the web in epidemics. Except from various information systems and methods created for data analysis of the web data, new terms were introduced to describe this new approach and trend, such as *Infoveillance* or *Infodemiology* (Eysenbach, 2006; Spruit & Lytras, 2018).

In this study, we examine the publications until the year of 2018. This examination was applied on an initial collection of 337 published items, of which 225 were found to be relevant. These publications consist of many different types. Most of them (86.22%) are published articles based on researches from various organizations, universities, or research centers which study the fields of syndromic surveillance or monitor epidemics. Other publications are based on dissertations, conference announcements, reviews or systematic reviews of articles, books, and one Google patent. In Fig. 2.1, we can see these types and their percentage in relation to the sum of the published items.

As we can see in Fig. 2.1, most of the publications are published articles. Nevertheless, we allocated 19 reviews or systematic reviews.

With this work we try to give a detailed analysis of the works published by identifying the most relevant ones, concerning syndromic surveillance using the Web, presenting the biggest collection of related articles ever made on this subject. By using the methodology of systematic review, there is an in-depth description and analysis of the main areas covered by these publications: the time (year) they were published, the diseases that were examined, the web data sources used by the researchers, the countries in which these diseases were

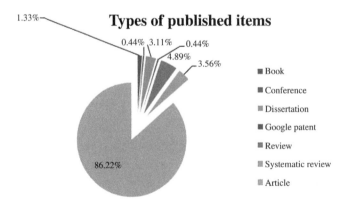

Figure 2.1
Types of all published items.

spread, the approaches of the data analysis used by the scientists, and finally, the number of scientists that have worked until now. The detailed analysis refers to 225 relevant publications that were extracted from the online database of Google Scholar (2018), which is a powerful tool for every researcher.

To conduct this review, we used a variation of the *PRISMA statements* methodology (Moher, Liberati, Tetzlaff, & Altman, 2009) and we also examine the previous reviews or systematic reviews. We identified 19 previous reviews that were conducted to analyze various articles in the previous years. Of the total reviews, most of them focus on the influenza disease or other diseases, while others examine epidemics using web data in a more general way. We consider the work of Rattanaumpawan, Boonyasiri, Vong, and Thamlikitkul (2018) as the one with the biggest collection of articles, 110 in total, without ignoring of course the good work that has been done by other scientists who conducted reviews.

Considering the above, this study is a both quantitative and qualitative analysis, and the aims of this review are:

1. To make a complete collection of articles, related to syndromic surveillance using web, available to any researcher.
2. To investigate the academic interest on this field, based on the number of published items every year. Is this growing or declining?
3. To analyze other aspects, such as the epidemic characteristics (diseases), the geographical spread of the researches and researchers, the used data, and the way the data analysis is described in these reteaches.
4. To estimate and evaluate what areas has been explored so far and what could be the possible research in the future.
5. To elaborate a novel way of systematic review on this research field that can help in deciding the importance of this research field.
6. To showcase, evaluate and align the results to the new Smart Healthcare technologies

2.2 Methodology: research protocol and stages

Our research took place from May 1 to June 30, 2018. The research model used was a variation of the PRISMA model, including a research protocol, which was created for this purpose and consists of five research stages plus a writing phase. The five stages are as follows: preparation, data retrieval, data analysis, data synthesis, and results. Below, we briefly present each stage.

2.2.1 Stage 1: Preparation, research questions, and queries

The preparation stage includes all the necessary decisions and tools to be used, such as the scope, the method designing, and the research questions. The definitions of the methods, appropriate for the implementation of this research was critical, meaning that it should be decided at first.

Three research questions were created to examine and understand the current literature regarding syndromic surveillance using the Web. The motivation of this review is to categorize and summarize the previous work that has been done until today and find the explored and unexplored areas toward a future work. These questions are as follows:

RQ1: Is the academic interest growing or declining?
To answer this question, we must base on the current literature and examine this in a yearly basis.
RQ2: What aspects have been explored until now in the available literature?
In addition, it is useful to understand which areas are underexplored. Generally, there is a very wide field of research, since there are lots of diseases and lots of countries, which can be researched. With this question, we are seeking what has been researched and at what extend. So, the next research question should be as follows:
RQ3: What topics have been covered and which ones need further development and research in the future?
This stage was concluded with some sample data that were gathered to help in finalizing the methods and tools needed to complete this research.

The present review has gone through with the help of the search queries that were inserted in the Google Scholar search engine. The criterion for the relevance of publications is whether each one includes the following keywords in the analysis, or the variants of them: *syndromic surveillance* OR *detecting epidemics* AND *using web*.

We conducted an extensive search through Google Scholar for research papers, articles, books, dissertations, reports, and conference presentations. The main keywords (which were expected to be prevalent in the relevant papers) were *syndromic surveillance*, *predicting epidemics*, and *using web*. These keywords are generally broad terms, while some others, more specific, were used such as *Google, Twitter, Yahoo*, or *Web*. There were two final search strings (for each of the two searches made) and can be expressed in one Boolean statement as follows:

$$((A \text{ OR } B) \text{ AND } (C1 \text{ OR } C2 \text{ OR } C3 \text{ OR } C4))$$

where A, syndromic surveillance; B, predicting epidemics; C1, using Web; C2, Google; C3, Yahoo; C4, Twitter.

The search strategy contained the following design decisions:

Searched databases: Google Scholar, which contains articles from Springer Link, Science Direct, IEEE Xplore, Web of Science, etc.

Searched items: Journal articles, conference papers, workshop papers, technical reports, books reviews, and dissertations.

Search applied on: Full text, to avoid exclusion of papers that didn't include the searched keywords in abstracts or titles or used a different variant of the terms but were relevant for this review.

Language: The search was limited to papers written in English. All other languages are excluded.

Publication period: All years (2004–18).

Syndromic surveillance using web started to receive attention after 2004, as already mentioned. Therefore the chosen publication period is set to be since 2004. The outcome of the search process resulted a total of 225 relevant papers, of which 19 are relevant reviews or systematic reviews.

2.2.2 Stage 2: Data retrieval

The data were retrieved in a period of two weeks and initially included 337 published items, possible to be eligible in the review. All needed information was entered in a centralized Microsoft Excel spreadsheet for further analysis, as follows.

2.2.3 Stage 3: Data analysis: study selection and excluding criteria

The objective of the study selection was to identify papers relevant to the objectives of the review, according to the agreed scope. The search strings were set to avoid excluding relevant studies in a relatively small category or when some data were missing, for example, when there was a research using web data, but not for a specific disease. In addition, some articles were entered twice, since there were present in each one of the queries entered in the Google Scholar search engine.

2.2.4 Stage 4: Data synthesis

During this phase, extensive analysis (quantitative and qualitative) has been done regarding the information gathered from the reviewed papers and articles. This was necessary for supporting data categorization and data synthesis. Our goal was to summarize, in a quantitative way, the main areas of research related to syndromic surveillance using web data. These quantitative summaries have been included in the results section, assisted with graphs that are supplemented by the references to the included papers.

The statistical analysis has been performed in all areas concerned with the synthesis of the studies that were identified. We used multiple perspectives to indicate interesting relationships and trends within the reviewed articles, since the available literature is not limited. By doing so, we believe that a scientist can better understand the perspectives and the trends of this type of research that has been conducted and goes into depth, finding interesting questions and views of the research field, potentially for a future work. The classification of the results includes the required characteristics to summarize, include or exclude features, to help the synthesis, and finally, the proper evaluation of all the researches included in this review.

2.2.5 Stage 5: Results analysis

This stage includes the outcomes of this research. The scope is not only to compare the previous published research to each other, but also to determine the importance of the research field of syndromic surveillance using web data.

2.2.6 Stage 6: Writing

The final stage is to write the procedures and results of this extensive research. This stage consists of all the procedures taken place during this research and we present them all in a way that helps in understanding each stage.

The entire research model can be briefly described in Fig. 2.2.

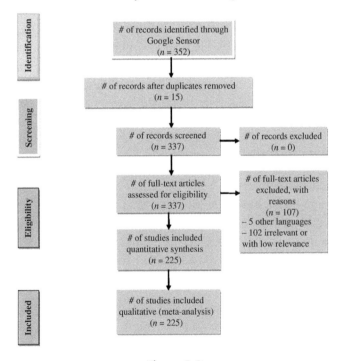

Figure 2.2
The PRISMA research model.

2.3 Results and analysis

In this section, the results of this systematic review are presented based on the 225 papers that are relevant to the examined subject and finally selected.

2.3.1 RQ1: Is the academic interest growing or declining?

To be able to answer this question, we must see the development of the articles and other items that were published each year from 2004. That means that we must find when these publications were made and determine the trend.

The first (relevant) one is published in 2004 and concerns the study of Johnson et al. (2004), while the last one was published in 2018. Many studies occurred after 2009 as a result of the 2009 influenza pandemic. A lot of articles refer to influenza and particularly to the H1N1 virus that was responsible for many cases with severe symptoms during that year. This virus type has an unusual characteristic: it does not affect people over 60 years old but many young people, adults, and children. This virus type can lead to pneumonia if not early diagnosed and treated. The term *swine flu* was used by the news media in America and a lot of money were directed to the treatment of this disease. For instance, in Russia, the government has allocated 4 billion rubles (US$140 million) to buy the initial 43 million doses of vaccines, to perform mass swine flu vaccinations during the year 2009. Russia planned to have 35.5 million doses before the end of that year (Russian News & Information Agency, 2018). This virus had implications in many people across the world in many countries. Since 2009, a lot of relevant articles have been published, as shown in Fig. 2.3.

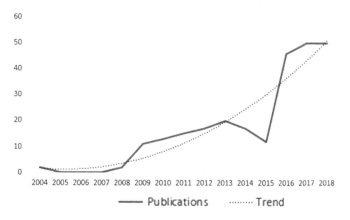

Figure 2.3.
Relevant publications by year.

In Fig. 2.3, the thicker line represents the number of publications per year, while the dotted thinner line represents the trend, as it was calculated from the following polynomial formula:

$$y = 0.3042x^2 - 1.3639x + 2.7626$$

where y is the expected number of publications and x is the current year—2003

Most articles per year are observed in 2017 (50 articles), but from 2013 until 2017, each year over 20 articles have been published regarding syndromic surveillance using the Web, except from the year 2015, in which we observe 12 publications. It seems that many scientists, research centers, or organizations appreciate the usability of the Web to provide data and tools for monitoring epidemics and outbreaks when they are effectively used along with the science of statistics. During the year 2018, we have allocated only 20 articles, but this is normal since this systematic review is conducted in June 15, 2018. As a result, the number of publications for the year 2018 is calculated as 50, using the abovementioned formula.

The results of this analysis answers to the first research question that the academic interest grows over time.

2.3.2 RQ2: Regarding syndromic surveillance using web data, what aspects have been explored until today in the available literature?

To answer this question, an analysis based on five perspectives of the current literature about the field of syndromic surveillance is conducted. The following categories of information represent the five perspectives to answer which disease, where, from what data source, with what techniques these researches have been conducted and the total number of authors of these publications, as follows in the summary:

- Disease analyzed, and health subjects used for the investigation (which disease)
- Geographical location of the studies (where)
- Web data source included in the studies (from what)
- With what statistical tools the data were handled (with what)
- How many scientists have worked to produce the published studies?

2.3.2.1 Which diseases have been explored?

Health issues are widely discussed in this research field as it is critical for modeling and predicting purposes concerning public health. Of the 225 publications, 161 (71.55%) refer explicitly to one or more health subject or disease.

Some researchers conducted researches for more than one health subject (6.22%), while others focused on one disease (65.33%). There is a relatively large percentage of researches that did not examine specific diseases, but the syndromic surveillance generally (28.45%). Table 2.1 includes all cases.

The relative % column indicates the percentage of the publications containing at least one health subject/disease. As we can see in this table, 103 published articles are related

Table 2.1: Health subjects.

n	Diseases	Publications	%	Relative %
1	AIDS, hepatitis B, tuberculosis, influenza, and foot-and-mouth disease	1	0.44	0.62
2	Influenza and pertussis	1	0.44	0.62
3	Ebola, cholera, respiratory epidemics, syndrome coronavirus outbreak, meningitis, influenza A H7N913, chikungunya, dengue fever, mumps	1	0.44	0.62
4	African swine fever	1	0.44	0.62
5	Breast cancer	1	0.44	0.62
6	Cancer	2	0.88	1.34
7	Cholera	1	0.44	0.62
8	Cholera, dengue	1	0.44	0.62
9	Communicable diseases	1	0.44	0.62
10	Dementia	1	0.44	0.62
11	Dengue	10	4.44	6.21
12	Depression	1	0.44	0.62
13	Diseases with diverse modes of transmission (e.g., airborne droplet, vector, sexual, and fecal-oral), biology (virus, bacteria, protozoa), dengue, tuberculosis	1	0.44	0.62
14	Ebola	3	1.33	1.86
15	Ebola, Zika	1	0.44	0.62
16	Ebola, Zika, and swine flu	1	0.44	0.62
17	Foodborne illness	2	0.89	1.24
18	Hand, foot, and mouth disease epidemics	2	0.89	1.24
19	Hantavirus syndromes	1	0.44	0.62
20	HIV/AIDS	5	2.22	3.11
21	Human papillomavirus	1	0.44	0.62
22	Influenza	103	45.78	63.98
23	Influenza, cholera, rabies virus	1	0.44	0.62
24	Influenza, dengue	1	0.44	0.62
25	Influenza, tuberculosis	1	0.44	0.62
26	Listeria	1	0.44	0.62
27	Listeria, influenza	1	0.44	0.62
28	Lyme disease	1	0.44	0.62
29	Malaria	4	1.78	2.48
30	Measles	2	0.88	1.32
31	Respiratory syncytial virus	1	0.44	0.62
32	Syphilis	1	0.44	0.62
33	Systemic lupus erythematosus	1	0.44	0.62
34	Zika virus	4	1.78	2.48
35	n/a	64	28.44	

exclusively to influenza (45.78%, relative percentage 63.98%), 10 articles are about dengue, 5 articles are about HIV/AIDS, 4 articles are about malaria, 4 articles about cancer or breast cancer, and 3 articles about Ebola exclusively. There are also two references for foodborne illnesses and two for hand, foot, and mouth epidemics. Other health subjects are discussed once, such as the African swine fever, malaria, Lyme disease, listeria, foodborne illness, Ebola, depression, dementia, communicable diseases, cholera, human papillomavirus, measles, respiratory syncytial virus, syphilis, and systemic lupus erythematosus. As we see, not all the abovementioned are diseases that can be transmitted, although depression is s special case of psychological phenomenon (disorder) related to individuals. However, regarding public health, the research revealed that the Web can be a useful source of data for other nontransmitted diseases or disorders as cancer (Foroughi, Lam, Lim, Saremi, & Ahmadvand, 2016), or depression (Yang, Huang, Peng, & Tsai, 2010). There are also articles which examine more than one disease and we include them separately in the table. Such cases are influenza and listeria, influenza and pertussis, cholera and dengue, influenza, cholera and rabies virus, influenza and dengue, and influenza and tuberculosis. Three studies include more than three diseases in their area of examination.

Another aspect is the keywords used to retrieve data from the internet for those researchers who have built specific databases for this purpose. In 78 studies, the scientists used as a search term, the name of the disease, in the language of the country they examined or using the English-speaking terms. Others used the words for their symptoms or other keywords, for example, "cold" to detect influenza, based both on the weather conditions of this common disease and on social media (Shikha, Younghee, & Mihui, 2017). Weather is an important factor for the development of epidemics and we will come back to this matter, since there are some researches from scientists that are classified as relevant. We will further discuss the potential of weather forecast to help syndromic surveillance using the Web.

2.3.2.2 Where did studies take place (region, country)?

A major aspect is where the relevant published researches have been conducted, but also which regions or countries of the earth these researches concern. We may assume that there is a similarity between these two aspects, since it is usual for a study to be made in the United States, for the United States. This is only a general rule applied to most publications, but there are exceptions. For instance, a scientist in Italy conducts a research about Africa. Such a case is the study of Alicino et al. (2015), which examines the spread of Ebola virus in West Africa based on the findings of the researchers from the University of Genoa (Italy). In our case, we believe that it is more appropriate to analyze the geographical location that has been under research with the use of the internet. This is important, taking into account that the use of internet is globally available and this makes

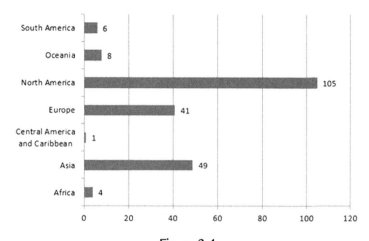

Figure 2.4
Regions examined for epidemics.

easy for data to be accessed by people in almost all countries of the world. Fig. 2.4 shows explicitly the geographic regions from which surveillance data were used.

In this figure we can see that the most explored region is North America with 105 publications. This occurs since most researchers originated from the countries of the United States and Canada, but also some other scientists have conducted researches for these countries, especially for the United States. It is important to notice that for Africa, there are only four studies conducted for the countries of West Africa (Liberia, Sierra Leone, and Guinea) for Ebola virus, since this virus is generally very common in the regions of Africa. For Europe, there are 41 publications and for Asia 49. For Asia, 17 of the articles concern China. For Oceania (Australia and New Zealand), there are eight publications, while for South America we found six publications. For Central America and Caribbean, only one publication has been made, referring to Haiti.

It is worth mentioning that eleven publications are made, examining more than one geographical region, for example, a study was made using data for Australia, Canada, Ireland, New Zealand, South Africa, the United Kingdom (England and Wales, Scotland, Northern Ireland), and the United States (Paul, Dredze, Broniatowski, & Generous, 2015). In the regional analysis, we separate the regions that were exclusively studied, while there are eleven publications concerning countries more than one. Another example is a study for Australia, Canada, and Ireland, regions quite different to each other, but they are included in one article. Other publications concern the United States and Australia or Brazil, Ukraine, Turkey, and Venezuela. We see that, in the last case, there are four countries belonging to two different geographical continents, South America and Europe. The above observations mean that the current publications concern all the continents of the world, except from Antarctica and the North Pole, since very few people live there.

Table 2.2: List of countries with publications.

n	Country	Sum	n	Country	Sum	n	Country	Sum
1	Australia	9	12	Italy	9	23	Republic of Korea	1
2	Brazil	3	13	Japan	6	24	Saudi Arabia	1
3	Canada	12	14	Korea	1	25	South Korea	5
4	China	19	15	Madagascar	1	26	Spain	4
5	Colombia	1	16	Malaysia	2	27	Sweden	3
6	Denmark	5	17	Netherlands	2	28	Taiwan	2
7	France	3	18	New Zealand	1	29	Thailand	1
8	Hong Kong	1	19	Norway	1	30	United Kingdom	18
9	India	5	20	Pakistan	1	31	United States	102
10	Indonesia	1	21	Philippines	1	32	Israel	1
11	Iran	2	22	Portugal	2			

It is also interesting to locate the countries, where the research has been conducted. All 225 researches were conducted in 32 countries. Most of the studies (102) were made in the United States. In the second place, far away, we find China with 19 publications, and the third place is taken by the United Kingdom with 18. Australia and Italy have nine publication each one. The complete list of countries is shown in Table 2.2.

From Europe, there are totally 47 publication from 9 countries on this research field. Surprisingly, Central Europe does not have too many publications, as Germany has none and France only three. In Europe, there are totally nine countries, in which researches are made: Denmark (5), France (3), Italy (9), Netherlands (2), Norway (1), Portugal (2), Spain (4), Sweden (3), and United Kingdom (18). On the contrast, it is quite interesting that countries, which are not considered as very developed or they are very small, have at least one publication, such as Madagascar, Pakistan, Philippines, and Thailand.

2.3.2.3 What is the web data source used or mentioned?

Scientists referred to or use various sources of data from the web for their experiments or/ and their analysis. We have found 169 different web sources that were used. The most popular is Twitter, as shown in Fig. 2.5.

In Fig. 2.5, we can see all the 169 web data sources. Fifty-nine publications (34.91%) have been conducted about Twitter. The next popular data source is Google Trends (30, 17.75%), which include both Google Trends and Goggle Flu Trends (GFT). Naver Trends search engine is used in one occasion. Other 18 (10.65%) researches include a combination of two or more data sources, for example, using social media and web search logs. The 15 publications (8.88%) which are mentioned as *other* include special systems developed in some countries. These systems are basically local systems used in countries to gather epidemiological data. They have been developed in specific countries and can be accessed to provide useful data and information, for example, recorded incidents by physicians,

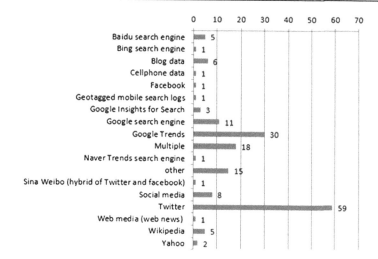

Figure 2.5
The web data sources.

cloud-based electronic health records, various other databases, or emergency medicine internet sites, such as the medical website Vårdguiden.se of Sweden (Hulth, Rydevik, & Linde, 2009).

The Google search engine follows with 11 publications (6.51%), while the Chinese Baidu search engine and Microsoft Bing were used in 6 researches (3.55%). The same number is found to blog data. Wikipedia is a web data source, used in five studies (2.96%) and data from Yahoo were used in two instances.

We can see that various web data have been used, in correlation to the syndromic surveillance data. It is important to mention that the data extraction was executed using traditional methods (use of internet sites) or by using specific API's (Application Programming Interfaces), written in programming languages, such as Python, C++, C#, .NET, etc.

2.3.2.4 What is the method(s) used for analysis and interpretation of the data?

There are many techniques regarding the data analysis approach used by various researchers that made estimations, analysis, or predictions. We have identified 109 published items with an explicit data analysis method (48.44%). The data analysis methods or statistical approach cannot easily be categorized, as scientists use sometimes multiple methods but, as a rule, all tried to find correlations between data from the official authorities for diseases and the data obtained from the web to create prediction rules.

Twenty-four correlation techniques are used to correlate health data to data from the internet. The correlation techniques used are mentioned as Pearson correlation *R*, Spearman correlation coefficient, cross correlation function, simple correlation, or autocorrelation function. Others use the R^2 coefficient. It must be noticed that many researchers use combinations of models, which is very common in statistics, when the probability or the validity of the results must be examined and verified in depth before they are announced. Thirty-two types of regression or autoregression models were found. These models can be summarized as follows: linear regression and the ARGO model (autoregression with Google search data) which uses publicly available online search data and not only incorporates the seasonality in influenza epidemics, but also captures changes in people's online *search behavior* over time. GARMA model is the generalized autoregression moving average model, ARIMA (Autoregressive Integrated Moving Average model) or ARMA is the Autoregressive Moving Average model, and SARIMA is the Seasonal Autoregressive Integrated Moving Average model. It must be said that in all cases, the dependent variable is the data from the official health authorities, while independent variables are the data from the sources on the internet.

Six studies have been conducted using linear, simple, and multivariate or multiple models. Seven use nonlinear models, such as logistic (logit), nonlinear regression, etc. Six researches use frequency analysis, for example, frequency of queries submitted in the internet.

It must be mentioned that there are some other models used, such as the Support Vector Machine (SVM) in two studies, and two used the Ailment Topic Aspect Model (ATAM). Of course, there are some cases that the statistical analysis requires more than one technique, for example, a research (Yanga, Santillana, & Kou, 2015) was conducted, using multiple techniques, such as:

- Auto Regression with Google search data (lag3) (ARGO),
- Root-Mean-Squared Error (RMSE),
- Mean Absolute Error (MAE), and
- Mean Absolute Percentage Error (MAPE).

Other scientists use the LASSO (Least Absolute Shrinkage and Selection Operator) models, referring to them as LASSO regression or LASSO algorithm, while others use other models, such as ANOVA, or other machine learning algorithms, or a combination of them.

Regarding an early prediction, some researchers conclude that, using web data, prediction is possible. In nine studies, early prediction time (period) varies from one day up to 6–13 weeks.

2.3.2.5 *How many scientists have worked so far?*

There are totally 786 authors, which contributed in the 225 publications. Some of them worked in more than one research. John S. Brownstein has the most publications, as he has participated in 17 published researches. Michael J. Paul has 10 publications as an author, while Mark Dredze and Mauricio Santillana have nine and eight, respectively. Vasileios Lampos has seven, Elad Yom-Tov has six, and Elaine O. Nsoesie has five. Below, in Table 2.3, we see that 29 scientists have three or more publications and other 72 have two publications as authors.

Table 2.3: List of authors with more than one publication.

n	Author	Count	*n*	Author	Count	*n*	Author	Count
1	John S. Brownstein	17	36	Alina Deshpande	2	71	Loukas Samaras	2
2	Michael J. Paul	10	37	Alireza Ahmadvand	2	72	Mathieu Roche	2
3	Mark Dredze	9	38	Alok Choudhary	2	73	Megan S.C Lim	2
4	Mauricio Santillana	8	39	Andrea Freyer Dugas	2	74	Miguel-Angel Sicilia	2
5	Vasileios Lampos	7	40	Anette Hulth	2	75	Ming-Hsiang Tsou	2
6	Elad Yom-Tov	6	41	Ankit Agrawal	2	76	Mizuki Morita	2
7	Elaine O. Nsoesie	5	42	Anna C. Nagel	2	77	Naren Ramakrishnan	2
8	Ingemar J. Cox	4	43	Antonino Mazzeo	2	78	Nassim Saremi	2
9	Nicholas Generous	4	44	Avinash Gandhe	2	79	Nattiya Kanhabua	2
10	Rumi Chunara	4	45	B. Aditya Prakash	2	80	Nicola Luigi Bragazzi	2
11	Wenbiao Hu	4	46	Benjamin M. Althouse	2	81	Paolo Missier	2
12	Adam Sadilek	3	47	Benyuan Liu	2	82	Philip M. Polgreen	2
13	Aron Culotta	3	48	Brian H. Spitzberg	2	83	Qingpeng Zhang	2
14	Christina Lioma	3	49	C.R. Macintyre	2	84	Qingyu Yuan	2
15	Daniela Paolotti	3	50	Cecile Viboud	2	85	Ross Lazarus	2
16	Eiji Aramaki	3	51	Clark C. Freifeld	2	86	S.C. Kou	2
17	Eunyoung Shim	3	52	Courtney D. Corley	2	87	S.J. Yan	2
18	Gabriel J. Milinovich	3	53	Daniela Perrotta	2	88	Sachiko Maskawa	2
19	Geoffrey Colin Fairchild	3	54	Dave Osthus	2	89	Sara Romano	2
20	Gunther Eysenbach	3	55	David A. Broniatowski	2	90	Sara Y. Del Valle	2
21	Henry Kautz	3	56	Diane J. Cook	2	91	Sean D. Young	2
22	Hyekyung Woo	3	57	Diego Cedrim	2	92	Sergio Di Martino	2
23	Kåre Mølbak	3	58	Dipak K. Gupta	2	93	Seth Foldy	2
24	Lawrence C. Madoff	3	59	Elena García-Barriocanal	2	94	Shannon Rutherford	2
25	Niels Dalum Hansen	3	60	Forough Foroughi	2	95	Shihao Yang	2
26	Nigel Collier	3	61	George W. Rutherford	2	96	Simon Pollett	2
27	Reid Priedhorsky	3	62	Gustaf Rydevik	2	97	Ssu-Hsin Yu	2
28	Shilu Tong	3	63	Harshavardhan Achrekar	2	98	Sumiko R. Mekaru	2
29	Vincent Silenzio	3	64	J. Mark Gawron	2	99	Suzanne Lindsay	2
30	A.A. Chughtai	2	65	Jianfeng He	2	100	Wolfgang Nejdl	2
31	Alessandro Garcia	2	66	Jiue-An Yang	2	101	Youngtae Cho	2
32	Alessio Signorini	2	67	Josh Gray	2			
33	Alex Lamb	2	68	K. Michael Peddecord	2			
34	Alexander Romanovsky	2	69	Kumanan Wilson	2			
35	Alfred K-Y Lam	2	70	Li An	2			

2.3.3 RQ3: What topics need further development and research?

Although many aspects of the research regarding syndromic surveillance using the Web have been used and analyzed, we believe that the field of research is still very wide. Besides influenza, other diseases have been explored but not to a very wide extend.

Lately, since 2017, another aspect is under examination; the role of weather. Four studies examine the role of weather into an integrated method based on weather data to assist the epidemics prediction.

According to Van Noort, Águasa, Ballesterosb, and Gomes (2011), *a more direct approach in determining the seasonal variation of the ILI factor* p, *for example, could be the confirmation of the presence of ILI symptoms in influenza infected persons.* The above statement is important, since indicates the use of weather data to track the presence of influenza. If this is true, then future information systems could be based both on web data and weather data. Such an effort is described in the research of Shikha et al. (2017). This is a very interesting aspect, since it is not widely researched and could be researched further. A surveillance system may be created, based on weather forecasts that can be accessed through the internet and give warnings about a possible spread of a disease, for example, influenza based on weather conditions. Regarding influenza, it is considered that the spread can be extensive in areas with cold and dry weather conditions (World Health Organization, Media Center, Influenza Overview, Fact Sheet no 211, March 2003) (World Health Organization, 2003). Furthermore, it might be interesting to analyze the spread and the outbreak of diseases with discrimination between urban and rural regions, taking into account that most infectious diseases are developed in a considerable extend in crowded cases, such as big and populous areas, for example, large metropolitan cities. This could be interesting, as in rural areas, internet data may be less or more difficult to be discovered, especially in some countries with vast territories or less developed.

2.4 Discussion and conclusions

2.4.1 Results

The above results show an analysis regarding the time, the epidemics, the location, the web data, and the data analysis methods, which are presented in the examined researches and included in this review. Regarding the time, more publications are made every year based on researches from various countries from the world. This is normal, as technology and web continuously advances. The data from the web are now abundant and many scientists can take advantage of it. Many fields of science are now included in this effort to harness the web and estimate epidemics and health issues. Computer science, statistics, sociology, and medicine work together to investigate the appropriate method to exploit the web data.

Various methods are used to analyze the data in a complex framework with the ultimate goal for the social benefit. While broadband internet is nowadays widely used as the data speeds are growing with VDSL and ADSL lines (Very high speed digital subscriber line, Asymmetric digital subscriber line) by using fiber optics cables, there is still a part of the world undeveloped, such as Africa, Central America, or South America. As we saw, only four studies examine web data for Africa, one for Central America, and six for South America, as people in these countries may still have not the economy power, the expertise, or the infrastructure to widely use web services. That's why the data volume is limited in these geographical areas. On the other hand, more advanced countries seek the way of using web data for health purposes.

Regarding epidemics, influenza seems to provide plenty of data and this explains the big percentage of studies that use data for this disease. It is also a disease with many health complications and a large number of deaths annually and worldwide. Twitter is found to be used in a large scale, as it may give many and useful advantages. Through the special APIs (REST and STREAMING API), there is the capability to track messages real-time, geolocated from almost every part of the world. The messages from Twitter, called *tweets*, provide the sufficient amount of data that can be further analyzed to help in the estimation of epidemics, although this procedure requires more computer programming techniques and algorithms. Google services, on the other hand, such as the search engine or the Trends, are also extensively used and are found to be also accurate enough to track epidemics. Nevertheless, as we have conducted researches with these two popular data sources, we believe that the potential of social media and Twitter particularly is bigger, despite certain constraints and limitations.

2.4.2 Information systems and epidemics

There is a lot of discussion about the usability of internet data to track epidemics. The key focus a researcher must have under consideration is how an internet system can be managed and function as a replacement system, a supplementary system, a support system, or an extension to traditional monitoring systems. Peek, Holmes, and Sun (2014) research is about the effective management of big data, collected through both traditional and internet surveillance systems. The scientists of this research believe that data for health and biomedicine have become so big and complex that the traditional methods and tools for managing them are not efficient any more. They call this development *a big data revolution*. They examine and discover the technical aspects of big data and the infrastructure needed for the management of them, to provide useful information. They also review analytical information about health and biomedicine regarding selection of cases and control, bias and confounding in observational data and techniques for mining health dimensional data. These data come from medical records, administrative data, web search logs, and social media. It is widely recognized that internet and electronic health data are quickly growing as technology advances. Capturing health data from various sources needs a change in the technical and management techniques regarding, such as the infrastructure, the file systems as well as the multidimensional data processing. To catch data from the internet, this can be done either with real-time techniques and nonreal-time techniques. Nevertheless, if we need early prediction of epidemics, we must support real-time data gathering and new technologies must be introduced to do so, such as Apache *Spark* and *Storm*.

Bernardo et al. (2013) examined various studies about the usability of data from the social media. Many authors claim that social media programs should primarily be used to support existing surveillance programs. The researchers of this study concluded that *the use of search queries and social media for disease surveillance are relatively recent phenomena* and there is also an evolution of the tools and the methodology to exploit them. Although these surveillance systems, based on internet data, have a support function to the traditional ones, they require a high level of familiarity about capturing social behavior through social media. The data from social media, such as Twitter, YouTube, and Facebook, are abundant, but the quality of health information among users in these media is highly variable and this may raise some concerns (Schein, Wilson, & Kealan, 2011) that social media users are exposed to unopposed viewpoints that counter core public health recommendations. We believe that this is logical but partly true as people interact with each other through social media about health issues, but it is hard to imagine that an individual could ignore the official treatment and medication or precaution measures for severe health issues just based on what people say in the social media. On the other hand, a person could be further alerted using social media.

Infoveillance (Guy, Ratzki-Leewing, Bahati, & Gwadry-Sridhar, 2011) is a term to describe the capability of real-time retrieval of internet data regarding syndromic surveillance. It is a strategy to capture real-time online data. These data can be systematically mined, aggregated, and analyzed to inform public health and policy. Social media are also considered as a real-time source of epidemic intelligence. Epidemics can be monitored through accessing the expected magnitude, peek time, and intensity, and the duration (Nsoesie, Brownstein, & Ramakrishnan, 2013). The data from the internet can inform healthcare practitioners on when to expect changes in demand for healthcare resources. A surveillance system based on real-time data could provide the means to do so. Nevertheless, in some cases, a precise estimation is not always successful. GFT is an online system that provides useful data, based on Google searches made for influenza. This system was developed by Google and during the first working period, it could also provide estimates and predictions. GFT is now no longer publishing current estimates, since it missed the emergence of the 2009 influenza pandemic and overestimated the 2012−13 influenza season epidemic (Olson, Konty, Paladini, Viboud, & Simonsen, 2013). Google searches though were used by many scientists and researchers to track epidemics, using various statistical methods that were very successful. Generally, we must consider that a general rule cannot be found for all countries and all diseases, but each one of the latter requires deep statistical analysis; a pattern of a disease in one country may differ in another. It is possible, however, to build systems based on internet data, social media, search engines, etc., but each system requires methods, which can be similar or not. The global pattern of human behavior and globalization can help this, since internet allows people to interact to an electronic system (such as Google Search) or to each other (social media). It is true that internet-based approaches are logistically and economically appealing. However, they do not have the capacity to replace traditional surveillance systems; they should not be viewed as an alternative, but rather as an extension (Milinovich, Williams, & Hu, 2014). Of course, many people could say that the previous statement is thought to be based on today's technology. In the future, as the research continues, technology will further advance and the credibility of internet-based systems will probably be better and wide across the world. The findings of the researches until today show that the potential of creating such internet surveillance systems becomes more possible over time.

2.4.3 Impact to society, ethics, and challenges

The impact of syndromic surveillance using web data has been shown to be large, both to the academic community and to the world in general. This is revealed not only from the numerous publications made, from the large number of authors and researchers, but also from the variety of techniques and sources used. The available tools to estimate and predict epidemics or health issues are undeniably a big conquest of science by humanity. Using web data, syndromic surveillance could be accurate in a less expensive way than traditional systems. Nevertheless, traditional surveillance systems must not stop existing. Web systems could be thought as supplementary or supportive systems. Hardware and software still go on getting better. Despite the evolution of electronic systems, the role of human is still important. Moran et al. (2016) describe the role of human interaction, comparing the weather forecast models to the ones for a weather forecast and found that *epidemic forecasting is messier than weather forecasting.*

Google data and Twitter data represent almost the two-thirds (65.70%) of the total web data, used to estimate epidemics. However, we must not forget that there is significant difference between these popular tools. Using Google logs or data from other searched engines, there is the ability to track the search volume and not the search text itself, because what we really need is the aggregated number of searches, provided by these search engines. Twitter on the other side has this ability, but it first requires and it's easy enough to get the whole text which is included in a message. This means that we can read the detailed view of an individual regarding epidemics, but almost on every opinion a person has about a topic and not just for epidemics. This is not of course a privacy violation, but it must not be used for evil purposes. Human interaction in the social media must be conceptualized as a *moment view*, which is depicted in a specific time and place through internet. This is moreover what syndromic surveillance does; an estimation of time and place.

2.4.4 Smart Healthcare innovations

Regarding modern healthcare systems, this work reveals the potential of internet syndromic surveillance systems to perform as adaptive analytic systems or as a novel research perspective in many ways, critical for Smart Healthcare: by enhancing Smart Healthcare data preprocessing and modeling and by using big data analytic techniques, model evaluation, knowledge deployment is possible through new forms of information infrastructure, as described in the work of Spruit and Lytras (2018). The key concepts applied to Smart Healthcare systems may be the following:

- How applied data science for patient-oriented healthcare can empower medical scientist and patients to more effectively and efficiently improve healthcare,
- The discipline of applied data science,
- The knowledge discovery process (KDP), and
- The meta algorithmic modeling.

Since gathering data from the internet is shown to be easy nowadays across the world, Smart Healthcare systems may drive the derived information to people in various directions: governments, scientists, medical doctors, national or international medical organizations or institutions, patients, or people who travel a lot and need direct and constant knowledge of what is happening in the world, regarding epidemics. This spread of data and information, within the framework of Smart Healthcare, could be valuable. Considering the advance of Internet of Things (IoT), the latest and future introduction of 5G networks, or smart home perspectives, internet surveillance systems could lead to a better warning and dealing with epidemics health plans and health policy decisions.

Under the above aspect, health decision policies might need a closest and greater attention to emerging technologies, such as the IoT, *cognitive computing, advanced analytics and business intelligence, 5G networks, anticipatory and context-aware computing, and advanced distributed data warehouse platforms* (Visvizi, Lytras, Damiani, & Mathkour, 2018). We believe that the key perspective would not be just the change of the technology infrastructure and social behavior, but the proper handling of health data itself for health policies.

Extending further the above into the future smart cities or villages (Lytras & Visvizi, 2018; Visvizi &Lytras, 2019) within the framework of IoT, another debate comes up regarding data on epidemics: first, citizens' awareness of applications and solutions that are considered *smart* and secondly, their ability to use these applications and solutions. In any case, to enhance traditional surveillance systems with internet systems for epidemics, given the proper use of the health data, can lead to social-driven decisions and policies for better living conditions for humans. At the end, both syndromic surveillance using internet data and Smart Healthcare will have the impacts in society, technology, and in medical science.

2.4.5 Conclusions and outlook

The main conclusions of this review can be summarized as follows:

1. **Research**

   There is an extensive literature related to the field of syndromic surveillance using the web. This review has gathered the biggest collection of articles and publications on this field ever made, totally 225. Of course, we may assume that more publications can be found except from Google Scholar or using other search queries, but the bulk of the gathered literature in this review is quite enough to extract useful results and conclusions.

   The academic interest is still growing, especially after 2009. The years containing relevant publications extend from 2004 to the year of 2018. Since 2009, the number of publications has risen, after the 2009 pandemic of influenza. The total number of authors in publications is 786 worldwide. These two facts are important as they reveal the significance and the future perspectives of this research field.

   Many health topics have been discussed, while most of them are about influenza. It seems that for influenza a lot of data are available through internet, but the fact that totally 34 severe diseases have been included is also important, as it shows the potential of the web data to be used for syndromic surveillance.

   Most articles examine North America, the United States, Canada, Europe, and Asia, since these are mainly the origins of scientists and data are broadly available in these areas of the world. Almost all regions of the earth have been examined for epidemics, but some areas, such as Africa, South America, or Central America, are underexamined. The contribution of scientists across the world is also extensive, since researchers from 32 countries of the world have published works on this field.

2. **Internet surveillance systems**

   Twitter at first and secondly Google are the most referred and used web data sources, although other social media, search engines, health records, and web logs have been widely used. There is a rich collection of various web data and electronic systems that have been built to present an internet surveillance system.

   Various models for data analysis and techniques are used to correlate health data to data from the internet. In some occasions, scientists show that a prediction of epidemics is possible before the official data are announced from the competent health authorities. This prediction was achieved 6−13 weeks prior to the official data. Another important aspect is that, using web data, we could estimate a disease development in shorter surveillance time intervals; while most of traditional surveillance systems monitor epidemics on weekly or monthly basis, information systems based on web data could provide daily monitoring or even for shorter periods.

3. **Smart Healthcare systems**

   Smart Healthcare innovations can use internet-based surveillance systems to assist in the awareness and direction of information to people, medical science and organizations, as well as the policy decisions. With the continuous use of internet, Global System for mobile communication networks, smart mobile devices, and health information could lead to a better understanding and informative techniques regarding epidemics. Within the concept and realization of IoT, early detection and prevention of epidemics could be the common policy for the future, rather than treatment, by reducing costs and procedures. Technology infrastructure will change to deal with the *big data revolution*, as not only humans, but also smart devices would probably be constantly connected and interact with each other.

   KDP is a constant effort to derive knowledge out of data. This can be thought as an adaptive procedure in relation to the technology progress. Health data have been always sensitive and not easy to use. The same applies for internet data, even though they are not considered as epidemical, but inspect and reveal an epidemic from other sources, for example, social media, web searches, etc. Internet, but mainly *Smart* technologies, could become irrepressible, if not treated under the previous assumption. Future research could also be dedicated on this matter. Both Internet surveillance systems and Smart Healthcare have the same destination: to improve the quality of life.

4. **Outlook**

   The potential of the research on this field remains broad and other diseases except from influenza could be further examined. In addition, the research could be driven to other aspects of syndromic surveillance, such as the weather conditions or the distinction of epidemics in between urban and rural regions with the use of data from the web. Furthermore, although the impacts of internet data for monitoring epidemics may be obvious, it could be more discussed in the future.

   Web can be a useful tool for obtaining data and make predictions for epidemics despite sometimes the restrictions of accuracy or the size of the data. Internet-based surveillance systems can be established to track epidemics and could work as alternative, supportive or as an extension to traditional systems.

   Finally, we believe that the contribution of this study is that it showcases the extended research and use of internet surveillance systems, the techniques, and the future perspectives within the concept and framework of Smart Health. Technology advance requires change of the way we think of data, information, and how to deliver them to accomplish the improvement of public health.

2.5 Teaching assignments

- Extensiveness of surveillance systems with internet data
- Data acquiring techniques and programming languages
- Social media interaction
- Early prediction and real-time monitoring of epidemics
- Smart Healthcare with the use of internet data for epidemics

Acknowledgments

We acknowledge the University of Alcala de Henares which gave us the opportunity and support to conduct this research.

Author contributions

Loukas Samaras conducted the research with the help of Dr. Miguel-Angel Sicilia and Dr.Elena García-Barriocanal. The conception and plan of the research conducted is part of Loukas Samaras' ongoing PhD work, and was done under the supervision of Miguel-Angel Sicilia and Elena García-Barriocanal.

References

Active Advice. (2017). *Smart Health — A new form of healthcare*. Available from <https://www.activeadvice. eu/news/concept-projects/what-is-smart-health-and-how-do-people-benefit/> Accessed 20.06.18.

Alicino, C., Bragazzi, N. L., Faccio, V., Amicizia, D., Panatto, D., Gasparini, R., . . . Orsi, A. (2015). Assessing Ebola-related web search behaviour: Insights and implications from an analytical study of Google Trends-based query volumes. *Infectious Diseases of Poverty, 4*, 54. Available from https://doi.org/10.1186/s40249-015-0090-9.

Bernardo, T. M., Rajic, A., Young, I., Robiadek, K., Pham, M. T., & Funk, J. A. (2013). Scoping review on search queries and social media for disease surveillance: A chronology of innovation. *JMIR, 15*(7). Available from https://doi.org/10.2196/jmir.2740.

Eysenbach, G. (2006). Infodemiology: Tracking flu-related searches on the web for syndromic surveillance. *AMIA Annual Symposium Proceedings Archive, 2006*, 244−248. PMID:17238340PMCID:PMC1839505.

Foroughi, F., Lam, A. K.-Y., Lim, M. S. C., Saremi, N. A., & Ahmadvand, A. (2016). "Googling" for cancer: An infodemiological assessment of online search interests in Australia, Canada, New Zealand, the United Kingdom, and the United States. *JMIR Cancer, 2*(1), e5. Available from https://doi.org/10.2196/cancer.5212. PMID: 28410185, PMCID: 5369660.

Google Scholar. (2018). Available from <http://scholar.google.gr/> Accessed 20.05.18.

Guy, S., Ratzki-Leewing, A., Bahati, R., & Gwadry-Sridhar, F. (2011). *Social media: A systematic review to understand the evidence and application in infodemiology*, Electronic Healthcare. eHealth 2011. *Lecture Notes of the Institute for Computer Sciences, Social Informatics and Telecommunications Engineering* (Vol. 91). Berlin, Heidelberg: Springer. Available from https://doi.org/10.1007/978-3-642-29262-0_1.

Henning, K. J. (2004). Overview of syndromic surveillance. What is syndromic surveillance? *Centres of Disease Control and Prevention, Morbidity and Mortality Weekly Report (MMWR), 53*(Suppl), 5−11. <https://www.cdc.gov/MMWr/preview/mmwrhtml/su5301a3.htm/> Accessed 20.06.18.

Hulth, A., Rydevik, G., & Linde, A. (2009). Web queries as a source for syndromic surveillance. *PLoS ONE, 4* (2), e4378. Available from https://doi.org/10.1371/journal.pone.0004378.

Johnson, H. A., Wagner, M. M., Hogan, W. R., Chapman, W., Olszewski, R. T., Dowling, J., & Barnas, G. (2004). Analysis of web access logs for surveillance of influenza (2004). *Medinfo*, *107*(Pt 2), 1202−1206. Available from https://doi.org/10.3233/978-1-60750-949-3-1202.

Lytras, M. D., & Visvizi, A. (2018). Who uses smart city services and what to make of it: Toward interdisciplinary smart cities research. *Sustainability*, *10*(6), 1−16. Available from https://doi.org/10.3390/su10061998.

Milinovich, G. J., Williams, G. M., & Hu, W. (2014). Internet-based surveillance systems for monitoring emerging infectious diseases. *The Lancet Infectious Diseases*, *14*(2), 160−168. Available from https://doi.org/10.1016/S1473-3099(13)70244-5.

Moher, D., Liberati, A., Tetzlaff, J., & Altman, D. G. (2009). The PRISMA group, preferred reporting items for systematic reviews and meta-analyses: The PRISMA statement. *PLoS Medicine*, *6*(7), e1000097. Available from https://doi.org/10.1371/journal.pmed.1000097.

Moran, K. R., Fairchild, G. C., Generous, N., Hickmann, K., Osthus, D., Priedhorsky, R., . . . Del Valle, S. Y. (2016). Epidemic forecasting is messier than weather forecasting: The role of human behavior and internet data streams in epidemic forecast. *The Journal of Infectious Diseases*, *214*(suppl_4), S404−S408. Available from https://doi.org/10.1093/infdis/jiw375.

Nsoesie, E. O., Brownstein, J. S., & Ramakrishnan, N. (2013). A systematic review of studies on forecasting the dynamics of Influenza outbreaks. *Influenza and Other Respiratory Viruses*, *8*(3). Available from https://doi.org/10.1111/irv.12226.

Olson, D. R., Konty, K. J., Paladini, M., Viboud, C., & Simonsen, L. (2013). Reassessing Google Flu Trends data for detection of seasonal and pandemic Influenza: A comparative epidemiological study at three geographic scales. *PLoS Computational Biology*, *9*(10), e1003256. Available from https://doi.org/10.1371/journal.pcbi.1003256.

Patient@home. (2018). Smart Helath technology: The next step in healthcare technology. Available from <https://path2025.dk/smart-health-technology/> Accessed 20.06.2018.

Paul, M. J., Dredze, M., Broniatowski, D. A., & Generous, N. (2015). Worldwide influenza surveillance through twitter. In *AAAI workshop: WWW and public health intelligence*.

Peek, N., Holmes, J. H., & Sun, J. (2014). Technical challenges for big data in biomedicine and health: Data sources, infrastructure, and analytics. *Yearbook of Medical Informatics*, *9*, 42−47. Available from https://doi.org/10.15265/IY-2014-0018.

Rattanaumpawan, P., Boonyasiri, A., Vong, S., & Thamlikitkul, V. (2018). Systematic review of electronic surveillance of infectious diseases with emphasis on antimicrobial resistance surveillance in resource-limited settings. *American Journal of Infection Control*, *46*(2), 139−146. Available from https://doi.org/10.1016/j.ajic.2017.08.006.

Russian News & Information Agency. (2018). *RIA Novosti*, Article of 20.11.2009. Available from <http://en.rian.ru/world/20091120/156921735.html/> Accessed 20.06.2018.

Schein, R., Wilson, K., & Kealan, J. (2011). *Literature review on effectiveness of the use of social media: A report for Peel Public Health*. [Region of Peel], Peel Public Health, 2011, Carleton Univercity, Ottawa, Ontario, Canada.

Shikha, V., Younghee, P., & Mihui, K. (2017). Predicting flu-rate using big data analytics based on social data and weather conditions. *Advanced Science Letters*, *23*(12), 12775−12779. Available from https://doi.org/10.1166/asl.2017.10897.

Spruit, M., & Lytras, M. D. (2018). Applied data science in patient-centric healthcare: Adaptive analytic systems for empowering physicians and patients. *Science Direct Telematics and Informatics*, *35*(4), 643−653. Available from https://doi.org/10.1016/j.tele.2018.04.002.

Van Noort, S. P., Águasa, R., Ballesterosb, S., & Gomes, M. G. (2011). The role of weather on the relation between Influenza and Influenza-like illness. *Journal of Theoretical Biology*, *298*, 131−137. Available from https://doi.org/10.1016/j.jtbi.2011.12.020.

Visvizi, A., Lytras, M. D., Damiani, E., & Mathkour, H. (2018). Policy making for smart cities: Innovation and social inclusive economic growth for sustainability. *Journal of Science and Technology Policy Management*, *9*(e:2), 126−133. Available from https://doi.org/10.1108/JSTPM-07-2018-079.

World Health Organization (2003). Media center, influenza overview, Fact Sheet no. 211 (revised March 2003). Available from <http://www.who.int/mediacentre/factsheets/2003/fs211/en/> Accessed 20.06.2018.

World Health Organization. (2011). *mHealth: New Horizons for health through mobile technologies: Based on the findings of the second global survey on eHealth (Global Observatory for eHealth Series, Volume 3). Author. ISBN 978 92 4 156425 0 (NLM classification: W 26.5).*

Yang, A. C., Huang, N. E., Peng, C.-K., & Tsai, S.-J. (2010). Do seasons have an influence on the incidence of depression? The use of an internet search engine query data as a proxy of human affect. *PLoS ONE, 5*(10), e13728. Available from https://doi.org/10.1371/journal.pone.0013728.

Yanga, S., Santillana, M., & Kou, S. C. (2015). Accurate estimation of influenza epidemics using Google search data via ARGO. *Proceedings of the National Academy of Sciences of the United States of America, 112* (47), 14473−14478. Available from https://doi.org/10.1073/pnas.1515373112.

Appendix: Included studies (alphabetical)

Achrekar, H., Gandhe, A., Lazarus, R., Yu, S.-H., & Liu, B. (2011). *Predicting flu trends using twitter data. International workshop on cyber-physical networking systems. Available from https://doi.org/10.1109/INFCOMW.2011.5928903.*

Achrekar, H., Gandhe, A., Lazarus, R., Yu, S.-H., & Liu, B. (2012). *Twitter improves seasonal influenza prediction.* International conference on health informatics (HEALTHINF'12) (pp. 61−70). Vilamoura, Portugal: Nature Publishing Group.

Alessa, A., & Faezipour, M. (2018). A review of influenza detection and prediction through social networking sites. *Theoretical Biology and Medical Modelling, 15*, 2. Available from https://doi.org/10.1186/s12976-017-0074-5.

Al-garadia, M. A., Khan, M. S., Varathan, K. D., Mujiaba, G., & Al-Kabsi, A. M. (2016). Using online social networks to track a pandemic: A systematic review. *Journal of Biomedical Informatics, 62*, 1−11.

Alicino, C., Bragazzi, N. L., Faccio, V., Amicizia, D., Panatto, D., Gasparini, R., . . . Orsi, A. (2015). Assessing Ebola-related web search behaviour: Insights and implications from an analytical study of Google Trends-based query volumes. *Infectious Diseases of Poverty, 4*, 54. Available from https://doi.org/10.1186/s40249-015-0090-9.

Al-Surimi, K., Khalifa, M., Bahkali, S., EL-Metwally, A., & Househ, M. (2016). The potential of social media and internet-based data in preventing and fighting infectious diseases: From internet to Twitter. In G. Rezza, & G. Ippolito (Eds.), *Emerging and re-emerging viral infections. Advances in experimental medicine and biology* (972, pp. 131−139). Cham: Springer. Available from https://doi.org/10.1007/5584_2016_1.

Althouse, M. B., Ng, Y. Y., & Cummings, A. T. D. (2011). Prediction of dengue incidence using search query surveillance. *PLoS Neglected Tropical Diseases, 5*(8), e1258. Available from https://doi.org/10.1371/journal.pntd.0001258.

Anggraeni, W., & Aristiani, L. (2016). Using Google Trend data in forecasting number of dengue fever cases with ARIMAX method case study: Surabaya, Indonesia. *Procedia Computer Science, 124*(2017), 189−196.

Apreleva, S., & Lu, T.-C. (2017). Disease prediction system using open source data. US20170308678A1, US Application. Available from <https://patents.google.com/patent/US20170308678A1/en/> Accessed 20.06.2018.

Aramaki, E., Maskawa, S., & Morita, M. (2011). *Twitter catches the flu: Detecting influenza epidemics using Twitter. Proceedings of the conference on empirical methods in natural language processing (EMNLP'11)* (pp. 1568−1576).

Arsevska, E., Roche, M., Sylvain, F., Lancelot, R., Chavernac, D., Hendrikx, P., & Barbara, D. (2016). *Monitoring disease outbreak events on the web using text-mining approach and domain expert knowledge. International conference on language resources and evaluation 10. Portoroz, Slovénie, 23 May 2016/28 May 2016, Version publieé − Anglais.*

Aryal, A. (2016). *Developing a prototype system for syndromic surveillance and visualization using social media data* (Thesis). Rochester Institute of Technology, ProQuest Dissertations Publishing. Available from <http://scholarworks.rit.edu/cgi/viewcontent.cgi?article = 10343&context = theses/>

Aslam, A. A., Tsou, M.-H., Spitzberg, B. H., Li, A., Gawron, M., Gupta, D. K., . . . Lindsay, S. (2014). The reliability of tweets as a supplementary method of seasonal influenza surveillance. *Journal of Medical Internet Research, 16*(11), e250. Available from https://doi.org/10.2196/jmir.3532.

Bahk, G. J., Kim, Y. S., & Park Myoung, S. (2015). Use of internet search queries to enhance surveillance of foodborne illness. *Emerging Infectious Diseases, 21*(11), 1906−1912. Available from https://doi.org/10.3201/eid2111.141834.

Basile, L., De la Fuente, M. O., Torner, N., Martínez, A., & Jané, M. (2018). Real-time predictive seasonal influenza model in Catalonia, Spain. *PLoS ONE, 13*(3), e0193651. Available from https://doi.org/10.1371/journal.pone.0193651.

Bernardo, T. M., Rajic, A., Young, I., Robiadek, K., Pham, M. T., & Funk, J. A. (2013). Scoping review on search queries and social media for disease surveillance: A chronology of innovation. *JMIR, 15*(7). Available from https://doi.org/10.2196/jmir.2740.

Bhatasharrya, L., Ramashandran, A., Bhatasharrya, J., & Dogra, N. K. (2013). Google trends for formulating GIS mapping of disease outbreaks in India. *International Journal of Geoinformatics, 9*(3), 9−19. Available from <https://www.researchgate.net/profile/Indrajit_Bhattacharya/publication/259591652_Google_Trends_for_Formulating_GIS_Mapping_of_Disease_Outbreaks_in_India/links/53d621ab0cf220632f3d86ad.pdf/>.

Bhattara, A. K. (2015). An investigation of the public health informatics research and practice in the past fifteen years from 2000 to 2014: A scoping review. In *MEDLINE, UWSpace*. Available from <http://hdl.handle.net/10012/10084/>

Bodnar, T., & Salathé, M. (2013). Validating models for disease detection using twitter. In *Companion proceedings of the 22nd international conference on world wide web (WWW'13)*, pp. 699−702. doi:10.1145/2487788.2488027.

Boit, J., & Alyami, H. (2018). Malaria surveillance system using social media. In *Association for information systems AIS electronic library (AISeL), in MWAIS 2018 proceedings*. Available from <http://aisel.aisnet.org/mwais2018/10/> Accessed 20.06.18.

Bragazzi, N. L., Barberis, I., Rosselli, R., Gianfredi, V., Nucci, D., Moretti, M., . . . Martini, M. (2017). How often people google for vaccination: Qualitative and quantitative insights from a systematic search of the web-based activities using Google Trends. In *Human vaccines & immunotherapeutics, Vol. 13, Issue 2: 10th world congress on vaccines, immunisation and immunotherapy*.

Breton, D., Bringay, S., Marques, F., Poncelet, P., & Roche, M. (2013). *Mining web data for epidemiological surveillance, PAKDD. Lecture Notes in Computer Science* (7769). Berlin, Heidelberg: Springer. Available from https://doi.org/10.1007/978-3-642-36778-6_2.

Briscoe, E., Appling, S., Clarkson, E., Lipskiy, N., Tyson, J., & Burkholde, J. (2017). Semantic analysis of open source data for syndromic surveillance. *Online Journal of Public Health Informatics, 9*(1), e072. Available from https://doi.org/10.5210/ojphi.v9i1.7651.

Broniatowski, D. A., Paul, M. J., & Dredze, M. (2013). National and local influenza surveillance through Twitter: An analysis of the 2012−2013 influenza epidemic. *PLoS ONE, 8*(12), e83672. Available from https://doi.org/10.1371/journal.pone.0083672.

Brownstein, J. S., Freifeld, C. C., & Madoff, L. C. (2009). Digital disease detection—harnessing the Web for public health surveillance. *The New England Journal of Medicine, 360*, 2153−2157. Available from https://doi.org/10.1056/NEJMp0900702.

Byrd, K., Mansurov, A., & Baysal, O. (2016). Mining Twitter data for influenza detection and surveillance. In *Proceedings of the international workshop on software engineering in healthcare systems (SEHS'16)*, Austin, TX, pp. 43−49, May 14−22.

Dalum Hansen, N., Mølbak, K., Cox, I. J., & Lioma, C. (2017). Time-series adaptive estimation of vaccination uptake using web search queries. In *Proceedings of the 26th international conference on world wide web companion (WWW'17)*, pp. 773−774. arXiv:1702.07326

Carneiro, H. A., & Mylonakis, E. (2009). Google trends: A web-based tool for real-time surveillance of disease outbreaks. *Clinical Infectious Diseases*, *49*(10), 1557−1564. Available from https://doi.org/10.1086/630200.

Chakraborty, S., & Sub, L. (2016). Extracting signals from news streams for disease outbreak prediction. In *IEEE global conference on signal and information processing (GlobalSIP)*, Washington, DC, pp. 1300−1304. Available from https://doi.org/10.1109/GlobalSIP.2016.7906051

Chen, L., Hossain, K. S. M. T., Butler, P., Ramakrishnan, N., & Prakash, A. B. (2016). Syndromic surveillance of Flu on Twitter using weakly supervised temporal topic models. *Data Mining and Knowledge Discovery*, *30*(3), 681−710. Available from https://doi.org/10.1007/s10618-015-0434-x.

Chiu, A. P. Y., Lin, Q., & He, D. (2017). News trends and web search query of HIV/AIDS in Hong Kong. *PLoS ONE*, *12*(9), e0185004. Available from https://doi.org/10.1371/journal.pone.0185004.

Choi, J., Cho, Y., Shim, E., & Woo, H. (2016). Web-based infectious disease surveillance systems and public health perspectives: A systematic review. *BMC Public Health*, *16*(1), 1238. Available from https://doi.org/10.1186/s12889-016-3893-0.

Chunara, R., Andrews, J. R., & Brownstein, J. S. (2012). Social and news media enable estimation of epidemiological patterns early in the 2010 Haitian cholera outbreak. *The American Journal of Tropical Medicine and Hygiene*, *86*(1), 39−45. Available from https://doi.org/10.4269/ajtmh.2012.11-0597.

Collier, N., Son, N. T., & Nguyen, N. M. (2011). OMG U got flu? Analysis of shared health messages for bio-surveillance. *Journal of Biomedical Semantics*, *2*(Suppl 5), S9. Available from https://doi.org/10.1186/2041-1480-2-S5-S9.

Corle, C. D. (2009). *Social network simulation and mining social media to advance epidemiology* (PhD thesis). University of North Texas, ProQuest Dissertations Publishing. Available from <http://digital.library.unt.edu/ark:/67531/metadc11053/m2/1/high_res_d/dissertation.pdf/> Accessed 20.06.2018.

Corley, C. D., Armin, R. M., Singhy, K. P., & Cook, D. J. (2009). Monitoring influenza trends through mining social media. In *International conference on bioinformatics & computational biology*, pp. 340−346.

Corley, C. D., Cook, D. J., Mikler, A. R., & Singh, K. P. (2010). Text and structural data mining of influenza mentions in web and social media. *International Journal of Environmental Research and Public Health*, *7*(2), 596−615. Available from https://doi.org/10.3390/ijerph7020596.

Costa, F. F. (2013). Social networks, web-based tools and diseases: Implications for biomedical research. *Drug Discovery Today*, *18*(5-6), 272−281. Available from https://doi.org/10.1016/j.drudis.2012.10.006.

Coviello L., Franceschetti M., García-Herranz M. Iyad R. (2016). Predicting and containing epidemic risk using friendship networks. In Information *theory and applications workshop (ITA)*, La Jolla, CA, pp. 1−7, Available from https://doi.org/10.1109/ITA.2016.7888201

Culotta, A. (2010a). Detecting influenza outbreaks by analyzing Twitter messages. CoRR, abs/1007.4748. Available from <http://arxiv.org/abs/1007.4748/> Accessed 20.06.18.

Culotta, A. (2010b). Towards detecting influenza outbreaks by analyzing Twitter messages. In *Proceedings of the first workshop on social media analytics (SOMA'10)*, 115−122, Washington, DC, July 25−28. ACM, New York, NY ©2010, table of contents. ISBN: 978-1-4503-0217-3.

Culotta, A. (2012). Lightweight methods to estimate Influenza rates and alcohol sales volume from Twitter messages. *Language Resources and Evaluation*, *47*(1), 217−238. Available from https://doi.org/10.1007/s10579-012-9185-0.

Curtis, S., Fair, A., Wistow, J., Val, D. V., & Oven, K. (2017). Impact of extreme weather events and climate change for health and social care systems. *Environmental Health*, *16*(Suppl 1), 128. Available from https://doi.org/10.1186/s12940-017-0324-3.

D'Avanzo, E., Pilato, G., & Lytras, M. D. (2017). Using Twitter sentiment and emotions analysis of Google Trends for decisions making. *Program*, *51*(3), 332−350. Available from https://doi.org/10.1108/PROG-02-2016-0015.

Dalton, C., Carlson, S., Hons, B., Butler, M., Cassano, D., Clarke, S., . . . Durrheim, D. (2017). Insights from flutracking: Thirteen tips to growing a web-based participatory surveillance system. *JMIR Public Health and Surveillance*, *3*(3), e48. Available from https://doi.org/10.2196/publichealth.7333.

Deiner, M. S., Fathy, C., Kim, J., Niemeyer, K., Ramirez, D., Ackley, S. F., . . . Porco, T. C. (2017). Facebook and Twitter vaccine sentiment in response to measles outbreaks. *Health Informatics Journal*. Available from https://doi.org/10.1177/1460458217740723.

Doan, S., Ohno-Machado, L., & Collier, N. (2012). Enhancing Twitter data analysis with simple semantic filtering: Example in tracking Influenza-like illnesses. In *IEEE HISB 2012 conference*, La Jolla, CA, September 27−28. USarXiv:1210.0848v1 [cs.SI].

Dredze, M., Paul, M. J., Bergsma, S., & Tran, H. (2012). Carmen: A twitter geolocation system with applications to public health. In *AAAI workshop on expanding the boundaries of health informatics using artificial intelligence (HIAI)*. Available from <https://pdfs.semanticscholar.org/9bc4/6fb12f2c7fae0e9e56e734e6efb9ca07fd98.pdf/> Accessed 20.06.18.

Dugas, A. F., Hsieh, Y.-H., Levin, S. R., Pines, J. M., Mareiniss, D. P., Mohareb, A., . . . Rothman, R. E. (2012). Google Flu Trends: Correlation with emergency department Influenza rates and crowding metrics. *Clinical Infectious Diseases*, *54*(4), 463−469. Available from https://doi.org/10.1093/cid/cir883.

Dugas, A. F., Jalalpour, M., Gel, Y., Levin, S., Torcaso, F., Igusa, T., & Rothman, R. E. (2013). Influenza forecasting with Google flu trends. *PLoS ONE*, *8*(2), e56176. Available from https://doi.org/10.1371/journal.pone.0056176.

Elkin, L. S., Topal, K., & Bebek, G. (2017). Network based model of social media big data predicts contagious disease diffusion. *Information Discovery and Delivery*, *45*(3), 110−120. Available from https://doi.org/10.1108/IDD-05-2017-0046.

Eysenbach, G. (2006). Infodemiology: Tracking flu-related searches on the web for syndromic surveillance. In *AMIA annual symposium proceedings*, pp. 244−248.

Eysenbach, G. (2009). Infodemiology and infoveillance: Framework for an emerging set of public health informatics methods to analyze search, communication and publication behavior on the internet. *Journal of Medical Internet Research*, *11*(1), e11. Available from https://doi.org/10.2196/jmir.1157.

Eysenbach, G. (2016). Impact of predicting health care utilization via web search behavior: A data-driven analysis. *Journal of Medical Internet Research*, *18*(9), e251. Available from https://doi.org/10.2196/jmir.6240.

Fairc, G. C. (2014). *Improving disease surveillance: Sentinel surveillance network design and novel uses of Wikipedia* (PhD thesis). The University of Iowa, ProQuest Dissertations Publishing. Available from <https://search.proquest.com/openview/df82c68765800af587dbf53ef6d8e8a7/1?pq-origsite = gscholar&cbl = 18750&diss = y/> Accessed 20.06.18.

Fleming, E., & Pamelá, P. (2014). *Using social media as a method for early indications & warnings of biological threats*. Capstone Project, Florida International University, Dr. Stack, April 9, 2014. Available from <http://maga.fiu.edu/academic-tracks/capstone-project/2014-capstone-working-papers/southcom-pam_eric_social-media-and-biosurveillance-capstone-april-2014-edited-by-dawndavies.pdf > .

Foldy, S., Foldy, S., Biedrzycki, P. A., Barthell, E. N., Healy-Haney, N., Baker, B. K., . . . Pemble, KimR. (2004). Syndromic surveillance using regional emergency medicine internet. *Annals of Emergency Medicine*, *44*(3), 242−246. Available from https://doi.org/10.1016/j.annemergmed.2004.01.019.

Foroughi, F., Lam, A. K.-Y., Lim, M. S. C., Saremi, N., & Ahmadvand, A. (2016). "Googling" for cancer: An infodemiological assessment of online search interests in Australia, Canada, New Zealand, the United Kingdom, and the United States. *JMIR Cancer*, *2*(1), e5. Available from https://doi.org/10.2196/cancer.5212.

Friesema, I. H. M., Koppeschaar, C. E., Donker, G. A., Dijkstra, F., Van Noort, S. P., Smallenburg, R., . . . van der Sande, M. A. B. (2009). Internet-based monitoring of Influenza-like illness in the general population: Experience of five Influenza seasons in The Netherlands. *Vaccine*, *27*(45), 6353−6357. Available from https://doi.org/10.1016/j.vaccine.2009.05.042.

Generous, N., Fairchild, G., Deshpande, A., Del Valle, S. Y., & Priedhorsky, R. (2014). Global disease monitoring and forecasting with Wikipedia. *PLoS Computational Biology*, *10*(11), e1003892. Available from https://doi.org/10.1371/journal.pcbi.1003892.

Ginsberg, J., Mohebbi, M. H., Patel, R. S., Brammer, L., Smolinski, M. S., & Brilliant, L. (2009). Detecting influenza epidemics using search engine query data. *Nature*, *457*, 1012−1014. Available from https://doi.org/10.1038/nature07634.

Girond, F., Randrianasolo, L., Randriamampionona, L., Rakotomanana, F., Randrianarivelojosia, M., Ratsitorahina, M., . . . Piola, P. (2017). Analysing trends and forecasting malaria epidemics in Madagascar using a sentinel surveillance network: A web-based application. *Malaria Journal, 16*. Available from https://doi.org/10.1186/s12936-017-1728-9, 72.

Guo, P., Zhang, J., Wang, L., Yang, S., Luo, G., Deng, C., . . . Zhang, Q. (2017). Monitoring seasonal influenza epidemics by using internet search data with an ensemble penalized regression model. *Scientific Reports, 7*. Available from https://doi.org/10.1038/srep46469, Article number: 46469.

Guy, S., Ratzki-Leewing, A., Bahati, R., & Gwadry-Sridha, F. (2011). *Social media: A systematic review to understand the evidence and application in infodemiology*, Electronic Healthcare. eHealth 2011. *Lecture Notes of the Institute for Computer Sciences, Social Informatics and Telecommunications Engineering* (Vol. 91). Berlin, Heidelberg: Springer. Available from https://doi.org/10.1007/978-3-642-29262-0_1.

Hansen, N. D., Lioma, C., & Mølbak, K. (2016). Ensemble learned vaccination uptake prediction using web search queries. In *Proceedings of the 25th ACM international on conference on information and knowledge management (CIKM'16)*, pp. 1953−1956.

Hansen, N. D., Mølbak, K., Cox, I. J., & Lioma, C. (2018). Predicting antimicrobial drug consumption using web search data. In *Proceedings of the 2018 international conference on digital health (DH'18)*, pp. 133−142.

Hart, M., Stetten, N., Islam, S., & Pizarro, K. (2017). Twitter and Public Health (Part 2): Qualitative analysis of how individual health professionals outside organizations use microblogging to promote and disseminate health-related information. *JMIR Public Health and Surveillance, 3*(4), e54.

Hartley, D., Nelson, N., Walters, R., Arthur, R., Yangarber, R., Madoff, L., . . . Lightfoot, N. (2010). The landscape of international event-based biosurveillance. *Threats Journal, 3*(1), 7096. Available from https://doi.org/10.3402/ehtj.v3i0.7096.

Hartley, D. M., Giannini, C. M., Wilson, S., Frieder, O., Margolis, P. A., Kotagal, U. R., . . . Macaluso, M. (2017). Coughing, sneezing, and aching online: Twitter and the volume of influenza-like illness in a pediatric hospital. *PLoS ONE, 12*(7), e0182008. Available from https://doi.org/10.1371/journal.pone.0182008.

Harvey, D. (2010). Informatics research proposal predicting influenza trends from blogspsu.edu. doi: 10.1.1.577.12.

Hill, S., Mao, J., Ungar, L., Hennessy, S., Leonard, C. E., & Holmes, J. (2011). Natural supplements for H1N1 Influenza: Retrospective observational infodemiology study of information and search activity on the Internet. *Journal of Medical Internet Research, 13*(2), e36.

Hirose, H., & Wang, L. (2012). Prediction of infectious disease spread using Twitter: A case of Influenza. *The 5th international symposium on parallel architectures*, Vol. 100. Available from https://doi.org/10.1109/PAAP.2012.23.

Ho, C. Ching, Ting, C.-Y., & Raja, D. B. (2018). Using public open data to predict dengue epidemic: Assessment of weather variability, population density, and land use as predictor variables for dengue outbreak prediction using support vector machine. *Indian Journal of Science & Technology, 11*(4). Available from https://doi.org/10.17485/ijst/2018/v11i4/115405.

Huang, D.-C., & Wang, J.-F. (2018). Monitoring hand, foot and mouth disease by combining search engine query data and meteorological factors. *Science of the Total Environment, 612*, 1293−1299. Available from https://doi.org/10.1016/j.scitotenv.2017.09.01.

Huang, J., Zhao, H., & Zhang J. (2013). Detecting flu transmission by social sensor in China. *In Green computing and communications (GreenCom), In 2013 IEEE and internet of things (iThings/CPSCom), IEEE International Conference on and IEEE Cyber, Physical and Social Computing*, IEEE. Available from https://doi.org/10.1109/GreenCom-iThings-CPSCom.2013.216.

Hulth, A., & Rydevik, G. (2011). GET WELL: An automated surveillance system for gaining new epidemiological knowledge. *BMC Public Health, 11*, 252. Available from https://doi.org/10.1186/1471-2458-11-252, Published: 21 April 2011.

Hulth, A., Rydevik, G., & Linde Annika. (2009). Web queries as a source for syndromic surveillance. *PLoS ONE., 4*(2), e4378. Available from https://doi.org/10.1371/journal.pone.0004378.

Hwang, S., Clarite, D. S., Elijorde, F. I., Gerardo, B. D., & Byun, Y. (2016). A web-based analysis for dengue tracking and prediction using artificial neural network. In *Advanced science and technology letters*. Science & Engineering Research Support Society: Sandy Bay, TAS, Australia, Vol. 122, pp. 160−164.

Iso, H., Wakamiya, S., & Aramaki, E. (2016). Forecasting word model: Twitter-based influenza surveillance and prediction. In *Proceedings of COLING 2016, the 26th international conference on computational linguistics: Technical papers*, Osaka, Japan, December 11−17, pp. 76−86.

Jadhav, A., Andrews, D., Fiksdal, A., Kumbamu, A., McCormick, J. B., Misitano, A., . . . Pathak, J. (2014). Comparative analysis of online health queries originating from personal computers and smart devices on a consumer health information portal. *Journal of Medical Internet Research*, *16*(7), e160. Available from https://doi.org/10.2196/jmir.3186.

Jena, A. B., Mandic, P. K., Weaver, L., & Seabury, S. A. (2013). Predicting new diagnoses of HIV infection using internet search engine data. *Clinical Infectious Diseases*, *56*(9), 1352−1353. Available from https://doi.org/10.1093/cid/cit022.

Ji, X., Chun, S. A., & Gelle, J. (2012). Epidemic outbreak and spread detection system based on twitter data. In *International conference on health information science*, Vol. 7231. Springer, Berlin, Heidelberg. Available from https://doi.org/10.1007/978-3-642-29361-0_19, Online ISBN 978-3-642-29361-0.

Johnson, H. A., Wagner, M. M., Hogan, W. R., Chapman, W., Olszewski, R. T., Dowling, J., & Barnas, G. (2004). Analysis of web access logs for surveillance of influenza. *Medinfo*, *107*(Pt 2), 1202−1206. Available from https://doi.org/10.3233/978-1-60750-949-3-1202.

Kandula, S., Hsu, D., & Shaman, J. (2017). Subregional nowcasts of seasonal influenza using search trends. *Journal of Medical Internet Research*, *19*(11), e370. Available from https://doi.org/10.2196/jmir.7486.

Kang, M., Zhong, H., He, J., Rutherford, S., & Yang, F. (2013). Using google trends for Influenza surveillance in South China. *PLoS ONE*, *8*(1), e55205. Available from https://doi.org/10.1371/journal.pone.0055205.

Kangbai, J. B. (2016). Social network analysis and modeling of cellphone-based syndromic surveillance data for Ebola in Sierra Leone. *Asian Pacific Journal of Tropical Medicine*, *9*(9), 851−855. Available from https://doi.org/10.1016/j.apjtm.2016.07.005.

Kazemi, D. M., Borsari, B., Levine, M. J., & Dooley, B. (2017). Systematic review of surveillance by social media platforms for illicit drug use. *Journal of Public Health*, *39*(4), 763−776. Available from https://doi.org/10.1093/pubmed/fdx020.

Khatua, A., & Khatua, A. (2016). Immediate and long-term effects of 2016 Zika outbreak: A twitter-based study. In *2016 IEEE 18th international conference on e-Health Networking, Applications and Services (Healthcom)*, Munich, pp. 1−6. Available from https://doi.org/10.1109/HealthCom.2016.7749496.

Lamb, A., Paul, M. J., & Dredze, M. (2012). Investigating Twitter as a source for studying behavioral responses to epidemics. In *AAAI fall symposium: Information retrieval and knowledge discovery in biomedical text*, Arlington, VA, pp. 81−83.

Lamb, A., Paul, M. J., & Dredze, M. (2013). Separating fact from fear: Tracking flu infections on twitter. In *Conference of the North American chapter of the association for computational linguistics: Human language technologies*, pp. 789−795.

Lampos, V. (2016). Flu detector: Estimating influenza-like illness rates from online user-generated content. arXiv preprint arXiv:1612.03494, 2016 - arxiv.org.

Lampos, V. (2017). Assessing public health interventions using Web content. arXiv:1712.08076. Available from <https://arxiv.org/pdf/1712.08076/> Accessed 20.06.18.

Lampos, V., Bie, T. D., & Cristianini, N. (2010). *Flu detector-tracking epidemics on Twitter*, *ECML PKDD 2010. Lecture Notes in Computer Science* (6323). Berlin, Heidelberg: Springer. Available from https://doi.org/10.1007/978-3-642-15939-8_42.

Lampos, V., Yom-Tov, E., Pebody, R., & Cox, I. J. (2015). Assessing the impact of a health intervention via user-generated Internet content. *Data Mining and Knowledge Discovery*, *29*, 1434. Available from https://doi.org/10.1007/s10618-015-0427-9.

Lane, I., Bryce, A., Ingle, S. M., & Hay, A. D. (2018). Does locally relevant, real-time infection epidemiological data improve clinician management and antimicrobial prescribing in primary care? A systematic review. *Family Practice*. Available from https://doi.org/10.1093/fampra/cmy008.

Laurent, M. R., & Vickers, T. J. (2009). Seeking health information online: Does Wikipedia matter? *Journal of the American Medical Informatics Association, 16*(4), 471−479. Available from https://doi.org/10.1197/jamia.M3059.

Lee, B., Yoon, J., Kim, S., & Hwang, B.-Y. (2012). Detecting social signals of flu symptoms. In *Proceedings of the 8th IEEE international conference on collaborative computing: Networking, applications and worksharing*, pp. 544−545, IEEE. Print ISBN: 978-1-4673-2740-4.

Lee, K., Agrawal, A., & Choudhary, A. (2017). Forecasting influenza levels using real-time social media streams. *2017 IEEE international conference on healthcare informatics (ICHI)*, Park City, UT, pp. 409−414. Available from https://doi.org/10.1109/ICHI.2017.68.

Li, J., & Cardie, C. (2013). Early stage influenza detection from twitter. *Computer Science − Social and Information Networks, Computer Science − Computation and Language.* arXiv1309.7340L.

Li, T., Ding, F., Sun, Q., Zhang, Y., & Kinney, P. L. (2016). Heat stroke internet searches can be a new heatwave health warning surveillance indicator. *Scientific Reports, 6.* Available from https://doi.org/10.1038/srep37294, Article number: 37294.

Li, Y. E., Tung, C.-Y., & Chang, S.-H. (2016). The wisdom of crowds in action: Forecasting epidemic diseases with a web-based prediction market system. *International Journal of Medical Informatics, 92,* 35−43. Available from https://doi.org/10.1016/j.ijmedinf.2016.04.014.

Li, Z., Liu, T., Zhu, G., Lin, H., Zhang, Y., He, J., ... Ma, W. (2017). Dengue Baidu Search Index data can improve the prediction of local dengue epidemic: A case study in Guangzhou, China. *PLoS Neglected Tropical Diseases, 11*(3), e0005354. Available from https://doi.org/10.1371/journal.pntd.0005354.

Liu, K., Wang, T., Yang, Z., Huang, X., Milinovich, G. J., Lu, Y., ... Lu, J. (2016). Using Baidu search index to predict Dengue outbreak in China. *Scientific Reports, 6.* Available from https://doi.org/10.1038/srep38040, Article number: 38040.

Lu, F. S., Hou, S., Baltrusaitis, K., Shah, M., Leskovec, J., Sosic, R., ... Santillana, M. (2018). Accurate influenza monitoring and forecasting using novel Internet data streams: A case study in the Boston Metropolis. *JMIR Public Health and Surveillance, 4*(1), e4. Available from https://doi.org/10.2196/publichealth.8950.

Luo, Y., Zeng, D., Cao, Z., Zheng, X., Wang, Y., Wang, Q., & Zhao, H. (2010). Using multi-source web data for epidemic surveillance: A case study of the 2009 influenza A (H1N1) pandemic. In *Beijingin 2010 IEEE international conference on service operations and logistics and informatics*, Qingdao, China. Piscataway, NJ: IEEE. Available from https://doi.org/10.1109/SOLI.2010.5551614.

Madoff, L. C., Fisman, D. N., & Kass-Hout, T. (2011). A new approach to monitoring dengue activity. *PLoS Neglected Tropical Diseases, 5*(5), e1215. Available from https://doi.org/10.1371/journal.pntd.0001215.

Madoff, L. C., & Li, A. (2014). Web-based surveillance systems for human, animal, and plant diseases. In R. M. Atlas, & S. Maloy (Eds.), *One health, people, animals and the environment.* Washington, DC: American Society for Microbiology. Available from https://doi.org/10.1128/microbiolspec.OH-0015-2012.

Malik, M. T., Gumel, A., Thompson, L. H., Strome, T., & Mahmud, S. M. (2011). Google flu trends and emergency department triage data predicted the 2009 pandemic H1N1 waves in Manitoba. *Canadian Journal of Public Health/Revue Canadienne de Santé Publique, 102*(4), 294−297.

Marques-Toledo, Cd. A., Degener, C. M., Vinhal, L., Coelho, G., Meira, W., Codeço, C. T., & Teixei, M. M. (2017). Dengue prediction by the web: Tweets are a useful tool for estimating and forecasting dengue at country and city level. *PLoS Neglected Tropical Diseases, 11*(7), e0005729. Available from https://doi.org/10.1371/journal.pntd.0005729.

Marquetoux, N., Stevenson, M. A., Wilson, P., Ridler, A., & Heue, C. (2016). Using social network analysis to inform disease control interventions. *Preventive Veterinary Medicine, 126,* 94−104. Available from https://doi.org/10.1016/j.prevetmed.2016.01.022.

Martin, A., & Rino, S. M. (2016). Predicting the spread of pandemic influenza based on air traffic data and social media. *Norwegian University of Science and Technology, NTNU Open.* Available from <https://brage.bibsys.no/xmlui/bitstream/handle/11250/2415312/14623_FULLTEXT.pdf?sequence = 1/> Accessed 20.06.18.

Martin, L. J., Lee, B. E., & Yasui, Y. (2016). Google Flu Trends in Canada: A comparison of digital disease surveillance data with physician consultations and respiratory virus surveillance data. *Epidemiology and Infection*, *144*(2), 325−332. Available from https://doi.org/10.1017/S0950268815001478, Epub 2015 Jul 2.

Martino, S. D., Romano, S., Bertolotto, M., Kanhabua, N., Mazzeo, A., & Nejdl, W. (2017). Towards exploiting social networks for detecting epidemic outbreaks. *Journal of Flexible Systems Management*, *18*, 61. Available from https://doi.org/10.1007/s40171-016-0148-y.

Mavragani, A., & Ochoa, G. (2018). Forecasting AIDS prevalence in the United States using online search traffic data. *Journal of Big Data*, *5*, 17. Available from https://doi.org/10.1186/s40537-018-0126-7.

McClellan, C., Mir, A., Mutter, R., Kroutil, L., & Landwehr, J. (2017). Using social media to monitor mental health discussions—evidence from Twitter. *Journal of the American Medical Informatics Association*, *24*(3), 496−502. Available from https://doi.org/10.1093/jamia/ocw133.

McGough, S. F., Brownstein, J. S., Hawkins, J. B., & Santillana, M. (2017). Forecasting Zika incidence in the 2016 Latin America outbreak combining traditional disease surveillance with search, social media, and news report data. *PLoS Neglected Tropical Diseases*, *11*(1), e0005295. Available from https://doi.org/10.1371/journal.pntd.0005295.

McIver, D. J., & Brownstein, J. S. (2014). Wikipedia usage estimates prevalence of Influenza-like illness in the United States in near real-time. *PLoS Computational Biology*, *10*(4), e1003581. Available from https://doi.org/10.1371/journal.pcbi.1003581.

McMillan, N., Feng, J., Stamps, K., & Burr, R. E. (2014). Use of web-based symptom checker data to predict incidence of a disease or disorder. US Patent App. 14/180,683, US20140236613A1, US Application. Available from <https://patents.google.com/patent/US20140236613/> Accessed 20.06.18.

Merkord, C. L., Liu, Y., Mihretie, A., Gebrehiwot, T., Awoke, W., Bayabil, E., . . . Wimberly, M. C. (2017). Integrating malaria surveillance with climate data for outbreak detection and forecasting: The EPIDEMIA system. *Malaria Journal*, *16*, 89. Available from https://doi.org/10.1186/s12936-017-1735-.

Milinovich, G. J., Williams, G. M., & Hu, W. (2014). Internet-based surveillance systems for monitoring emerging infectious diseases. *The Lancet Infectious Diseases*, *14*(2), 160−168. Available from https://doi.org/10.1016/S1473-3099(13)70244-5.

Missier, P., Romanovsky, A., Miu, U., Pal, A., Daniilakis, M., Garcia, A., . . . Da Silva So, L. (2016). Tracking dengue epidemics using twitter content classification and topic modelling. In S. Casteleyn, P. Dolog, & C. Pautasso (Eds.), *Current trends in web engineering. ICWE 2016. Lecture notes in computer science* (Vol. 9881). Cham: Springer, arXiv:1605.00968v1 [cs.SI] 3 May 2016.

Moran, K. R., Fairchild, G. C., Generous, N., Hickmann, K., Osthus, D., Priedhorsky, R., . . . Del Valle, S. Y. (2016). Epidemic forecasting is messier than weather forecasting: The role of human behavior and internet data streams in epidemic forecast. *The Journal of Infectious Diseases*, *214*(suppl_4), S404−S408. Available from https://doi.org/10.1093/infdis/jiw375.

Morita M., Maskawa S., Aramaki E. (2013), Comparing social media and search activity as social sensors for the detection of influenza, In *The 5th international symposium on languages in biology and medicine (LBM 2013)*, Tokyo, Japan, December.

Moss, R., Zarebski, A., Dawson, P., & McCaw, J. M. (2016). Forecasting influenza outbreak dynamics in Melbourne from Internet search query surveillance data. *Influenza and Other Respiratory Viruses*, *10*(4). Available from https://doi.org/10.1111/irv.12376.

Moulton, A. D., & Schramm, P. J. (2017). Climate change and public health surveillance: Toward a comprehensive strategy. *Journal of Public Health Management & Practice*, *23*(6), 618−626. Available from https://doi.org/10.1097/PHH.0000000000000550.

Mowery, J. (2016). Twitter influenza surveillance: Quantifying seasonal misdiagnosis patterns and their impact on surveillance estimates. *Online Journal of Public Health Informatics*, *8*(3), e198. Available from https://doi.org/10.5210/ojphi.v8i3.7011.

Nagar, R., Yuan, Q., Freifeld, C. C., Santillana, M., Nojima, A., Chunara, R., & Brownstein, J. S. (2014). A case study of the New York City 2012-2013 Influenza season with daily geocoded Twitter data from temporal and spatiotemporal perspectives. *Journal of Medical Internet Research*, *16*(10), e236. Available from https://doi.org/10.2196/jmir.3416. , PMID: 25331122, PMCID: 4259880.

Nagel, A. C., Tsou, M.-H., Spitzberg, B. H., An, L., Gawron, J. M., Gupta, D. K., . . . Sawyer, M. H. (2013). The complex relationship of real space events and messages in cyberspace: Case study of Influenza and pertussis using tweets. *Journal of Medical Internet Research*, *15*(10), e237. Available from https://doi.org/10.2196/jmir.2705.

Nawa, N., Kogaki, S., Takahashi, K., Ishida, H., Baden, H., Katsuragi, S., . . . Ozono, K. (2016). Analysis of public concerns about Influenza vaccinations by mining a massive online question dataset in Japan. *Vaccine*, *34*(27), 3207−3213. Available from https://doi.org/10.1016/j.vaccine.2016.01.008.

Nawaz, M. S., Mustafa, R. U., & Lali, M. I. U. (2018). Role of online data from search engine and social media in healthcare informatics. In *Applying Big Data analytics in bioinformatics and medicine*, Chapter 11, pp. 272−293, IGI Global, 2017.

Neill, D. B., & Soetebier, K. A. (2011). Monitoring Twitter content related to influenza-like-illness in Spanish-speaking populations. *Emerging Health Threats Journal*, *4*(88), 88. Available from https://doi.org/10.3402/ehtj.v4i0.11185.

Nsoesie, E. O., & Brownstein, J. S. (2015). Computational approaches to influenza surveillance: Beyond timeliness. *Cell Host and Mocrob*, *17*(3), 275−278. Available from https://doi.org/10.1016/j.chom.2015.02.004.

Ocampo, A. J., Chunara, R., & Brownstein, J. S. (2013). Using search queries for malaria surveillance, Thailand. *Malaria Journal*, *12*, 390. Available from https://doi.org/10.1186/1475-2875-12-390.

Ofoghi, B., Mann, M., & Verspoor, K. (2016). Towards early discovery of salient health threats: A social media emotion classification technique. In *Proceedings of the Pacific symposium, biocomputing 2016*, pp. 504−515.

Ofran, Y., Paltiel, O., Pelleg, D., Rowe, J. M., & Yom-Tov, E. (2012). Patterns of information-seeking for cancer on the internet: An analysis of real world data. *PLoS ONE*, *7*(9), e45921. Available from https://doi.org/10.1371/journal.pone.0045921.

Olson, D. R., Konty, K. J., Paladini, M., Viboud, C., & Simonsen, L. (2013). Reassessing Google Flu Trends data for detection of seasonal and pandemic Influenza: A comparative epidemiological study at three geographic scales. *PLoS Computational Biology*, *9*(10), e1003256. Available from https://doi.org/10.1371/journal.pcbi.1003256.

Oren, E., Frere, J., Yom-Tov, E., & Yom-Tov, E. (2018). Respiratory syncytial virus tracking using internet search engine data. *BMC Public Health*, *18*, 445. Available from https://doi.org/10.1186/s12889-018-5367-z.

O'Shea, J. (2017). Digital disease detection: A systematic review of event-based internet biosurveillance systems. *International Journal of Medical Informatics*, *101*, 15−22. Available from https://doi.org/10.1016/j.ijmedinf.2017.01.019.

Parrella, A., Dalton, C. B., Pearce, R., Litt, J. C. B., & Stocks, N. (2009). ASPREN surveillance system for Influenza-like illness: A comparison with flutracking and the national notifiable diseases surveillance system. *Australian Family Physician*, *38*(11), 932−936.

Patwardhan, A., & Bilkovski, R. (2012). Comparison: Flu prescription sales data from a retail pharmacy in the US with Google Flu trends and US ILINet (CDC) data as flu activity indicator. *PLoS ONE*, *7*(8), e43611. Available from https://doi.org/10.1371/journal.pone.0043611.

Paul, M. J., & Dredze, M. (2011). You are what you Tweet: Analyzing Twitter for public health. In *Proceedings of the 5th international AAAI conference on weblogs and social media (ICWSM)*. Available from <http://www.aaai.org/ocs/index.php/ICWSM/ICWSM11/paper/viewFile/2880/3264/> Accessed 20.06.18.

Paul, M. J., & Dredze, M. (2012). *A model for mining public health topics from Twitter. Technical report*. Johns Hopkins University. Available from <https://pdfs.semanticscholar.org/41cb/ae26fe87307e6878e87b0a08056206a5c4c1.pdf/> Accessed 15.06.18.

Paul, M. J., Dredze, M., & Broniatowsk, D. A. (2014). Twitter improves Influenza forecasting. *PLOS Currents Outbreaks*. Edition 1. Available from https://doi.org/10.1371/currents.outbreaks.90b9ed0f59bae4ccaa683a39865d9117.

Paul, M. J., Dredze, M., Broniatowski, D. A., & Nicholas, G. (2015). Worldwide influenza surveillance through twitter. In *AAAI workshop: WWW and public health intelligence*. Available from <https://pdfs.semanticscholar.org/6327/7acf07927625df96e668b8e812e6781f2a6b.pdf/> Accessed 20.06.18.

Paul, M. J., Sarker, A., Brownstein, J. S., Nikfajiam, A., Scotch, M., Smith, K. L., & Gonzalez, G. (2016). Social media mining for public health monitoring and surveillance. *Pacific symposium on biocomputing*, Vol. 21, 468.

Peek, N., Holmes, J. H., & Sun, J. (2014). Technical challenges for big data in biomedicine and health: Data sources, infrastructure, and analytics. *Yearbook of Medical Informatics*, *9*(1), 42−47. Available from https://doi.org/10.15265/IY-2014-0018. Published online 2014 Aug 15. PMCID: PMC4287098, PMID: 25123720.

Perrotta, D., Bella, A., Rizzo, C., & Paolotti, D. (2017). Participatory online surveillance as a supplementary tool to sentinel doctors for influenza-like illness surveillance in Italy. *PLoS ONE*, *12*(1), e0169801. Available from https://doi.org/10.1371/journal.pone.0169801.

Perrotta, D., Tizzoni, M., & Paolotti, D. (2017). Using participatory Web-based surveillance data to improve seasonal influenza forecasting in Italy. In *Proceedings of the 26th international conference on world wide web (WWW17)*, pp. 303−310, Perth, Australia—April 03−07, 2017, International World Wide Web Conferences Steering Committee Republic and Canton of Geneva, Switzerland ©2017 table of contents. ISBN: 978-1-4503-4913-0. Available from https://doi.org/10.1145/3038912.3052670.

Petersen, J., Simons, H., Patel, D., & Freedman, J. (2017). Early detection of perceived risk among users of a UK travel health website compared with internet search activity and media coverage during the 2015−2016 Zika virus outbreak: An observational study. *BMJ Open*, *7*, e015831. Available from https://doi.org/10.1136/bmjopen-2017-015831.

Polgreen, P. M., Chen, Y., Pennock, D. M., Nelson, F. D., & Weinstein, R. A. (2008). Using internet searches for Influenza surveillance. *Clinical Infectious Diseases*, *47*(11), 1443−1448. Available from https://doi.org/10.1086/593098.

Pollett, S., Althouse, B. M., Forshey, B., Rutherford, G. W., & Jarman, R. G. (2017). Internet-based biosurveillance methods for vector-borne diseases: Are they novel public health tools or just novelties? *PLoS Neglected Tropical Diseases*, *11*(11), e0005871. Available from https://doi.org/10.1371/journal.pntd.0005871.

Pollett, S., Boscardin, W. J., Azziz-Baumgartner, E., Tinoco, Y. O., Soto, G., Romero, C., . . . Rutherford, G. W. (2017). Evaluating Google Flu Trends in Latin America: Important lessons for the next phase of digital disease detection. *Clinical Infectious Diseases*, *64*(1), 34−41. Available from https://doi.org/10.1093/cid/ciw657.

Prakash, B. A. (2016). Prediction using propagation: From flu trends to cybersecurity. *IEEE Intelligent Systems*, *31*(1), 84−88. Available from https://doi.org/10.1109/MIS.2016.1.

Priedhorsky, R., Osthus, D., Daughton, R., Moran, K. R., Generous, N., Fairchild, G., . . . DelValle, S. Y. (2017). Measuring global disease with Wikipedia: Success, failure, and a research agenda. In *Proceedings of the 2017 ACM conference on computer supported cooperative work and social computing (CSCW'17)*, pp. 1812−1834, Portland, Oregon, USA—February 25−March 01, 2017, ACM New York, NY, USA ©2017, table of contents. ISBN: 978-1-4503-4335-0. Available from https://doi.org/10.1145/2998181.2998183.

Qiu, R., Hadzikadic, M., & Yao, L. (2017). *Estimating disease burden using google trends and wikipedia data advances in artificial intelligence: From theory to practice*, IEA/AIE 2017. *Lecture notes in computer science* (10351). Cham: Springer. Available from https://doi.org/10.1007/978-3-319-60045-1_39, Print ISBN 978-3-319-60044-439, Online ISBN 978-3-319-60045-1.

Radzikowski, J., Stefanidis, A., Jacobsen, K. H., Croitoru, A., Crooks, A., & Delamater, P. L. (2016). The measles vaccination narrative in twitter: A quantitative analysis. *JMIR Public Health and Surveillance*, *2*(1), e1. Available from https://doi.org/10.2196/publichealth.5059. Published online 2016 Jan 4. PMCID: PMC4869226, PMID: 27227144.

Rattanaumpawan, P., Boonyasiri, A., Vong, S., & Thamlikitkul, V. (2018). Systematic review of electronic surveillance of infectious diseases with emphasis on antimicrobial resistance surveillance in resource-limited settings. *American Journal of Infection Control*, *46*(2), 139−146. Available from https://doi.org/10.1016/j.ajic.2017.08.006.

Rekatsinas, T., Ghosh, S., Mekaru, S. R., Nsoesie, E. O., Brownstein, J. S., Getoor, L., & Ramakrishnan, N. (2017). Forecasting rare disease outbreaks from open source indicators. *The ASA Data Science Journal*, *10*(2), 136−150. Available from https://doi.org/10.1002/sam.11337.

Richterich, A. (2016). Using transactional big data for epidemiological surveillance: Google flu trends and ethical implications of 'infodemiology'. In B. Mittelstadt, & L. Floridi (Eds.), *The ethics of biomedical Big*

Data. Law, governance and technology series (29). Cham: Springer. Available from https://doi.org/10.1007/978-3-319-33525-4_3.

Robertson, C., & Yee, L. (2016). Avian influenza risk surveillance in North America with online media. *PLoS ONE, 11*(11), e0165688. Available from https://doi.org/10.1371/journal.pone.0165688.

Robin, M.-H., Bancal, M.-O., Cellier, V., Délos, M., Felix, I., Launay, M., . . . Aubertot, J.-N. (2017). IPSIM-Web, an online resource for promoting qualitative aggregative hierarchical network models to predict plant disease risk: Application to brown rust on wheat. *APS Jourals, Plant Disease, 102*(3), 488−499. Available from https://doi.org/10.1094/PDIS-12-16-1816-SR, March 2018.

Rohart, F., Milinovich, G. J., Avril, S. M. R., Cao, K.-A. L., Tong, S., & Hu, W. (2016). Disease surveillance based on Internet-based linear models: An Australian case study of previously unmodeled infection diseases. *Scientific Reports, 6.* Available from https://doi.org/10.1038/srep38522, Article number: 38522.

Romano, S., Di Martino, S., Kanhabua, N., Mazzeo, A., & Nejdl, W. (2016). Challenges in detecting epidemic outbreaks from social networks. In *2016 30th international conference on advanced information networking and applications workshops (WAINA)*, NSPEC Accession Number: 16022255, Available from https://doi.org/10.1109/WAINA.2016.111

Sadilek, A., Kautz, H., DiPrete, L., Labus, B., Portman, E., Teitel, J., & Silenzio, V. (2016). Deploying nEmesis: Preventing foodborne illness by data mining social media. In *The IAAI conference on artificial intelligence (IAAI)*, pp. 3982−3990.

Sadilek, A., Kautz, H., & Silenzio V. (2012), Modeling spread of disease from social interactions. In *Proceedings of the ICSWM'11.* Available from <https://pdfs.semanticscholar.org/699c/3faeac25ebf5ebbb4e2641f3f4fb5a9a7720.pdf/> Accessed 20.06.18.

Sadilek, A., Kautz, H., & Silenzio, V. (2012). Predicting disease transmission from geo-tagged micro-blog data. In *Proceedings of the 26th AAAI conference on artificial intelligence*, December.

Samaras, L., García-Barriocanal, E., & Sicilia, M.-A. (2012). Syndromic surveillance models using Web data: The case of scarlet fever in the UK. *Informatics for Health and Social Care, 37*(2), 106−124.

Samaras, L., García-Barriocanal, E., & Sicilia, M.-A. (2017). Syndromic surveillance models using web data: The case of influenza in Greece and Italy using google trends. *JMIR Public Health and Surveillance, 3*(4), e90. Available from https://doi.org/10.2196/publichealth.8015.

Sandhu, R., Harsuminder, K. G., & Sandeep, K. S. (2016). Smart monitoring and controlling of Pandemic Influenza A (H1N1) using Social Network Analysis and cloud computing. *Journal of Computational Science, 12,* 11−22. Available from https://doi.org/0.1016/j.jocs.2015.11.001.

Santillana, M., Nguyen, A. T., Dredze, M., Paul, M. J., Nsoesie, E. O., & Brownstein, J. S. (2015). Combining search, social media, and traditional data sources to improve Influenza surveillance. *PLoS Computational Biology, 11*(10), e1004513. Available from https://doi.org/10.1371/journal.pcbi.1004513.

Santillana, M., Nguyen, A. T., Louie, T., Zink, A., Gray, J., Sung, I., & Brownstein, J. S. (2016). Cloud-based electronic health records for real-time, region-specific influenza surveillance. *Scientific Reports, 6.* Available from https://doi.org/10.1038/srep25732, Article number: 25732.

Santillana, M., Nsoesie, E. O., Mekaru, S. R., Scales, D., & Brownstein, J. S. (2014). Using clinicians' search query data to monitor Influenza epidemics. *Clinical Infectious Diseases, 59*(10), 1446−1450. Available from https://doi.org/10.1093/cid/ciu647.

Santos, J. C., & Matos, S. (2013). Predicting flu incidence from Portuguese Tweets. In *IWBBIO proceedings*, Granada, Spain, March 18−20, pp. 11−18.

Santos, J. C., & Matos, S. (2014). Analysing Twitter and web queries for flu trend prediction. *Theoretical Biology and Medical Modelling, 11*(Suppl 1), S6. Available from https://doi.org/10.1186/1742-4682-11-S1-S6.

Schein, R., Wilson, K., & Kealan, J. (2011). *Literature review on effectiveness of the use of social media: A report for Peel Public Health.* [Region of Peel], Peel Public Health, 2011, Carleton University, Ottawa, Ontario, Canada.

Schellpfeffer, N., Collins, A., Brousseau, D. C., Martin, E. T., & Hashikawa, A. (2014). Web-based surveillance of illness in childcare centers. *Health Security*, *15*(5). Available from https://doi.org/10.1089/hs.2016.0124.

Schirmer, P., Lucero, S., Oda, G., Lopez, J., & Holodniy, M. (2010). Effective detection of the 2009 H1N1 Influenza pandemic in US Veterans Affairs medical centers using a national electronic biosurveillance system. *PLoS ONE*, *5*(3), e9533. Available from https://doi.org/10.1371/journal.pone.0009533.

Schwab-Reese, L., Hovdestad, W., Tonmyr, L., & Fluke, J. (2018). The potential use of social media and other internet-related data and communications for child maltreatment surveillance and epidemiological research: Scoping review and recommendations. *Child Abuse & Neglect*. Available from https://doi.org/10.1016/j.chiabu.2018.01.014, ISSN: 1873-7757, Publication Year: 2018, PMID:29366596.

Sciascia, S., & Radin, M. (2017). What can google and wikipedia can tell us about a disease? Big Data trends analysis in systemic lupus erythematosus. *International Journal of Medical Informatics*, *107*, 65−69. Available from https://doi.org/10.1016/j.ijmedinf.2017.09.002, November 2017.

Seifter, A., Schwarzwalder, A., Geis, K., & Aucott, J. (2010). The utility of "Google Trends" for epidemiological research: Lyme disease as an example. *Geospatial Health*, *4*, 135−137. Available from https://doi.org/10.4081/gh.2010.195.

Şerban, O., Thapen, N., Maginnisa, B., Hankina, C., & Foot, V. (2018). Real-time processing of social media with SENTINEL: A syndromic surveillance system incorporating deep learning for health classification. *Information Processing & Management*. Available from https://doi.org/10.1016/j.ipm.2018.04.011, ISSN: 0306-4573, Publication Year: 2018.

Seyyed Hosseini, S. (2018). An infodemiology study on breast cancer in Iran: Health information supply versus health information demand in PubMed and Google Trends. *Emerald Inside*, *36*(2), 258−269. Available from https://doi.org/10.1108/EL-03-2017-0062, 2018/04/03, N1 -doi:10.1108/EL-03-2017-0062.

Sharpe, J. D., Hopkins, R. S., Cook, R. L., & Strile, C. W. (2016). Evaluating Google, Twitter, and Wikipedia as tools for influenza surveillance using Bayesian change point analysis: A comparative analysis. *JMIR Public Health and Surveillance*, *2*(2), e161. Published online 2016 Oct 20. Available from DOI: 10.2196/publichealth.5901, PMCID: PMC5095368, PMID: 27765731.

Shikha, V., Younghee, P., & Mihui, K. (2017). Predicting flu-rate using big data analytics based on social data and weather conditions. *Advanced Science Letters*, *23*(12), 12775−12779. Available from https://doi.org/10.1166/asl.2017.10897. (5), Publisher: American Scientific Publishers.

Shin, S.-Y., Kim, T., Seo, D.-W., Sohn, C. H., Kim, S.-H., Ryoo, S. M., ... Lim, K. S. (2016). Correlation between national influenza surveillance data and search queries from mobile devices and desktops in South Korea. *PLoS ONE*, *11*(7), e0158539. Available from https://doi.org/10.1371/journal.pone.0158539.

Signorini, A. (2015). *Use of social media to monitor and predict outbreaks and public opinion on health topics* (PhD thesis). University of Iowa. Available from <http://ir.uiowa.edu/etd/1503/> Asceesed 19.06.18.

Signorini, A., Segre, A. M., & Polgreen, P. M. (2011). The use of Twitter to track levels of disease activity and public concern in the US during the Influenza A H1N1 pandemic. *PLoS ONE*, *6*(5), e19467. Available from https://doi.org/10.1371/journal.pone.0019467.

Sivasankari, S., Kavitha, M., & Saranya, G. (2017). Medical analysis and visualisation of diseases using Tweet data. *Research Journal of Pharmacy and Technology*, *10*(12), 4306−4312. Available from https://doi.org/10.5958/0974-360X.2017.00788.0.

Sousa, L., De Mello, R., Cedrim, D., Garcia, A., Missier, P., Uchôa, A., ... Romanovsky, A. (2018). VazaDengue: An information system for preventing and combating mosquito-borne diseases with social networks. *Information Systems*, *75*, 26−42.

Spruit, M., & Lytras, M. (2018). Applied data science in patient-centric healthcare: Adaptive analytic systems for empowering physicians and patients. *Telematics and Informatics*, *35*(4), 643−653. Available from https://doi.org/10.1016/j.tele.2018.04.002, 2018.

Suzumura, T. (2011). StreamWeb: Real-time web monitoring with stream computing. In *2011 IEEE international conference on web services*, July 4−9, INSPEC Accession Number: 12219322, Available from https://doi.org/10.1109/ICWS.2011.16.

Teng, Y., Bi, D., Xie, G., Jin, Y., Huang, Y., Lin, B., ... Tong, Y. (2017). Dynamic forecasting of Zika epidemics using Google Trends. *PLoS ONE*, *12*(1), e0165085. Available from https://doi.org/10.1371/journal.pone.0165085.

Tilston, N. L., Eames, K. T. D., Paolotti, D., Ealden, T., & Edmunds, W. J. (2010). Internet-based surveillance of Influenza-like-illness in the UK during the 2009 H1N1 Influenza pandemic. *BMC Public Health*, *10*, 650. Available from https://doi.org/10.1186/1471-2458-10-650.

Tony, Yang Y., Horneffer, M., & DiLisio, N. (2013). Mining social media and web searches for disease detection. *Journal of Public Health Research*, *2*(1), 17−21. Available from https://doi.org/10.4081/jphr.2013.e4. Published online 2013 May 31. PMCID: PMC4140326, PMID: 25170475.

Valdivia, A., López-Alcalde, J., Vicente, M., Pichiule, M., Ruiz, M., & Ordobas, M. (2010). Monitoring Influenza activity in Europe with Google Flu Trends: Comparison with the findings of sentinel physician networks-results for 2009-10. *EuroSurveillance*, *15*(29). Available from https://doi.org/10.2807/ese.15.29.19621-en.

Verdery, A. M., Siripong, N., & Pence Brian, W. (2017). Social network clustering and the spread of hiv/aids among persons who inject drugs in 2 cities in the Philippines. *JAIDS Journal of Acquired Immune Deficiency Syndromes*, *76*(1), 26−32. Available from https://doi.org/10.1097/QAI.0000000000001485.

Visvizi, A., & Lytras, M. D. (Eds.), (2019). *Smart Cities: Issues and Challenges: Mapping Political, Social and Economic Risks and Threats*. Amsterdam, The Netherlands: Elsevier.

Walker, J. G. (2013). New media methods for syndromic surveillance and disease modelling. *CAB reviews perspectives in agriculture veterinary science nutrition and natural resources*, February. Available from https://doi.org/10.1079/PAVSNNR20138031.

Wang, F., Wang, H., Xu, K., Raymond, R., Chon, J., Fuller, S., & Debruyn, A. (2016). Regional level influenza study with geo-tagged Twitter data. *Journal of Medical Systems*, *40*, 189. Available from https://doi.org/10.1007/s10916-016-0545-y.

Wang, H.-W., Chen, D.-R., Yu, H.-W., & Chen, Y.-M. (2015). Forecasting the incidence of dementia and dementia-related outpatient visits with google trends: Evidence from Taiwan. *Journal of Medical Internet Research*, *17*(11), e264. Available from https://doi.org/10.2196/jmir.4516. Published online 2015 Nov 19. PMCID: PMC4704919, PMID: 26586281.

Wasim, A. (2018). *Using Twitter data to provide qualitative insights into pandemics and epidemics* (PhD thesis). University of Sheffield, UK, Available from <http://etheses.whiterose.ac.uk/20367/1/Final%20PhD%20Thesis%2011%20MAY.pdf/> Accessed 20.06.18.

Wilson, K., & Brownstein, J. S. (2009). Early detection of disease outbreaks using the Internet. *CMAJ*, *180*(8), 829−831. Available from https://doi.org/10.1503/cmaj.1090215.

Woo, H., Cho, H. S., Shim, E., & Lee, J. K. (2017). Identification of keywords from Twitter and web blog posts to detect influenza epidemics in Korea. *Disaster Medicine and Public Health Preparedness*. Available from https://doi.org/10.1017/dmp.2017.84, Published online: 31 July 2017.

Woo, H., Cho, Y., Shim, E., Lee, J.-K., Lee, C.-G., & Kim, S. H. (2016). Estimating influenza outbreaks using both search engine query data and social media data in South Korea. *Journal of Medical Internet Research*, *18*(7), e177. Available from https://doi.org/10.2196/jmir.4955.

Xiao, Q. Y., Liu, H. J., & Feldman, M. W. (2017). Tracking and predicting hand, foot, and mouth disease (HFMD) epidemics in China by Baidu queries. *Epidemiology & Infection*, *145*(8), 1699−1707. Available from https://doi.org/10.1017/S0950268817000231, June 2017.

Xie, Y., Chen, Z., Cheng, Y., Zhang, K., Agrawal, A., Liao, W.-K., & Choudhary, A. (2013). Detecting and tracking disease outbreaks by mining social media data. In *Proceedings of the 23rd international joint conference on artificial intelligence*. AAAI Press, pp. 2958−2960.

Xu, Q., Gel, J. R., Ramirez, L., Nezafati, K., Zhang, Q., & Tsu, K.-L. (2017). Forecasting influenza in Hong Kong with Google search queries and statistical model fusion. *PLoS ONE*, *12*(5), e0176690. Available from https://doi.org/10.1371/journal.pone.0176690.

Xu, W., Han, Z.-W., & Ma J. (2010). A neural network based approach to detect Influenza epidemics using search engine query data. In *e-Business engineering (ICEBE) 2011 IEEE 8th international conference*, pp. 9−15, Available from https://doi.org/10.1109/ICMLC.2010.5580851.

Yan, S. J., Chughtai, A. A., & Macintyre, C. R. (2017a). Effectiveness of web-based social sensing in health information dissemination—A review. *Telematics and Informatics*, *34*(1), 194−219. Available from https://doi.org/10.1016/j.tele.2016.04.012.

Yan, S. J., Chughtai, A. A., & Macintyre, C. R. (2017b). Utility and potential of rapid epidemic intelligence from internet-based sources. *International Journal of Infectious Diseases*, *63*, 77−87. Available from https://doi.org/10.1016/j.ijid.2017.07.020.

Yang, A. C., Huang, N. E., Peng, C.-K., & Tsai, S.-J. (2010). Do seasons have an influence on the incidence of depression? The use of an internet search engine query data as a proxy of human affect. *PLoS ONE*, *5*(10), e13728. Available from https://doi.org/10.1371/journal.pone.0013728.

Yang, M., Li, Y.-J., & Kiang, M. (2011). Uncovering social media data for public health surveillance, Association for Information Systems AIS Electronic Library (AISeL). In *PACIS 2011 Proceedings*. ISBN: [978-1-86435-644-1]; Full paper.

Yang, S., Kou, S. C., Lu, F., Brownstein, J. S., Brooke, N., & Santillana, M. (2017). Advances in using Internet searches to track dengue. *PLoS Computational Biology*, *13*(7), e1005607. Available from https://doi.org/10.1371/journal.pcbi.1005607.

Yang, S., Santillana, M., Brownstein, J. S., Gray, J., Richardson, S., & Kou, S. C. (2017). Using electronic health records and Internet search information for accurate influenza forecasting. *BMC Infectious Diseases*, *17*, 332. Available from https://doi.org/10.1186/s12879-017-2424-7.

Yang, W. (2017). *Early warning for infectious disease outbreak: Theory and practice* (p. 388) Cambridge, MA: Academic Press, ISBN: 978-0-12-812343-0.

Yanga, S., Santillana, M., & Kou, S. C. (2015). Accurate estimation of Influenza epidemics using Google search data via ARGO. *Proceedings of the National Academy Sciences*, *112*(47), 14473−14478. Available from https://doi.org/10.1073/pnas.1515373112, published ahead of print November 9, 2015.

Ye, X., Li, S., Yang, X., & Qin, C. (2016). Use of social media for the detection and analysis of infectious diseases in China. *ISPRS International Journal of Geo-Informatics*, *5*(9), 156. Available from https://doi.org/10.3390/ijgi5090156.

Yom-Tov, E., Borsa, D., Cox, I. J., & McKendry, R. A. (2014). Detecting disease outbreaks in mass gatherings using Internet data. *Journal of Medical Internet Research*, *16*(6), e154. Available from https://doi.org/10.2196/jmir.3156. PMID: 24943128, PMCID: 4090384.

Yom-Tov, E., Cox, I. J., & Lampos, V. (2015). Learning about health and medicine from Internet data. In *Proceedings of the 8th ACM international conference on web search and data mining (WSDM'15)*, pp. 417−418, Shanghai, China, February 02−06, ACM, New York, NY, ©2015, table of contents. ISBN: 978-1-4503-3317-7. https://doi.org/10.1145/2684822.2697042.

Yom-Tov, E., White, R. W., & Horvitz, E. (2014). Seeking insights about cycling mood disorders via anonymized search logs. *Journal of Medical Internet Research*, *16*(2), e65. Available from https://doi.org/10.2196/jmir.2664. PMID: 24568936, PMCID: 3961703.

Young, S. D., Rivers, C., & Lewis, B. (2014). Methods of using real-time social media technologies for detection and remote monitoring of HIV outcomes. *Preventive Medicine*, *63*, 112−115. Available from https://doi.org/10.1016/j.ypmed.2014.01.024, ISSN: 1096-0260 Publication Year: 2014.

Young, S. D., Torrone, E. A., Urata, J., & Aral, S. O. (2018). Using search engine data as a tool to predict syphilis. *Epidemiology*, *29*(4), 574−578. Available from https://doi.org/10.1097/EDE.0000000000000836.

Yuan, Q., Nsoesie, E. O., Lv, B., Peng, G., Chunara, R., & Brownstein, J. S. (2013). Monitoring influenza epidemics in China with search query from Baidu. *PLoS ONE*, *8*(5), e64323. Available from https://doi.org/10.1371/journal.pone.0064323.

Zhang, Y., Bambrick, H., Mengersen, K., Tong, S., & Hu, W. (2018). Using Google Trends and ambient temperature to predict seasonal influenza outbreaks. *Environment International*, *117*, 284−291. Available from https://doi.org/10.1016/j.envint.2018.05.016.

Zhou, X., Yang, F., & Feng, Y. (2017). A spatial-temporal method to detect global influenza epidemics using heterogeneous data collected from the Internet. *Journal IEEE/ACM Transactions on Computational Biology and Bioinformatics (TCBB)*, *15*(3), 802−812. Available from https://doi.org/10.1109/TCBB.2017.2690631.

Zou, B., Lampos, V., & Cox, I. J. (2018). Multi-task learning improves disease models from web search. In *Proceedings of 2018 IW3C2 (International World Wide Web Conference Committee) (WWW'18)*, published under Creative Commons CCBY4.0 License. ACMISBN978-1-4503-5639-8/18/04, Available from https://doi.org/10.1145/3178876.3186050.

Zou, B., Lampos, V., Gorton, R., & Cox, I. J. (2016). On infectious intestinal disease surveillance using social media content. In *Proceedings of the 6th international conference on digital health conference (DH'16)*, pp. 157−161, Montréal, Québec, Canada, April 11−13. ACM New York, NY, ©2016, table of contents. ISBN: 978-1-4503-4224-7. Available from https://doi.org/10.1145/2896338.2896372.

Natural Language Processing, Sentiment Analysis, and Clinical Analytics

Adil Rajput

Information Systems Department, Effat University An Nazlah Al Yamaniyyah, Jeddah, Saudi Arabia

3.1 Introduction

The Big Data revolution has changed the way scientists approach problems in almost every (if not all) area of research (Lytras, Raghavan, & Damiani, 2017). The Big Data field culls concepts from various fields of Computer Science. These include Natural Language Processing (NLP), Information Retrieval (IR), Artificial Intelligence, Machine Learning (ML), network analysis, and graph theory to name a few. The aforementioned fields have been part and parcel of research in Computer Science for many decades. However, the advent of Web 2.0 and social media resulted in the three Vs of the Big Data—variety, veracity, and volume (Laney, 2001).

3.1.1 Natural Language Processing and Healthcare/Clinical Analytics

One of the challenges that researchers and practitioners face in both psychology and psychiatry is access to data that truly reflect the mental state of the subject/patient. The traditional approaches depend on gathering data from the subject and the immediate family/friends and/or asking select individuals belonging to a certain group to fill put surveys/questionnaires that might provide an insight into mental state of various individuals/groups.

Sentiment analysis domain—also known as Opinion Mining—allows scientists to sift through the text gathered via various sources and glean how the subject at hand feels. The area depends heavily on techniques in NLP. The NLP allows a machine to process a natural human language and translates it to a format that the machine understands. NLP dates back to the 1960s but became very popular with the advent of the World Wide Web and search engines. The query processing capabilities of search engines required to add context to the terms entered by users and in turn present a set of results that the user can choose from.

Innovation in Health Informatics.
DOI: https://doi.org/10.1016/B978-0-12-819043-2.00003-4

3.1.2 Sentiment analysis

Utilizing the techniques from NLP, sentiment analysis field looks at users' expressions and in turn associate emotions with what the user has provided. The cultural norms add a different twist to this area. For example, the following statement could be interpreted very differently.

This new gadget is bad!

While the obvious meaning alludes to the user's dislike of the gadget, user community belonging to a certain age group would consider the above statement as a resounding endorsement of the gadget at hand. Furthermore, the sentiment analysis looks at the time at which the user expressed the sentiment or opinion. The same user can be under certain stressors which can cloud their judgment and hence gathering statements on a time continuum can provide better assurance of the sentiments expressed.

The social media platform provides both challenges and opportunities in this area. On a positive note, it grants anonymity to the person writing on the web thus allowing him/her to express their feelings freely (Rajadesingan, Zafarani, & Liu, 2015). Moreover, the data can be gathered for a given interval that can prove vital in ensuring consistency. The data gleaned in this manner will offer a preponderance of evidence supporting the researcher's hypothesis and can provide a solid foundation for scientific deductions. Gathering data from the web has become the choice of many fields such as Marketing, etc. Google, YouTube, and Amazon are examples of how companies can provide customized content to the end-user. Many such fields can depend greatly on objective metrics such as number of likes, total number of items sold given an age range, etc. However, the fields of psychology/psychiatry do not have such luxury as the data are in form of text written by users on the various media such as blogs, social media, etc. This dimension adds more complexity due to (1) use of different languages on a certain topic/blog, (2) use of nonstandard words that cannot be found in a dictionary, and (3) use of emojis and symbols. These questions are tackled by experts in the NLP domain along with those working in the sentiment analysis area.

There is a need of providing social scientists and psychiatrists the requisite vocabulary and the basic tools to scavenge data from the web, parse it appropriately and glean the contextual information. This work is intended to be a step in this direction. Specifically, the paper provides the following:

1. Provide a basic understanding on various prevalent theories in NLP
2. Explain the traditional and the statistical approaches to NLP
3. Look at the work done in the area of sentiment analysis and the challenges faced in the light of mental health issues
4. Present a brief synopsis of various applications in applying NLP concepts to mental health issues and sentiment analysis

This paper will introduce the key concepts and definitions pertaining to each section rather than lumping it altogether in a separate section.

3.2 Natural Language Processing

The field of NLP dates back to few decades and has matured quite significantly over the years. Initially confined to gathering data from a limited set of digitized documents, the advent of World Wide Web saw an explosion in information in many different languages. Significant amount of work was done in the IR field which is considered an application of the NLP domain. Before discussing the IR techniques, a bit more, let us delve into the theoretical and practical aspects of NLP.

3.2.1 Traditional approach—key concepts

Initially, the NLP approach followed the following discrete steps.

1. Text preprocessing/tokenization
2. Lexical analysis
3. Syntactical analysis
4. Semantic analysis

3.2.1.1 Preprocessing/tokenization

The first challenge is to segment a given document into words and sentences. The word token—initially confined to programming languages theory—is now synonymous with segmenting the text into words. Most of the languages use the white space as the delimiter but it can be a bit tricky in certain languages. While seeming straightforward, the challenges include separating words such as "I'm" into "I am" and deciding whether or not to separate a token such as "high-impact" into two words. Complicating the matter further would be the language of the document. The unicode standard helps tremendously as each character is assigned a unique value and therefore makes it practical to decide upon the underlying language.

Another concept that NLP experts use quite often is "Regular Expression (RE)." Also finding its root in the computer programming language theory, RE specifies the format of the string that needs to be looked at. As an example, a password string (token) that can contain upper case letters only will be specified as [A−Z], while a string counting numbers will be specified as [0−9]. The importance of RE will become apparent in the next subsection.

In addition to segmenting the text into token/words, the NLP domain places great emphasis on finding the boundary of sentences. While many languages will use punctuation marks to define sentence boundaries, other languages such as Chinese, Korean, etc. prove to be much more difficult in this regards. Complicating the matter further are short forms that use the period symbol ".". While used for ending a sentence, a token such as "Mr." might send the wrong signal.

3.2.1.2 Lexical analysis

After processing the text, the next challenge is to divide the text into lexemes. A lexeme in linguistics represents a meaning and is considered the unit of lexicon. A lexeme can have different endings—known as inflectional endings. As an example, the term "sleep" is the unit that can take various forms such as "sleeping," "slept," or "sleeps." The unit token is also known as lemma. A lexeme is composed of morphemes—bound and unbound/free. An unbound morpheme is "tokens" that can be independent words such as cat. Bound morphemes are affixes and suffixes such as "un," "-tion," etc.

After preprocessing of text and segmenting it into words, the NLP practitioners would take each token and reduce it to its unit lexeme form. Thus the words "depression" and "depressed" will both be reduced to one-unit form—"depress." This process is also known as stemming where each token is reduced to a root form called stem. This term is more prevalent in Computer Science and in certain cases might not be the same as the lemma. The most famous algorithm for this technique is the Porter algorithm (Porter, 1980) which was later improved to Porter2 or Snowball algorithm. Lancaster Stemmer is also used frequently but is considered a bit more aggressive. This will be discussed in more detailed in the practical section.

One of the most important benefits of stemming is to gather a frequency distribution of various words in a given text. The frequency distribution helps surmise the topic of the text being considered at hand. The famous tf–idf algorithm in Linguistics and Computer Science is widely used. The tf measures the frequency of the terms present in the document and infers the subject/keywords describing the document. The idf factor focuses on eliminating the commonly used words such as prepositions, articles, etc. allowing the tf factor to accurately represent the subject of the document at hand. While many other techniques have been proposed and tested, tf–idf algorithm is usually the starting point when dealing with texts.

3.2.1.3 Syntactical analysis

Now that we understand how a text can be broken down into sentences and words using the concept of tokens, the next challenge is to ensure that the text being processed is following rules of grammar and is conveying certain meaning. Syntactical analysis is the process that ensures that rules of grammar are being followed. As an example, consider the sentence "Mary Joe road deer drive." The tokens and the period will indicate a full sentence but does not convey any meaning. The grammars are described as sets of rules. The following rules, for example, describe the rules for representing numbers and the four operators namely addition, subtraction, division, and multiplication.

$$<E> \rightarrow Number$$
$$<E> \rightarrow (<E>)$$
$$<E> \rightarrow <E> + <E>$$
$$<E> \rightarrow <E> - <E>$$
$$<E> \rightarrow <E> / <E>$$
$$<E> \rightarrow <E> \times <E>$$

The Grammar (referred to as mathematical grammar) is composed of terminal and nonterminal symbols. In the above example, Number is a terminal symbol while $<E>$ is a nonterminal symbol. If we assume that the Number symbol represents integers then the following expressions when parsed will conform to the above grammar.

$$134 + 256, \quad 134, \quad (256)$$

However, expressions such as "−134," "134," "25," and "134/12 34" will not conform to the grammar described above. The process of ensuring the tokens follow a particular grammar is also referred to parsing by Computer Scientists/Computational Linguists. The lexical analyzer described in the previous subsection and a parser is needed to process text. While the above might seem overwhelming a bit at first, think of it as this: If the text has the following two sentences, how can it be decided that the sentences are conforming to English grammar?

The dog ran after the ball

The ball dog ran ball the

A human looking at the two sentences above will dismiss the second sentence as gibberish right away, but it is not so easy for a computer to discern. The question computer scientists and computational linguists traditionally faced was whether or not a natural language can be represented by a mathematical grammar (also referred to as formal grammar). The grammars that have been traditionally the subject of researchers are best described by Chomsky hierarchy (Chomsky et al., 2012). The formal grammars can be divided as follows:

1. Unrestricted grammars: These are grammars that would have a rule like $\alpha \rightarrow \beta$, where α and β can both be terminals, nonterminals, or null. Such the unrestricted grammars are the most general and include all the remaining grammars. The problem with such grammars is that they are too general to describe any programming or natural language.
2. Context-sensitive grammars: These grammars are described by rules such as $\alpha A \beta \rightarrow \alpha \gamma \beta$, where α and β can be nonterminals, terminals, or empty, γ can be nonterminals or terminals but never empty, and A has to be a nonterminal. In simple terms, the context-sensitive grammars refer to the fact that certain words can only be

appropriate in a certain context—a problem that is intuitive to humans. The issue with such grammars is that they are extremely difficult computationally (if decidable at all). Note that context-sensitive grammars contain the context-free grammars and regular grammars but not vice versa.

3. Context-free grammars: These grammars are described by the rules such as $A \rightarrow \gamma$, where γ can be can be nonterminals or terminals but never empty, and A has to be a nonterminal. These grammars are used to describe the syntax of most programming languages such as C, etc. The context-free grammars contain the regular grammar but not vice versa.

4. Regular grammars: These grammars are described by $A \rightarrow aB$ or $A \rightarrow Ba$, where a is a terminal and both A and B are nonterminals. The regular grammars are used to define the search patterns and lexical structure of the programming languages.

The problem researchers in Computer Science and Computational Linguistics faced for the longest time was that while the above was enough to describe the programming languages, it was not sufficient for natural languages. This was addressed by statistical approach as we shall see in Section 3.2.

3.2.1.4 Semantic analysis

Finally, we will briefly discuss the semantic analysis before taking a look at the statistical. Recall that when we want to process a text, we need to preprocess the text where we break down the text into words and sentences. Next, we perform a lexical analysis where we will group various words who have the same root token called lemma together. The syntactical parsing allows us to ensure that the text is following a grammatical structure and hence can be part of a given language. Also recall that most of the languages can be processed by this approach while few languages such as Chinese and Thai face difficulty in the process of tokenization and lemmatization. Once this is accomplished, we need to ensure whether or not the sentence written is conveying a meaning. In addition to the example in syntactical analysis where one sentence was termed as gibberish, consider the following sentences:

I am going down

I am feeling down

I am walking down

The three sentences can be interpreted differently. Moreover, the first and third sentence could mean that the person is going to a floor down or the first sentence could mean the person is about to have a flu if the symptoms of flu were discussed prior to this sentence (recall the context-sensitive grammar where the text requires history of the text). It can also mean a player mentioning that he/she might lose the game. In summary, one can surmise that there are many possibilities that any given sentence can convey. Linguistics over the past century has seen many theories crop up that have been the basis for the work of Computer Scientists/Computational Linguists. While covering all the theories here is beyond the scope of this work, we will briefly summarize four such theories here.

1. Formal semantics: The key premise in formal semantics is that there is no difference between natural and artificial languages. Both can be represented as a set of rules and based on such rules we can make deductions. As an example, consider the following rules:

    Every man is mortal

    John is a man

    John is Mortal

    This can be represented mathematically as follows:

    Man → Mortal

    Man(John)

    ⇒ Mortal(John).

2. Cognitive semantics: As opposed to the formal semantics, cognitive semanticists believe in intuition/psychological aspect of the communication. In other words, they argue that each sentence has an intuitive aspect that delivers the message. For example, "He is going down" can be interpreted as becoming sick or the physical action of heading down. The difference lies in the context/intuition. Furthermore, various cultures can add meanings to various sentences.

3. Lexical semantics: The lexical semantics deal with the meanings of individual lexemes and the meanings entailed by them. The lexemes can have suffixes and affixes and they can alter the meaning of the individual word. Moreover, the individual lexemes might have sensory meaning associated with them. For example, the following sentences are correct in terms of grammar but the second one will not be deemed a correct sentence.

    The cat chased a mouse

    The mouse chased a cat

4. Compositional semantics: The compositional semantics do not look at the individual meaning of the lexemes but rather look at how a sentence is composed. For example, a sentence can be composed of a noun phrase (NP) or a verb phrase (VP). So the following two sentences will be considered correct:

    Jack is a boy

    J is a B

The key premise behind the above is that minus the lexical parts what remains are the rules of composition.

The traditional approach to processing text yields descent results when it comes to preprocessing and tokenization phase. However, one can surmise from the examples above that the task increases in complexity in the syntactical and semantical analysis phase. This has given rise to the statistical approach to NLP which will be discussed later in this paper. However, understanding the above concepts is paramount to comprehending and implementing the statistical approaches.

3.2.2 Statistical spproach—key concepts

As we saw in the previous section, the traditional approach has its share of challenges when performing the syntactical and semantical analysis. The statistical approach takes its motivation from the ML approach. Simply put the ML approach takes a subset of data and studies the underlying structure and behavior of the input and the output. Specifically, the process finds the optimal way to convert the given input to the desired output—known as "supervised learning." The data utilized in the supervised learning is known as the training dataset. Once the algorithm is discovered, the algorithm is applied to a new dataset—test dataset—to see the effectiveness of the algorithm. This process is termed as "unsupervised learning." While many complexities underlie the above process, the following concepts describe the key ideas in this approach.

3.2.2.1 Corpus and its intricacies

While many definitions exist for corpus, we chose the following from (Sinclair, 1991):

> A collection of naturally occurring text, chosen to characterize a state or variety of a language

For NLP purposes, the text needs to be machine readable, so it can be annotated. The annotation process in NLP takes a text and adds special tags known as metadata to various words—described in more detail in a later section.

Researchers over the past decades have provided us with many corpora. These include the Brown corpus (Marcus, Marcinkiewicz, & Santorini, 1993), British National corpus (Aston & Burnard, 1998), and International corpus of English and Google Ngram corpus (Lin et al., 2012). Such corpora relieve us from the legal aspect as pointed out in Chen et al. (2016). However, the choice of corpus is important given the task at hand and the results can be highly domain specific (Gordon, Van Durme, & Schubert, 2009). Intuitively, someone working intending to study British population would naturally look at the British National corpus to get better insights. Despite having many copra available to us, there is a constant need to build new corpora. For example, Rajput et al. (2019b) described the need to have a corpus for psychology and psychiatry. This begs the question: What are the key characteristics of a corpus? The size, balance, and representativeness are three aspects that need to be looked at.

3.2.2.1.1 Size

The very first question that needs to be answered is how big a corpus should be in order to represent the desired text. Since corpora depend on sampling, the answer to this question will help build a corpus that can provide the researchers they are looking for. While intuitively it might make sense to keep the corpus as large as possible, having a small corpus fulfills a very important purpose—performing annotation and studying grammatical/underlying text structure. Thus someone focused on annotating a given text heavily and/or studying the grammatical structure of a particular text would find it very difficult if not impossible to work with a corpus that is too big. Loosely speaking a large corpus helps in studying the occurrences of lexemes, their frequencies and concordances of various tokens (Berber-Sardinha, 2000). A concordance is when certain words occur together in certain text. For example, when Google fills certain words such as "have" when someone types "I can" is based on the study of various queries and corpora. This will become more evident when we discuss Part-of-Speech (POS) tagging.

3.2.2.1.2 Balance

The Balance of a corpus refers to the ability of a corpus to represent the language being studied. Even before the era of acronyms of the chat era, one would expect that the text scripts of spoken language would be quite different from the written texts. Furthermore, languages having more than one spoken dialect will have different text scripts representing different regions. As an example, Arabic-speaking community in Tunisia will have different choices of word/lexemes compared to someone from Egypt. Adding to the complexity is the choice of colloquial words specific to that particular community. Furthermore, a particular lexeme can have different connotations across different communities. As an example, consider the word "unionized" that can be pronounced as "union-ized" (specific to unions) or "un-ionized" (specific to Chemistry). Similarly, the acronym ROE will be read as "Return on Equity" by the finance community while the military community would read it as "Rules of Engagement." As one can imagine, various corpora are specific to different domains and hence the continuous need to build corpora.

3.2.2.1.3 Representativeness

Consider studying/tagging a Shakespeare act to represent how a daily dialogue commences between people. Obviously, this will not be representative of the times we live in. A better example would be to revisit the way people chatted when instant messaging made its debut. With the advent of time, terms such as "lol" (laugh out loud) and "imo" (in my opinion) have been added to the everyday jargon. So how can a text continue to represent a language over a period of time? How often it needs to be updated? These are the questions one needs to keep in mind when building a corpus. However, there are corpora which should not be updated at all. As an example, the text scripts representing the phone records of conversation during the 1990s represent the choice of words in that decade. On the other hand, the advent of social media and various terminologies/acronyms requires a frequent update to certain corpora. For example, should a corpus representing behavior of various psychological disorder be limited to answers of individuals selected for a survey? or should it incorporate lexemes/words that are gleaned from various tweets discussing depression? How should one deal with the Out of Vocabulary (OOV) words that cannot be found in a dictionary but are prevalent among such communities? While answers to such questions are subject to scrutiny by many researchers and beyond the scope of this tutorial, they underlie the importance of corpus building and selection in human, social, and medical sciences.

3.2.2.2 Part-of-Speech tagging

So far, we have discussed creating the corpus which will be either our training or test dataset or both. The POS tagging is a process akin to what kids are taught when studying any grammar namely recognizing the type of word they come across. For example, the sentence "The dog jumped over the fence" can be tagged as the following:

> The/Determiner (Definite Article) dog/Noun jumped/Verb over/Preposition the/ Determiner fence/Noun

Let us make few observations. First of all, while the above seems easy (once we learn the grammatical rules), the problem is much more complex in NLP as many words van have different possible tags. The word "over" can be a preposition (as shown above) or an adverb (consider the sentence "He fell over"). Secondly, we would recognize the word "jumped" as a verb after the process of lemmatization as described earlier in this primer. As we noted earlier, the preprocessing and lexical analysis process specific to traditional approaches is equally beneficial and applicable to the statistical approach. Thirdly, in the corpus creation, we discussed that all corpora are especially helpful in annotation and POS tagging. A small corpus usually would represent the rules of a given language quite comprehensively and hence the benefit of a small corpus (Brants, 2000). We will also discuss the application of taggers in the next section which will discuss annotations in some detail.

There are three main prevalent techniques for POS tagging widely used.

1. Rule-base POS tagging: The rule-based tagging where manual rules are encoded. For example, one rule could be that a noun always follows a determiner. This can be very helpful if consider the word "excuse" which can be both tagged as a noun or a verb. Now consider the following two sentences:

    The excuse was not accepted

    The employee was not excused

A rule-based tagger would thus tag the "excuse" as a noun. The problem with rule-based taggers is that it takes many iterations over a text and hence computational time and space. To alleviate this problem, researchers take a probabilistic approach know as Markov Model approach.

2. Markov model POS tagging: The Markov model is a concept in probability and statistics which states that events are not always independent (such as tossing a coin where each outcome is independent of the previous one). Rather, the events might be related to the history. Markov models in its simplest form assume that given a number of sequential events say E_1, E_2, ... E_n, the next event E_{n+1} is simply dependent on the previous event. This is known as the memoryless property. As an example, some would argue that the probability of a basketball player making the second free throw goes up if he makes the first one. Conversely, the probability will go down if the player misses the first shot.

   Revisiting the example from the rule-based tagging, the probability of a noun following a determiner can be set to 1. Hence the word "excuse" will be tagged as a noun in the first sentence. This can be very helpful in ensuring that the sentence follows the grammatical rules of a particular language. Markov model makes the assumption that the information about the last state is available. In certain cases, more history is available as is the case in speech tagging. Specifically, we can look for other words that appear in the sentence on a high frequency basis. Hidden Markov model is the mathematical model that interest's researchers and there are many variations that have been tried and tested such as variable Markov memory models. Taking it a step further, researchers also look for words that frequently occur together in a document—a concept known as concordances.

3. Feature-base POS tagging: Certain features of a language can help the tagging process further. Such features are known a priori such as proper names are always capitalized. These features can become quite complex and have been the subject of researchers for quite some time. Features help in providing context to the tagging process. For example, the word "Citibank" would provide the context that the document at hand is probably related to Finance.

The tagging approaches help NLP practitioners in gleaning information about the document at hand. The metadata can include the author name, the subject matter, date of publishing, etc. Regardless of the choice of taggers employed (or combination of them), POS tagging offers a great value to NLP practitioners. One such application is "Annotation."

3.2.2.3 Treebank annotation

Simply put, the annotation process takes a text corpus and attaches metadata information to the text. Many such corpora are available and have been developed over the years. The Brown Corpus developed at Brown University is heavily annotated as there are many other corpora. The annotation traditionally was done manually but many computational

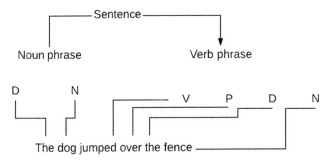

Figure 3.1
Constituency-based annotation.

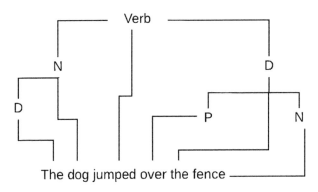

Figure 3.2
Dependency-based annotation.

algorithms now exist to perform the annotation automatically. Recall from the syntactical analysis section that a text must conform to a particular grammar. While the traditional approaches had limited results approaching this problem, POS tagging and treebank annotation improve the grammatical accuracy quite significantly.

The key premise behind treebank annotation is that it views a sentence as a tree. The tree can be built using a constituency-based annotation or dependency-based annotation (Marcus et al., 1993). A constituency-based approach divides a sentence to an NP or a VP as shown below (Fig. 3.1).

A dependency-based annotation on the other hand focuses on the verb and builds the tree around it. Such an approach is very helpful for certain languages such as Arabic (Fig. 3.2).

Both the constituency- and dependency-based annotations have pros and cons. While we will defer this discussion to other work in the future, treebank annotations address many problems in semantic analysis that we saw in the traditional approach.

3.3 Applications

Work done by Landers, Brusso, Cavanaugh, and Collmus (2016) provides a framework that helps in extracting Big Data from the Web. The authors specifically promote a "theory-driven" web scraping, where researchers are encouraged to formulate questions and hypotheses before embarking on scavenging data from the web. This can include various criteria such as age and demographics. The authors put forward a case study in which the gender identity is deduced and prove a hypothesis regarding women behavior. Lastly, the authors point out the importance of web crawlers work and how Application Programming Interfaces (APIs) play in the Big Data field. Most if not all the social media platforms provide APIs that help the researchers gather data.

Both NLP and sentiment analysis have been applied in many areas such as marketing. However, both social sciences and medicine have just started to feel the impact. Researchers have recently started looking at how Big Data techniques can be applied to mental health issues such as detection of depression. In this section, we present an overview of various applications both in the field of sentiment analysis and detecting mental health issues.

3.3.1 Sentiment analysis

The basic application of sentiment analysis lies in gathering the opinion of people. Such opinions are precursors to many business decisions. Similar to the stop words, sentiment analysis domain depends on list of words that describe the effect of the writer. Nielsen (2011) explained how ANEW list is used to classify the opinions of users as negative, neutral, or positive. Wang, Wei, Liu, Zhou, and Zhang (2011) applied the sentiment analysis concepts to topics rather than the actual opinions and gleaned how the discussion would follow the sentiment of a topic.

Pang and Lee (2008) also looked at the user reviews and the possible mistakes that can occur during the data entry when it comes to providing ratings. Goldberg, Zhu, and Wright (2007) and Hopkins and King (2007) looked at the opinions of democrat voters and how they felt about the presidential elections. Bansal, Cardie, and Lee (2008) looked at the long-term aspect of sentiment analysis in the political domain where the voters can get a long-term view of how the politicians act during their tenure. Other projects have as a long-term goal the clarification of politicians' positions.

Jin, Li, Mah, and Tong (2007) used applied sentiment analysis concepts to detect inappropriate ads. Cheong and Lee (2011) tackled the problem of finding content related to terrorism. The work looked at the sentiments of civilians and how the twitter data can be harvested to glean such information. More work has been done in the field of twitter harvesting by Agarwal, Xie, Vovsha, Rambow, and Passonneau (2011), Saif, He, and Alani

(2012), and Rosenthal, Farra, and Nakov (2017). Twitter data were also used to build a corpus that could be specific to twitter as explained by Pak and Paroubek (2010). Finally, Cobb, Mays, and Graham (2013) has applied sentiment analysis to smoking-cessation techniques given certain drug choices.

3.3.2 Natural Language processing application in medical sciences

Work done by Youyou, Kosinski, and Stillwell (2015) focuses on the Facebook platform where the authors compare the human perception to that being gleaned from the social media. Specifically, the authors judge the judgments of users by the numbers of "likes" the users press. On the other hand, they build two samples of more than 14,000 users where they ask the users' friends to rate the judgment of the user. The results showed that the results gleaned from Facebook likes were more accurate. The results once again provide the researches evidence that information gleaned from the social media can prove to be both valuable and accurate. The results do not reflect the comments that the users make on various sites/items which can grant more accuracy to the results. Moreover, there is no corpus involved in the process. Work done by Rajput et al. (2019b) can be leveraged in this regards.

Work done by Chen and Wojcik (2016) provides an overview of Big Data application to Psychology. The authors focus on the four steps necessary for such endeavors namely planning, acquisition, planning, and analytics. They also provide three tutorials for the users. They introduce the user to the MapReduce framework that has garnered lot of attention lately. The paper also explains the concept of supervised and unsupervised learning as explained above. The work while providing an excellent overview does skip certain details that the user might need. Specifically, they glance over the preprocessing part of data processing and the many underlying details such as text normalization.

The work done by Han, Cook, and Baldwin (2013) focuses on text normalization for the OOV words. Specifically, the users target words such as "smokin" and find a mechanism to convert it into "smoking." The work focuses primarily on SMS messages and also delves into a decent sample size for Twitter. The authors proposed method produces very encouraging results comparing it to a corpus obtained from *New York Times*. The OOV words are first normalized using a dictionary-based matching and based on the results the authors move further to test in a context setting. Rajput et al. (2019b) showed results in a psychology/psychiatry context—specifically depression. One of the issues the authors do not look into is converting OOV synonyms into actual dictionary-based words—as an example "imo" into "in my humble opinion." A similar approach of normalization was also taken by Gordon et al. (2009) where the authors construct a normalization dictionary for Weblogs. The work provides an excellent way of preprocessing blogs—another social media platform. The work is not domain specific and hence the ideas can be applied to the more domain-specific context.

Work done at Stanford University (Kosinski, Wang, Lakkaraju, & Leskovec, 2016) looks at the concept of digital footprint of a user and two mathematical ways to analyze data. The work is based on R language (as opposed to Python) and helps predict real life outcomes. The work is based in the unsupervised learning domain and uses Facebook data as a case study. While the work is not focused in the medical/social sciences domain, it is an excellent introduction to digital footprint of a user and can come in very handy in detection symptoms specific to various conditions.

De Choudhry et al. have done some work in detecting mental illness. The authors started the work by focusing on detecting postpartum depression. The authors chose reddit as their platform and studied the linguistic changes that happened in new mothers. They showed the prevalence of negative affect in certain cases among other results. The work was an excellent first step in this realm and was followed by De Choudhury (2013), De Choudhury, Counts, and Horvitz (2013), and De Choudhury, Gamon, Counts, and Horvitz (2013) where they predict depression in Twitter users. One of the prerequisites of their work is that the users identify themselves as depressed and gave consent to follow their Twitter account. The next step in this field should be to detect symptom of depression from random set of tweets. Moreover, the DSM V guidelines should also be followed and brought in line with the social media text.

De Choudhury, Sharma, and Kiciman (2016) also did some work in focusing on the anonymity factor of the social media and the disinhibitions that accompany such anonymity. Specifically, they looked at the "throwaway" accounts that the users used to express their opinions. The authors also applied more Big Data and ML techniques to the Nutrition area where they used social media to understand dietary choices among the social media users (Pavalanathan & De Choudhury, 2015). While the work is not directly related to mental illness, it can be leveraged in various situations such as cases of eating disorders occurring with other conditions such as depression or bipolar. Authors in Rajput and Ahmed (2019a, 2019b) did a brief overview of the state of art in application of Big Data in mental health. Furthermore, Rajput and Ahmed (2019a, 2019b) make a case for having a corpus specific to mental health issues.

Saha and De Choudhury (2017) modeled stress among a group of college students after cases of shooting on campus. The authors used reddit campus community and looked at the linguistic style of the students making posts to detect high level of stress after such traumatic incidents. They looked at 12 incidents of gun violence over a period of 5 years and analyzed both the time and linguistic dimension of the posts. The work done gives a great platform to spring from and see whether clinical inferences can be done given such data.

It is worth mentioning the work in O'Callaghan, Harrigan, Carthy, and Cunningham (2012) where the authors choose YouTube platform and focus on detecting spam in the comments section. The authors use graph and network theory to look at bot (automatic programs) behavior. Such work can be combined with other work and help researchers classify various videos from myriad of dimensions. Once such classification is accomplished, the researchers can look at the embedded comments and tie the content to user mental state and how they are expressing it.

While the aforementioned work analyzed from a psychology point of view (also applicable to clinical part of psychiatry), Monteith, Glenn, Geddes, and Bauer (2015) presented a list of projects that are underway in the realm of psychiatry. The authors look at the Big Data field from a medical sciences perspective and emphasize how Big Data in a clinical setting can provide benefits such as pinpointing rare events. The work done in this area ranges from the use of psychotropic drugs to comparing the risk of dementia in a certain age group.

3.4 Conclusion

Sentiment analysis and NLP offer a great opportunity to mental health practitioners to be able to mine text data from the web and detect symptoms that could be harbinger to various mental health issues. In this chapter, we have presented a detailed overview of NLP and sentiment analysis. In addition, we have given a brief synopsis of strength of Python language and the NLTK toolkit. Lastly, we have presented various applications in the sentiment analysis domain and application of NLP to the medical field. In the future, the author would like to apply sentiment analysis in detection of mental health diseases such as cyberbullying and depression.

3.4.1 Future research directions

To begin with, social media (Alkhammash, Jussila, Lytras, & Visvizi, 2019) offers the best source of data for mental health practitioners. The data are produced by real users and the anonymity provided by the Internet allows the practitioners to gather authentic data that can provide valuable insights into the mindset of patients suffering from mental illness.

The social media allows patients to post comments using their language of choice. Such data should be segregated and compared to see whether there are any commonalities between patients irrespective of their cultural background. For example, an interesting question to ask will be: Are the underlying drivers of depression as reported by users suffering from depression in the United States and an Arabic speaking country the same?

Furthermore, while English remains the language of choice for majority of the users on the Internet, there are subtle differences in the way people write their comments. Thus an interesting area to look into is ways to segregate English-speaking patients based on their cultural and geographical backgrounds and glean the differences. For example, do users hailing from India and Pakistan display the same symptoms as the users from United Kingdom?

Lastly, another area to look into will be the ability to glean the socioeconomic status (SES) of the users that are posting to the social media. The SES is a valuable piece of information that the healthcare practitioners use to predict the onset of various diseases. One facet of SES is the level of education of the user who is posting. Smart Healthcare interventions and applications require a strategic fit to smart cities strategies and a deep understanding of clusters of users (Lytras, Visvizi, & Sarirete, 2019)

3.4.2 Teaching assignments

- Perform a literature review of the work done on cyber bullying and identify how sentiment analysis and NLP techniques can be helpful.
- Perform a literature survey on various techniques that can rank the writing style of various users.
- Research the bi-gram and tri-gram data made available by Google and how it can be helpful in application to the domain of healthcare analytics.

References

Agarwal, A., Xie, B., Vovsha, I., Rambow, O., & Passonneau, R. (June 2011). *Sentiment analysis of twitter data. Proceedings of the workshop on languages in social media* (pp. 30−38). Association for Computational Linguistics.

Alkhammash, E. H., Jussila, J., Lytras, M. D., & Visvizi, A. (2019). *Annotation of Smart Cities Twitter Micro-Contents for Enhanced Citizen's Engagement* (Volume 7). IEEE Access, Digital Object Identifier 10.1109/ACCESS.2019.2935186.

Aston, G., & Burnard, L. (1998). *The BNC handbook: Exploring the British National Corpus with SARA.* Capstone.

Bansal, M., Cardie, C., & Lee, L. (2008). The power of negative thinking: Exploiting label disagreement in the min-cut classification framework. *COLING (Posters)*, 15−18.

Berber-Sardinha, T. (October 2000). *Comparing corpora with WordSmith Tools: How large must the reference corpus be? Proceedings of the workshop on comparing corpora* (pp. 7−13). Association for Computational Linguistics.

Brants, T. (April 2000). *TnT: A statistical part-of-speech tagger. Proceedings of the sixth conference on applied natural language processing* (pp. 224−231). Association for Computational Linguistics.

Chen, E. E., & Wojcik, S. P. (2016). A practical guide to big data research in psychology. *Psychological Methods, 21*(4), 458.

Cheong, M., & Lee, V. C. S. (2011). A microblogging-based approach to terrorism informatics: Exploration and chronicling civilian sentiment and response to terrorism events via Twitter. *Information Systems Frontiers, 13*(1), 45−59.

Cobb, N. K., Mays, D., & Graham, A. L. (2013). Sentiment analysis to determine the impact of online messages on smokers' choices to use varenicline. *Journal of the National Cancer Institute Monographs, 47,* 224−230.

De Choudhury, M. (2013). *Role of social media in tackling challenges in mental health. Proceedings of the 2nd international workshop on socially-aware multimedia.* ACM.

De Choudhury, M., Counts, S., & Horvitz, E. (2013). *Predicting postpartum changes in emotion and behavior via social media. Proceedings of the SIGCHI conference on human factors in computing systems.* ACM.

De Choudhury, M., Gamon, M., Counts, S., & Horvitz, E. (2013). Predicting depression via social media. *Proceedings of the 7th international AAAI conference on weblogs and social media, 13*, 1−10.

De Choudhury, M., Sharma, S., & Kiciman, E. (February 2016). *Characterizing dietary choices, nutrition, and language in food deserts via social media. Proceedings of the 19th acm conference on computer-supported cooperative work & social computing* (pp. 1157−1170). ACM.

Goldberg, A. B., Zhu, X., & Wright, S. J. (2007). *Dissimilarity in graph-based semi-supervised classification, . AISTATS* (2, pp. 155−162).

Gordon, J., Van Durme, B., & Schubert, L. (September 2009). *Weblogs as a source for extracting general world knowledge. Proceedings of the 5th international conference on knowledge, capture* (pp. 185−186). ACM.

Han, B., Cook, P., & Baldwin, T. (2013). Lexical normalization for social media text. *ACM Transactions on Intelligent Systems and Technology (TIST), 4*(1), 5.

Hopkins, D., & King, G. (2007). Extracting systematic social science meaning from text. Available from <http://gking.harvard.edu/files/words.pdf>.

Jäger, G., & Rogers, J. (2012). Formal language theory: refining the Chomsky hierarchy. *Philosophical Transactions of the Royal Society B: Biological Sciences, 367*(1598), 1956−1970.

Jin, X., Li, Y., Mah, T., & Tong, J. (2007). *Sensitive webpage classification for content advertising. Proceedings of the 1st international workshop on data mining and audience intelligence for advertising (ADKDD'07)* (pp. 28−33). ACM.

Kosinski, M., Wang, Y., Lakkaraju, H., & Leskovec, J. (2016). Mining big data to extract patterns and predict real-life outcomes. *Psychological Methods, 21*(4), 493.

Landers, R. N., Brusso, R. C., Cavanaugh, K. J., & Collmus, A. B. (2016). A primer on theory-driven web scraping: Automatic extraction of big data from the Internet for use in psychological research. *Psychological Methods, 21*(4), 475.

Laney, D. (2001). 3-D data management: Controlling data volume, velocity and variety. META Group Research Note, February 6.

Lin, Y., Michel, J. B., Aiden, E. L., Orwant, J., Brockman, W., & Petrov, S. (July 2012). *Syntactic annotations for the google books ngram corpus. Proceedings of the ACL 2012 system demonstrations* (pp. 169−174). Association for Computational Linguistics.

Lytras, M., Raghavan, V., & Damiani, E. (2017). Big Data and Data Analytics Research: From Metaphors to Value Space for Collective Wisdom in Human Decision Making and Smart Machines. *Int. J. Semantic Web Inf. Syst. 13*(1), 1−10.

Lytras, M. D., Visvizi, A., & Sarirete, A. (2019). Clustering Smart City Services: Perceptions, Expectations, Responses. *Sustainability, 11*(6), 1669.

Marcus, M. P., Marcinkiewicz, M. A., & Santorini, B. (1993). Building a large annotated corpus of English: The Penn Treebank. *Computational Linguistics, 19*(2), 313−330.

Monteith, S., Glenn, T., Geddes, J., & Bauer, M. (2015). Big data are coming to psychiatry: a general introduction. *International Journal of Bipolar Disorders, 3*(1), 21.

Nielsen, F. Å. (2011). A new ANEW: Evaluation of a word list for sentiment analysis in microblogs. arXiv preprint arXiv:1103.2903.

O'Callaghan, D., Harrigan, M., Carthy, J., & Cunningham, P. (2012, June). Network analysis of recurring YouTube spam campaigns. In *ICWSM*.

Pak, A., & Paroubek, P. (May 2010). Twitter as a corpus for sentiment analysis and opinion mining. *LREc, 10*, 1320−1326.

Pang, B., & Lee, L. (2008). Opinion mining and sentiment analysis. *Foundations and Trends in Information Retrieval, 2*(1−2), 1−135.

Pavalanathan, U., & De Choudhury, M. (May 2015). *Identity management and mental health discourse in social media. Proceedings of the 24th international conference on world wide web* (pp. 315−321). ACM.

Porter, M. F. (1980). An algorithm for suffix stripping. *Program, 14*(3), 130−137.

Rajadesingan, A., Zafarani, R., & Liu, H. (February 2015). *Sarcasm detection on twitter: A behavioral modeling approach. Proceedings of the 8th ACM international conference on web search and data mining* (pp. 97−106). ACM.

Rajput, A. E., & Ahmed, S. M. (2019a). Big Data and social/medical sciences: State of the art and future trends. arXiv preprint arXiv:1902.00705.

Rajput, A. E., & Ahmed, S. M. (2019b). Making a case for social media corpus for detecting depression. arXiv preprint arXiv:1902.00702.

Rosenthal, S., Farra, N., & Nakov, P. (2017). SemEval-2017 task 4: Sentiment analysis in Twitter. *Proceedings of the 11th international workshop on semantic evaluation (SemEval-2017)*, 502−518.

Saha, K., & De Choudhury, M. (2017). Modeling stress with social media around incidents of gun violence on college campuses.

Saif, H., He, Y., & Alani, H. (November 2012). *Semantic sentiment analysis of twitter. International semantic web conference* (pp. 508−524). Berlin, Heidelberg: Springer.

Sinclair, J. (1991). *Corpus, concordance, collocation.* Oxford University Press.

Wang, X., Wei, F., Liu, X., Zhou, M., & Zhang, M. (October 2011). *Topic sentiment analysis in twitter: A graph-based hashtag sentiment classification approach. Proceedings of the 20th ACM international conference on information and knowledge management* (pp. 1031−1040). ACM.

Youyou, W., Kosinski, M., & Stillwell, D. (2015). Computer-based personality judgments are more accurate than those made by humans. *Proceedings of the National Academy of Sciences, 112*(4), 1036−1040.

Further reading

Andreu-Perez, J., Poon, C. C., Merrifield, R. D., Wong, S. T., & Yang, G. Z. (2015). Big data for health. *IEEE Journal of Biomedical and Health Informatics, 19*(4), 1193−1208.

Eisenstein, J. (2013). *What to do about bad language on the internet. Proceedings of the 2013 conference of the North American Chapter of the association for computational linguistics* (pp. 359−369). Human language technologies.

Greene, S. C. (2007). *Spin: Lexical semantics, transitivity, and the identification of implicit sentiment.* Ann Arbor, MI: ProQuest.

Jindal, N., & Liu, B. (2006). *Identifying comparative sentences in text documents. Proceedings of the 29th annual international ACM SIGIR conference on research and development in information retrieval, SIGIR'06* (pp. 244−251). ACM.

Jurafsky, D., & Martin, J. H. (2014). *Speech and language processing* (Vol. 3). London: Pearson.

Kouloumpis, E., Wilson, T., & Moore, J. D. (2011). *Twitter sentiment analysis: The good the bad and the omg!. Proceedings of the 5th international conference on weblogs and social media,* Barcelona, Catalonia, Spain, July 17−21.

Liu, B. (2012). *Sentiment analysis and opinion mining.* San Rafael, CA: Morgan & Claypool.

Nakov, P., Ritter, A., Rosenthal, S., Sebastiani, F., & Stoyanov, V. (2016). SemEval-2016 task 4: Sentiment analysis in Twitter. *Proceedings of the 10th international workshop on semantic evaluation (semeval-2016)*, 1−18.

NLTK toolkit. Available from <www.nltk.org>.

Partee, B. B., ter Meulen, A. G., & Wall, R. (2012). *Mathematical methods in linguistics* (Vol. 30). Springer Science & Business Media.

Wang, S., & Manning, C. D. (July 2012). *Baselines and bigrams: Simple, good sentiment and topic classification, Proceedings of the 50th annual meeting of the association for computational linguistics: Short papers* (Vol. 2, pp. 90−94). Association for Computational Linguistics.

Wiebe, J. M., Bruce, R. F., & O'Hara, T. P. (1999). *Development and use of a gold-standard data set for subjectivity classifications. Proceedings of the 37th annual meeting of the association for computational linguistics on computational linguistics (ACL'99)* (pp. 246−253). Association for Computational Linguistics.

Advanced Decision Making and Artificial Intelligence for Smart Healthcare

CHAPTER 4

Clinical decision support for infection control in surgical care

Marco Spruit and Sander van der Rijnst
Utrecht University, Utrecht, The Netherlands

4.1 Introduction

Healthcare organizations around the world are challenged by pressures to reduce the costs of giving care, improve coordination, deliver more and higher quality patient care, provide more with less financial resources, less manpower while being more patient centric. With increasing demands from regulatory bodies for enhanced healthcare quality and increased value, healthcare providers are under pressure to deliver better health outcomes through smarter healthcare (Spruit, Vroon, & Batenburg, 2014).

The majority of medical errors result from faulty systems and processes, not individuals (Institute of Medicine, 1999, 2001). Processes that are inefficient and variable, changing case mix of patients, health insurance, differences in provider education and experience, and numerous other factors contribute to the complexity of healthcare. Another element lies in improving the quality of healthcare by reducing waste in processes and by adhering to standardized protocols (Porter, 2010).

In 2004 the Dutch Government decided that all hospitals systematically have to manage the safety of care provision with the aid of a patient safety management system (PSMS). Its origins can be traced back to a study performed in the United States which investigated the incidence of adverse events, preventable adverse advents, and potentially preventable deaths in the Netherlands (Zegers et al., 2009). The authors argue that the incidence of adverse advents is substantial and needs to be reduced. The study also identified priority areas for improvement by recommending that patient safety efforts should focus on surgical procedures and elderly patients.

The concerned parties have chosen a number of specific initiatives for use in the Dutch hospital patient safety program, a PSMS (VMS, 2009). The idea behind the program is to select priority areas that present the greatest opportunity to narrow the gap between what the healthcare system is routinely doing now and what is currently known to be best clinical practice.

Innovation in Health Informatics.
DOI: https://doi.org/10.1016/B978-0-12-819043-2.00004-6

This paper describes a compelling healthcare problem for information system (IS) researchers for which IS researchers can provide design solutions, methodologies, and tools. The surgical process has been designated by scientific research as the most high priority clinical process and serves as the starting point for the acquisition of raw data to demonstrate a decision support system (DSS) prototype. A successful DSS-prototype can create new opportunities for operations research and six sigma capabilities as a tool for intervention in surgical care delivery processes. Our research aim is to draw on achievements regarding quantifying efficiency and efficacy of DSS prototyping in primary care to help guide this research (Meulendijk et al., 2013, 2015, 2016).

Evidence-based best practice guidelines have been disseminated by the Dutch government to support the aim of reducing surgical site infections (SSIs). The "Prevention of surgical site infections" theme introduces an SSI-bundle and provides guidelines for implementing the infection prevention bundle to prevent the development of postoperative SSIs (VMS, 2009).

However, even though measuring instruments (performance indicators) are provided by the patient safety management program, properly translating these requirements into IS-constructs remains elusive. To provide clinical decision makers with reliable, useful and meaningful information regarding process compliance, we pursue an Applied Data Science approach by demonstrating a working prototype to close the widening gap in monitoring progress toward measurable goals (Spruit & Jagesar, 2016; Spruit & Lytras, 2018). Therefore this study examines the following research question: "How can surgical data from electronic patient records (EPRs) be automatically collected and utilized for infection control purposes to support evidence-based clinical decision-making?"

4.2 Research methodology

To do so, the current use of clinical information systems in the surgical care domain is examined. Two classes of ISs play a critical role in this study, which are electronic patient records (EPRs) and DSSs. EPRs with clinical decision support (CDS) capabilities hold great promise to improve the efficiency and quality of patient care while reducing cost and medical errors (Chaudry & Koehler, 2005).

We conducted our single case study within an infection control unit of a large academic university hospital in Western Europe, in an action research setting to investigate its efforts to develop a more patient and process oriented information delivery approach regarding process-of-care measurements, process compliance and patient outcomes in operation rooms. Due to obvious confidentiality reasons, the care provider will remain anonymous.

This study performs an Applied Data Science research (Spruit & Lytras, 2018) where the design-science paradigm serves as the main approach for this study. Hevner, March, Park, and Ram (2004) provided an IS research framework and a set of seven design-science guidelines which help IS researchers conduct, evaluate, and present design-science research. It provides the opportunity to investigate the complex healthcare environment at the source of its occurrence, by collecting data from key clinical ISs and key stakeholders directly involved in the surgical care delivery process.

Lastly, this study extends the existing research and body of knowledge related to clinical ISs, CDS, and clinical business intelligence pertaining to surgical care.

4.2.1 Data collection methods

Data that have relevance for clinical decisions are accumulating at an incredible rate due to a host of technological advances and innovations. Electronic data capture has become inexpensive and ubiquitous as a by-product of innovations such as EPRs.

The lack of an effective measurement system for empirical patient safety reporting calls for a better understanding of design solutions. The design-science approach is used in this research to gain more insight in the challenges associated with instantiating a decision support prototype that facilitates distributing reliable information and insights to clinical decision makers. A conceptual model of the reporting and analysis prototype has been constructed by using the design-science guidelines.

The first goal is to design an information model which links surgical care delivery and data entry activities to an information model using metaprocess modeling and metadata modeling. A process-deliverable diagram (PDD) was created based on scientific literature, guidelines by the healthcare inspectorate, documents of Dutch and international working groups, and through observations. Weerd and Brinkkemper (2008) described PDDs as "a technique to reveal relations between activities (the process of the method) and concepts (the deliverables produced in the process)." The PDD serves as a reference model (minimal data set) and can be used as a conceptual model for the development of a prototype, validation, and finalization into a usable software product. The prototype, when instantiated, can be used to identify patterns, relationships, trends, similarities, and differences across OR-theaters and surgical practices.

By outlining all the required and relevant data necessary in the surgical process and by transforming the raw data into information and performance indicators (i.e., knowledge), it should lead to the possibility of quantifiable, transparent and above all, improvable surgical processes, and care delivery.

Design experiments are used to determine how process-of-care variables can be properly related to a reporting template regarding infection control and for use in compliance monitoring. By charting the surgical workflows and their related information flows, a list of relevant variables was constructed. By deploying the prototype as a pilot and iterating on each design, the researcher was able to pretest the design artifact on applicability and usability.

The aim is to collect numerous different data points from the surgical process using traditional transactional ISs (EPRs) and related subsystems as the main foundation. Key to this process is to collect data on a highly granular level and storing the data in a data repository. Kimball and Ross (2011) extensively described the dimensional modeling concepts that are used as a base for designing the blueprints of the data mart prototype. The designs allow for the collection and further analysis of large amounts of data elements recorded during surgical care practices. For example, the required data elements in this study range from the patient's temperature to data streamed from door sensors to general descriptive categorical variables about the patient.

4.2.2 Design objectives

The following design objectives are formulated:

- Enable compliance measurement and monitoring in surgical care for infection prevention and control;
- Gain access to a broad range of surgical and patient variables enabling data analysis;
- Enable basic data quality monitoring for a complete and accurate surgical record;
- Provide predefined visualizations and dashboards for reoccurring surgical questions (weekly, monthly, quarterly, yearly) for complementary use in decision-making processes (i.e., multidimensional analysis);
- A highly interactive and dynamic environment with the ability to construct, reorganize, and customize your own data set;
- Ability to define multiple patient groups (children, elderly, cancer patients among others) based on OR-site location or by hand picking and assigning individual patients to a group (e.g., clinical trial groups);
- Analyze and track key metrics to identify trends, highlight issues, and pitch improvements to key clinical stakeholders;
- Increase awareness of patterns, trends, and variances in surgical care to enable continuous improvement and to ensure the best possible surgical outcomes.

4.3 Clinical decision support prototype

This chapter provides an understanding and review of the case study domain for the design of the prototype and translates requirements from governmental and regulatory bodies into a prototype using information science concepts and constructs.

4.3.1 Contextual background

Hospitalization brings associated risks, including risk of infection. Healthcare-associated infections (also known as nosocomial infections or hospital infections) are acquired as a result of healthcare interventions and have serious implications for hospitalized adults and children. Hospital infections have been identified as one of the most serious patient safety issues in healthcare (Kleinpell, Munro, & Giuliano, 2008; Stone, Larson, & Kawar, 2002). This type of adverse event increases morbidity, mortality, and lengths of stay, as well increases hospital costs. SSIs are the most common postoperative infection (Setiawan, 2011).

The SSI-bundle contains four process-of-care measures which first need to be implemented in surgical practice and second, be measured with the intent to reach a total compliance of at least 90%. The goal of the priority area is to reduce SSIs by 50% by implementing the following four process-of-care variables:

1. Employment of appropriate hair removal methods;
2. Appropriate use of prophylactic antibiotics;
3. Maintenance of (perioperative) normothermia;
4. Appropriate hygienic discipline in operating rooms regarding door movements.

The assumption is that adherence to a series of evidence-based surgical practices can partly prevent SSIs through suitable use of abovementioned preventive measures (Fig. 4.1).

Porter's causality chain is adapted to fit the domain-specific requirements for measuring value in surgical processes related to infection prevention to drive continuous improvement. The causality chain in Fig. 4.2 starts with patients present for surgical care with initial or preexisting conditions. Initial conditions can affect both the surgical

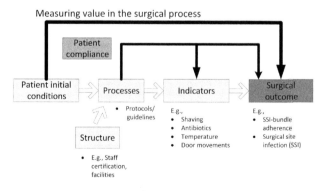

Figure 4.1

Measuring value in the surgical process. Source: *Adapted from Porter, M. E. (2010). What is value in health care?* The New England Journal of Medicine, 363, 2477–2481.

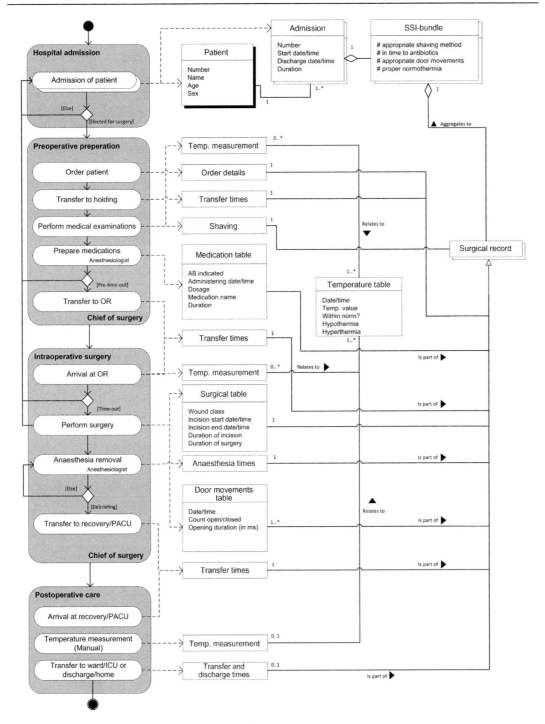

Figure 4.2
Process-deliverable diagram of the surgical care process.

procedure chosen and the likelihood or degree of success. The next step is processes of surgical care, the services, or interventions delivered. In between the processes and outcomes are indicators. These indicators can reflect (biologic) measures in patients and are predictors of outcomes. The final step in the chain of causality is outcomes themselves, which are the actual results of surgical care, in this case reducing the development of postoperative SSIs.

A deeper and complete discussion about the causality chain is considered out of the scope; therefore, this thesis refers to the work of Porter (2010) for a more detailed explanation. The surgical variables for infection control purposes are introduced and further explained in the next section.

4.3.2 Describing the surgical process using process-deliverable diagrams

Presently, there is little quantitative data available for comparing SSI-bundle compliance across OR-theaters at the local hospital level. To collect data from the surgical process, IS researchers need to bring data together from different data sources (i.e., EPRs and their subsystems) and then enrich the data with other patient and surgical data to measure the effectiveness of national and local infection control policies. Existing literature and documents were used as a starting point to gain a better understanding of the business domain under investigation. Unfortunately, documentation of the IS contained process overviews that were incomplete, out-of-date, nonexistent, or not fit for purpose. Therefore the surgical process was first analyzed and formalized to serve as a reference surgical process model from an infection control point of view. Designing the right information models and artifacts requires a comprehensive understanding of the surgical domain, its data, information needs, and the actual capabilities of the ISs in use. In addition, validated, standardized definitions by small and medium-sized enterprises (SMEs) are critical to the design of the prototype. The PSMS guide for preventing SSIs (VMS, 2009) provided the following key terms and definitions (Table 4.1).

To obtain pertinent data related to the overarching perioperative surgical process, the surgical process is divided into three phases of surgery: preoperative, intraoperative, and postoperative. A simplified version of the surgical care PDD is depicted in Fig. 4.3.

The model contains several layers. The first layer entails all data elements at the most granular level and corresponds with the medical activities during surgery relevant for data capture. The second layer consists of an aggregation level where the calculation rules of the algorithms are applied automatically by the DSS-prototype. Lastly, a visualization model can be constructed on top of the aggregation level for reporting and analysis purposes. In addition, derived variables can be added to the prototype with ease. The simplified reference process model serves as a template for each process-of-care measure. It provides

Table 4.1: List of key terms and definitions.

Label	Definition
Duration of admission	The number of minutes between the time the patient arrives at the hospital and the moment the patient is discharged.
Duration of surgery	The number of minutes between the time the patient arrives at the OR and the moment they depart the premises of the OR (to be admitted to the recovery room, PACU, nursing ward, or intensive care).
Duration of incision (surgical time)	The number of minutes between the start of the surgery (knife enters skin) and the moment the surgeon closes the wound.
Hygienic discipline (Y/N)	Is the total number of door movements in the OR (of all available doors combined in the OR-complex) during the surgical time within norm?
Antibiotics prophylaxis (Y/N)	Is antibiotic prophylaxis administered 15–60 min prior to incision and repeated if the surgery lasts longer than 4 h or if more than 2 L of blood loss occurred (adults only)?
Hair removal (Y/N)	Is hair removal around the surgical site properly performed? Y: No hair removal or removal with clippers. N: Other means of hair removal.
Normothermia (Y/N)	Was a normal body temperature maintained between 35.5°C and 37.5°C (nonrectal) or 36°C and 38°C (rectal) for the patient when the patient arrives at the recovery room at the end of the surgery?
Surgical site infection (Y/N)	Has a surgical site infection be determined during a follow-up meeting?

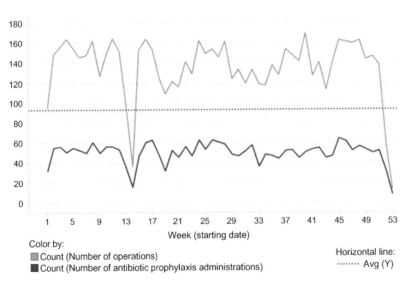

Color by:
■ Count (Number of operations)
■ Count (Number of antibiotic prophylaxis administrations)

Horizontal line:
········ Avg (Y)

Figure 4.3
AB-prophylactics and adherence to norm per week (2013).

the building blocks for monitoring and maintaining compliance and to identify deviations from the reference process (i.e., normalized throughput times, bundle adherence).

By identifying key surgical activities, relationships, data elements, and representing them by formal business process models, it allows for subject matter experts to communicate about these processes in an efficient and effective manner. The reference model can be used to identify similarities and differences in surgical practice and in subsequent clinical ISs (across OR-departments) in a systematic way.

The explicit representation of a reference surgical process information model is a core concept to achieve a better understanding. Workflow verification and validation verify the soundness of the surgical process workflows, including a sound clinical information model. However, it is important to note that it does not attempt to fully describe the surgical process for simplicity and scoping reasons. Only the most relevant surgical activities and necessary items to perform the analysis for the prevention of SSIs are depicted in the model.

4.3.3 Data sources, data collection procedure, and data description

Computerizing the surgical process opens up the possibility to automatically collect data. The data sources, the central infrastructure, and possible data applications are based on industry proven methods, mainly from the field of data warehousing. First of all, raw data from the multitude of data sources (subsystems of the EPR) are transported to the central data infrastructure. From there, the data are transformed and fed into a research repository for further statistical computation.

The DSS-prototype provides the ability to aggregate data about surgical patients and surgical practice from numerous different sources to provide a view of the complete surgical value chain. Visualizing the data is conducted as a last step to deliver extra added value and insights for further improving bundle compliance and surgical practices.

4.3.4 Algorithms

This section describes algorithms for automating multiple clinical rules. They are of varied complexity and are designed to calculate and computerize the process-of-care variables from the underlying data stored in EPRs. Note that the variable for correct shaving is absent since an algorithm is not required due to simplicity reasons. The clinical rules are mainly comprised of "If-then" rules and can be updated with new developments in the knowledge base.

In short, the DSS incorporates the medical knowledge and a mechanism to communicate with the data sources as part of the data infrastructure. By processing surgical information,

Table 4.2: Algorithm for determining timely administering of prophylactic AB.

Prophylactic antibiotics

1. Select all surgical patients, including the surgical operation date and times and patient identifier.
2. Determine, in advance, if the patient has an indication for administering antibiotic prophylactic medicine. If so, set the "antibiotic prophylactic indication" to true (1) and proceed to step 3. If not, set the "antibiotic prophylactic indication" variable to false (0) and the timely AB-variable to "1." Proceed to step 9.
3. Select, for all patients with AB indicated, all administered medications for the patient using the surgical date/time as a starting point by combining the list of surgical patients (with indicated prophylactic antibiotics) and the administered medications before surgery.
4. Select all administered medications *2 h in advance* of the surgical operation start date until the surgical operation end date.
5. Within the selected time window, check if the administered medications are classified as prophylactic antibiotics (see Boolean flag). If so, proceed to step 6, else go to step 8.
6. Select the incisional start moment (moment that the knife enters a tissue or organ) and check if the antibiotic prophylactic is administered within a timeframe of 15–60 min before the incisional start time.
7. If the antibiotic prophylactic is timely administered, then the variable scores positively (1), else it scores negatively (0).
8. NB: If the required incisional moments and/or values are missing, then the administered antibiotic prophylactic medication should remain visible in the final data set. No records are allowed to go missing from the medication subset. In this situation, the variable scores negatively.
9. End.

Table 4.3: Algorithm for determining pre-, intra-, and postoperative normothermia (holding area, operating room, and recovery room).

Normothermia

1. Select all surgical patients, including the surgical operation date/time and patient identifier.
2. Select all temperature measurements before, during, and after surgery. Start with 2 h in advance of the surgical operation start date and 2 h after the surgical operation end date.
3. Within the selected time window:
   a. determine the last temperature measurement at the holding area;
   b. determine the lowest (minimum) and highest (maximum) temperature value during surgery;
   c. determine the first temperature measurement on arrival at the recovery room.
4. For each returned value, determine if the temperature value is in range of 36.5°C and 38.5°C.
5. If the temperature value is within acceptable boundaries, then the variable scores positively (1). In all other cases, the variable scores negatively (0).
6. NB: If the required surgical moments and/or values are missing, then the temperature measurements should remain visible in the final data set. No records are allowed to go missing from the temperature measurements subset. In this situation, the variable scores negatively.
7. End.

Table 4.4: Algorithm for determining total number of door movements.

Door movements
1. Select all surgeries and the surgical operation date/time and operating room number.
2. Select all door movement data from the door sensors including the operating room number.
3. Combine the two data sets based on the operating room number and the surgical time window. Select each door movement between the incisional start date and time (moment when the knife enters the body tissue or organ) and incisional end date and time (closing of the wound).
4. Summarize the total number of door movements between the incisional start date/time and incisional end date/time (surgical time).
5. NB: If the required surgical and incisional moments are missing, then the door movements cannot be aggregated. Display a NULL value in these cases.
6. End.

Table 4.5: Key performance indicator example 1: process outcome.

Percentage adherence to SSI-bundle (process outcome)		
All surgical patients with all four process-of-care variables applied / All surgical patients	$\times 100$	... % SSI-bundle adherence (per department, per medical specialty, per surgical team, among others)

Table 4.6: Key performance indicator example 2: patient outcome.

Percentage SSI (patient outcome)		
All surgical patients who developed a postoperative SSI / All surgical patients	$\times 100$	... % SSI (per department, per medical specialty, per surgical team, among others)

all the combined data result in a specific true-or-false outcome regarding the individual process-of-care variables and the full bundle of care variable (Tables 4.2–4.4).

4.3.5 Key performance indicators

Compliance monitoring is enabled by automatically calculating the following process and outcome indicators using abovementioned algorithms. The definitions for the process and outcome indicators related to surgical patients and the surgical process are provided by the Dutch Patient Safety Programme (VMS, 2009). Tables 4.5 and 4.6 present two key performance indicators that are important to monitor. On an aggregated level, the four process-of-care measures of the bundle should be met with a total compliance of at least 90% (all surgical patients), according to an all-or-nothing principle. This means that if one intervention measure is out of range, then the whole SSI-bundle for the surgical patient scores negatively.

Table 4.7: Data variables per data source.

Data variable	Data source
Unique patient identifier	Electronic patient record
Unique surgical procedure identifier	Surgical information system
Chief of surgery	Surgical information system
Date of admission	Electronic patient record
Date of discharge	Electronic patient record
Surgery start	Surgical information system
Surgery end	Surgical information system
Start time of incision	Perioperative suite
End time of incision	Perioperative suite
Age	Electronic patient record
Sex	Electronic patient record
Urgency (i.e., elective vs emergency)	Surgical information system
OR-theater/environment (site location)	Surgical information system
OR-number	Surgical information system
Use of prophylactic antibiotics (i.e., # in time to antibiotics)	Perioperative suite
Temperature measurements (i.e., proper perioperative normothermia)	Perioperative suite
Number of door movements in the OR (i.e., hygienic discipline)	Door sensor system
Duration of surgery/procedure	Surgical information system (derived)
Duration of pre-, intra-, and postoperative processes	Surgical information system (derived)

4.3.6 Opportunities for local improvements

The prototype allows for analysis on the following variables that relate to the preoperative, the intraoperative, and the postoperative subprocesses. Table 4.7 lists all the data variables that were collected including its source of origin.

It is important to note that the availability of high-quality surgical data is a key requirement to enable good compliance measurement and monitoring. By storing the data generated in the surgical process in a research repository, it enables analysis of the data using methods such as the Cross-Industry Standard Process for Data Mining (CRISP-DM; Chapman et al., 2000) or the Three-Phases Method (3PM; Vleugel, Spruit, & van Daal, 2010).

4.4 Exploratory data analysis

We have performed an exploratory data analysis to raise questions for further exploration. We applied the CRISP-DM to structure our analysis. More specifically, we investigate as to why differences exists across and within departments, medical specialties, and operating rooms theaters. The extent to which medical specialties and departments are compliant to the infection prevention bundle will be investigated using the four predefined process-of-care variables. The main goal of the data analysis is to establish a baseline for further and deeper analysis, to assess the current state of the data quality, and to enable the opportunity to measure and monitor interventions.

One year of historical transactional data were extracted from the EPRs and carefully studied. There have been very few ways in which the compliance of surgical teams has been formally measured, other than basic summary reporting. The goal of this exploratory data analysis is to give concrete recommendations to devise a safer surgical environment for patients and contribute to the aim of reducing hospital acquired infections associated with care delivery for the hospital. The intentions are better treatment, lower costs, more prevention, and reducing (preventable) surgical harm.

Some descriptive statistics: 7451 surgeries were analyzed out of a total of approximately 50,000 surgical procedures performed from January 1, 2012 to December 31, 2013; no cases were excluded even if that means they did not meet all inclusion criteria. In total, 7195 surgeries for one operating room-complex (subpopulation) are analyzed, measured over a period of 1 year. Of these 7195 surgeries studied, 5396 were elective cases (75%), 1531 were operations performed urgently (21.3%), and 268 were performed emergently (3.7%). Furthermore, 3763 were men (52.3%), 3980 were between the ages of 0 and 6 years (55.3%), 7190 were not infected with the Methicillin-resistant *Staphylococcus aureus* (MRSA)-bacteria upon admission (99.9%), and 2941 stayed 1 day or less in the hospital (40.9%). The following sections will analyze and identify two of the possible causes to improve bundle compliance. Note that other causes also worth investigating, but which we do not pursue in this work, includes employment of appropriate hair removal methods.

4.4.1 Appropriate use of prophylactic antibiotics

Timely antibiotic prophylaxis administration significantly reduces the incidence of SSIs. When indicated, short-term antibiotic should be given 15−60 minutes prior to incision to reduce the risk of postoperative SSIs. The selection on timing and appropriately administered antibiotic prophylaxis is critical to maximize the effect.

4.4.2 Maintenance of (perioperative) normothermia

Proper monitoring, maintenance, and regulation of the body temperature during surgery can decrease the likelihood of the development of SSIs. Patients who have had a $90°C$ decrease of only $1°C$ or $2°C$ were three times as likely to develop postoperative wound infections as were those in whom a normal body temperature of $37°C$ was maintained.

Each 5 minutes the body temperature is automatically measured if the patient is connected to the surveillance monitors. In addition, and if necessary, manual temperature measurements are recorded in the system at the designated fields. Ideally, the temperature

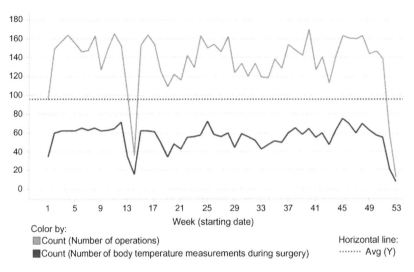

Figure 4.4
Normothermia and adherence to norm per week (2013).

of the patients stays within the agreed boundaries of 36.5°C and 38.5°C during all stages of the surgical process. Hypothermia (temperature value $\leq 36.5°C$) and hyperthermia (temperature value $\geq 38.5°C$) should be avoided in all cases and is also part of the analysis. Patients who arrive at the OR or leave the OR with temperatures below 36.5°C or higher than 38.5°C are susceptible to a higher degree of postoperative wound infections. Finally, the temperature at the end of the procedure (measured at the recovery room) is used as the reference value for adherence to the norm.

In our analysis, normothermia per month within the agreed boundaries (if recorded) does not show much variation on a month-by-month basis. Fig. 4.4 depicts the difference between the numerator and denominator and nonadherence to the normothermia intervention measure on a weekly basis for all operated patients. The negative spikes can most likely be explained due to holiday seasons. Ideally, the difference should be zero or one should strive for zero defects or full compliance. It is possible to drill down to departmental level, specialty level, or individual patient level to further investigate root causes.

4.4.3 Hygienic discipline in operating rooms regarding door movements

Hygienic discipline (measurement of the number of times the operating doors moved) in operating rooms has been implicated as a cause of SSI by several clinical studies (VMS, 2009). To automatically measure the door movements, the decision was made to install automatic door sensors for each operating room (up to three or four door sensors per OR, one for each door). The operating rooms at the case site were equipped with two systems from two different manufacturers, which is not uncommon in these types of studies but also not preferable. The recorded data from the two systems are in turn added to the central infrastructure and made available for analysis.

Door movements are counted during the surgical time (start of incision until end of incision) and checked if the total number of door movements is in accordance with the norm. The target has been arbitrarily set at a maximum of <10 door movements on average per hour.

A distinction has been made between surgical time and incisional time due to required values sometimes missing from fields in the IS indicating data entry issues. Some fields are mandatory, which increases the usability of the data for this analysis, while other important process-of-care variables are often documented using informal recording practices, and thus, are lacking in the surgical record from time to time. This makes it harder to calculate derived variables that are dependent on the before mentioned required fields.

Given the current state of this context, analysis for door movements will most likely provide suboptimal results which should be treated as such. However, it does reflect the current state of recording practices and usage of IS from an information science and clinical point of view to a large degree and holds the potential to identify areas for improvement and enhancement.

In addition, monitoring OR-traffic, such as frequent opening of the OR doors, could possibly indicate short-comings in the discipline of the surgical team. For example, in the preoperative preparation stage, it could be made sure that all required tools are within hand reach, thus reducing the number of door movements. With proper adjustments, most door movements could be reduced and adhere to the norm with ease. The collected data can be used to promote good hygienic discipline (less traffic) and increase awareness for the importance of these activities in the OR.

Fig. 4.5 depicts the total number of door movements versus the duration of surgery. As the total duration of surgery increases, the total number of door movements increases as well. A norm curve has been added based on a maximum of 10 door openings per hour. The results show that a large majority (in this data set) do not adhere to the norm.

Fig. 4.6 shows the difference between the numerator and denominator and the nonadherence to the hygienic discipline preventative measure on a weekly basis for all operated patients. Duration during surgery is added since the start and end moments are mandatory fields in the administrative system whereas the incisional moments are not. However, in 2013 not all door sensors were installed or configured properly to allow for reliable data collection. The negative spikes can most likely be explained due to holiday seasons. Ideally, the difference should be zero or one should strive for zero defects or full

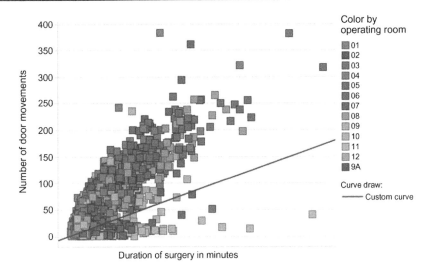

Figure 4.5

Number of door movements versus duration of surgery in minutes.

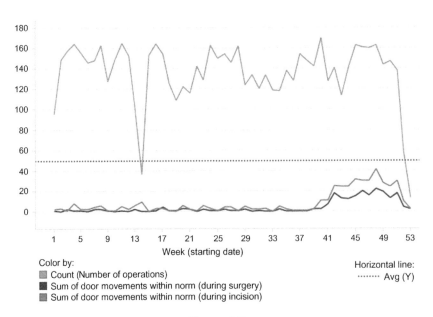

Figure 4.6

Door movements and adherence to norm per week.

compliance. It is possible to zoom into departmental level, specialty level, patient group level, individual patient level, or individual surgeon level to further investigate root causes. One meaningful conclusion can be drawn for certain, that is, that OR-traffic is too high.

However, more reliable data need to be acquired to draw more informed conclusions and are partly caused due to the abovementioned data quality and prototype design issues.

4.5 Discussion and implications

The prototype and subsequent analysis have succeeded in establishing a baseline for bundle compliance over 2013 for pediatric patients with the ability to track progress and further increase bundle compliance over time. The automated data collection method currently captures and enforces industry standards and compliance requirements in the underlying data infrastructure. This research has also demonstrated that there is a need for improved surgical ISs and DSSs that span the whole surgical process.

This study described the inner workings of a prototype to quantify the surgical process by collecting data of the studied bundle variables pertaining to antibiotics, temperature, door movements, and SSI-bundle compliance. An automated and standardized data collection method for routine measurement was established, and a prototype for measuring compliance to the SSI-bundle was built. The results were used to determine the usability and applicability of the design to enable decision support capabilities for infection control purposes.

Usability and applicability could be further increased by improving data and information sharing which should result in measurable improved surgical practice compliance and surgical outcomes for patients over time. The prototype and the acquired baseline provide an initial starting point for further discussion on how to narrow the gap between what surgical operations are routinely doing and what is currently known to be best surgical practice.

The importance of taking a hospital-wide approach to data analysis regarding surgical operations covering all OR-theaters should be emphasized where performing analysis of the data should become a more fundamental activity as part of the core business process, as part of research and development (which is a strategic driver for academic university hospitals), or as an outsourced process. Outsourcing data mining and analytics processes are further elaborated in Vleugel et al. (2010) by introducing the 3PM. In addition, the notion of "data analytics as a service," which is currently being popularized, could be further explored on a nationwide level in support of economy of scale requirements (e.g., Spruit & Boer, 2014). Governmental agencies, universities, and relevant commercial parties (e.g., EPR-vendors, service providers) could provide assistance and make contributions toward solving compelling healthcare and IS challenges.

For example, a national data repository could contain surgical data from all OR-theaters to support benchmark activities and future scientific usages among other usages. Meaningful information regarding surgical care could be complemented with data profiling results to be distributed to local data stewards and information managers. This increases the quality and thus the usability and applicability of the prototype solution. In general, the quality and usability of data are critical to the success and acceptance of any decision support solution.

By supporting small-scale initiatives and by disseminating preliminary findings, establishing a positive feedback flow on a regular basis, continuous improvement initiatives can be sustained. The first preliminary findings with expected low compliance should be disseminated to surgeons, surgical teams, and care managers as soon as possible. Over time, this should lead toward a higher bundle compliance rate from the current baseline to at least 90% or higher while following national evidence-based guidelines.

From the above we conclude that Healthcare Innovations in general and Future Generation Medical Systems in particular can indeed thrive, when adaptive analytic systems can be constructed and extended from the functionalities as implemented and evaluated in our clinical surgery analysis prototype. This study further demonstrates the viability of a Model-Driven Analytic Systems perspective as an attractive framework to take such a potential healthcare innovation to the next level: from a successful computational experiment to, ultimately, improving daily healthcare practices by empowering healthcare professionals and patients, defining and integrating evidence-based models where possible to more meaningfully interpret analytic outcomes (Spruit & Lytras, 2018).

4.5.1 Limitations and further research

Current primary issues in the collection of high-quality data have (1) to do with the use of EPRs by surgical teams in their workflows, (2) the underlying data structures of the EPR, (3) the availability of the key data elements, (4) achieving consensus about the mandatory terms and definitions, and (5) the lack of a positive feedback flow for increasing awareness of before mentioned issues. Another limitation entails the automated data collection method which is heavily tailored and localized to the case site. It is difficult to generalize without significantly changing programming code. While the core conceptual models and prototype support general use, the data collection method and its code are deeply tailored to the local situation.

Further studies could extent the simplified surgical process to include other relevant surgical activities enabling measurement on other subjects and variables that are not related to the variables investigated in this study. For instance, the data set and underlying design models can be extended by including other variables such as the ASA score, wound class, type of wound class (superficial or deep), number of surgical team members, infection present at admission among other variables. The prototype can also be directed into supporting SSI outcome measurement or by providing insights into financial areas such as cost per surgical outcome. This would allow to compare surgical outcomes with the total costs of achieving them over the full cycle of surgical care. Lastly, further case studies in different sized healthcare institutions, including international institutions, should be undertaken to confirm, strengthen the results and provide more external validity.

Finally, it is easy to underestimate the amount of resources and resilience one must muster to transition from a successful analytic prototype onto an analytic system that is ready for daily practices. We discuss here our Top-3 Knowledge Deployment Considerations: usability, compliance, and acceptance. First, outside of a controlled computational laboratory environment, the perceived utility of such a system is often mainly governed by usability requirements, whereas a computational experiment prototype is primarily designed for effectiveness and then efficiency. This requires substantial engineering efforts to streamline the process flow and improve the user interface (Spruit & Jagesar, 2016). Second, another substantial factor is General Data Protection Regulation (GDPR) compliance in Europe: especially in healthcare systems which contain many Protected Health Information attributes, additional privacy and security measures are required by law before an analytic system can be introduced into daily practices or high fines may be incurred. Typical measures include IP address whitelisting, end-to-end encrypted communication including encrypted password storage, role-based access control to restrict medical professionals' access to patient-sensitive information to those that are crucial for user acceptance. This, again, requires substantial engineering efforts to implement adequately. Third, for DSSs including adaptive analytic systems, the golden rule is to never be perceived as replacing its user. This can be implemented by providing options to overrule generated advices and by optimally integrating the systems into the current process flow, among others (Tijssen, Spruit, van de Ridder, & van Raaij, 2011). This, again, requires substantial engineering efforts to implement data or even process integrations with external software adequately and may even require explicit and written permission from the external software vendors, as these remain legally responsible for the patients' privacy under the GDPR (Visvizi & Lytras, 2018).

4.6 Conclusion

This study aimed to quantify the surgical process from an infection control perspective to support in the overall aim of reducing SSIs. Using mandatory and optional EPR data, a minimum basic data set for reporting on SSI compliance was compiled. This work presents a high-level surgical process model as a reference model for OR-theaters to monitor, maintain, and sustain compliance to infection control policies. In addition, an analytic prototype solution was designed and instantiated. This model-driven analytic system prototype quantifies the surgical process and thereby makes deviations from evidence-based practices and the reference surgical process model visible and transparent, allowing for necessary improvement initiatives at the level of local OR-theaters. Lastly, the

DSS-prototype creates new opportunities for operations research and six sigma capabilities. The results can be used to further streamline and strengthen surgical practices by continuously eliminating waste from the surgical process until a satisfactory result has been attained, grounded in the Applied Data Science framework.

4.7 Teaching assignments

- The Applied Data Science framework is structured around the CRISP-DM process model. Map the steps described in this chapter to the phases and subtasks of the CRISP-DM model and elaborate on your findings regarding task coverage and gaps.
- Based on the provided algorithms in Section 4.3, construct a meta-algorithmic model as described in Spruit and Jagesar (2016) that balances the algorithmic complexities and communicative expression capabilities of at least one analytic task.
- Using the Top-3 Knowledge Deployment Considerations in the Further Research section as a guideline, reflect on the knowledge deployment issues to be expected for the surgical care process as shown in Fig. 4.2. Can you think of more considerations? Are some considerations irrelevant for this particular process?

References

Chapman, P., Clinton, J., Kerber, R., Khabaza, T., Reinartz, T., Shearer, C., & Wirth, R. (2000). *CRISP-DM 1.0 step-by-step data mining guide*. IBM.

Chaudry, Z., & Koehler, M. (2005). *Electronic clinical decision support systems should be integral to any healthcare system*. Gartner.

Hevner, A., March, S., Park, J., & Ram, S. (2004). Design science in information systems research. *MIS Quarterly, 28*(1), 75−105.

Institute of Medicine. (1999). *To err is human: Building a safer health system* (pp. 223−240). National Academy Press.

Institute of Medicine. (2001). Crossing the quality chasm: A new health system for the 21st century. National Academy Press.

Kimball, R., & Ross, M. (2011). *The data warehouse toolkit: The complete guide to dimensional modeling*. John Wiley & Sons.

Kleinpell, R. M., Munro, C. L., & Giuliano, K. K. (2008). Targeting health care-associated infections: Evidence-based strategies. *Patient safety and quality: An evidence-based handbook for nurses*.

Meulendijk, M., Spruit, M., Drenth-van-Maanen, A., Numans, M., Brinkkemper, S., & Jansen, P. (2013). General practitioners' attitudes towards decision-supported prescribing: An analysis of the Dutch primary care sector. *Health Informatics Journal, 19*(4), 247−263.

Meulendijk, M., Spruit, M., Drenth-van Maanen, C., Numans, M., Brinkkemper, S., Jansen, P., & Knol, W. (2015). Computerized decision support improves medication review effectiveness: An experiment evaluating the STRIP Assistant's usability. *Drugs & Aging, 32*(6), 495−503.

Meulendijk, M., Spruit, M., Willeboordse, F., Numans, M., Brinkkemper, S., Knol, W., & Askari, M. (2016). Efficiency of clinical decision support systems improves with experience. *Journal of Medical Systems, 40* (4), 1−7.

Porter, M. E. (2010). What is value in health care? *The New England Journal of Medicine, 363*, 2477−2481.

Setiawan, B. (2011). The role of prophylactic antibiotics in preventing perioperative infection. *Acta Medica Indonesiana, 43,* 262–266.

Spruit, M., & Boer, T. de (2014). Business intelligence as a service: A vendor's approach. *International Journal of Business Intelligence Research, 5*(4), 26–43.

Spruit, M., & Jagesar, R. (2016). Power to the people! Meta-algorithmic modelling in applied data science. In A. Fred, et al. (Eds.), *Proceedings of the 8th international joint conference on knowledge discovery, knowledge engineering and knowledge management* (pp. 400–406). Porto: ScitePress, KDIR 2016, November 11–13, 2016.

Spruit, M., & Lytras, M. (2018). Applied data science in patient-centric healthcare: Adaptive analytic systems for empowering physicians and patients. *Telematics and Informatics, 35*(4), 643–653.

Spruit, M., Vroon, R., & Batenburg, R. (2014). Towards healthcare business intelligence in long-term care: An explorative case study in the Netherlands. *Computers in Human Behavior, 30,* 698–707.

Stone, P. W., Larson, E., & Kawar, L. N. (2002). A systematic audit of economic evidence linking nosocomial infections and infection control interventions: 1990-2000. *American Journal of Infection Control, 30,* 145–152.

Tijssen, R., Spruit, M., van de Ridder, M., & van Raaij, B. (2011). BI-FIT: Aligning business intelligence end-users, tasks and technologies. In M. Cruz-Cunha, & J. Varajão (Eds.), *Enterprise information systems design, implementation and management: Organizational applications* (pp. 162–177). .

Van de Weerd, I., & Brinkkemper, S. (2008). *Meta-modeling for situational analysis and design methods. Handbook of research on modern systems analysis and design technologies and applications* (pp. 35–54). .

Visvizi, A., & Lytras, M. (2018). Rescaling and refocusing smart cities research: from mega cities to smart villages. *Journal of Science and Technology Policy Management (JSTPM).* Available from https://doi.org/10.1108/JSTPM-02-2018-0020.

VMS. (2009). *Voorkomen van wondinfecties na een operatie.* Utrecht: VMS Zorg.

Vleugel, A., Spruit, M., & van Daal, A. (2010). Historical data analysis through data mining from an outsourcing perspective: The three-phases method. *International Journal of Business Intelligence Research (IJBIR), 1*(3), 42–65.

Zegers, M., de Bruijne, M. C., Wagner, C., Hoonhout, L. H. F., Waaijman, R., Smits, M., & van der Wal, G. (2009). Adverse events and potentially preventable deaths in Dutch hospitals: Results of a retrospective patient record review study. *Quality & Safety in Health Care, 18*(4), 297–302.

Further reading

De Bruijne, M., Zegers, M., Hoonhout, L., & Wagner, C. (2004). *Onbedoelde schade in Nederlandse ziekenhuizen Dossieronderzoek van ziekenhuisopnames in 2004.* Retrieved from http://www.nivel.nl/sites/default/files/bestanden/onbedoelde-schade-in-nederlandse-ziekenhuizen-2007.pdf

Kaplan, R. S., & Porter, M. E. (2011). How to solve the cost crisis in health care. *Harvard Business Review, 89,* 46–52, 54, 56–61 passim.

CHAPTER 5

Human activity recognition using machine learning methods in a smart healthcare environment

Abdulhamit Subasi[1], Kholoud Khateeb[1], Tayeb Brahimi[2] and Akila Sarirete[3]

[1]Information Systems Department, College of Engineering, Effat University, Jeddah, Saudi Arabia, [2]Natural Sciences, Mathematics, and Technology Unit, College of Engineering, Effat University, Jeddah, Saudi Arabia, [3]Effat College of Engineering, Effat University, Jeddah, Saudi Arabia

5.1 Introduction

A noteworthy percentage of the elderly population complains age-related health problems such as diabetes, cardiovascular disease, osteoarthritis, Alzheimer's disease, dementia, or other chronic diseases. These common diseases, together with the obviously happening progressive weakening in cognitive and physical abilities of elderly people prevent them from living independently. Current developments in information and communication technologies (ICTs), along with improvements in ambient smart technologies, such as sensors, smartphones have brought a quick development of smart environments (Lytras, Visvizi, Daniela, Sarirete, & Ordonez De Pablos, 2018; Visvizi, Jussila, Lytras, & Ijäs, 2019). Smart healthcare appeared as a promising solution to the challenge of a growing aging population. They can offer smart health services to encounter the requirements of this growing population. Especially, smart healthcare systems monitor and assess any critical health condition of elderly people in their daily activities. The smart healthcare frameworks not only permit the elderly people to live independently, but they may also provide healthcare services more sustainable by decreasing the burden on the whole health system by the elderly and dependent individuals. In order to implement a smart healthcare system, there are many challenges in several features of the development process. These challenges contain the remote monitoring of the environment, the communication technology needed for the environment, the existence of intelligent processing systems, and the delivery of context-aware services. Therefore in order to eliminate these challenges, additional investigation is essential to enhance the design (Mshali, Lemlouma, Moloney, & Magoni, 2018).

Innovation in Health Informatics.
DOI: https://doi.org/10.1016/B978-0-12-819043-2.00005-8

Smart healthcare monitoring systems (SHMSs) are the incorporation of ICTs with pervasive computing. These schemes have appeared as a talented solution to deliver smart health services, which match the real requirements of subjects. In this manner, numerous solutions and researches have been developed to address various features of these systems. The main objective of these solutions is to offer a smart environment in which the system monitors and analyses the health conditions of subjects and delivers them with timely smart health services (Mshali et al., 2018). Fig. 5.1 shows a general framework of an SHMS.

Advances in ICT have led to the broader employment of smart sensors and smartphones. In modern smart healthcare applications, the utilization of smart body sensors and smartphones brings patients and physicians together for real-time health monitoring in a smart environment. Smart body sensors and smartphones enable to monitor and analyze real-time health conditions in a pervasive manner. Moreover, the combination of smart devices in healthcare initiates smart applications such as smart healthcare and mobile healthcare monitoring systems. Smart healthcare is a crucial feature of improvement at the forefront of this revolution. This chapter presents a smart healthcare system which is principally deliberate to stimulate the potential of wearable body sensors and mobile devices. These devices are increasingly utilized for the monitoring of personal healthcare and wellbeing. Moreover, a smart healthcare system based on both body sensor and mobile technology is presented to deliver pervasive human activity recognition (HAR) by using machine learning methods. Healthcare services have experienced incredible improvements in the last decade. Smart healthcare is the main engine of development in the frontend of this revolution. Banos, Garcia, et al. (2014) developed mHealthDroid framework for mobile healthcare to enable the ease of progress of biomedical applications. The assembly is creative for the

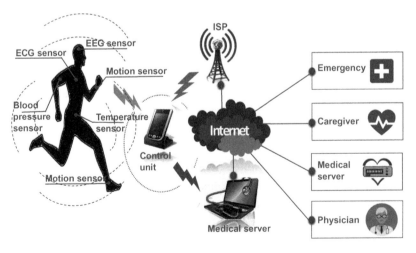

Figure 5.1
A general framework for smart healthcare monitoring systems (SHMS).

effectiveness of mobile devices such as wearable sensors, mobile devices, and ambulant biomedical devices. Smart healthcare is a medical health infrastructure supported by smart body sensors and mobile devices and it involves the employment of core utility of general packet radio service, 4G systems, global positioning system, and Bluetooth technology (Kay, Santos, & Takane, 2011; Subasi, Radhwan, Kurdi, & Khateeb, 2018).

Recently numerous improvements in emerging technologies in Internet protocols and computing systems have achieved communication between several devices easier than ever before (Mahdavinejad et al., 2017). Thus with the recently developed concept of smart sensors and smartphones, all stuff in life become part of the Internet and it became ubiquitous. As smart sensors allow integrated communications between numerous types of devices, it became more productive in different fields such as smart healthcare system. In smart healthcare applications, smart sensors include several kinds of wearable sensors that enable people to appreciate contemporary medical healthcare services anytime, anywhere. Additionally, the body sensor network technology is one of the most efficient technologies utilized in the smart healthcare system. It is mainly an integration of low-power and lightweight wireless sensor nodes that are used to monitor the HAR (Gope & Hwang, 2016). Smart healthcare is still required to create and assess the whole spectrum of smart healthcare technologies. Influential structures and smart body sensors or smartphones that support the justification and improvement of multidisciplinary smart healthcare applications are needed (Banos, Garcia, et al., 2014; Subasi et al., 2018).

HAR turn out to be a prominent research area due to its noteworthy contributions in human-centered areas of a study aiming to improve the quality of life, contribute to the safety, transportation and health in smart cities and smart villages, and help policy makers react effectively to improve the qualification of services (Lytras & Visvizi, 2018; Mshali et al., 2018; Spruit & Lytras, 2018). HAR framework provides information about the behavior and activity of the subjects (Clarkson, 2002). This is generally achieved by recording signals from smart sensors or smartphones and processing them by utilizing machine learning methods for recognition. HAR is employed for continuous patient monitoring with diverse diseases (Avci, Bosch, Marin-Perianu, Marin-Perianu, & Havinga, 2010) daily living activities, locomotion, sports and transportation (Nham, Siangliulue, & Yeung, 2008; Reyes-Ortiz, Oneto, Sama, Parra, & Anguita, 2016; Tapia, Intille, & Larson, 2004). Since smart sensors are the main sources of new data, machine learning, and pattern recognition methods accomplished an excessive contribution to form more smart sensor applications. These techniques composed of several methods suitable for diverse areas. The data processing with machine learning methods involves substantial data types such as variety, volume, velocity; data models such as supervised and unsupervised algorithms and employing efficient algorithms that might be suitable for the data characteristics. As data is generated by several sources with precise data types, it is crucial to implement or adopt algorithms that can handle the data characteristics. Additionally, discovering the best data model which suits the data is one of the critical stages for pattern recognition and for better analysis of sensor data (Mahdavinejad et al., 2017; Subasi et al., 2018).

In this chapter, we will present different machine learning techniques for HAR based on smart sensors and smartphones. The presented HAR system is employed to analyze the human activity that can be one of the most prominent areas in smart healthcare. A robust and precise smart healthcare model will be presented with a user-independent machine learning approach for HAR based on sensor technology.

With the advance of wireless network technology, wearable body sensors are gradually implemented for intelligent daily activity monitoring for various application domains such as emergency help, cognitive assistance, and safety (Majumder et al., 2017; Neves, Stachyra, & Rodrigues, 2008). HAR is employed to recognize different human activities and gesture from the actions of subjects via smart sensors as well as using smartphones equipped with numerous sensors. HAR can be realized to take the benefit of smart body sensors. In terms of the recognition of complex activity, mostly data-driven approaches suffer from problems of portability, expansion, and interpretation, while knowledge-based methods are often weak in dealing with complex temporal data (Liu, Peng, Liu, & Huang, 2015). One of the objectives of machine learning is to reduce the large amounts of data so that they simply reflect the entire data without circulation (Xu et al., 2017). The sensor-based activity recognition is becoming more popular than video-based to protect privacy (Liu, Nie, Liu, & Rosenblum, 2016; Wang, Chen, Hao, Peng, & Hu, 2017). HAR can be realized utilizing smart sensors to benefit pervasive applications. With increased accessibility of wearable smart sensors and smartphones, it has raised attention in the progress of HAR techniques in pervasive computing (Liu et al., 2015). Information collected from the wearable smart sensors and smartphones can be processed by machine learning algorithms. Because HAR is a very fast-growing field of research, it has wide applications in healthcare, assisted living, home monitoring, personal fitness assistants, and terrorist detection. Similarly, HAR systems could be adapted in a smart home healthcare system to enhance and develop the rehabilitation processes of patients (Hassan, Uddin, Mohamed, & Almogren, 2018). Therefore, in order to deliver elderly people with proactive assistance, the caregivers use smart sensors to track and analyze the activity of daily living of them (Liu et al., 2016). Moreover, this may assist elderly people in living in their own homes and sometimes it becomes one of the challenges for recognizing everyday life activities more accurately. A lot of research has been published about the sensor and investigated for HAR but is not accurate enough and with more additional sensors are introduced nowadays to open new possibilities for tracking more details of human activity. However, it is needed to discover which machine learning method is more suitable to recognize human activity in high accuracy. With the expanding number of wearable smart sensors and smartphones, HAR has attracted in many types of research. A HAR framework with different wearable sensors contains segments for information securing and preprocessing, information division, include extraction and determination, grouping or order, and performance assessment (He, Tan, & Zhang, 2018).

5.2 Background and literature review

5.2.1 Human activity recognition with body sensors

In the literature, with the progress of smart sensors and smartphones with different sensors, there is a tendency to HAR and applications on cell phones, including wellbeing observation, self-overseeing framework and wellness following. However, the main difficulties of the current HAR are the accuracy is moderately low and high computation power is required. Understanding individuals' activities and their connections with the physical condition is a crucial component for the improvement of the smart sensors and digital empowered applications. HAR is an examination area which precisely manages this problem for detecting and inspiring. Keeping in mind the end goal to convey setting mindful information that can be employed to give customized support in several applications. The HAR has turned into therapeutic, security, and military applications. Hence, distinguishing human exercises in regular daily existence, for example, walking, running, or upstairs turns out to be very helpful to give criticism to the caregiver about the patient's situation (Cao, Wang, Zhang, Jin, & Vasilakos, 2018).

Studies on sensor-based HAR have been growing in the past decade. A lot of methods have been proposed to recognize human daily life. One of the research (Wang et al., 2017) compared deep learning approaches with conventional pattern recognition approaches for sensor-based activity recognition. So the recent advance of deep learning approach has been adopted and explored sensor-based activity recognition tasks from three categories: sensor modality, deep model, and application. Köping, Shirahama, and Grzegorzek (2018) presented a model for sensor-based HAR that can be improved and integrated easily to the sensors in mobile devices. The framework has two characteristics: first, a smartphone is used for temporary data storage recorded from diverse sensors with their own programming interface and send those data to the central server. Second, the codebook-based learning approach is employed to analyze sensor data and extract valuable information for HAR. The results revealed that the success of the model proven in real time where they integrate eight sensors from different wearable devices such as smartphone, smart glasses, and smartwatch.

Recently many efforts have been made toward recognizing human activity utilizing wearable sensors. In spite of the diversity of proposed systems, current solutions share operating only according to predefined settings and restricted sensor settings. Real-world activity recognition applications require users to configure more flexible sensors that deal with potential negative situations such as faulty or lost sensors. In order to provide interoperability and retrofitting, the heterogeneous sensors are used in HAR should be derived to some extent from the actual network infrastructure. Villalonga, Pomares, Rojas, and Banos (2017) proposed several techniques to eliminate measurement characteristics and wearable sensor characteristics, including their location on the body. The proposed sensor selection method adopts a set of guidelines for determining sensors locations under different conditions.

Liu et al. (2016) studied several algorithms to recognize temporal patterns from simple actions for presenting complex activities. Most of the researches focused on recognition of simple actions to fulfill a simple purpose like walking and standing only, while the activity of multiple actions over time also is much more representative of human's real life like cooking and coffee time. The result confirms that the accuracy of this approach is able to recognize complex activities from temporal patterns to deal with the error. Ignatov (2018) proposed a deep learning approach for online HAR by using convolutional neural networks with statistical features which maintain global attributes of the accelerometer time series. Xu et al. (2017) proposed a multilevel feature learning model for sensor-based HAR using a single body-worn inertial sensor. The model was based on the low-level, mid-level, and high-level features. The low-level features collect signal-based information. The mid-level features learn component-based representation. The high-level features semantic descriptions. The results revealed that the success of the framework has been achieved the state-of-the-art performances on different datasets.

Cao, Li, Ma, and Tao (2018) proposed wearable activity recognition systems by utilizing multiple heterogeneous or homogeneous sensors to get effective information. In the proposed framework, sensor-based activity recognition system implemented with a multisensor fusion designed with ensemble pruning system. Two new ensemble pruning methods are suggested (mRMR and discriminative pruning) to balance the sensor size and system performance. The mRMR pruning utilizes mutual information and is the complex standard of classifier redundancy and relevance to the selected classifier set. The pruning measure of discriminative pruning combines reduced-error pruning and complementary pruning presented as mutual information. The pruning learner with lower error is chosen as final ensemble classifier by utilizing a suitable pruning method which is better than traditional ensemble methods.

Espinilla et al. (2017) implemented a smart environment with heterogeneous architectures in a wide area of heterogeneous electronic devices. It delivers a solution to treat problem related to the growing of size and aging of the population by offering monitoring activities of daily life and adapted environment. By using feature selection methods, the subset of sensors of a smart environment to handle sensors are optimized and higher accuracy is achieved. The proposed sensor system reduces the costs from a technological perspective, while it maintains the accuracy for activity recognition and reduces the sensor data and computational complexity. Wen and Wang (2016) offered a scheme that integrates dynamically available contexts to enhance the activity recognition system in a dynamic environment where the original data source might fail and new data sources can be available. The experimental results revealed that the performance of the activity recognition can be enhanced with dynamically discovered data sources.

5.2.2 Human activity recognition with mobile phone sensors

Smart sensor and mobile phone technology are going on developing everyday, and it is all for the sake of simplifying people lives. But, in order to accomplish this, different efforts need to be carried out on the population to know what their most needed activities are, what they are doing, and how technology is willing to support them to achieve their task. Ignatov (2018) affirmed that intelligent mobile devices, including smartphones, smartwatches, and fitness trackers combined several sensors can be used for HAR. Once sensors integrated to these smart devices, the data recorded via these sensors for HAR can be analyzed using machine learning techniques. HAR has played a major role in promoting the improvement of people's quality of life (Ortiz, 2015). It is now focused also on healthcare areas and how HAR can improve infected people with a certain disease to be healed. Even though that now it can be also implemented in an online pattern, through the more powerful resources that smartphones (Shoaib, Bosch, Incel, Scholten, & Havinga, 2015). Moreover, just because smartphones resources are a handful that does not mean it cannot be affected by this process. So integration is needed to ensure that activity recognition is not affecting smartphone power in a negative way. This is proposed by Wang, Chen, Yang, Zhao, and Chang (2016) by constructing an online activity recognizer through a novel feature selection approach. This can generate a better generalization ability, plus reducing smartphone power consumption. An experiment was conducted by Arif, Bilal, Kattan, and Ahamed (2014) in order to handle obesity issues through HAR by acceleration sensors presented within a smartphone, to monitor user's physical activities, such as walking, jogging, sitting, and so on. HAR goes through the process of classification, such as base-level and meta-level classifiers. However, in HAR the most used one is the base level, although when putting base-level and meta-level classifiers on the comparison on a variety of activity recognition tasks, it shows us that meta-level classifiers (such as boosting, bagging, and plurality voting) outperform base-level classifiers (Reiss, Hendeby, & Stricker, 2015). Classification can go through beyond many conditions of HAR, taken that in an experiment conducted by Bayat, Pomplun, and Tran (2014) to measure activity classification at two situations, one where the smartphone is in-hand and the other is where it is in-pocket, their results are showing that the highest performance was by multilayer perceptron (MLP) with an 89.48% accuracy for in-hand position and 89.72% for in-pocket position.

A problem that faces classification technique within HAR that the "classification accuracy is relatively low." Hence, Cao et al. (2018) proposed a framework to improve the accuracy by implementing GCHAR, which stands for group-based connect-aware classification method for HAR within smartphones. This technique takes the advantage of a hierarchical group-based scheme that helps to improve classification efficiency. Another classification issue is pointed out by Yang and Wang (2016) where smartphone users tend to keep their devices in a fixed position, such as a trousers' pocket. Hence, such behavior affects the recognition accuracy. Hence, they proposed a position-independent method known as parameters adjustment corresponding to smartphone position. That way this method can enhance the performance of activity recognition. HAR can also be combined with other methods for a deep activity recognition such as early diagnosing of a stroke. This is made through a novel HAR method proposed for stroke early diagnosing along the adaption of the genetic fuzzy finite state machine method (González et al., 2015). HAR is a technique used to analyze human motion and activity. HAR can be used for single or multiple participants. The sensors are used to surveillance user via various tools such as a camera. These sensors are designed to be flexible and small in order to recognize human movements. It does not need any extra devices that provide a comfortable experience for users. One of the obstacles that face HAR is the correct information because of the huge amount of data it's difficult to gain the correct information. The supervised learning uses correct information that raises the privacy concerns due to the need for Activities of Daily Living (ADL) and truth information together (Hossain, Khan, & Roy, 2017). However, to solve the privacy issue, researcher came up with smartphones sensor that works in background mode, which is achieving a good result in low-cost matter (Martín, Bernardos, Iglesias, & Casar, 2013). Furthermore, the scholars search about new method and techniques that help improve accuracy and integrity level of smartphone sensors. They found out a new method that used the smartphone accelerometer pair with dedicated chest sensor to recognize the human activity by 98% accuracy (Guiry, van de Ven, Nelson, Warmerdam, & Riper, 2014). This encourages the researcher who interested in HAR to contribute to this field by search about new method and tools. Hence Zhong, Wen, Hu, and Indulska (2017) came up with a new technique which is compressed sensing method to recognize human motion based on compressed sensing theory, and the outcomes of their paper reach 86% accuracy. On the other hand, the authors to improve the activity recognition field. They study the cases and scenarios of accuracy level when the results can be accepted or rejected. The quality of metrics has been a dialectic issue between researchers who seek to improve the method and tools the used to measure the performance. This highlights the importance of comparing between micro- and macrosignal that performance that speed throughout the multiclass classification. This creates a new method used by model parameter optimization in application to enhance the quality of recognition (Safonov, Gartseev, Pikhletsky, Tishutin, & Bailey, 2015). Some authors studied the performance issue related to sensors. Performance is important metrics to evaluate your overall all work and outcomes. Especially, in HAR, this encourages searching into a systematic analysis of motion sensor behavior for HAR (Chen & Shen, 2017). According to Uddin, Billah, and Hossain (2016), the results of their paper show 100% accuracy on benchmark dataset and point out that signals generated from recognition are the best. However, the activity recognition is not only on information technology environment but it can be used by the medical researcher in order to enhance the health services (Woznowski, Kaleshi, Oikonomou, & Craddock, 2016). Moreover, Ronao and Cho (2016) argued how deep learning network helps HAR at smartphones. They used this technique to increase HAR efficient by searching the ingrained feature of activities.

5.3 Machine learning methods

5.3.1 Artificial neural networks

Artificial neural network (ANN) models are inspired from the human brain and characterizes device that can processes information and has some extraordinary abilities that outreach current engineering research in biomedical signal analysis. MLP can realize nonlinear discriminants, if used for classification, and can give an approximation of nonlinear functions of the input if used for regression. The output of the MLP is the linear combination of the nonlinear basis function values given by the hidden units. Hidden units perform a nonlinear mapping from the d-dimensional input space to the H-dimensional space spanned by the hidden units, and, in this space, the second output layer realize a linear function. As MLP is not restricted to have one hidden layer, more hidden layers with their own weights can be located after the first layer with sigmoid hidden units in order to calculate nonlinear functions of the first layer of hidden units and realizing more complex functions of the inputs (Alpaydin, 2014; Rumelhart, Hinton, & Williams, 1986).

5.3.2 k-Nearest neighbor

The k-nearest neighbor (k-NN) classifier has been widely used in the biomedical signal analysis. Learning is carried out by comparing a given test set with training sets that are similar. The training sets are defined by n attributes. As each set signifies a point in an n-dimensional space, all the training sets are stored in n-dimensional pattern space. When it is applied to the unknown set, k-NN searches for the k training sets that are the closest to the unknown set in its pattern space. These k training sets represent the k "NN" of the unknown sets. "Closeness" of the sets is defined with a distance metric, such as Euclidean distance. For k-NN classification, the unknown set is assigned the most common class among its k-NN. For $k = 1$, the unknown set is given the class of the training set that is closest to it in pattern space. In general, when the number of the training set is larger, the value of k will be also larger (Han, Pei, & Kamber, 2011)

5.3.3 Support vector machine

Among all well-known machine learning algorithms, the most robust and accurate method is a support vector machine (SVM). In the case of two-class learning problem, the objective of the SVM is to determine the best classification function to differentiate members of the two classes in the training set. For a dataset that is linearly separable, a linear classification function represents a separating hyperplane that passes through the middle of the two classes. As there are many of such hyperplanes, SVM shows that the best function is determined by maximizing the margin between two classes. The margin represents the amount of space or separation between two classes. Geometrically, the margin is the shortest distance between a point on the hyperplane and the closest data points. Despite there is an infinite number of hyperplanes, only a few can be eligible as the solution to SVM. SVMs offer the best generalization ability and it gives not only the best classification performance but also leaves much space for the exact classification of future data (Wu et al., 2008).

5.3.4 Naïve Bayes

When given a set of objects where each belongs to a known class and has a known vector of variables, the aim is to create a rule which will assign a future object to a class, given only the vectors of variables describing the future objects. As Naïve Bayes does not need any complicated iterative parameter estimation scheme, it is very easy to build. In other words, Naïve Bayes can be easily applied to huge datasets and users that are unskilled in classifier technology can understand easily. In any particular application, it may not be the best possible classifier but it can easily be relied on to be robust and to perform quite well (Wu et al., 2008).

5.3.5 Classification and regression tree

Classification and regression tree (CART) is a major innovation in the evolution of artificial intelligence, machine learning, and data mining. The CART represents a binary recursive partitioning procedure that performs processing of continuous and nominal attributes, both as targets and predictors. Trees are grown to a maximum size without the use of stopping rule. Then it is pruned back to the root by cost-complexity pruning. The split, which is contributing least to the overall performance of the tree on training data, is the next split to be pruned. The CART model has the aim to produce a sequence of nested pruned trees, all of which are candidate optimal trees. CART gives no internal performance measures for tree selection based on the training data as such measures are considered suspicious. The CART mechanism allows cost-sensitive learning dynamic feature construction and probability tree estimation and contains automated class balancing and automated missing value handling. As Gini criterion is calculated more quickly than information gain, and as it can be extended to involve symmetrized costs, the CART uses Gini instead of information gain (Wu et al., 2008).

5.3.6 C4.5 decision tree

C4.5 uses classifiers defined as decision trees. However, it can make classifiers in more comprehensible ruleset form. In order to rank possible tests, C4.5 uses two heuristic criteria: information gain that minimizes total entropy of the subsets, and default gain ratio that is represented as a division of information gain by the information provided by the test outcomes. The format of the test outcomes is defined with attributes, as they can be numeric or nominal. In order to avoid overfitting, the initial tree is pruned. The pruning algorithm uses a pessimistic estimate of the error rate that is associated with a set of N cases, and it does not belong to the most frequent class. Pruning procedure is done from the leaves to the root. If the subtree is replaced by a leaf, C4.5 adds the estimated errors of the branches and compares them to the estimated error. If the former is higher than the latter, the subtree is pruned. As information about one class is usually distributed through the tree, the understanding of the complex decision trees can be difficult (Wu et al., 2008).

5.3.7 REPTree

REPTree is an algorithm that constructs a decision or regression tree using the reduction of information gain and prunes it employing reduced-error pruning. As it only sorts the values for the numeric attributes once, it is optimized for speed. Similarly, to C4.5, REPTree handles missing values by dividing instances into pieces. Parameters that can be set include the minimum number of instances per leaf, maximum tree depth, minimum proportion of the training set variance for a split for numeric classes only, and the number of folds for pruning (Witten, Frank, Hall, & Pal, 2016).

5.3.8 LADTree algorithm

The LADTree learning algorithm employs the logistic boosting (LogitBoost) algorithm to implement an alternating decision tree (ADTree). The LogitBoost algorithm is merged with the induction of ADTrees in two ways. In the first, separate trees are grown-up for each class in parallel. In the second approach called LADTree, only one tree is grown predicting all class probabilities at the same time. A single attribute test is selected as the splitter node for the tree at every iteration with the original algorithm. The aim is to fit the working response to the mean value of the instances, in a specific subset, by minimizing the least-squares value among them. After choosing tests to add to the tree, the maximum gain is looked for, that is, the highest decrease in the least-squares calculation (Holmes, Pfahringer, Kirkby, Frank, & Hall, 2002).

5.3.9 Random tree classifiers

The random tree which is an ensemble learning algorithm produces numerous individual learners using bagging to yield a random set of data for building a decision tree. In an ordinary tree, nodes are divided employing the best split between the variables. The random tree which is an ensemble of tree classifiers receives the input feature vectors and predicts them with each tree in the forest employing the majority voting. The performance of single decision trees is significantly enhanced by using tree diversity and randomization. First, for every single tree, the training data are resampled with replacement, and only a random subset of all attributes is taken at every node instead of always computing the best split for each node. This result is employed by the random tree to yield split selection and accordingly produce practically balanced trees, hence the optimization procedure is simplified (Hall, Witten, & Frank, 2011; Kalmegh, 2015)

5.3.10 Random forests

The random forest (RF) classifier represents another modified version of the bagging. It is more justified than boosting, as RF uses bootstrap data samples as training sets for the creation of the base models. Improvement in RF consists of stimulating the greater base model diversity by randomizing the modeling algorithm, which is a decision tree or regression tree algorithm. The algorithm uses two approaches to the creation of the base model: instance sampling and algorithm nondeterminism. Nondeterminism is achieved by performing a random split selection that is used for tree growing. RF draws a random subset of available attributes in each node and restricts the subsequent split selection process to split using those attributes. In order to not have the growing process unchanged, the usual criteria for the split assessment for decision trees or regression trees are employed. Stopping criteria for decision or regression tree growing are set up to achieve comparatively big, precisely fitted trees and no pruning is used. This approach achieves several splits being chosen and produces a high level of base model diversity unless the number of existing splits is too small. The square root of the number of all existing attributes is used as the size of the randomly drawn subset of attributes. Individual overfitting of the models is canceled out by the aggregation process that makes the RF ensemble to be highly resistant to overfitting (Cichosz, 2014).

5.4 Results

In this study, we presented two types of SHMS: one with body sensors and the other one with smartphone sensors. The HAR data are collected from body sensors or smartphone sensors, and then processed and classified. The general experimental set-up is shown in Fig. 5.2.

K-fold cross-validation, which is the preferred practical method mostly in limited-data situations, used for the evaluation of classifiers' performance. In cross-validation, a fixed number of partitions of the data or folds is decided. During the cross-validation, the dataset is divided into *k* subset in a way that each class is denoted roughly the same sizes. Every subset is kept in turn and the classification algorithm is trained on the residual nine-tenths. Then the classifier error is calculated on the holdout set. Consequently, the learning procedure is performed totally *k* times on different training sets. Lastly, in order to calculate the overall error estimate, the *k* error estimates are averaged (Hall et al., 2011).

The true negatives (TNs) and the true positives (TPs) are accurate classifications whereas a false positive (FP) is as the result is wrongly classified as positive while it is essentially negative and a false negative (FN) is as the result is wrongly classified as negative while it is essentially positive (Hall et al., 2011). Biomedical researchers describe parameters for classifier performance such as recall and precision:

$$\text{Recall} = \frac{\text{TP}}{\text{TP} + \text{FN}} \tag{5.1}$$

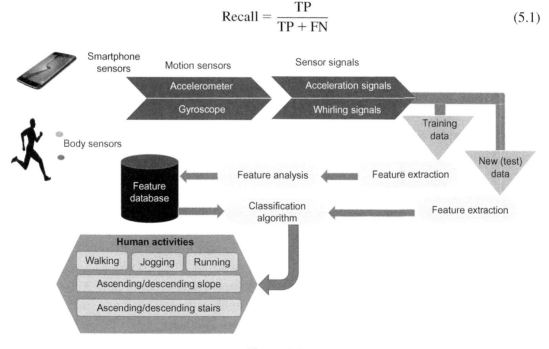

Figure 5.2
The general experimental setup for smart healthcare monitoring systems (SHMS).

$$\text{Precision} = \frac{\text{TP}}{\text{TP} + \text{FP}} \tag{5.2}$$

The additional performance measure is the *F*-measure, which is represented by

$$F\text{-measure} = 2 \times \frac{\text{Precision} \times \text{Recall}}{\text{Precision} + \text{Recall}} = \frac{2 \times \text{TP}}{2 \times \text{TP} + \text{FP} + \text{FN}} \tag{5.3}$$

Finally, the overall success rate is given by the ratio of the correct classifications to the total number of classifications

$$\text{Accuracy} = \frac{\text{TP} + \text{TN}}{\text{TP} + \text{FN} + \text{TN} + \text{FP}} \times 100\% \tag{5.4}$$

A graphical method for assessing classifier performance is represented by the receiver operating characteristic (ROC) curves. ROC curves represent the performance of a classifier without considering the error costs or the class distribution. The vertical axis represents the TP rate and the horizontal axis represents the TN rate. Sometimes, the area under the ROC curve (AUC) is used since the larger the area the better the model. AUC is convenient if class distributions and costs are unknown and one model is chosen to represent all cases (Hall et al., 2011).

The kappa statistic is a measure which takes the expected figure into account by taking it from the classifier's achievements and articulating the output as a percentage of the sum of the classifiers. Hence the kappa statistic represents the agreement between the observed and the predicted classes, whereas adjusting for an agreement which happens by chance. Nevertheless, it does not take into consideration costs like the simple success rate (Hall et al., 2011)

5.4.1 Experimental results for human activity recognition data taken from body sensors

5.4.1.1 Dataset information

In this present work, the open access activity recognition dataset REALDISP[1] (REAListic sensor DISPlacement) has been used. This dataset investigates the effects of sensor displacement in HAR process; it is available at the Center for Machine Learning and Intelligent Systems (Banos, Toth, Damas, Pomares, & Rojas, 2014). The dataset contains recordings of 7 females and 10 males aging 22−37 years old and performing 33 physical activities with different intensity involving diverse combinations of the body such as walking, jogging, running, jumping up-front-back-sideways, jump legs/arms opened and closed, trunk twist (arms outstretched), trunk twist (elbows bended), waist rotation, etc.

---

[1] Downloaded from https://archive.ics.uci.edu/ml/datasets/REALDISP + Activity + Recognition + Dataset

(Boonkrong, Unger, & Meesad, 2014). The activities were measured by a total of nine on-body sensors located in different parts of the body that permit a normal daily living behavior. Each sensor measures four sensor modalities namely: 3D acceleration (accX, accY, accZ), the 3D rate of turn or gyro (gyrX, gyrY, gyrZ), 3D magnetic field orientation (magX, magY, magZ), and 4D quaternions (Q1, Q2, Q3, Q4). In the present work, we used a reduced version of the REALDISP original dataset containing seven activities. However, to guarantee a fair distribution of the various exercises recorded for this dataset, we selected exercises involving the motion of different parts of the users' body. Seven activities have been selected: elliptical bike, cycling, jogging, jump-up, rowing, running, and walking. The dataset comprises the readings of motion sensors recorded while users execute typical daily activities. There is a total of 120 attributes (Banos, Toth, et al., 2014).

5.4.1.2 Experimental results

The main objective of this study is to represent machine learning methods to recognize human activities using wearable sensors located in different parts of the body. In this context, several classification techniques have been applied and the performances of the classifiers were evaluated in terms of total classification accuracy, *F*-measure, ROC area, and Kappa which are defined in the previous section. Seven activities have been selected for the dataset namely: elliptical bike, cycling, jogging, jump-up, rowing, running, and walking. To validate the model, different classification methods have been applied such as SVMs, k-NNs, Naive Bayes, ANNs, C4.5 decision tree, and RFs. For the sake of comparison, the same parameters settings have been applied to all the classifiers used. To investigate the accuracy of each model and how it performs, the whole HAR data have been broken into training and test sets, and then *k*-fold cross-validation has been applied. The reason why *K*-fold cross-validation has been used is to prevent bias presented by choosing a specific training and test set.

According to the results given in Table 5.1 and based on the total classification accuracy, AUC, *F*-measure, and Kappa statistics, it is clear that all selected methods performed

Table 5.1: Classification results for HAR data taken from body sensors.

	Accuracy (%)	F-Measure	ROC	Kappa
SVM	99.43	0.994	0.999	0.9933
k-NN	98.92	0.989	1	0.9874
ANN	99.33	0.993	0.993	0.9922
Naïve Bayes	93.97	0.94	0.994	0.9296
RF	99.19	0.992	0.995	0.9906
CART	98.71	0.987	0.995	0.985
C4.5	98.83	0.988	0.996	0.9863
REPTree	98.25	0.983	0.997	0.9796
LADTree	84.05	0.837	0.976	0.8139

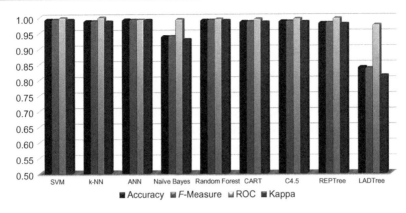

Figure 5.3
Performance of classifiers for HAR using body sensors.

reasonably. The best level of accuracy for SVM shows 99.43% which is the best among all the selected classification methods. The rest of the classifiers performed, respectively, at follows: SVM 99.43%, *k*-NN 98.92%, ANN 99.33%, Naïve Bayes 93.97%, RF 99.19%, CART 98.71%, C4.5 98.83%, and REPTree 98.25%. In the second column of Table 5.1, the *F*-measure of each classifier is displayed. The *F*-measure ranges from 0.837 to 0.994. SVM provides best *F*-measure while LADTree is the least with 0.837 value. Investigating other measures such as ROC in column 3 and Kappa in column 4, we can notice that SVM is on the top of the list of all classifier methods. The accuracy and a comparison of classification algorithms for body sensor HAR are shown in Fig. 5.3.

5.4.2 Experimental results for human activity recognition data taken from smartphone sensors

5.4.2.1 Dataset information

In this experiment, smartphone sensors are used to investigate the ADL of a person based on some observations including the surrounding environment.[2] The objective is to predict human activity based on data recorded and collected by a smartphone. The experiment has been carried out with a group of 30 volunteers performing ADL (Reyes-Ortiz et al., 2016). The age of the group ranges from 19 to 48 years old, and by wearing a smartphone attached to the waist of each person who has the ability to perform a total of six activities namely: walking, walking upstairs, walking downstairs, sitting, standing, and laying. A video-recorded is then used to manually label the data. The acquired database has been randomly divided into two sets, where 70% of the volunteers (21 subjects) have been utilized for

---

[2] Downloaded from https://archive.ics.uci.edu/ml/datasets/Smartphone-Based + Recognition + of + Human + Activities + and + Postural + Transitions

training purposes and 30% of the volunteers (9 subjects) as test information data. Overall, there are a total of 10,299 records, 7352 for train data and 2947 for test data. Each record has the following attributes:

- Triaxial acceleration from the accelerometer and the assessed body acceleration.
- Triaxial angular velocity took from the gyroscope.
- Each vector has 561 features including time and frequency domain variables and activity label.
- Each vector has a subject identifier who carried out the experiment.

By using embedded accelerometer and gyroscope of a smartphone, the three-axial linear acceleration and the three-axial angular velocity are sampled at a constant rate of 50 Hz. Both accelerometer and gyroscope were preprocessed to remove any noise from the signal then sampled in fixed-width sliding windows of 2.56 seconds and 50% overlap (128 readings/window). The sensor acceleration signal has three components: the noise, the gravitational, and the movement. Since the gravitational component is assumed to have a low frequency, a 0.3 Hz cutoff frequency filter was used. By computing the variables from the time and frequency, a vector of the feature is generated (Anguita, Ghio, Oneto, Parra, & Reyes-Ortiz, 2013).

5.4.2.2 Experimental results

The main objective of this study was to investigate and predict the ADL of a person using a smartphone attached to the waist of a person who is capable of performing a total of six main activities, walking, walking upstairs, walking downstairs, sitting, standing, and laying. Nine classification methods have been applied and results are shown in Table 5.2. The different classification methods performed are SVM, k-NN, ANN, Naïve Bayes, RF, CART, C4.5, REPTree, and LADTree. According to these results, SVM, RF, and k-NN performed sensibly well with an accuracy of 98.91%, 98.61%, and 97.66%, respectively. A good result was also obtained by C4.5, CART, and REPTree classifiers with an accuracy of 94.84%, 93.76%, and 93.42%, respectively. However, k-NN, ANN, and Naïve Bayes show poor results.

Table 5.2: Classification results for HAR data taken from smartphone sensors.

	Accuracy (%)	F-Measure	ROC area	Kappa
SVM	98.91	0.989	0.997	0.987
k-NN	97.66	0.977	0.986	0.9719
ANN	56.26	0.531	0.912	0.4712
Naïve Bayes	76.79	0.75	0.959	0.7217
RF	98.61	0.986	1	0.9833
CART	93.76	0.938	0.977	0.925
C4.5	94.84	0.948	0.974	0.938
REPTree	93.42	0.934	0.983	0.9209
LADTree	88.06	0.881	0.988	0.8565

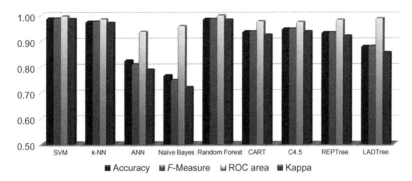

Figure 5.4
Performance of classifiers for HAR using smartphone sensors.

The *F*-measures of SVM, *k*-NN, ANN, Naïve Bayes, RF, CART, C4.5, REPTree, and LADTree were 0.989, 0.977, 0.531, 0.75, 0.986, 0.938, 0.948, 0.934, and 0.881, respectively. On the other hand, the ROC area of all the classifiers shows the high score. However, the Kappa results show the high score for all classifiers except for ANN with a very low value of 0.4712, and an average score of 0.7217 and 0.8565 for Naïve Bayes and LADTree, respectively. The accuracy and a comparison of classification algorithms for smartphone sensor HAR are shown in Fig. 5.4.

5.5 Discussion and conclusion

Future trends in smart sensors and smartphones are making a flourishing in the wearable market, where scientists can improve wearable models for several applications. Improvements in smart sensors and smartphone technologies and the increasing awareness in SHMSs in different areas claim that spreading the use of wearable devices into the clinical applications and medical home monitoring will be attractive. Continuous and precise remote monitoring of critical health condition of elderly people in their daily activities is a crucial task. HAR utilizing wearable devices for abnormal situation detection is a new direction and can play a crucial role in healthcare systems. The aim is to detect any crucial situation such as fall detection by applying in smart HAR. In this chapter, we have presented a smart HAR using real-time sensor data. The aim of this chapter is to present the usability of smart HAR system for the detection of abnormal activities. The framework was demonstrated by a use case, in which body sensor and smartphone sensor data sent to a remote server at a certain frequency, and data analysis was completed in real time after the data were sent to the server. The system has been confirmed to be practical, precise, and effective for HAR. The improvements in smartphones and body sensor technology offer vital solutions to improve the quality of healthcare for patients with several diseases.

The main aim of this chapter is to present how to implement an automatic, efficient, and scalable HAR system to detect any critical health condition in real time using body sensors or smartphone sensors. Hence two experiments have been conducted to investigate human activities. The first one uses wearable body sensors on different parts of a user body, and the second one uses a smartphone inertial sensor. The objective was to predict human activity based on data recorded and collected using machine learning techniques to evaluate results in terms of total classification accuracy, F-measure, ROC area, and Kappa. For wearable sensors and according to the results given in Table 5.1, it has been found that SVM gives better accuracy in terms of accuracy, F-measure, ROC area, and Kappa. SVM is better than all classifier methods used in this study, namely SVMs, k-NNs, Naive Bayes, ANNs, C4.5 decision tree, and RFs. For the smartphone inertial sensors, nine different classification methods have been investigated: SVM, k-NN, ANN, Naïve Bayes, RF, CART, C4.5, REPTree, and LADTree. According to these results in Table 5.2 and in terms of accuracy, it has been found that SVM, RF, and k-NN achieved better accuracy compared to ANN, Naïve Bayes, CART, C4.5, REPTree, and LADTree, and three classifiers k-NN, ANN, and Naïve Bayes showed poor results. It is also important to note here that the HAR data taken from body sensors achieve better accuracy than the HAR data taken from the smartphone sensors.

With the expanding number of wearable sensors and cell phones, HAR has attracted many researches to automatically recognize human behavior and provide accurate information on their activities, for example, in smart homes environment or for health monitoring assistance applications, emergency services, and transportation assistance services. The present study showed that HAR based on the sensor data is very challenging, in particular with the existence of a diversity of machine learning techniques. There is no standalone solution to all when it comes to machine learning methods, as shown in this study, not all the classification techniques can be performed well, consequently, it is important to systematically investigate and analyze each technique. Moreover, it is also important to extend HAR to other activities such as sleeping or bicycling and extract more features that could help in analyzing human-to-human interaction and interpersonal relationships.

Despite all the recent development in health informatics, machine learning, and data mining techniques, one should not forget that human behavior is not only naturally spontaneous, but human may perform several activities at the same time or even perform some activities that are not relevant. Another issue is the challenge encountered in the prediction of the speed of the motion, or activity. It is our believe that future HAR should be designed to predict and recognize these concurrent activities and be capable of handling uncertainty to achieve high accuracy and improve healthcare functionality, quality, and safety.

5.6 Teaching assignments

- Develop a smartphone-based HAR using boosting classifiers
- How to use HAR for healthcare using smartphone
- Analyze HAR in smart homes
- Analyze HAR using wearable sensors
- Compare and analysis machine learning algorithms for HAR
- Analyze the application of HAR for smart cities
- Use WEKA to compare different classifiers

References

Alpaydin, E. (2014). *Introduction to machine learning*. MIT Press.

Anguita, D., Ghio, A., Oneto, L., Parra, X., & Reyes-Ortiz, J. L. (2013). A public domain dataset for human activity recognition using smartphones. *Presented at the ESANN*.

Arif, M., Bilal, M., Kattan, A., & Ahamed, S. I. (2014). Better physical activity classification using smartphone acceleration sensor. *Journal of Medical Systems*, *38*(9), 95. Available from https://doi.org/10.1007/s10916-014-0095-0.

Avci, A., Bosch, S., Marin-Perianu, M., Marin-Perianu, R., & Havinga, P. (2010). Activity recognition using inertial sensing for healthcare, wellbeing and sports applications: A survey. In *Presented at the architecture of computing systems (ARCS), 2010 23rd international conference on, VDE*, pp. 1−10.

Banos, O., Garcia, R., Holgado-Terriza, J. A., Damas, M., Pomares, H., Rojas, I., & Villalonga, C. (2014). *mHealthDroid: A novel framework for agile development of mobile health applications. Presented at the international workshop on ambient assisted living* (pp. 91−98). Springer.

Banos, O., Toth, M. A., Damas, M., Pomares, H., & Rojas, I. (2014). Dealing with the effects of sensor displacement in wearable activity recognition. *Sensors*, *14*(6), 9995−10023.

Bayat, A., Pomplun, M., & Tran, D. A. (2014). A study on human activity recognition using accelerometer data from smartphones. *Procedia Computer Science*, *34*, 450−457.

Boonkrong, S., Unger, H., & Meesad, P. (2014). *Recent advances in information and communication technology*. Springer.

Cao, J., Li, W., Ma, C., & Tao, Z. (2018). Optimizing multi-sensor deployment via ensemble pruning for wearable activity recognition. *Information Fusion*, *41*, 68−79.

Cao, L., Wang, Y., Zhang, B., Jin, Q., & Vasilakos, A. V. (2018). GCHAR: An efficient Group-based Context—Aware human activity recognition on smartphone. *Journal of Parallel and Distributed Computing*, *118*, 67−80.

Chen, Y., & Shen, C. (2017). Performance analysis of smartphone-sensor behavior for human activity recognition. *IEEE Access*, *5*, 3095−3110.

Cichosz, P. (2014). *Data mining algorithms: Explained using R*. John Wiley & Sons.

Clarkson, B.P. (2002). *Life patterns: Structure from wearable sensors*. PhD Thesis, Massachusetts Institute of Technology, School of Architecture and Planning, Program in Media Arts and Sciences.

Espinilla, M., Medina, J., Calzada, A., Liu, J., Martínez, L., & Nugent, C. (2017). Optimizing the configuration of an heterogeneous architecture of sensors for activity recognition, using the extended belief rule-based inference methodology. *Microprocessors and Microsystems*, *52*, 381−390.

González, S., Sedano, J., Villar, J. R., Corchado, E., Herrero, Á., & Baruque, B. (2015). Features and models for human activity recognition. *Neurocomputing*, *167*, 52−60.

Gope, P., & Hwang, T. (2016). BSN-Care: A secure IoT-based modern healthcare system using body sensor network. *IEEE Sensors Journal*, *16*(5), 1368−1376.

Guiry, J. J., van de Ven, P., Nelson, J., Warmerdam, L., & Riper, H. (2014). Activity recognition with smartphone support. *Medical Engineering & Physics*, *36*(6), 670−675.

Hall, M., Witten, I., & Frank, E. (2011). *Data mining: Practical machine learning tools and techniques.* Burlington: Kaufmann.

Han, J., Pei, J., & Kamber, M. (2011). *Data mining: Concepts and techniques.* Elsevier.

Hassan, M. M., Uddin, M. Z., Mohamed, A., & Almogren, A. (2018). A robust human activity recognition system using smartphone sensors and deep learning. *Future Generation Computer Systems*, *81*, 307−313.

He, H., Tan, Y., & Zhang, W. (2018). A wavelet tensor fuzzy clustering scheme for multi-sensor human activity recognition. *Engineering Applications of Artificial Intelligence*, *70*, 109−122.

Holmes, G., Pfahringer, B., Kirkby, R., Frank, E., & Hall, M. (2002). Multiclass alternating decision trees. In *Presented at the European conference on machine learning*, Springer, pp. 161−172.

Hossain, H. S., Khan, M. A. A. H., & Roy, N. (2017). Active learning enabled activity recognition. *Pervasive and Mobile Computing*, *38*, 312−330.

Ignatov, A. (2018). Real-time human activity recognition from accelerometer data using convolutional neural networks. *Applied Soft Computing*, *62*, 915−922.

Kalmegh, S. (2015). Analysis of WEKA data mining algorithm REPTree, Simple CART and RandomTree for classification of Indian news. *International Journal of Innovative Science, Engineering and Technology*, *2* (2), 438−446.

Kay, M., Santos, J., & Takane, M. (2011). mHealth: New horizons for health through mobile technologies. *World Health Organization*, *64*(7), 66−71.

Köping, L., Shirahama, K., & Grzegorzek, M. (2018). A general framework for sensor-based human activity recognition. *Computers in Biology and Medicine*, *95*, 248−260.

Liu, L., Peng, Y., Liu, M., & Huang, Z. (2015). Sensor-based human activity recognition system with a multilayered model using time series shapelets. *Knowledge-Based Systems*, *90*, 138−152.

Liu, Y., Nie, L., Liu, L., & Rosenblum, D. S. (2016). From action to activity: Sensor-based activity recognition. *Neurocomputing*, *181*, 108−115.

Lytras, M., & Visvizi, A. (2018). Who uses smart city services and what to make of it: Toward interdisciplinary smart cities research. *Sustainability*, *10*(6), 1998.

Lytras, M. D., Visvizi, A., Daniela, L., Sarirete, A., & Ordonez De Pablos, P. (2018). Social Networks Research for Sustainable Smart Education. *Sustainability*, *10*(9), 2974. Available from https://doi.org/10.3390/su10092974.

Mahdavinejad, M. S., Rezvan, M., Barekatain, M., Adibi, P., Barnaghi, P., & Sheth, A. P. (2017). Machine learning for Internet of Things data analysis: A survey. *Digital Communications and Networks*, *4*, 161−175.

Majumder, S., Aghayi, E., Noferesti, M., Memarzadeh-Tehran, H., Mondal, T., Pang, Z., & Deen, M. J. (2017). Smart homes for elderly healthcare—Recent advances and research challenges. *Sensors*, *17*(11), 2496.

Martín, H., Bernardos, A. M., Iglesias, J., & Casar, J. R. (2013). Activity logging using lightweight classification techniques in mobile devices. *Personal and Ubiquitous Computing*, *17*(4), 675−695.

Mshali, H., Lemlouma, T., Moloney, M., & Magoni, D. (2018). A survey on health monitoring systems for health smart homes. *International Journal of Industrial Ergonomics*, *66*, 26−56.

Neves, P., Stachyra, M., & Rodrigues, J. (2008). Application of wireless sensor networks to healthcare promotion, Journal of Communications Software And Systems, 4(3), 181−190.

Nham, B., Siangliulue, K., & Yeung, S. (2008). *Predicting mode of transport from iphone accelerometer data.* Standford University Class Project.

Ortiz, J. L. R. (2015). *Smartphone-based human activity recognition.* Springer.

Reiss, A., Hendeby, G., & Stricker, D. (2015). A novel confidence-based multiclass boosting algorithm for mobile physical activity monitoring. *Personal and Ubiquitous Computing*, *19*(1), 105−121. Available from https://doi.org/10.1007/s00779-014-0816-x.

Reyes-Ortiz, J.-L., Oneto, L., Sama, A., Parra, X., & Anguita, D. (2016). Transition-aware human activity recognition using smartphones. *Neurocomputing*, *171*, 754−767.

Ronao, C. A., & Cho, S.-B. (2016). Human activity recognition with smartphone sensors using deep learning neural networks. *Expert Systems with Applications, 59*, 235−244.

Rumelhart, D. E., Hinton, G. E., & Williams, R. J. (1986). Learning representations by back-propagating errors. *Nature, 323*(6088), 533.

Safonov, I., Gartseev, I., Pikhletsky, M., Tishutin, O., & Bailey, M. (2015). An approach for model assissment for activity recognition. *Pattern Recognition and Image Analysis, 25*(2), 263−269.

Shoaib, M., Bosch, S., Incel, O. D., Scholten, H., & Havinga, P. J. (2015). A survey of online activity recognition using mobile phones. *Sensors, 15*(1), 2059−2085.

Spruit, M., & Lytras, M. (2018). Applied data science in patient-centric healthcare: Adaptive Analytic Systems for Empowering Physicians and Patients. Telematics and Informatics, 35(4), 643−653.

Subasi, A., Radhwan, M., Kurdi, R., & Khateeb, K. (2018). IoT based mobile healthcare system for human activity recognition. In *Presented at the learning and technology conference (L&T), 2018 15th, IEEE*, pp. 29−34.

Tapia, E. M., Intille, S. S., & Larson, K. (2004). *Activity recognition in the home using simple and ubiquitous sensors, Presented at the pervasive* (Vol. 4, pp. 158−175). Springer.

Uddin, M. T., Billah, M. M., & Hossain, M. F. (2016). Random forests based recognition of human activities and postural transitions on smartphone. *Presented at the informatics, electronics and vision (ICIEV), 2016 5th international conference on, IEEE*, pp. 250−255.

Villalonga, C., Pomares, H., Rojas, I., & Banos, O. (2017). MIMU-Wear: Ontology-based sensor selection for real-world wearable activity recognition. *Neurocomputing, 250*, 76−100.

Visvizi, A., Jussila, J., Lytras, M. D., & Ijäs, M. (2019). Tweeting and mining OECD-related microcontent in the post-truth era: a cloudbased app. *Computers in Human Behavior*. Available from https://doi.org/10.1016/j.chb.2019.03.022.

Wang, A., Chen, G., Yang, J., Zhao, S., & Chang, C.-Y. (2016). A comparative study on human activity recognition using inertial sensors in a smartphone. *IEEE Sensors Journal, 16*(11), 4566−4578.

Wang, J., Chen, Y., Hao, S., Peng, X., & Hu, L. (2017). Deep learning for sensor-based activity recognition: A survey. *ArXiv Preprint ArXiv, 1707*, 03502.

Wen, J., & Wang, Z. (2016). Sensor-based adaptive activity recognition with dynamically available sensors. *Neurocomputing, 218*, 307−317.

Witten, I. H., Frank, E., Hall, M. A., & Pal, C. J. (2016). *Data mining: Practical machine learning tools and techniques*. Morgan Kaufmann.

Woznowski, P., Kaleshi, D., Oikonomou, G., & Craddock, I. (2016). Classification and suitability of sensing technologies for activity recognition. *Computer Communications, 89*, 34−50.

Wu, X., Kumar, V., Quinlan, J. R., Ghosh, J., Yang, Q., Motoda, H., & Philip, S. Y. (2008). Top 10 algorithms in data mining. *Knowledge and Information Systems, 14*(1), 1−37.

Xu, Y., Shen, Z., Zhang, X., Gao, Y., Deng, S., Wang, Y., & Chang, C. (2017). Learning multi-level features for sensor-based human action recognition. *Pervasive and Mobile Computing, 40*, 324−338.

Yang, R., & Wang, B. (2016). PACP: A position-independent activity recognition method using smartphone sensors. *Information, 7*(4), 72.

Zhong, M., Wen, J., Hu, P., & Indulska, J. (2017). Advancing Android activity recognition service with Markov smoother: Practical solutions. *Pervasive and Mobile Computing, 38*, 60−76.

CHAPTER 6

Application of machine learning and image processing for detection of breast cancer

Muhammad Kashif[1], Kaleem Razzaq Malik[1], Sohail Jabbar[2] and Junaid Chaudhry[3]

[1]Department of Computer Science, Air University Multan Campus, Multan, Pakistan, [2]Department of Computer Science, National Textile University, Faisalabad, Pakistan, [3]College of Security and Intelligence, Embry-Riddle Aeronautical University, Prescott, AZ, United States

6.1 Introduction

The implementation of an advanced computer application in healthcare requires integrated approaches. These approaches have social, economic, political, and cultural impacts. These approaches also have the challenges of communication and information technologies. Data analysis and smart data with computation are the technologies which make great attention for the domain of healthcare (Spruit & Lytras, 2018).

In the modern era, many developed countries are going to the smart cities concept. In a smart city, everything is controlled by a computer. Every field of the world is emerging toward the computer. Human wants to control everything by computer. Decision-making is a big challenge in a smart environment. This modern era is also known as data world. Because on daily basis data are generated by the users. These data are very useful to make the environment smart. Decisions based on data. Artificial intelligence (AI) allows the computer to make decisions. To make decisions, data should be available to the computer (Lytras & Visvizi, 2018; Razzaq Malik et al., 2017).

Healthcare is a big challenge in the world. Use of computer, intelligent systems, and intelligent device play an important role in healthcare. Early stage detection of disease can reduce the risk of human lives. The risk of human lives can be reduced new innovations.

Cancer is the deadliest disease in the world. The critical condition is that every year thousands of people die from cancer. Because cancer cannot be diagnosed in its early stage by a physician. Sometimes cancer disease symptoms cannot be seen from outside of the body. At the second or third stage, cancer cannot be cured. Some latest techniques can cure

Innovation in Health Informatics.
DOI: https://doi.org/10.1016/B978-0-12-819043-2.00006-X

the disease but those techniques also have some side effects. So the early stage detection of cancer can reduce the risk of patient life.

Breast cancer is the second leading disease which causes woman deaths. According to report, 2.5 million cases of cancer identified in 2017 and 40,000 women expected to die in the United States (DeSantis, Ma, Goding Sauer, Newman, & Jemal, 2017).

A report by IARC shows 8.2 million deaths were caused by cancer in 2012. Before 2030 is expected that 27 million new cancer cases (Patel, Uvaid, & Suthar, 2012).

A report by the International Agency of Cancer says that 79,000 women are facing the disease of breast cancer (Sreeja, Rathika, & Devaraj, 2012).

This ratio is increasing in developed countries. This is a critical problem in healthcare. The cells that uncontrolled and grow rapidly given the name of cancer. Breast cancer occurs due to growth of cells in the breast. Group of extra tissues is known as tumor. The second name of a tumor is cancer.

In this paper, we developed a model to predict breast cancer from mammogram images. We used a hybrid approach having mammogram processing and machine learning (ML) algorithms. The mammogram processing technique is used to extract features from mammogram images. The images having abnormalities Malignant or Benign are classified by ML. These images are taken from a mammogram image analysis society (MIAS) cancer dataset (Suckling et al., 2015). In the first phase, images preprocessed and then passed through the segmentation phase. In the second phase, features were extracted. In the third phase, classification is done on the basis of features. In the last phase, the comparison is done for different classification techniques. The classification technique gave the best results that can be used for prediction of cancer for new mammograms.

6.1.1 Mammograms

To check, the symptoms of breast cancer disease mammograms can be used. X-ray picture of woman breast is known as a mammogram. When a woman has no symptoms of breast cancer, then screening mammography is done. This process can reduce the deaths of women from breast cancer at the age of 40–70. This process also has some disadvantages. Sometimes breast has no symptoms but mammogram shows abnormality. This caused anxiety because more test has been done. Mammograms are taken from those younger women which has the symptoms of breast cancer.

X-ray images of the breast which have abnormalities are known as a mammogram. The x-ray beam is applied to the breast which compressed between two plates to take the image. Breast cancer can be diagnosed using these images. The technique which is performed before symptoms occur in woman breast is known as screening mammography. The technique which is performed after symptoms occur in woman breast is known as diagnosing mammography. Mammography is currently the most effective technique to detect early breast cancer (Sundaram, Sasikala, & Rani, 2014).

6.1.2 Preprocessing

The objective of preprocessing is to enhance the mammogram image. Because enhancement gives the more accurate results. In this phase, we remove noise from a mammogram. Noise is removed from mammogram to sharp the image. This sharpness gives the sharp edges and boundaries. Enhancement cannot increase or decrease the mammogram image. It only increases the features sharpness.

Mammogram preprocessing is a technique which is used to improve the quality of the mammogram image. The objective of mammogram preprocessing is to clean noise and enhancement of quality of mammogram to proceed for further processing. Image filters are used to remove irrelevant artifacts and enhance the quality of the image (John & Nallathambi, 2017).

6.1.3 Segmentation

Segmentation is the process of finding the region of interest (ROI). In this phase that region is selected which has a tumor. This phase is necessary to get our results. Because if the ROI is not extracted then the whole image is processed to extract features. So the ROI helps to get the required features. In this process, the tumor area is extracted from the mammogram image. After this feature extraction process is applied to the ROI image.

Two methods are used for image segmentation. In the first method, the author differentiates the region of the image by locating edges. This method is known as edge-based technique for image segmentation. In the second method, the author slices up the image into small blocks by combining separate pixels into blocks. This method is known as region-based segmentation (Bandyopadhyay, 2010).

6.1.4 Machine learning

ML is a subfield of AI. It has two major types. Algorithms are trained using labeled data. Unsupervised algorithms are trained using unlabeled data. In labeled data, classification labels are known. In my case, label "0" indicates normal case and label "1" indicates Cancerous case. ML is subcategories in four types.

- Supervised ML
- Unsupervised learning

- Semisupervised learning
- Reinforcement and deep learning

6.1.4.1 Supervised machine learning

In supervised ML, two variables are used in practice. One variable is (T) which is the input variable. Second variable is (P) which is the output variable. A mapping function is learned to the algorithm from input to output.

$$P = f(T)$$

The objective of this mapping function is to predict output value for the variable (P) from new input data for the variable (T). It is known as supervised learning. The algorithm learns from training dataset and makes predictions for new data. At the acceptable performance, learning is stopped.

Supervised learning is subclassified into two categories.

- Classification
- Regression

6.1.4.1.1 Classification

Classification is used when the output variable is like "yes" or "no." When output variable has "disease" or "Normal," then classification is applied.

6.1.4.1.2 Regression

Regression is used when the output variable has real or continuous values like "salary" or "weight."

6.1.4.2 Unsupervised learning

Unsupervised learning is applied where only (T) variable is given. It means only input data are given. The output variable is unknown. The objective of unsupervised learning is to understand the structure of data or distribution of data. It is known as unsupervised learning because there is no output variable. It means we don't know the actual answer of the input data. In unsupervised learning, the algorithm finds the pattern on its own devises in given data distribution. Unsupervised learning is subcategorized into association and clustering.

- Clustering
- Association

6.1.4.2.1 Clustering

Clustering is the process of grouping the same type of data in a way that data are similar within a cluster. Which means data are more similar within a group or cluster and differences between other groups or cluster of data. For example, a college will group students according to their IQ in sections like super section, average section, and weak section. In another example, books are grouped in a shelf according to their field.

6.1.4.2.2 Association

Association means finding interesting patterns in data. Mostly used in unsupervised learning to find a frequent pattern in data. For example, we can find a frequent pattern in superstore data, like [butter, egg] = > [bread] rule tells that, a customer who buys butter and egg from the superstore is likely to buy bread.

6.1.4.3 Semisupervised learning

It is similar to supervised learning but the difference is that it also uses unlabeled data for training. Mostly, it has less labeled data and more unlabeled data. Which mean it lies between supervised and unsupervised.

6.1.4.4 Reinforcement and deep learning

Both techniques are autonomous and self-learning. Millions of data are given to these algorithms for learning. But the difference between both is that reinforcement learning learns by trial and error mechanism and deep learning learns finding patterns from millions of data (Haider, Malik, Khalid, Nawaz, & Jabbar, 2017). For example, in order to recognize dinosaur photos, millions of dinosaur photos are given to algorithm in order to self-learn.

6.2 Literature review

Authors used three ML techniques to predict breast cancer. They used ICBC dataset to extract results from experiments at National Cancer Institute of Tehran. They applied three machine algorithms (ANN, D-Tree, and SVM) on ICBC dataset. They observed that SVM has the highest accuracy of 95%, ANN 94%, and Decision Tree has a low accuracy of 93% (Ahmad, Eshlaghy, Poorebrahimi, Ebrahimi, & Razavi, 2013).

In this paper, authors develop a system which combines CFRSFS, *K*-Mean clustering, and LS-SVM. The author proposed a feature selection algorithm called CFRSFS. CFRSFS select only eight features that are given to only *K*-Mean clustering to further feature processing. Their method has 99.54% accuracy (Suji & Rajagopalan, 2015).

In this paper, the authors applied different ML algorithms according to the dataset. They used the WDBC dataset to get experimental results. They calculated the accuracy of

Table 6.1: Previous work.

No.	Authors	Technique or algorithm	Dataset	Accuracy (%)
1	Ahmad et al. (2013)	Decision TreeANNSVM	ICBC	93
				94
				95
2	Suji and Rajagopalan (2015)	CFRSFS, *K*-Mean	Wisconsin Diagnostic Breast Cancer (WDBC)	99.54
3	Rana et al. (2015)	KNN	WDBC	72
		SVM		68
		Logic Reg.		68
		Naïve Byes		67

algorithms as SVM-linear 68%, Logic regression 68%, KNN 72%, and Naïve Byes 67% (Rana, Chandorkar, Dsouza, & Kazi, 2015).

In this paper, the authors used Neural Networks to detect breast cancer. They used 1808 cases of cancer. They used 387 cases for testing. They calculated accuracy 95.80% for Neural Network algorithm (Singh, Gupta, & Sharma, 2010).

Previous related work is presented in Table 6.1.

6.3 Proposed work

See Fig. 6.1.

6.3.1 Dataset

Sample dataset is taken from MIAS (Suckling et al., 2015). It is a United Kingdom research group. This research group is interested in understanding mammogram images. These images are taken from United Kingdom National Breast Screening center. This dataset contains 322 instances. The original image from this dataset is shown in Fig. 6.2. It is displayed in Mat lab tool. This image is sent to preprocess block or module.

6.3.2 Noise removal (preprocessing)

The objective of preprocessing is to enhance the mammogram image. Because enhancement gives the more accurate results. In this phase, we remove noise from a mammogram. Noise is removed from mammogram to sharp the image. This sharpness gives the sharp edges and boundaries. Enhancement cannot increase or decrease the mammogram image. It only increases the features sharpness. Mammogram preprocessing is a technique which is used to improve the quality of the mammogram image. The objective of mammogram preprocessing is to clean noise and enhancement of quality of mammogram to proceed for

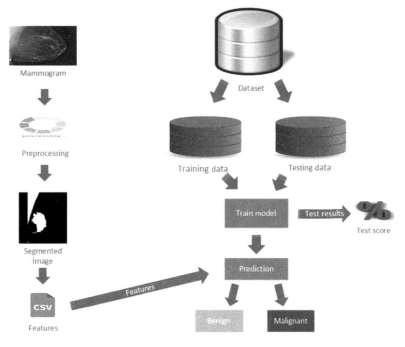

Figure 6.1
Proposed architecture.

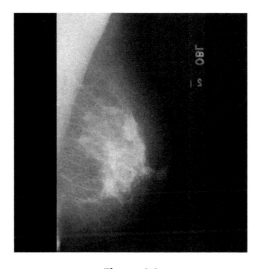

Figure 6.2
Original mammogram from MIAS database (Suckling et al., 2015).

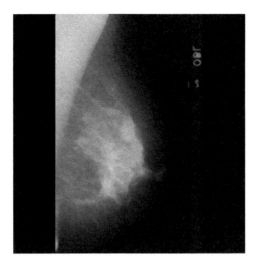

Figure 6.3
Preprocessed mammogram.

further processing. Image filters are used to remove irrelevant artifacts and enhance the quality of the image. In this step, the image is load from database and preprocessed to remove the noise from the image. This step increases the quality of the image. This step is necessary because the original mammogram image has noise and other artifacts. I will apply the 2D median filter to remove noise from the image. The average and adaptive filter can also be applied to remove noise. But the median filter is enough to remove noise in my case. In Fig. 6.3, preprocessed image is shown. This image is noise free. To remove, noise median filter is applied. This module is also executed in Mat lab tool.

6.3.3 Segmentation process

Segmentation is the process to select the ROI. In this process that area is selected that has a tumor after noise removal. This step is necessary because it is very difficult to extract features from the whole image. We are interested to extract a feature from that region which has a tumor or cancer. Segmentation can be done from using Grab cut algorithm, thresh-holding, and watershed algorithm. So I will apply thresh-holding for segmentation. The segmented image will be used for feature extraction. Segmentation is the process of finding the ROI. In this phase that region is selected which has a tumor. This phase is necessary to get our results. Because if the ROI is not extracted then the whole image is processed to extract features. So the ROI helps to get the required features. In this process, the tumor area is extracted from the mammogram image. After this feature extraction process is applied to the ROI image. Two methods are used for image segmentation. In the

Figure 6.4
Noise-free image converted in binary.

first method, the author differentiates the region of the image by locating edges. This method is known as edge-based technique for image segmentation. In the second method, the author slices up the image into small blocks by combining separate pixels into blocks. This method is known as region-based segmentation. Fig. 6.4 binary image is given. Pixels that are contained white color having "1" and black pixels having "0" value.

After combining, the binary and original image got a masked image that shows tumor as shown in Fig. 6.5.

In Fig. 6.6, segmented image is shown that is required for feature extraction.

6.3.4 Feature extraction

In this step, I will use the segmented image to extract features. Features will describe the condition of cancer. A Features that will be extracted from the segmented image are:

1. the radius of the highlighted region;
2. the entropy of highlighted region;
3. the smoothness of highlighted region;
4. mean texture of highlighted region; and
5. texture-based features.

Figure 6.5
Tumor highlighted picture.

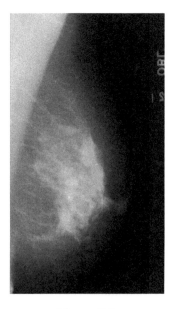

Figure 6.6
Segmented image.

6.3.5 Training model and testing

In this step, features label data will be divided into two parts. One part is training and the second part is testing. Training data train the model. We measure the precision and recall by providing unlabeled testing data.

6.3.6 Classification

In this step, prediction or test data will be given to model and the classified label will be extracted. Classification model that is applied is Support Vector Machine (SVM), Ada Boost, Decision Tree, Logistic regression, K Nearest Neighbor, and Random Forest Classifiers. Each algorithm gives us the result in binary classification. Using these binary classification results performance measures will be calculated. This measure will help us to compare the results. On the basis of comparisons of the algorithm, we can suggest the best technique that can be used to solve the given healthcare problem.

6.3.7 Performance evaluation metrics

To evaluate the performance of algorithms, the confusion matrix is used and some formulas of precision, recall, *f*-score, sensitivity, specificity, and accuracy were applied.

PT = true positive

PF = false positive

NT = true negative

NF = false negative

Confusion matrix divides the predicative instance into four outcomes as shown above. PT shows that the instances predicted no cancer are correct. It means these instances have no cancer. Algorithm predicted results are correct. PF means the predicted result is incorrect. Actual instances have no cancer but algorithm says cancer exist. This means algorithm predicted wrong results. NT is similar to PT in a way, there was cancer in instances, it predicts there is cancer in instances. Algorithm results are correct. Finally, NF shows the situation in which actual instances have cancer but the algorithm predicts that instances do not have cancer. The algorithm is again shown wrong results like in case of PF.

In Table 6.2, Confusion matrix is given that describes the relationship between predicted class and actual class. The predicted class is compared with actual class with four performance indices PT, NT, PF, and NF.

PT class shows correctly classified Benign tuples. Pf class shows False Classified Malignant tuples that are marked Benign. NT class shows Correctly classified Malignant tuples.

Table 6.2: Confusion matrix.

CM	Positive	Negative
Positive	PT	PF
Negative	NF	NT

PT, true positive; *PF*, false positive; *NT*, true negative; *NF*, false negative.

Table 6.3: Performance measurements.

Performance measure	Definition
PT	Correctly classified Benign tuples.
PF	False classified Malignant tuples that are marked Benign.
NT	Correctly classified Malignant tuples.
NF	False classified Benign tuples that are marked Malignant.

PT, true positive; *PF*, false positive; *NT*, true negative; *NF*, false negative.

NF class shows False Classified Benign tuples that are marked Malignant. Discussed classes are the performance measures. Definition of these measures are given in Table 6.3.

Sensitivity is the ratio between PT and all marked tumors (PT + NF).

$$\text{Sensitivity} = \frac{PT}{PT + NF} \tag{6.1}$$

Specificity is the relation between NT and marked a tumor (PF + NT).

$$\text{Specificity} = \frac{NT}{PF + NT} \tag{6.2}$$

Accuracy formula is given in Eq. (6.3).

$$\text{Accuracy} = \frac{PT + NT}{PT + PF + NF + NT} \tag{6.3}$$

6.3.8 f-Score measure

f-Score is an evaluation metrics for ML algorithm.

$$\text{Precision} = \frac{PT}{PT + PF} \tag{6.4}$$

$$\text{Recall} = \frac{PT}{PT + NF} \tag{6.5}$$

From Eqs. (6.4) and (6.5), precision and accuracy calculated and used in Eq. (6.6) to calculate *F*-measures:

$$F\text{-measure} = \frac{2(\text{precision·recall})}{\text{precision} + \text{recall}} \tag{6.6}$$

6.4 Results

In Table 6.4, output labels and their test score is given. "0" label indicates normal case and label "1" cancerous case. These predicated labels are compared with original labels from the dataset. Different measures are calculated that given in Tables 6.5 and 6.6.

Table 6.4: Predict labels by applied algorithms.

Algorithm	Output (predicted label)	Test score (%)
SVM	[0. 0. 0. 0. 0. 0. 0. 0. 0. 0. 0. 0. 0. 0. 0. 0. 0. 0. 0. 0. 0. 0. 0. 0. 0. 0. 0. 0. 0. 0. 0. 0. 0. 0. 0. 0. 0. 0. 0. 0. 0. 0.]	76
Ada Boost	[0. 0. 0. 1. 1. 0. 0. 0. 0. 0. 1. 0. 1. 0. 1. 0. 0. 0. 0. 0. 1. 0. 1. 0. 1. 0. 1. 1. 0. 0. 1. 1. 0. 0. 0. 1. 1. 1. 0. 1. 0. 0.]	66
Decision Tree	[1. 1. 0. 1. 0. 1. 0. 0. 0. 0. 0. 1. 0. 0. 1. 0. 1. 1. 0. 1. 0. 0. 0. 0. 0. 0. 1. 1. 0. 1. 1. 1. 1. 0. 0. 1. 1. 1. 0. 1. 0. 0.]	50
Logistic Regression	[0. 0. 0. 0. 0. 0. 0. 0. 0. 0. 0. 0. 0. 0. 1. 0. 0. 0. 0. 0. 0. 0. 0. 0. 0. 0. 0. 0. 0. 0. 0. 0. 0. 0. 0. 0. 0. 0. 0. 0. 0. 1.]	76
Random Forest	[0. 1. 0. 1. 0. 0. 0. 0. 0. 0. 1. 0. 1. 0. 1. 0. 0. 0. 0. 0. 1. 0. 1. 1. 0. 0. 1. 0. 0. 0. 1. 0. 1. 0. 0. 0. 0. 1. 0. 1. 0. 0.]	60
Gradient Boost	[1. 1. 0. 1. 0. 0. 0. 0. 0. 0. 1. 0. 1. 0. 1. 0. 0. 0. 0. 1. 0. 0. 1. 0. 0. 1. 1. 1. 0. 0. 0. 1. 1. 0. 0. 1. 1. 1. 0. 1. 0. 0.]	60
KNN	[0. 0. 0. 1. 0. 0. 0. 1. 0. 0. 0. 0. 1. 0. 0. 0. 0. 0. 0. 0. 0. 0. 1. 1. 0. 0. 1. 1. 0. 0. 0. 0. 0. 0. 1. 1. 0. 0. 0. 1. 0. 0. 0.]	63

Table 6.5: Predicted binary classification results of algorithms.

Model	Total instances	PT	NT	PF	NF
SVM	42	38	0	4	0
Ada Boost	42	23	1	3	15
Decision Tree	42	21	2	2	17
Logistic Regression	42	36	0	4	2
Random Forest	42	26	0	4	12
Gradient Boost	42	21	1	3	17
KNN	42	30	2	2	8

PT, true positive; *PF*, false positive; *NT*, true negative; *NF*, false negative.

Table 6.6: Performance of algorithms calculated from the above formulas.

Model	Test score	*f*-Score	Sensitivity	Specificity	Precision	Recall	Accuracy (%)
SVM	0.77	0.95	1	0	0.90	1	90
Ada Boost	0.67	0.71	0.61	0.25	0.88	0.60	57
Decision Tree	0.53	0.68	0.55	0.5	0.91	0.55	54
Logistic Regression	0.70	0.92	0.94	0	0.90	0.95	85
Random Forest	0.63	0.76	0.69	0	0.87	0.68	61
Gradient Boost	0.60	0.67	0.55	0.25	0.88	0.55	52
KNN	0.63	0.85	0.78	0.5	0.94	0.78	76

6.5 Discussions

Dataset is divided into training and testing data. Training data have 250 instances and testing data have 30 instances. After developing the model, 42 instances are predicted using different models. Their binary classification results are given in Table 6.5.

Using the above formulas, we have calculated the *f*-score, precision, sensitivity, specificity, recall, and accuracy of different algorithms applied to breast cancer dataset.

The graph given in Fig. 6.7 shows the outcomes of different algorithms. Each algorithm predicts different results as shown in the graph. Total tested instances were 42. SVM classifier predicted 38 instances as PT and 4 instances as PF. Ada Boost classifier predicted 23 instances as PT, 1 instance as NT, 3 instances as PF, and 15 instances as NF. Decision Tree classifier predicted 21 instances as PT, 2 instances as NT, 2 instances as PF, and 17 instances as NF. Logistic Regression classifier predicted 36 instances as PT, 4 instances as PF, and 2 instances as NF. Random Forest classifier predicted 26 instances as PT, 4 instances as PF, and 12 instances as NF. Gradient Boost classifier predicted 21 instances as PT, 1 instance as NT, 3 instances as PF, and 17 instances as NF. K Nearest Neighbor classifier predicted 30 instances as PT, 2 instances as NT, 2 instances as PF, and 8 instances as NF. These outcomes of the different classifier are very important for the calculation of test score, *f*-score, sensitivity, specificity, precision, recall, and accuracy. It means the whole results are dependent on the given outcomes of different algorithms or classifier.

Percentage accuracy of SVM is best with 90% accuracy as shown in Table 6.6. Similar way, Gradient Boost is the worst case with the lowest accuracy, precision, and *f*-score. Logistic regression comes in an average case where accuracy is 85% with average *f*-score, test score, and precision. My result concludes that the precision, recall, *f*-score, and

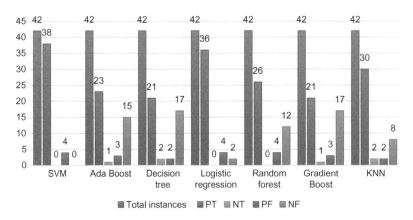

Figure 6.7
Graph for confusion matrix of different algorithms.

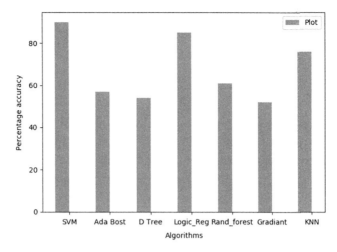

Figure 6.8
Accuracy graph of applied algorithms.

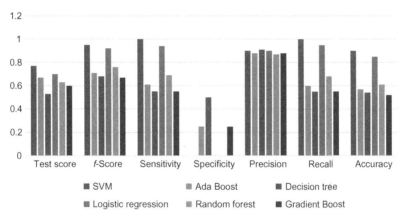

Figure 6.9
Graph of different measurements calculated.

precision increases out prediction will show the best results. But if we increase the training dataset, the accuracy of the model increases. On the basis of work, we suggest the SVM ML technique can be used to identify the critical disease because our work shows the highest accuracy that is obtained.

In Fig. 6.8, a graph is a plot. This plot is obtained from the calculated values of different measure given in Table 6.6. These values are calculated from different formulas that are given above. In the above graph, test score, *f*-score, sensitivity, specificity, precision, recall, and accuracy are given. These values are calculated using binary classification

Table 6.7: Classification symbols.

Cancer type	Binary symbol
Benign	0
Malignant	1

results. These results vary according to binary classification. This graph shows that the algorithm having high precision and recall show high accuracy. The technique having low precision and recall gives less accuracy (Fig. 6.9). In Table 6.7 Classification symbols are discussed. Benign is the type of image having no cancer. Malignant is the type of image having cancer.

SVM provides good results when its sigma value is small and "c" parameter is large. Similarly, logistic regression utilizes "lambda" to give better performance. Its performance depends on lambda. On the certain value of lambda, the performance of logistic regression is best as in our case.

6.6 Conclusion

Information technology is playing an important role in healthcare. Communication technologies enable the user to stay in contact with the physician. Physicians are also staying in contact with his patient. Smart wearable sensing devices are easily available in the latest environment. The patient wears these sensing devices and performs daily life routine actions. If there is any disturbance in the patient body than sensing devices, sense it and send the message to the doctor about the patient condition. Through this process, the physician can give the proper treatment to a patient according to the condition of the patient. Patient life can be saved using these innovations in smart healthcare.

Key findings of our work are introducing a new innovation in healthcare. The innovation is the use of the computer in healthcare. According to our work, computer techniques can be used for the early detection of critical disease. Our work is based on the detection of critical disease breast cancer.

Our work is beneficial to save human lives. Our work is based on the comparison of different algorithms that can be used for the classification of disease type. Our work shows that SVM algorithm gives reasonable accuracy for the prediction of cancer. So this technique is useful in healthcare systems to predict the diseases. In the field of healthcare system, computer is used to get the results at the earliest possible way to give treatment to a patient on time.

ML algorithms are used to predict cancer from mammogram images. The experimental results are good to predict cancer. Mammogram images are not suitable for direct mining of symptoms leasing to the prediction for this we needed a multistage strategy. At first step, this study required to apply segmentation consequently leading to feature extraction. A total of 322 instances have been used for MIAS cancer images datasets. In the later phase, this work applied ML mixed approach for cancer prediction. A combination of techniques consisting of supervised and unsupervised was used for classification. Based on classifications different measures are identified for each algorithm. Study observations reflect that SVM classifier has the highest accuracy leading to better prediction of cancer from complex images. On the other hand, Gradient Boost classifier shows worst results with 52% accuracy. Similarly, Gradient Boost algorithm has the lowest precision, recall, test score, and *f*-score. While SVM has the highest precision, recall, *f*-score, and test score. These characteristics make the SVM a better option to use for such dataset of images.

In future, our approach can be used to predict lungs cancer, liver cancer, skin cancer, brain tumor, heart disease, and diabetics. ML algorithms are trained using a dataset. In this world of Big Data, large datasets of MRI, CT scans, and mammograms are available in the research labs. Researchers use these datasets to train the ML algorithms and make the predictions for new data. In the future, these techniques will be used for every disease. Healthcare field is growing very fast. In the future, deep learning algorithm to predict and classify the disease with high accuracy and precision. Deep learning algorithms are more advanced from the algorithms used in this project. Deep learning algorithm demands high computing power. As computing powers increase, it enables the researcher to use latest and more accurate techniques to use.

6.7 Research contribution highlights

- Understanding of mammograms
- Reading of mammograms
- Finding of ROI
- Understanding features of mammograms
- Feature extraction from mammograms
- Comparison of ML algorithms
- Prediction for new data
- Suggestion a technique for critical healthcare problem

6.8 Teaching assignments

- Preprocessing of mammograms
- Feature extraction from mammograms
- Implementation of ML algorithms
- Differentiate between supervised and unsupervised learning
- The solution for classification problem by ML
- Which ML technique is best and why?

References

Ahmad, L. G., Eshlaghy, A., Poorebrahimi, A., Ebrahimi, M., & Razavi, A. (2013). Using three machine learning techniques for predicting breast cancer recurrence. *Journal of Health and Medical Informatics*, *4*(124), 3.

Bandyopadhyay, S. K. (2010). Pre-processing of Mammogram Images. *International Journal of Engineering Science and Technology*, *2*(11), 6753—6758.

DeSantis, C. E., Ma, J., Goding Sauer, A., Newman, L. A., & Jemal, A. (2017). Breast cancer statistics, 2017, racial disparity in mortality by state. *CA: A Cancer Journal for Clinicians*, *67*(6), 439—448.

Haider, K. Z., Malik, K. R., Khalid, S., Nawaz, T., & Jabbar, S. (2017). Deepgender: Real-time gender classification using deep learning for smartphones. *Journal of Real-Time Image Processing*. Available from https://doi.org/10.1007/s11554-017-0714-3.

John, B., & Nallathambi, S. (2017). Study and analysis of filters. *Advances in Computational Sciences and Technology*, *10*(3), 331—341.

Lytras, M., & Visvizi, A. (2018). Who uses smart city services and what to make of it: Toward interdisciplinary smart cities research. *Sustainability*, *10*(6), 1998.

Patel, V. K., Uvaid, S., & Suthar, A. (2012). Mammogram of breast cancer detection based using image enhancement algorithm. *International Journal of Emerging Technology and Advanced Engineering*, *2*(2012), 143—147.

Rana, M., Chandorkar, P., Dsouza, A., & Kazi, N. (2015). Breast cancer diagnosis and recurrence prediction using machine learning techniques. *IJRET: International Journal of Research in Engineering and Technology eISSN*, 2319-1163.

Razzaq Malik, K., Habib, M., Khalid, S., Ullah, F., Umar, M., Sajjad, T., & Ahmad, A. (2017). Data compatibility to enhance sustainable capabilities for autonomous analytics in IoT. *Sustainability*, *9*(6), 877.

Singh, S., Gupta, P., & Sharma, M. K. (2010). Breast cancer detection and classification of histopathological images. *International Journal of Engineering Science and Technology*, *3*(5), 4228.

Spruit, M., & Lytras, M. (2018). *Applied data science in patient-centric healthcare*. Elsevier.

Sreeja, G. B., Rathika, P., & Devaraj, D. (2012). Detection of tumours in digital mammograms using wavelet based adaptive windowing method. *International Journal of Modern Education and Computer Science*, *4* (3), 57.

Suckling, J., Parker, J., Dance, D., Astley, S., Hutt, I., Boggis, C.,... Savage, J. (2015). Mammographic image analysis society (MIAS) database v1.21 [Dataset]. Available from https://www.repository.cam.ac.uk/handle/1810/250394.

Suji, R. J., & Rajagopalan, S. (2015). A novel hybrid system for diagnosing breast cancer using fuzzy rough set and LS-SVM. *Research Journal of Applied Sciences, Engineering and Technology*, *10*(1), 49—55.

Sundaram, K. M., Sasikala, D., & Rani, P. A. (2014). A study on preprocessing a mammogram image using adaptive median filter. *International Journal of Innovative Research in Science, Engineering and Technology*, *3*(3), 10333—10337.

CHAPTER 7

Toward information preservation in healthcare systems

Omar El Zarif and Ramzi A. Haraty

Department of Computer Science and Mathematics, Lebanese American University, Beirut, Lebanon

7.1 Introduction

Information security is an integral part in any database system, taking into consideration the sensitive data that these systems harness (Mazzucelli & Visvizi, 2017). These data may vary from financial records, to military information, medical history, and many other fields, where it is essential to protect or rectify any occurring damage to ensure the correctness of the database. Information security in multilevel databases is a top concern. Because data secrecy and database integrity should be maintained. Information warfare defines attacks on the database system as any action that can disrupt the ACID properties (Atomicity, Consistency, Isolation, and Durability). These attacks can take the form of spoofing, viruses, worms, and denial of service (Bernstein, Hadzilacos, & Goodman, 1987).

Medical systems, in particular, adopt the multilevel database scheme due to the enhancements in the secrecy and confidentiality properties. These systems require special care for storing data as they encompass sensitive information that is personal to the patients and should be undisclosed. The clearance for some records is strictly limited to authorized personnel only as the medical history of patients is private and should only be accessed by the appointed doctor. Other cases of some specific medication or treatment can indicate severe illness of patients. Those also are secured by some security level that only doctors or medical experts with a higher clearance level can access. In our days big-data paradigm challenges also the management and the preservation of medical data (Lytras et al, 2017).

Prevention, detection, and recovery are the three main pillars to respond to a certain attack. Prevention is the first step, where many preventive measures can be taken to elude the attack; these methods use techniques such as firewalls, authentication, authorization, access control, and antiviruses that can work to a certain extent but cannot be relied on solely (Khochare, Chalurkar, Kakade, & Meshramm, 2011).

Innovation in Health Informatics.
DOI: https://doi.org/10.1016/B978-0-12-819043-2.00007-1

The second detection step is complimentary to the first, since any prevention method should be accompanied by a detection scheme. The intrusion detection system (IDS) is usually the driving force in this phase; it is in charge of detecting an attack, usually by identifying the malicious transactions following historical analysis (Lunt, 1993). Living in an interconnected world, where the Internet is the main role player in any system, information sharing is becoming inevitable. This facilitates the fact that an attack can virtually come from any place and can penetrate the system no matter how much the last is fortified. The weak-point in any system is the trust given to a user. When some systems blindly allow to perform any transaction from any user, others use approaches such as in Hua, Xiaolin, Guineng, and Ziyue (2011) where users are classified.

Identifying the malicious transactions and recovering the affected ones is the last line of defense in the system. The system provides a log file that can span in size to describe all the committed transactions in the system; so it is evident that algorithms relying on extensive I/O operations on the log file itself can cause denial of service for the recovering system. The algorithm for detection and recovery should then be efficient in time to reduce the amount of affected transactions and should adhere low system requirements to prevent a complete shutdown, allowing only restricted access to the affected part of the system.

The elapsed time between the attack and the detection of the malicious transactions could vary depending on the situation. In any system, the transactions that should be assessed should follow some set of rules to ensure the correctness of the algorithm. In this work, we care about the transactions that read from other affected or malicious transactions mainly that is the transactional dependency technique. The data dependency technique detects affected transactions if they read a data item written previously by a malicious transaction (Haraty & Kaddoura, 2017).

In this work, we present a model that relies on auxiliary data structures for an efficient and quick damage assessment and recovery (DAR) in multilevel databases. We define two structures, the first being the dependency matrix, while the second being the write buckets, which are highly involved in the clustering part of our hybrid approach. The approach requires access to the log file only once, it passes through it to record the writes in the buckets, and from there tracks the dependency. The log is scanned from the first affected transaction location, which improves further the performance of our algorithm. Then it progressively records the primary keys of the written tuples in the corresponding buckets. Our approach is then based on transaction dependency, the use of the buckets is strictly to track the written transactions and ease in the recovery process.

This proposed algorithm will be compared with few single level database approaches based on matrices mainly, as our proposition is in its core a matrix approach but tailored toward multilevel databases. We compare it also to classical approaches based on log files and clustering, to properly classify our work in the state of art. The algorithm will prove to be a contender with single level approaches, since tackling multilevel databases is new, and to the best of our knowledge, no previous work has been done in regard to DAR. Irrespective, our comparison will formulate a new perspective of what we can achieve in the multilevel scenario.

We have introduced our problem and approach in this section. In Section 7.2, we research the literature in information warfare for classical approaches in DAR, and more modern ones. We explain in depth our approach and the nature of multilevel databases in Section 7.3, then we compare our work with the previous presented approaches in Section 7.4. We conclude our work with a sight for future enhancements and suggestions in Section 7.5.

7.2 The literature review

Information warfare advancement has inspired many algorithms to help in the DAR. The main purpose for all these algorithms is to track the set of affected transactions and their operations to achieve a successful recovery. To track the set of affected transactions, the algorithm must follow one of the two schemes: transaction dependency or data item dependency. Many approaches emerged to implement either of the two dependencies. Some are log based, and use the log file itself by iterating to track the dependencies. Others use auxiliary data structures to record on fly the transactions. Affected transactions are then detected using, for example, graph approaches, or matrices, or cluster.

7.2.1 Log files

Panda et al. introduced two approaches based on log files in Panda and Zhou (2003) and Panda and Haque (2002). Both approaches treat the log file as the only available resource to track the dependencies. The first uses transactions and the relative read-from/write relations to track the dependencies, while the second tracks the dependencies from each read-from/write relation on the data items. The first approach divides the log file into multiple segments where all dependent transactions are stored, while the second mainly stores the dependent data items, where a graph is then constructed to assess the affected transactions. Ammann, Jajodia, and Liu (2002) presented a classic log file technique for recovery and damage assessment, the authors rely on two log files to track the dependencies. The first log file is for the writes, while the other is for the reads. Then they describe a two pass algorithm, to track the dependencies. The first pass is the damage assessment part, it starts by scanning forward from the first affected transaction in the log to detect all the affected or malicious transactions. And the second pass is the recovery part, it scans from the end of the log file in a backward direction to undo all the detected transactions.

Another approach relying on the log file is proposed by Bai and Liu (2009). They introduced a lightweight damage tracking, quarantine, and recovery method. The approach is called "Trace," it advocates for a zero downtime in the system by enforcing two rules: to recover the affected data on the fly, which happens by ensuring that DAR are done simultaneously, and to avoid blocking read-only transactions. "Trace" smart behavior is attained by using smart tagging techniques to identify the malicious transactions. The system also supports two modes of operation: the standby mode and the cleansing mode. The first is the normal mode of operation, whereas the second performs the DAR, it is usually triggered by the IDS when an intrusion is detected.

7.2.2 Graph

Panda and Giordano (1999) implemented two data dependency approaches. The main difference between the two approaches is that one of them performs DAR in parallel while the second performs them separately. Separating the two approaches introduces a higher burden of denial of service period, but in its turn, it saves resources and computing power. Both approaches use a directed graph to map the data items and the transactions that operated on them in the database. This will be built when the IDS detects an anomaly in the system, it will then help showcasing the spreading damage.

Ammann et al. (2002) also describe a classic graph recovery technique that sorts the transactions based on a graph. The graph is built by assuming two sets of transactions: the good and the suspicious, and will represent the transactions in a way where the malicious and affected transactions can be easily identified. The algorithm has two modes, a cold-start and a warm-start. The main difference between them is the time taken to perform the recovery with respect to the normal execution of the database. The first allows the normal execution suffering from a longer time to recover, while the second disables the execution performing at full power for recovering.

Zuo and Panda (2004) presented two graph-based recovery and assessment models that are targeted toward distributed databases. The usual two schemes for any distributed system are centralization or decentralization, respectively, the two algorithms follow the two concepts. Thus the first model requires a coordinator, which is elected based on its location, its processing capabilities and backup requirements, while the second model is a peer-to-peer model where communication is done in an ad hoc manner. In both cases, each site is only responsible of its local log file, where in the case of any attack the site manager will be responsible of detecting the threat locally.

Liu and Yu (2011) presented a distributed recovery and assessment model that spans along the sites in the system. The sites each have a local DAR manager responsible to detect the affected transactions. But transaction dependency can be present within multiple sites, so a global coordinator is required. The last will help in identifying the appropriate local DAR to forward to some affected transactions from another site as these transactions might be a subject of further dependencies.

7.2.3 Clustering

Another type of approach in assessment and recovery is based on clustering the log file. The log file would contain the transactions and their operations, and these algorithms are interested in classifying the lasts in clusters, by grouping the transactions affecting certain data items, to ease the tracking of the dependencies. Sometimes the clustering might be by imposing constraints on the logs. Ragothaman and Panda (2003) suggested a simple cluster technique by requiring a limitation on the log file based on size, the number of committed transactions, or a time window on the cluster.

Haraty and Zeitunlian (2007) proposed an approach that is an exact data item dependency approach. It assumes that the history is rigorously serializable first, and the transaction IDs are sequentially incremented by one starting by T_1. They use two data structures *transaction subcluster list* and *data subcluster list*. The first list stores transaction IDs and the relative *data subcluster list* ID for each transaction, the *data subcluster list* would then contain the data items of each transaction listed in the *transaction subcluster list*, whether the data item was read or written. These data structures are built from the log file itself and will be used whenever the IDS detects an attack to identify the list of the affected transactions. The algorithm furthermore builds in the detection phase two data structures *Damaged DI* that is the list of data items affected by the malicious transactions, and *Damaged PB* that contains the execution blocks of those transactions. The blocks will be essential for the recovery, since they contain the interaction of each transaction with the data items.

Lala and Panda (2001) worked on clustering the transactions with an objective of eliminating the harmless ones. The model creates a matrix that represents the dependency, where there is an extra column "ClusterID" to identify the cluster to which the transactions belong. The clustering is dynamic, and its size could vary, the algorithm then faces a trade-off of accuracy to size. Condensing the size could misplace some transactions in the clusters, when a bigger cluster size means a more accurate identification of dependencies.

7.2.4 Matrices

Haraty and Zbib (2014) and Haraty, Zbib, and Masud (2016) adopted an approach based on matrices to assess the damage and recover. The system assumes an active IDS that reports the set of malicious transactions. The history is rigorously serializable and checkpoints are used to track the stable states of the database in the log file. The matrix is a two-dimensional array that represents the data items in the system and the set of the committed transactions. The data items in the system could undergo three types of interactions: a blind write, a modification according to other transactions (in the example of a previous read then write), or left untouched (like a simple read). The matrix will then be built following these rules:

- **0:** will mark a transaction left intact.
- **1:** will mark that the data item is blindly written.
- **A positive transaction ID**: T_i means that the data item was modified according to the last value of the data item written by T_i.
- **A negative transaction ID:** T_i means that the data item was modified based on different reads by the transaction.

To adhere to the negative ID condition, an additional data structure is required to track all interactions of transactions on the data items. The recovery could then be achieved by checking against the initial matrix in the blind write and positive ID cases, while in the negative case the algorithm would have to traverse the additional data structure to track the affected transactions.

Another matrix-based approach is presented in Zhou, Panda, and Hu (2004). The authors built different types of matrices, to drop the use of the log file completely. Then they manipulate the matrices using logical AND or OR operators. The two needed matrices are one read matrix that stores all the data items and transactions that read from it, while the other is a write matrix that serves the same purpose for the writes. The algorithm also required two additional matrices; a damaged data vector containing identified damaged data items, and a damaged transactions list that contains the identified damaged transactions.

Kaddoura, Haraty, and Zekri (2015) also adopted a matrix approach. Their approach is based on matrices solely and it is a data dependency approach. They save in a matrix data items as columns and the transactions as rows, where each data item written is marked within the transaction row. The algorithm does not require any additional log file to detect the dependencies, and to speed up the performance of the algorithm, it tracks the number the affected data items in each row. Indexing is also used to save time in traversing the matrix, where each row keeps an index of the first affected data item. The approach used another matrix to store the details of the transactions in the system for recovery purposes.

7.3 Our approach

As mentioned in the introduction, our approach is inspired mainly from two techniques well used in information warfare for assessment and recovery. Our first being the graph approach, which relies solely on the transactional dependency to track the read/write relationships in the system. The second, the clustering technique that was used in another context in our work. In its classical form, the last is used mainly to group the transactions following common shared characteristics, either to cluster based on transactions and its data items, or by applying specific constraints to the logs. But in our case it was clustered based on the level of the transactions in the database, which is a common characteristic for them. To explain our approach further, we introduce two single level approaches that are adapted to our work.

7.3.1 Background

The following works by Haraty and Kaddoura (2017) and Haraty and El Sai (2017) are both a transaction dependency approach that are based on tracking the transactions in the system following the read/write relationships. Although there are differences between the two approaches, in their core both work on creating an adjacency list that is a graph representation where each row depicts a transaction dependent on the other transactions present in its columns. Both works assume a rigorously serializable history, where the transactions IDs are to be incremented sequentially in the system, and all current transactions can only read from the previous transactions only. Hence, the adjacency list can represent on each row a unique transaction dependency.

The read/write relationship that is tracked in the system is defined by the operation of reading from a previous transaction then writing. The data fields written or read are not of importance, as this is a generalized rule to carry the work with less complexity. In the work of Haraty and Kaddoura (2017), the adjacency list is represented as an array of lists. Each list corresponds to a transaction and its dependencies, the index of the list represents the transaction ID, and the content is the dependent transactions. The list stores only committed transactions in order based on the rule; if a transaction T_i reads from the write of another transaction T_j then wrote, the transaction T_j is recorded as a neighbor for T_i. We take for an example a small scenario representing this approach, shown in Fig. 7.1. T_0 wrote x only, T_1 read from T_0 and wrote. Hence, it is recorded as dependency.

T_0: $w(x)$
T_1: $r(x)w(y)$
T_2: $r(x)w(z)$

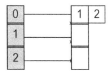

Figure 7.1
Adjacency list for the sample scenario.

In the approach of Haraty and El Sai (2017), the recording is done in an opposite manner, Haraty and Sai record for each transaction all other transactions that the last read from. For example, if a transaction with ID 200 read from the writes of transaction 150 and 151, then wrote, we would record for the transaction 200 two dependent transactions, which are 150 and 151.

To store the dependencies, the two algorithms pass through the log file once to check the read/write relationships. The log file can be completely abandoned in the following stages, since the lists represent the complete dependencies in the system. To find the set of affected transactions, the IDS would report malicious transactions that would be the initial point of entry for a simple graph search algorithm to detect all the affected transactions. The search in the case of Haraty and Kaddoura (2017) is more efficient since the graph stores for each transaction, the counterparts that read then write from. This facilitates the search since for each malicious transaction, the algorithm can directly track the first affected transactions, which are those in the malicious transactions content list. The search would repeat this process for all affected transactions until no neighbors are found. While in the case of Haraty and El Sai (2017), the process requires more extensive looping to track the set, since the read/write relationship is represented in the opposite way. The search starting from a malicious transaction knows the transactions that the last read from, so to get the affected ones, the algorithm searches within all the transactions to check if the malicious transaction is present in their content list, making the looping more expensive.

The recovery after the search is identical in the two approaches. It happens first by deleting the effects of the malicious transactions, in addition to restoring the affected transactions, either by re-executing their operations or by restoring the before images. Our algorithm integrates the algorithm in Haraty and Kaddoura (2017) adapted to a multilevel approach, together with a clustering technique to group the transactions by their appropriate levels.

7.3.2 Adaptation to multilevel

Typical relational databases used in the field are single level ones. The notion of multilevel has not caught the mainstream attention, but still some fields require this type of databases for the additional secrecy and security enhancements that it provides.

The key difference between multilevel and single level is in the storage of the data items. While single level databases store each data item strictly once, multilevel databases allow multiple values for each data item. The concept is close to multiversioning in the database, but the multiple versions presented here are related to views and clearances. Access control is a key concept here, where each user is allowed a clearance level that dominates certain security levels (Haraty & Bekaii, 2006).

The clearance to security level relationship is usually imposed by rules on the reads and writes in the system. Two simple properties to manage the transactions can be explained as:

- **The simple security property**: A transaction is allowed to read in an appropriate level, only if its clearance is of the same or higher level.
- **The * property**: A transaction is allowed to write in an appropriate level, if its clearance is of the same level.

Following the multilevel constraints imposed in the system, we can deduce that data insertion will not be handled as it was in the single level scheme. Suppose that a transaction at level UNCLASSIFIED—U wants to insert a new record in the database with a primary key that has been previously inserted in another level, supposedly CONFIDENTIAL—C. Naturally, in a single level database, this instance would be rejected, since the use of an existing primary key is forbidden in an INSERT query. But in the case of multilevel databases, multiple records with the same primary key had to be allowed. This concept is called polyinstantiation as defined in Jajodia and Sandhu (1991). It concerns the tuple itself by allowing multiple tuples with the same primary key but different access classes to be stored in the same table. This can happen in two cases referred to as visible and invisible polyinstantiation.

As preliminary to our approach, we consider that the history in our system is rigorously serializable, and the system also spawns transactions by plus one incremental IDs. The rigorous property guarantees strictness and ensures that no read data item is overwritten until the previous transaction carrying the read is committed or aborted (Breitbart, Georgakopoulos, Rusinkiewicz, & Silberschatz, 1991). This allows the scheduling of the transactions in the system in a sort of sequential manner where transactions with a higher ID would only interact with lower ID transactions.

This helps our algorithm in the assessment and detection phases. In the first phase, while reading from the log file to track the dependencies, starting from a transaction with ID x we can safely check for its interactions with other transactions with ID y where $y < x$, since transactions can only read/write from transactions with lower IDs. The rigorous scheduling enhances the performance in the second phase too. The search for affected transactions after reporting the malicious ones would require only a search starting from the malicious transaction ID going upwards in the IDs, following the same property described earlier.

The system respects polyinstantiation by allowing multiple tuples in the database with the same primary key, but with different security levels. We ensure the polyinstantiation property by restricting reads on the specified or lower security levels. If the clearance dominates the security level and the data item to be read was found, the read would be accomplished successfully on that specified level, else the system would search through the lower security levels sequentially to find the data item. The writes in our system are recorded on the same level only. Hence, a transaction would write with a clearance level that is equal to the corresponding security level it is attempting to access.

The system classifies the transactions on the record level, since we assume that a transaction would insert on one level only in a query. Formally, a transaction performing an insertion with a certain security level would write all its data items at that same security level. For a correct execution of the assessment, the algorithm needs to bypass the simple and * security properties in the multilevel databases, since the damage detection in the system should be across all the levels of the database. The writes clusters are then subject to be checked regardless the level of the transaction in question, to ensure that our algorithm is tracking all the dependencies. Thus we would give our algorithm the highest security level access on the database to ensure its correctness.

Our approach assumes the existence of four security levels: UNCLASSIFIED (U), CONFIDENTIAL (C), SECRET (S), and TOP SECRET ($T\,S$). We record the writes of transactions read from the log on the fly in four buckets corresponding to the level of each transaction, U, C, S, and $T\,S$. These writes will serve as the sufficient reference to record transaction dependencies. The algorithm does not require passing through the log file more than once, since the buckets will be used in their turn to check all read/write interactions in the system. Each bucket will be represented as a bipartite graph, since data items are stored on one side and the transactions are stored on the other. By definition, a bipartite graph is constituted from two sets of nodes, where no nodes in the same set are adjacent.

One data item would have multiple transactions overwriting it, but we can safely sort the transactions by ascending IDs to represent the last written one, since our history is rigorous. Formally a data item x, represented by a node, would have an edge to the node $T\,(n)$ in bucket i represented by; $x \rightarrow T\,(n)$, if $T\,(n)_i$: $w(x)$, where n is the primary key of the modified record. We record the primary key to identify the modified record to catch the dependencies by the primary key—foreign key relationships in the next stage. Another recorded element is the table name of the modified record, and this is essential to locate the change when we need to restore the database. We record also with each write in the bucket the before image (previous value). This would speed up the recovery time since even the operations to be rolled back are saved in memory. Hence, every node of a transaction would constitute of its ID, the primary key of the modified record, its relevant table name, and the before image.

The second phase for the damage assessment is for recording the dependencies in our adjacency list. A transaction executing in the system and after recording its writes in the buckets, if it read from a certain level then wrote, the algorithm will check for the last write on that data item in the corresponding bucket following the primary key—foreign key relationship on the record itself. It will then record a dependency with the last transaction

Table 7.1: The damage assessment process.

Input: Set of transactions S: $T_0...T_n$
Output: A graph tt, $tt = (V, E)$ where each E represents a transaction dependency

for each $T(n)$ in S **do**
  if $T(n)$ contains $W_i(x)$ **then**
  Record $x \rightarrow T(n)$ in bucket i
 end if
if $T(n)$ contains $r(x)_i w(y)_j$ && bucket i contains $x \rightarrow T(m)$ **then**
  Record $T(m) \rightarrow T(n)$ in tt
end if
end for

Table 7.2: The damage detection process.

Input: Set of malicious transactions S: $T_0...T_n$, empty queue Q, graph tt
of all transaction dependencies.
Output: A set of all affected transactions S^j

for each $T(n)$ in S
  do Add $T(n)$ to Q
  while $Q! = \emptyset$ **do**
  $T(m) = $ Pop Q
  Add $T(m)$ to S^j
  Add neighbors of $T(m)$ to Q
 end while
end for

---

carrying the write if the relationship was found. Formally, if $T(n)_j$: $r(x)_i w(y)_j$ where $i < j$, and bucket i contains $x \rightarrow T(m)$, we record dependency $T(m) \rightarrow T(n)$; where m and n are the relative primary and foreign keys. This process and the buckets write are described in Table 7.1.

After fully clustering the log file into buckets of writes, and recording all the dependencies in the adjacency list, the detection of affected transactions and their recovery is now simple. The detection starts when the IDS reports the malicious transactions in the system. The algorithm requires a search over the adjacency list to track the affected transactions. We choose this search to be breadth first. The algorithm is illustrated in Table 7.2, it mainly uses a queue to start with the first malicious transactions, then each neighbor visited is considered affected and entered into the queue, until the queue is empty, so all neighbors are visited. The recovery following this step, and since the before images are recorded in our system, requires only a traversal on the buckets to capture the writes and the before images of the affected transactions. The before images are then used to restore the database to its stable state.

The damage recovery process needs to ensure that all the effects of the malicious transactions are invalidated. The lasting effects of an affected transaction are its writes in

Table 7.3: The damage recovery process.

Input: Set of affected transactions S: $T_0...T_n$, Set of write buckets B: B_0 $...B_n$
Output: None
for each $T(n)$ in S **do for** each $B(n)$ in B **do**
for each $B(n)$ in B **do**
do
if $B(n)$ contains $T(n)$ **then**
Extract before image, primary key, and table name of $B(n)$
Update table with before image WHERE primary key $= T(n)$'s key
end if
end for
end for

Table 7.4: Our database schema.

Doctor: d-id(pk), d-name, d-major, d-experience.
Medication: m-id(pk), m-name, m-company name, m-phone.
Patient: p-id(pk), p-name, p-DOB, p-address.
Prescription: pre-id(pk), p-id(fk), d-id(fk), pre-date.
Prescription-Detail: pd-id(pk), m-id(fk), pre-id(fk), pd-frequency, pd-days.

the database. The lasts are considered invalid since they might be based on the read of a malicious transaction. Hence, the content of these writes is malicious by itself. To recover the database, we illustrate in Table 7.3 the process that should be executed. We are given the set of the affected transactions from the damage detection process. The first step is by looping all these transactions and buckets, to find all the writes that an affected transaction performed on all the levels in the system. And since our algorithm bypasses the security constraints of the multilevel database, we can safely identify all the transactions' writes and their relevant before images and primary keys. The last step in the process is simply by re-executing an update on the corresponding affected table, where the primary key is equal to the transaction's primary key, and the new value is the before image.

To be more elaborate explain how our data structures will be built, we illustrate the above mentioned algorithms in a real-life scenario. The system is a medical database, where information of doctor, patients, and prescriptions are tracked. The records in the system follow the schema shown in Table 7.4, *pk* signifies the primary key in the record, and *fk* is a foreign key. The database is consisted of five tables. The Doctor table contains the id of the doctor as a primary key, the name, the major, and the experience represented as years. The second table, Medication, is composed of the id, the name, the manufacturing company, and the company's phone number. The third table is the Patient table, it has the id of the patient, the name, the date of birth, and the address. The Prescription table is the fourth one, it has the prescription's id, the patient's id, the doctor's id, and the date when it was prescribed. The doctor and the patient ids signify the relation of a doctor prescribing that prescription to a patient. The last table is the Prescription-Detail, it contains an id, the medication id, and the prescription id, which serves as the relation of a medication that was prescribed in a prescription, the frequency that represents the number of times that a prescription should be taken per day, and the days that represent the number of days for the prescription to be taken.

The previously mentioned rules of simple and * security properties are respected in the scenario. The reads are performed on the same level of the transaction if the data item is found, else they traverse the levels down incrementally to find the appropriate data item. The writes are executed on the same level only. Polyinstantiation is respected in the visible and invisible form, but our notion is simplified since we are dealing with records classifications. All the records follow a single security level. Hence, if a transaction with level U is executed, all its writes will be performed on that level only. The execution is in the form of queries on the database, where all the queries would have reads and writes operations. We would track the dependencies from the relative primary key–foreign key relationships, since each query is reading from another record and writing a certain value. The following transactions are injected in the system:

T_0U: Doctor("1000", "John Macintosh", "Dermatologist", "10")

T_1S: Patient("2001", "Paul Revere", "18-08-90", "Beirut, Lebanon")

T_2S: Prescription("4109", "2001", "1000", "03-10-2017")

T_3U: Prescription("4115", "2021", "1000", "03-10-2017")

T_4U: Medication("3162", "Lexotanil", "Radiant Pharamaceutical", " + 88802-96603037")

T_5U: Prescription-Detail("5074", "4115", "3162", "1", "10")

T_6S: Prescription-Detail("5074", "4115", "3162", "3", "30")

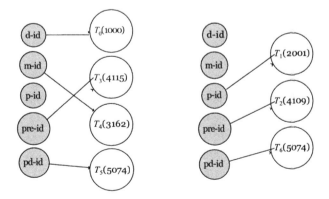

Figure 7.2

Bipartite graph representing the writes on the unclassified level from the left and on the secret level from the right.

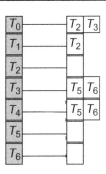

Figure 7.3
Adjacency list illustrating the transactions dependencies.

In Fig. 7.2, we illustrate the writes of the above transactions, tracking the writes of each transaction on the primary keys. Our bipartite graph is represented at two sides, where the left side represents the writes on the unclassified level and the right is on the secret level. Tracking the writes from the primary key–foreign key relationships as previously described, we represent the transaction dependencies also in an adjacency list, as shown in Fig. 7.3.

We start the execution by injecting the transactions in order. T_0 performs a write on the Doctor table. The field $T_0(1000)$ is recorded in bucket U of writes on the d-id. We have no foreign key reads in this transaction. The second transaction T_1 performed a write on the table Patient on the secret level. Hence we record $T_1(2001)$ on the p-id in the S bucket. The first transaction to record a dependency is T_2, it performs a write on the Prescription table on the secret level, it reads from the foreign key 1000 of the Doctor table. So far the only satisfied relationship is with the transaction T_0 on the unclassified level. Respecting the multilevel security property, the algorithm can safely record for T_0 a dependency with T_2. The second dependency is on the secret level, T_2 read from T_1 on the secret level. T_3 is executed on the unclassified level, the only relationship it has is with the d-id 1000. Thus the dependency T_0 is recorded with T_3. The transaction T_4 performs a simple write only, it is recorded on m-id in bucket U as $T_4(3162)$. The last two transactions illustrate the nature of polyinstantiation, they both have the same primary key, but are executed on different levels. T_5 was executed on the unclassified level, it read from both T_3 and T_4 on the unclassified level. Hence, T_5 is recorded as a dependency for both T_3 and T_4. T_6 has the same primary key of T_5 but was executed on the secret level. It is accepted in the system, and the primary key $T_6(5074)$ is recorded in the bucket S. It has read also from the writes of T_3 and T_4; therefore, the dependency of T_6 with those two is recorded. The dependencies are satisfied since the reads of T_6 were on the secret level, and the targeted data items in the secret level were not found. The system searched through the lower levels and found the appropriate data items on the unclassified level.

7.3.3 Complexity analysis

We explained in the previous section, three algorithms that embody our approach. We are interested in analyzing the complexity of these algorithms to ensure that all their running time is polynomial. This is essential in the work, since by definition, polynomial time complexity means that the algorithm's running time is upper bounded by a polynomial expression of its input: $T(n) = O(n^k)$ for some constant k. This ascertains that our running time is not growing exponentially depending on the size of the input.

The damage assessment algorithm presented in Table 7.1 is composed of two steps. Recording the writes in the bucket is the first one, it can be performed in $O(1)$ since it is a constant time operation. The second step, the recording of the dependency is executed in $O(n^2)$. It loops on the transactions in the log, and for each transaction that performs a read/write, it checks in the buckets if the read data item is present. That is two nested loops, which explains the order of n^2 for the operation.

The damage detection algorithm explained in Table 7.2 is the implementation of the breadth first search on the adjacency list recorded in the detection stage.

Breadth First Search is known to perform in $O(n \log_n)$, since it uses the queue to visit the neighbors in the graph in a breadth search manner. The algorithm loops over the malicious transactions, then uses the queue to push all their neighbors, where for each element in the queue its neighbors will be visited in turn. All these visited neighbors plus the initial set of malicious transactions should be recovered in the next step.

The last discussed algorithm is the recovery in Table 7.3. The recovery happens after retrieving all the affected transactions. The algorithm loops once over all the transactions that are received. The second loop is on the buckets to extract the appropriate fields for the rollback. We extract the primary key, the table, and the before image. These two nested loops indicate that the running time of the recovery is in the order of $O(n^2)$. These three processes are run sequentially in the system. Each process depends on the previous one, but checkpoints can be added when each process is completed. Their running time is shown to be polynomial, and the worst one was bounded by n^2 operations. We can assure then that our DAR approach is efficient. Notably since the log will not span for more than thousands of transactions in the system.

7.4 Experimental results

As we have seen in the previous section, our approach runs by detecting affected transactions sequentially from the malicious transactions themselves. It then recovers from the attack by reverting the work of these transactions on the database. This is due the nature of our rigorously serializable history. The experiment is run sequentially on multiple cases, where we specify the first affected transaction ID, and scan our data structure to track all affected transactions from this point. This shows a concrete relation between performance and number of affected transactions in the system.

Our approach was simulated on generated log files that represent multiple cases in the system. A random scenario where transactions are randomly dependent on each other, a worst case scenario where one transaction is dependent on all other transactions, and a best case scenario where each transaction is dependent on another one only. The simulation was done on a sqlite database with the schema specified in Table 7.4. The system is a personal computer with a CPU of 2.6*ttHz* Intel Core *i*5, and 8*ttB* RAM. The code was written in Python 3.4.3 where the integration with the sqlite database is native using *sqlite3* library.

7.4.1 Performance results of the detection algorithm

To start with the detection algorithm and taking into consideration the abovementioned requirements of our model, we need to prove the correctness of the detection phase. Following our history properties, scanning from the list of affected transactions should start from the first next transaction in the system after the attacker ID. In Fig. 7.4 we show that our algorithm is running proportionally to the ID of the smallest affected transaction, since the portions of the needed transactions to be scanned decrease with the increasing number of the smallest malicious ID, and we know that our history disallows the reads from a higher transaction ID.

The detection algorithm was tested on a log of 1000 transactions in the system, where the dependencies are ad hoc and random. We compare, in order, the performance of our detection

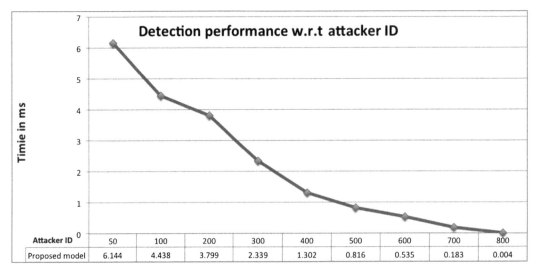

Figure 7.4
Performance of the detection algorithm.

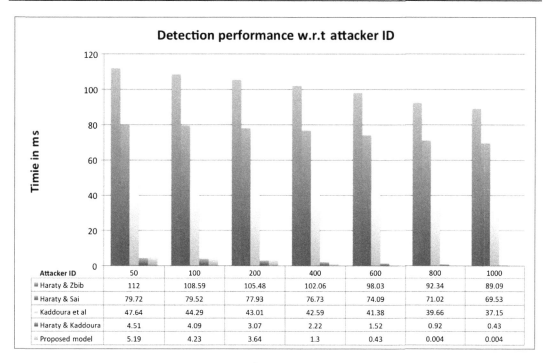

Figure 7.5
Performance of the detection in comparison with other recent models.

algorithm to other recent algorithms. In Fig. 7.5 we see that the time taken by Haraty and Zbib (2014) is by far the highest, since it is an approach where two matrices are used to track the dependencies, it needs more time to detect the affected transactions. In Haraty and El Sai (2017), the authors reach a better result because the tracking is based on one matrix. Kaddoura et al. (2015) implemented a data dependency approach but it uses smart indexing to tag the dependent transactions. Hence, the time was even better than the two previous mentioned transaction dependencies approaches. The approach in Haraty and Kaddoura (2017) is really similar to the one in Haraty and El Sai (2017), but Haraty and Kaddoura enhanced the performance by getting the list of affected transactions in one run, it is only sufficient to retrieve the list of affected transactions by retrieving the head of the adjacency list that represents the malicious one. Our approach proved to have similar running time to Haraty and Kaddoura (2017), since it is identical when it comes to detection.

Additionally, we compared our approach with other nonmatrix approaches as shown in Fig. 7.6. The classical approach being Bai and Liu (2009), and the clustering approaches were all proposed in Haraty and Zeitunlian (2007). We notice from the beginning that the matrix approach is by far more dominant in performance than these other approaches. The matrix in our model stores needed information only to describe transaction dependencies, enhancing the running time in detection phase. The deterioration in all these models is the

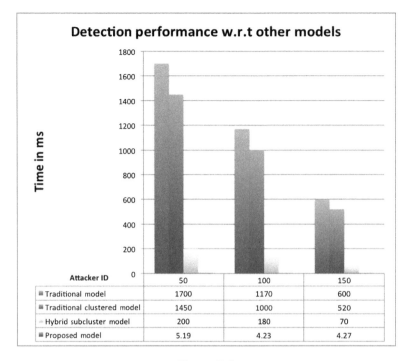

Detection performance w.r.t other models

Attacker ID	50	100	150
▨ Traditional model	1700	1170	600
▨ Traditional clustered model	1450	1000	520
Hybrid subcluster model	200	180	70
▨ Proposed model	5.19	4.23	4.27

Figure 7.6
Performance of the detection in comparison with classical models.

fact that they need to pass through logs multiple times, requiring expensive I/O operations, to track all dependent transactions. The other advantage in our model is that scanning begins from the first smallest transaction ID after the attacker ID, which is not the case in these other algorithms.

7.4.2 Performance results of the recovery algorithm

Regarding to the recovery, our algorithm running time should be increasing linearly to the number of affected transactions. Checking Fig. 7.7 we can see that the running time is increasing with a factor of 3−6 ms for each 50−100 transactions to be recovered. This proves that the recovery algorithm is steady in our system, since the running time is growing logically in proportion to the work that should be done to recover.

The recovery algorithm was also compared to the other classical approaches previously mentioned in the detection phase. We are interested in the differences with these approaches, since the recovery in all matrix approaches is similar. In Fig. 7.8 we compared our model to the traditional in Bai and Liu (2009), clustered and hybrid subclustered (Haraty & Zeitunlian, 2007), on a same set of a log of 1000 transactions where the

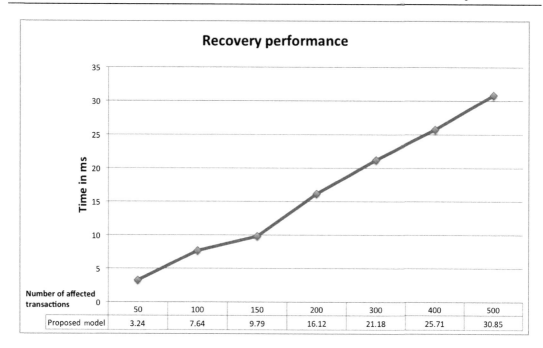

Figure 7.7
Performance of the recovery phase.

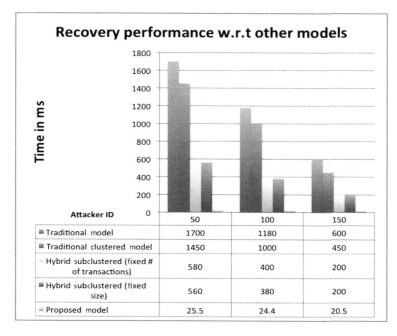

Figure 7.8
Performance of the recovery in comparison with classical models.

dependencies are random, starting from a malicious transaction ID. All these models fail to attain a better running time. We can attribute this failure to the difference in the strategy when it comes to representing the transactions. Our model passes through the log file once and saves in memory all the dependencies, represented in the adjacency list, and the multilevel writes in the in memory buckets. While the other models have to go through the log file multiple times to retrieve the transaction and its operation to recover it. It is a similar trade-off to the one in the detection phase, where they had to pass through the log files multiple times to track the dependencies, and here it is the case of tracking the transaction operations, nevertheless the price in memory in our model is not immense compared to the saved running time.

7.4.3 Memory footprint analysis

The memory analysis in the system is initiated from the point of the matrix creation and the writes buckets. We are merely interested in assessing the footprint when it comes to storing all these needed information in memory, since as we have seen in the previous sections, we are outperforming in running time some of the recent algorithms that were done on single level databases.

These results come at the price of memory as seen in Fig. 7.9, the memory is tracked in bytes on a log of 1000 transactions where the dependencies are random. The footprint in Haraty and Zbib (2014) is one of the worse, since they were using here two matrices to

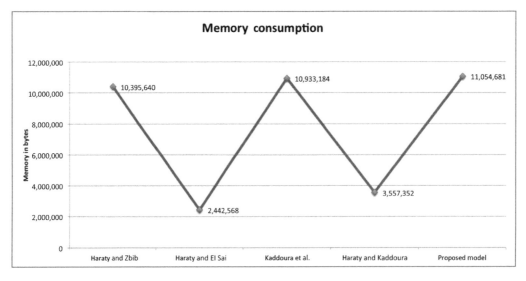

Figure 7.9
Memory consumption in comparison with recent models.

track dependencies, as discussed before. It is followed by the approach of Kaddoura et al. (2015), since it is a data dependency approach it needs to store a lot of data items, resulting with that increase in memory footprint. Haraty and El Sai (2017) reach the best result in storing just the dependency matrix. While their counterpart in Haraty and Kaddoura (2017) also reaches a great result but the difference is due to the randomness of transaction dependencies in the log file. Our proposed model is heavy in memory since we are handling a multilevel database, we are storing beside the transaction IDs in the dependency matrix all the writes in buckets corresponding the levels in the system.

7.5 Conclusion

The three pillars to defend in the information warfare are prevention, detection, and recovery. Prevention and as it was described by imposing barriers in the system from firewalls to antiviruses can certainly achieve in preventing many attacks, but still even the most secure system can be breached. Detection is then essential, it is usually carried by an IDS following historical studies. The system would catch the intruder work that is in our case the malicious transactions. Hence, recovery is a complementary aspect to continue the work of the detection. Recovery is the last line of defense in the system. The work that should be done to recover from the affected transactions should be quick, efficient, and ultimately prevent the events of denial of service. The requirements for such a work in multilevel databases are different from the traditional proposed approaches. The algorithm must comprehend the security levels to clearance relationship, polyinstantiation, and the structure of data.

We targeted medical systems in our study due to the nature of the data they store. The need for efficient DAR approach for these databases is of high importance. The corruption in the medical systems could lead to grave outcomes. Other than leaking the confidential medical history of patients, it can cause fatalities if prescriptions were altered. Hence, the necessity of a state of art algorithm to ensure the stabilization of the database to the correct state.

We proposed an algorithm that has proved to be a contender in the DAR with the best of the approaches proposed for single level database systems. Our running time for the detection of the malicious transactions was on par with the best single level approach to date. The only drawback in our system is the consumption of memory, but we think that it is acceptable since it did not exceed the consumption by a high margin in comparison with the work that incorporated matrices, taking into consideration that the algorithm is saving before images, and handling a multilevel environment. Our algorithm managed to track the dependencies, the writes, and the before images of the data items correctly. We can recover the system with high accuracy and speed, since all the needed information is saved in memory.

We believe that our work can enhance medical systems by providing an approach that can prove its usefulness in the industry. The approach and in its comparison to the latest single level approaches proved that in theory our work can be adopted by the medical systems and can attain worthy performance. Hence, we will help the medical databases in utilizing this algorithm as the third line of defense after the prevention and detection lines. The usage of this work in the industry would increase the resiliency of the medical databases to attacks in general. Whether the databases are hosted by large systems or a simpler personal computer, our work can consolidate the concerns and limitations in computing power.

As for future work we plan on experimenting with other approaches to ease the memory overhead, and reach an efficient quick recovery. We can try by flushing to another backup database the present information in memory, lazy load the needed data while recovering or even dropping our bucket clustering approach for another alternative.

7.6 Teaching assignments

1. Cloud computing is fast becoming a defacto choice for healthcare providers as it offers benefits such as improved access to data and cost efficiency. Discuss the impact of cloud computing on patient data privacy.
2. Insider threats to healthcare resources, such as clinics and hospitals are a major concern in the digital world era. These threats can be carried out by patients as well as staff. Discuss ways to mitigate insider dangers.
3. Healthcare systems tend to be interconnected. This may enable invaders to use one service provider as a way to breach another organization. Devise policies to alleviate the risk of attackers gaining access to private information through interconnected systems.

References

Ammann, P., Jajodia, S., & Liu, P. (2002). Recovery from malicious transactions. *IEEE Transactions on Knowledge and Data Engineering, 14*, 1167–1185.

Bai, K., & Liu, P. (2009). *A data damage tracking quarantine and recovery (DTQR) scheme for mission-critical database systems. Proceedings of the 12th international conference on extending database technology: Advances in database technology* (pp. 720–731). ACM.

Bernstein, P. A., Hadzilacos, V., & Goodman, N. (1987). *Concurrency control and recovery in database systems* (Vol. 370). New York: Addison-wesley.

Breitbart, Y., Georgakopoulos, D., Rusinkiewicz, M., & Silberschatz, A. (1991). On rigorous transaction scheduling. *IEEE Transactions on Software Engineering, 17*, 954–960.

Haraty, R., & Zeitunlian, A. (2007). Damage assessment and recovery from malicious transactions using data dependency for defensive information warfare. *ISESCO Science and Technology Vision, 3*, 43–50.

Haraty, R. A., & Bekaii, N. (2006). Towards a temporal multilevel secure database (TMSDB). *Proceedings Journal of Computer Science, 2*, 19–28.

Haraty, R. A., & El Sai, M. (2017). Information warfare: A lightweight matrix-based approach for database recovery. *Knowledge and Information Systems, 50,* 287−313.

Haraty, R. A., & Kaddoura, S. (2017). Transaction dependency based approach for database damage assessment using a matrix. *International Journal on Semantic Web and Information Systems (IJSWIS), 13,* 74−86.

Haraty, R. A., & Zbib, M. (2014). *A matrix-based damage assessment and recovery algorithm. 2014 14th International Conference on innovations for community services (I4CS)* (pp. 22−27). IEEE.

Haraty, R. A., Zbib, M., & Masud, M. (2016). Data damage assessment and recovery algorithm from malicious attacks in healthcare data sharing systems. *Peer-to-Peer Networking and Applications, 9,* 812−823.

Hua, D., Xiaolin, Q., Guineng, Z., & Ziyue, L. (2011). SQRM: An effective solution to suspicious users in database. In *Proceedings of the 3rd international conference on advances in databases, knowledge, and data applications (DBKDA).*

Jajodia, S., & Sandhu, R. (1991). Toward a multilevel secure relational data model. *ACM SIGMOD Record, 20,* 50−59.

Kaddoura, S., Haraty, R., & Zekri, A. (2015). *Information warfare: Fighting back through the matrix. 2015 IEEE symposium series on computational intelligence* (pp. 449−454). IEEE.

Khochare, N., Chalurkar, S., Kakade, S., & Meshramm, B. (2011). Survey on SQL injection attacks and their countermeasures. *International Journal of Computational Engineering & Management (IJCEM), 13,* 689−702.

Lala, C., & Panda, B. (2001). Evaluating damage from cyber attacks: A model and analysis. *IEEE Transactions on Systems, Man, and Cybernetics-Part A: Systems and Humans, 31,* 300−310.

Liu, P., & Yu, M. (2011). Damage assessment and repair in attack resilient distributed database systems. *Computer Standards & Interfaces, 33,* 96−107.

Lunt, T. F. (1993). A survey of intrusion detection techniques. *Computers & Security, 12,* 405−418.

Lytras, M. D., Raghavan, V., & Damiani, E. (2017). Big Data and Data Analytics Research: From Metaphors to Value Space for Collective Wisdom in Human Decision Making and Smart Machines. *International Journal on Semantic Web and Information Systems (IJSWIS), 13*(1), 1−10. Available from https://doi.org/10.4018/IJSWIS.2017010101.

Mazzucelli, C., & Visvizi, A. (2017). Querying the Ethics of Data Collection as a Community of Research and Practice The Movement toward the "Liberalism of Fear" to Protect the Vulnerable. *Genocide Studies and Prevention: An International Journal, 11*(1), 2−8. Available from http://doi.org/10.5038/1911-9933.11.1.149.

Panda, B., & Giordano, J. (1999). *Reconstructing the database after electronic attacks. Database security XII* (pp. 143−156). Springer.

Panda, B., & Haque, K. A. (2002). *Extended data dependency approach: A robust way of rebuilding database. Proceedings of the 2002 ACM symposium on applied computing* (pp. 446−452). ACM.

Panda, B., & Zhou, J. (2003). *Database damage assessment using a matrix based approach: An intrusion response system. Proceedings of the 7th international conference on database engineering and applications symposium* (pp. 336−341). IEEE.

Ragothaman, P., & Panda, B. (2003). *Analyzing transaction logs for effective damage assessment. Research directions in data and applications security* (pp. 89−101). Springer.

Zhou, J., Panda, B., & Hu, Y. (2004). *Succinct and fast accessible data structures for database damage assessment. ICDCIT* (pp. 420−429). Springer.

Zuo, Y., & Panda, B. (2004). *Fuzzy dependency and its applications in damage assessment and recovery. Proceedings from the 5th annual IEEE SMC information assurance workshop* (pp. 350−357). IEEE.

Emerging technologies and systems for smart healthcare

CHAPTER 8

Security and privacy solutions for smart healthcare systems

Yang Lu and Richard O. Sinnott

School of Computing and Information Systems, The University of Melbourne, Australia

8.1 Introduction

In the digital-rich era, online data management becomes increasingly essential. In the health domain, a seismic change is occurring from traditional, paper-based documents to electronic records stored in database systems (Nguyen, Bellucci, & Nguyen, 2014). This can cause many challenges. For instance, care providers may require the access to vital information in different locations; however, many safety issues arise in the handoff of patients among healthcare providers since necessary information cannot be shared. For clinical research, it is necessary to obtain approvals from cancer patients or their families before using their genomic data (Grossman et al., 2016). When it comes to distributed data analytics, the study goal can be balancing privacy and utility while attempting to share, integrate, and visualize health records (Grossman et al., 2016; Wang, Gui, Liu, Jin, & Chen, 2014; Takabi, Joshi, & Ahn, 2010). Due to the increasing use of Internet of Things (IoT) technology in the healthcare domain, certain e-health services are now equipped with more powerful communication and computing capabilities. As a result, connected objects can threaten system security and personal privacy by opening more interactive channels.

According to Solanas et al. (2014), the concept smart health (s-health) refers to "the provision of health services by using the context-aware network and sensing infrastructure of smart cities." Demirkan (2013) pointed that a smart healthcare system (SHS) should provide "opportunities for healthcare organizations to deploy solutions with fewer risks and increased context awareness, converging electronic medical records (EMRs), cloud platforms, social networks, advanced sensors, and data analysis techniques." The SHS technology can create values for taxpayers, care providers, and researchers by tracking, analyzing and processing healthcare information anytime, anywhere. For instance, elderly people can enjoy healthcare services at home (Amrutha, Haritha, Haritha Vasu, Jensy, & Charly, 2017). By building medical data centers for data collection and transmission, authorized individuals can access and decide whether to share their physiological data with

Innovation in Health Informatics.
DOI: https://doi.org/10.1016/B978-0-12-819043-2.00008-3

clinicians for disease diagnosis (Prakash & Balaji Ganesh, 2019). Due to the portable design, smart health services are especially helpful in emergency situations (Ambhati, Kota, Chaudhari, & Jain, 2017). For example, a diabetic patient suddenly faints in their workplace. In this medical scene, ambulance personnel often require his/her history records. With mobile applications tracking patients' diet, exercise, sleep, and blood sugar levels, it is now much easier to learn the basic health conditions immediately.

Policies are required to maintain system security and privacy so as to earn customers' and stakeholders' trust. In Australia, the National Statement on Ethical Conduct in Human Research (NHMRC) labels health data items as *individually identifiable*, *reidentifiable*, and *nonidentifiable*.[1] On this basis, security policies can be defined to constrain data collection and publishing, with the security categories and circumstantial information being considered. The Health Insurance Portability and Accountability Act 1996 (HIPPA)[2] suggests several privacy levels as the guidelines of anonymization. Specially, it identifies the "safe harbors" including 18 attribute types (name, address, date, biometric information, serial numbers of personal devices, etc.) to be removed from individual records before getting disclosed. Similar requirements can be found in the EU General Data Protection Regulation (GDPR).[3] In practice, researchers are required to use health data in an ethical and confidential manner. According to O'Keefe and Connolly (2010), the secured access to and use of health data can be guaranteed by following three procedures: (1) Obtaining consent from data owners (i.e., the patients) for using data; (2) gaining access by satisfying requirements defined for targeted resources, and (3) anonymizing personal data for secondary use, such as public health research activities (Lowrance, 2003). As wireless sensors such as wearable devices and environmental monitors intertwine into our daily lives, unprecedented challenges arise in maintaining security and minimizing privacy risks.

To help other researchers in the related fields, we identify security and privacy challenges by combining social (healthcare) and technical features of s-health applications. To see why such issues occured and how they might be tackled, the rest of this chapter is organized in the following sections: in Section 8.2, we clarify some key concepts related to SHSs (also known as s-health) and identify related technologies. Based on the functional characteristics, we determine the major focuses and review emerging strategies related to *Identification*, *Access Control*, and *Privacy Preservation* in Section 8.3. The key findings

---

[1] National Health and Medical Research Council (Australia). (2007). National statement on ethical conduct in human research. National Health and Medical Research Council.

[2] Centers for Medicare & Medicaid Services. (1996). The Health Insurance Portability and Accountability Act of 1996 (HIPAA). Online at: http://www.cms.hhs.gov/hipaa

[3] GDPR Regulation (EU) 2016/679 of the European Parliament and of the Council of 27 April 2016 on the protection of natural persons with regard to the processing of personal data and on the free movement of such data, and repealing Directive 95/46/EC (General Data Protection Regulation). Off J European Union, vol. L119/59, May 2016.

are discussed in Section 8.4. Finally, we conclude the study with a summary of key contributions and several research directions in Section 8.5.

8.2 Smart healthcare framework and techniques

Smart city infrastructures have brought great convenience to people. In the process of monitoring and collecting data from diverse domains, wireless sensor networks become commonplace and have been widely used in the intelligent transportation systems, mobile networks for remote healthcare, and smart meters used for metering gas usage. Collectively, these can be used to deliver the Internet of Things (IoT) applications. The main idea of IoT is to connect all sorts of things (sensors and IoTs) that can shape the lives of citizens more efficiently and conveniently. Existing projects such as Smart Santander greatly relied on IoT technologies. Through deploying sensors in different cities, a test bed was developed to monitor the traffic status and help drivers to quickly locate available parking spaces (Domingue, Galis, & Gavras, 2011). Different types of data can be collected by an urban IoT system, and exploited to promote the activities of local governments and serve their citizens. For instance, the London Oyster Card system can generate 7 million data records per day and 160 million records per month.[4] With a wide spectrum of data sets being collected in such sizes, big data technologies can be adopted to support a variety of smart city applications, from collecting, processing to analyzing multivariate data sets.

As shown in Fig. 8.1, smart health (s-health) research can be seen as the result of projecting an e-health plane over a smart city plane (Solanas et al., 2014). Both smart health (s-health) and mobile health (m-health) can be presented as subsets of e-health; however, in the sense of underlying infrastructures, s-health might not consist of mobile devices/applications but fixed sensors. Due to the support of big data analytic techniques (e.g., pattern recognition, predictive modeling, and other machine learning algorithms), an s-health framework can be provisioned through automatic services (Provost & Fawcett, 2013).

Another s-health framework was designed to apply a variety of analytic techniques on health-related databases (Sakr & Elgammal, 2016). As shown in Fig. 8.2, a layered, scalable s-health framework was designed with four functional layers for data connection, data storage, data analytics, and result presentation. After collecting data items from diverse scenarios, the first challenge is integrating heterogeneous datasets (e.g., hospital information, laboratory records, radiology records, and prescriptions from pharmacies). This can rely on modeling related semantic ontologies at the connection layer. At the storage layer, synthetic data can be accessed and operated flexibly by using cloud-based relational databases and/or NoSQL storage services to process structured, semistructured, and unstructured data sources. Building on this, the analytic layer can provide various functions

---

[4] Batty, M. Smart cities and Big Data. http://www.spatialcomplexity.info/.

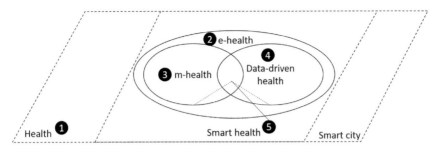

Figure 8.1
Diagram of smart health and related concepts[5].

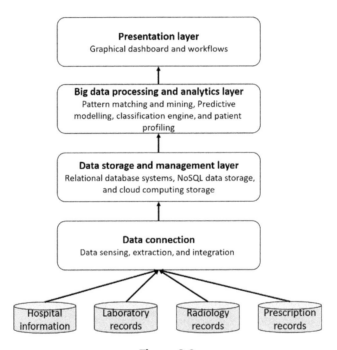

Figure 8.2
Architecture underlying smart healthcare systems (Sakr & Elgammal, 2016).

according to the data processing requirements. Finally, a user-friendly dashboard can be built to display the analytics results in the presentation layer. Throughout the treatment process, clinicians and researchers are able to make better, real-time decisions.

---

[5] (1) Health refers to health-related activities commonly occur in medical contexts; (2) e-health involves the use of the information communication technology, namely health-related activities relying on the access of electronic health records; (3) m-health practices are typically supported by the use of wireless infrastructures and mobile devices; (4) data-driven health business involves big data collecting, processing and analyzing; (5) smart health (s-health) is defined as the combination of (3) and (4), representing as m-health augmented with certain intelligence.

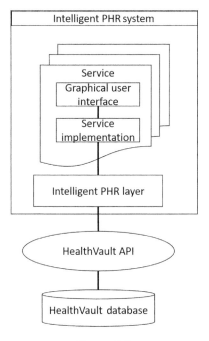

Figure 8.3
Intelligent PHR system built on Microsoft HealthVault (Kostadinovska et al., 2015).

Data-driven platforms such as HealthVault and Google health are widely adopted to provide s-health services. As shown in Fig. 8.3, a high-level architecture can be designed to underlie the intelligent personal health record (PHR) system (Kostadinovska, de Vries, Geleijnse, & Zdravkova, 2015). In this architecture, remote services can be delivered on the population-level data obtained through HealthVault APIs. Thus, a lightweight intelligent PHR system can be established without local storage. Another key principle of this approach is that patients are in control of their data, and thus they are encouraged to participate in their own treatment. In addition, the proposed PHR system can benefit care providers and researchers by supporting diverse analytical technologies. For instance, through monitoring health conditions, retrieving hospitalization and testing results, care providers can make better decisions at minimal cost, whilst public health researchers are able to predict and prevent adverse events from happening among a very large population through access to clinical and laboratory data in PHR records.

To make optimal use of wireless technologies, Catarinucci et al. (2015) designed an IoT-aware SHS by extending hospital services in an IoT network. Typically, the following three parts should be included in the architecture: (1) a sensing network built with wireless sensors for data acquisition; (2) an IoT smart gateway for authenticating local and remote users before they can access or use the sensitive information; and (3) a user interface allowing data management and real-time result display. An IoT-aware system should be able to collect and deliver patients' symptoms and environmental conditions to a operating center, such as processing data with intelligent algorithms and allowing alert messages to be sent in case of emergency.

Depending on the sensor types in use, Baig and Gholamhosseini (2013) further classified the s-health systems as wearable health monitoring system (WHMS), mobile health monitoring system (MHMS), and remote health monitoring system (RHMS). Specifically, a WHMS involves the use of wearable sensors while an MHMS is based on mobile devices. Through combining mobile communication and wearable monitoring technology, an RHMS can be established to transmit vital messages, such as from a health center to the patient's home. As shown in Fig. 8.4, wireless body area networks can provide patient symptom data such as blood pressure, ECG, and heartbeat through sensors placed on the human body. By using mobile devices, health-related data can be transmitted to the local network and e-health servers to support treatment and data analytics (Khan, Jilani, Khan, & Ahmed, 2017). Finally, the last layer provides services to patients living remotely. Data stored in the e-health server can be delivered to remote hospitals.

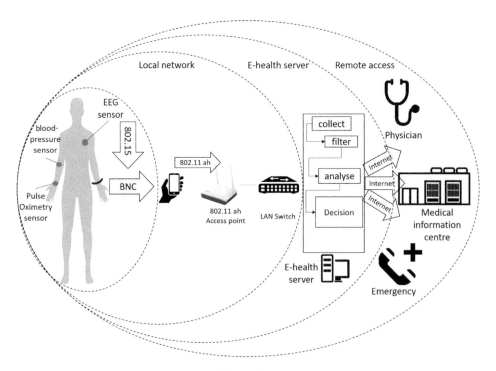

Figure 8.4
Smart health based in wireless body area networks (Ghamari et al., 2016).

In addition to healthcare, remote access to medical information also supports emergency services (Gope & Hwang, 2016). To generalize the use of such architecture, Sahi et al. (2018) designed a multitiered system to serve a larger group of users, including physicians, pharmacists, health insurance providers, etc. located at remote organizations. Through the adoption of communication technologies, multiple systems are connected to form a smart access solution. Smart health monitoring systems are often referred to as using advanced technologies to monitor patients' health conditions. Based on the behavioral models extracted from monitoring systems, Baig and Gholamhosseini (2013) proposed a generic s-health architecture and its communication within a smart city infrastructure. As shown in Fig. 8.5, it can be used in different contexts such as home, hospital and outdoors.

Due to the sensitive attributes included in PHRs, protection against unauthorized use/access is essential. Based on a systematic review of existing work, two main features are found in the s-health frameworks: the adoption of monitoring technologies (e.g., mobile, wearable sensors) in ubiquitous environments and complex data analytics (e.g., data integration and machine learning methods) on heterogenous datasets. Therefore, extra security measures are required in s-health infrastructures where diverse application functionalities need to be equipped with.

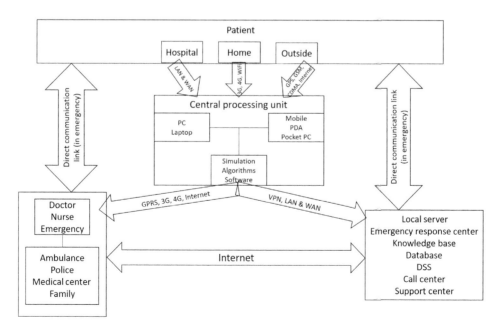

Figure 8.5
Health monitoring system (Baig & Gholamhosseini, 2013).

8.3 Identified issues and solutions

As a theoretical guideline for ICT, the *Confidentiality*, *Integrity*, and *Availability* (CIA) model has been widely used to safeguard online database systems (Cherdantseva & Hilton, 2013). As shown in Fig. 8.6, the CIA Security Principle addresses requirements in terms of *Confidentiality* through defining policies to prevent inappropriate data access; *Integrity* that protects data against unauthorized modification; and *Availability* that focuses on ensuring any reliable access/use of information (Samonas & Coss, 2014; Wang, Lee, & Wang, 1998; Zhao, You, Zhao, Chen, & Peng, 2010). Certain methods are designed by following appropriate guidelines. For instance, encryption algorithms can be applied to ensure confidentiality, whereby encrypted messages cannot be viewed by attackers who do not own the decryption keys (Kumar & Saxena, 2011). Authorization policies also restrict "editing" privileges to those who have the admin roles (Malik & Park, 2008).

In addition to CIA, Prasser, Kohlmayer, Spengler, and Kuhn (2018) suggested a general security framework for health information sharing. As shown in Fig. 8.7, it contains security principles related to *Trust, Controlled Data Access*, and *Deidentification* thereby offering a three-layer concept model. From the outermost layer, trust relations can be created (and strengthened) between organizations (Firth-Cozens, 2004) and thus provide the foundation for authentication (Cody-Allen & Kishore, 2006). The middle layer is tasked with protected data sources so as to satisfy requirements suggested in the CIA model. Finally, anonymizing strategies can help reduce (or eliminate) the chance of disclosing sensitive information (Fairchild et al., 2007; Shlomo, 2007). For instance, individual health records containing HIV test results must be kept anonymous before they are used for secondary purposes. Datasets containing such patient information may

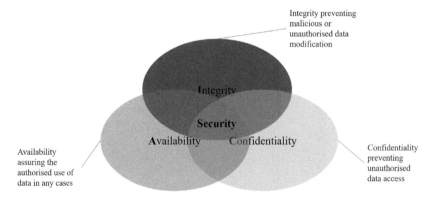

Figure 8.6
CIA: confidentiality, integrity, and availability model.

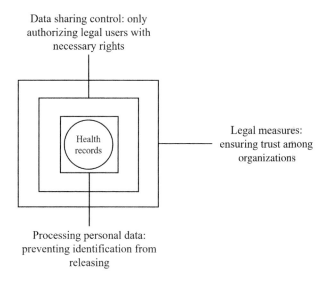

Data sharing control: only
authorizing legal users with
necessary rights

Health
records

Legal measures:
ensuring trust among
organizations

Processing personal data:
preventing identification from
releasing

Figure 8.7
Principles guaranteeing security and privacy of health records.

be accessible to people who are identified as "specialists" in the e-health platform. When it comes to collaborative research activities, cross-domain authentication can also ensure the secured data sharing.

Both conceptual models present a range of security issues that need to be carefully dealt with in online data sharing. As a subfield of smart cities (shown in Fig. 8.1), smart health enjoys the same group of technologies while heavily relies on the access to health information. As a result, security and privacy preserving solutions should be developed by taking all features into consideration. This requires the involved entities are truly connected to intelligent healthcare services. For instance, Fig. 8.8 outlines a "mind map" of this study: (1) identifying the technical features of smart cities such as *Wireless, Mobile, and Ubiquitous Computing*; (2) identifying smart health applications by combining available functionalities of existing e-health systems; and (3) determining security and privacy requirements for s-health applications, given the wide range of smart city technologies (shown in Fig. 8.1).

In this chapter, we review the innovative work that has been done to mitigate security or privacy risks within smart healthcare applications. In this study, we consider several procedures in the following order: *Technical Enablers → s-Health Applications → Security and Privacy Solutions*. Based on the key issues outlined in the two models (Figs. 8.6 and 8.7), strategies can be categorized into *Authentication, Privacy-aware access control*, and *Anonymization*.

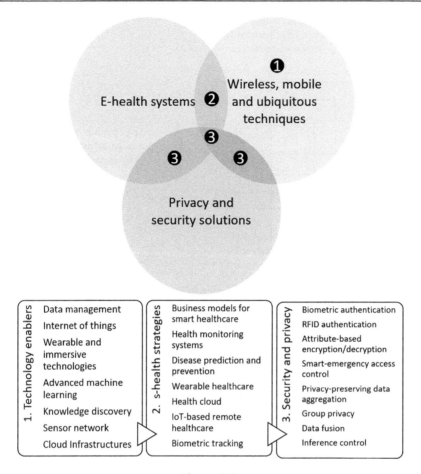

Figure 8.8
Mind map of this work.

8.3.1 Authentication

Identifying legitimate people and objects is paramount to s-health system design. Due to the functional characteristics, both subject and object authentication are required in using s-health applications. Technologies such as radio frequency identification (RFID) are widely used to identify physical objects and people in ubiquitous environments. Due to the system openness, authentication technologies can be further categorized as centralized and decentralized authentication, depending on how the processes are performed.

8.3.1.1 Internet of Things authentication

Thousands of connected things can be built within SHSs. As a result, authentication is an important security service, determining valid accessible objects in IoT networks. RFID is

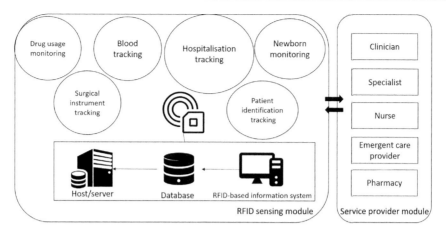

Figure 8.9
A generic RFID-enhanced hospital system (Rahman, Bhuiyan, & Ahamed, 2017).

widely used to identify IoT objects based on a serial number stored in a microchip (Amendola, Lodato, Manzari, Occhiuzzi, & Marrocco, 2014). It has the advantage of reading information without physical contact. As shown in Fig. 8.9, a generic hospital system consists of two modules: RFID Sensing Module including all RFID identifying and monitoring systems and Service Provider Module containing systems used for legitimate RFID identification data. For instance, with RFID sending patient information to a given monitoring system, the alarm can be activated in case of an emergency happening.

A major concern in RFID-based healthcare systems is how user privacy can be protected when using RFID identification data. In this regard, Rahman et al. (2017) suggested a healthcare service access control framework where unauthorized disclosures of health information need to be prevented by using access control techniques (Dafa-Alla, Kim, Ryu, & Heo, 2005). As shown in Fig. 8.10, through writing and managing privacy policies by an "Administrator," the use of and access to various data can be related to user-defined policies. A "Privacy Policy Manager" breaks down policies into unit policies and unit roles, which are respectively stored in "Privacy Policy Database" and "User Role Database" to deliver protection on real-time RFID tags that are read into the system.

8.3.1.2 User authentication

In IoT-based scenarios, there is a rise in the use of biometric authentication mechanism. Different from using traditional passwords, biometric data such as fingerprints, face scans can be used as an "unforgettable" means to authenticate individuals into various smart infrastructures. For instance, biometric systems such as Apple's Touch ID and Android's Face Unlock are designed for authenticating smartphone users (De Luca, Hang, Von Zezschwitz, & Hussmann, 2015). Based on the use of fingerprint information, a novel

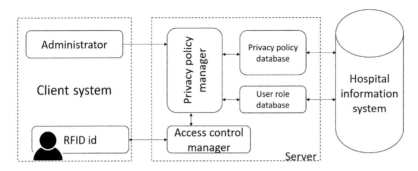

Figure 8.10
Architecture of healthcare service access control (Rahman et al., 2017).

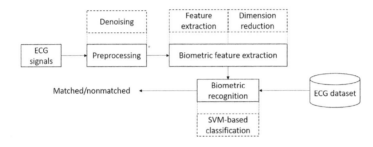

Figure 8.11
ECG authentication in smart healthcare systems (Hejazi et al., 2016).

authentication system is implemented for user registration and secured access control (Murillo-Escobar, Cruz-Hernández, Abundiz-Pérez, & López-Gutiérrez, 2015). Electrocardiogram (ECG) signals are monitored in nearly all healthcare systems, and thus, ECG-based authentication is considered in user authentication and medical information access (Zhang, Gravina, Lu, Villari, & Fortino, 2018).

The use of machine learning algorithms for processing patients' biometric data can support user authentication. For instance, Fig. 8.11 illustrates a generic framework describing how ECG signals can realize the user (patient) authentication (Hejazi, Al-Haddad, Singh, Hashim, & Aziz, 2016). Generally, it involves such procedures as data collection, preprocessing, feature extraction, and classification-based recognition. Based on the feature vectors extracted from cleaned ECG signals, a decision model can be learned by training feature vectors from the ECG dataset. Based on the evaluation, optimal testing results can be achieved by using SVM-based classification in the recognition phrase.

8.3.1.3 Distributed authentication

Due to the increasing complexity of smart healthcare business models, different types of attributes can be incorporated into the design of security measures. For instance, the attribute-based encryption (ABE) can be used as an effective cryptographic tool for secure communication in SHSs (Ambrosin et al., 2016). ABE variants such as ciphertext-policy attribute-based encryption (CP-ABE) and key-policy attribute-based encryption (KP-ABE) are explored to protect IoT devices (Bethencourt, Sahai, & Waters, 2007; Goyal, Pandey, Sahai, & Waters, 2006). According to Ambrosin et al. (2016), a secret key represents access policies in the KP-ABE mode. Therefore, users can decrypt the ciphertext whenever the access policy associated with the secret key (policy) can be satisfied by assigned attributes. In contrast, the CP-ABE method enforces access policies on data and associates a set of attributes to the secret key. As a result, a user can decrypt a ciphertext when the key (attributes) satisfies the access policies on the plaintext.

Based on trust relations among known certificate authorities (CAs), public key infrastructures (PKIs) can underpin a multitude of secure, collaborative platforms (Aberer, Datta, & Hauswirth, 2005). A typical PKI authentication scenario is depicted in Fig. 8.12. With a key certificate being created/issued at a CA, clients can securely communicate with each other by sharing public keys for encryption and limiting the access of encrypted contents to private key owners. In addition, a hierarchical trust model is implemented to allow more entities and CAs to participate (Perlman, 1999). Normally hierarchies reflect different security levels, each of which requires certain CAs to respond in a given interaction.

Single sign-on (SSO) has been widely applied to exempt legal users from repeated authentications to potentially remote services (Pashalidis & Mitchell, 2003). This scheme

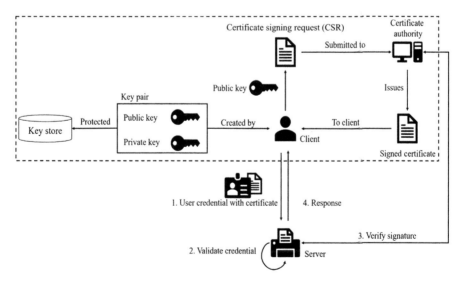

Figure 8.12
PKI certification and authentication.

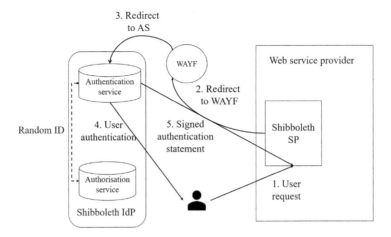

Figure 8.13
Shibboleth components and user authentication (Chadwick & Fatema, 2012).

can be implemented through configuring the Shibboleth system (Chadwick & Fatema, 2012; Watt & Sinnott, 2011). As shown in Fig. 8.13, the SSO process involves at least one identity provider (IdP), service provider (SP), as well as the "where-are-you-from" (WAYF) service. Upon receiving an access request, the SP can redirect the requestor to a WAYF site where he/she can select an IdP to verify the identity. Based on the trust associations among organizations, requested sites should be able to authenticate remote clients based on a local authentication at their home site, and thus enable the same clients to sign in and use multiple services (hosted by different SPs).

8.3.2 Privacy-aware access control

Access control policies are predominantly used to determine "who is allowed to access data and use services." Traditional access control can partially meet the demands in the s-Health context. With the implementation of monitoring, an emergency access control paradigm is demanded to allow save patient lives in some dangerous scenarios. Besides patient-centric methods are studied in smart healthcare. By returning data control back to patients (data owners), patients will be highly motivated to participate in various health-related activities.

8.3.2.1 Patient-centric access control

While using healthcare services, (patient) customers demand to store, use and share health information with their trusted professionals. To encourage their participation, current systems tend to return the control back to users. Here the core idea is to rely on user-centric authentication and authorization for secure data management. In this regard, OpenID and

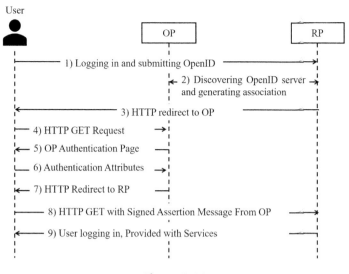

Figure 8.14
OpenID protocol flows.

OAuth can be used together to allow users to be signed in to multiple services with a single identifier and decide whether to authorize specific operations on resources by creating access tokens (Hardt, 2012; Recordon & Reed, 2006). As shown in Fig. 8.14, a typical process should involve at least one user, OpenID provider (OP) and Replaying Party (RP) (Recordon & Reed, 2006). On this basis, OAuth can be implemented among clients, resource owners, resource servers and authorization servers (Hardt, 2012). With this being implemented, resource servers will release online information only when the client presents the verified access tokens by the authorization server (Leiba, 2012).

Google Health and Microsoft HealthVault are featured as user control. Specifically, Google Health users can add their medical information (e.g., history medications, allergies, test results) and define access policies to protect their records at any time. What's more, Google assures that health records will not be shared without users' agreement.[6] Similarly, Microsoft's HealthVault brings users' medical records to an online platform. Through the web-based interface, patients can decide to upload, store in an encrypted database or share health documents with their providers (Gupta, Agrawal, Chhabra, & Dhir, 2016). In the e-health sector, similar access models are developed based on informed consent, one of the essential ethical principles (Kunneman & Montori, 2017; O'Keefe, Greenfield, & Goodchild, 2005). The idea is to let patients decide whether to permit access requests through issuing their consents.

---

[6] Lohr, S. Google and Microsoft Look to Change Health Care, 2007. Retrieved from https://www.nytimes.com/ 2007/08/14/technology/14healthnet.html.

8.3.2.2 Staff access control

The role-based access control (RBAC) model was designed for simplifying permission management by creating roles and permissions (Gilbert, 1995). Due to the flexibility, RBAC has been widely applied in e-health systems (Sahi et al., 2018). As shown in Fig. 8.15, nurses may need the writing privilege to input medical records to the database while reading is not necessary in typical healthcare scenarios. Due to their job contents, both pharmacists and physicians need to access related information before prescribing medicines to patients. In addition, some efforts are made to satisfy ethical and legitimate requirements, for example, as required to implement access control models underpinning clinical treatment and research (Brown, Brown, & Korff, 2010; Sicuranza & Esposito, 2013).

RBAC variants were proposed to satisfy special security demands from different systems. For instance, more powerful authorization can be realized by extending with contextual factors (Bertino, Bonatti, & Ferrari, 2001; Hansen & Oleshchuk, 2003). Considering the discrepancy of "roles" in different contexts, semantic technology was applied to formulate such a policy model (Lu & Sinnott, 2015). For general purposes, attribute-based access control was suggested to address requirements about the subject (user), object (health-related records), action (operations), and environment (accessing time, location, etc.), specified in eXtensible Access Control Markup Language (XACML) (Hu et al., 2013; Lu & Sinnott, 2016). Dealing with heterogeneous information silos, the access control should ideally incorporate inference capabilities rather than purely static description and comparison (Lu, Sinnott, & Verspoor, 2018; Lu, Sinnott, Verspoor, & Parampalli, 2018). As shown in Fig. 8.16, a semantic-enhanced framework enables reasoning on related knowledge formalized into ontology

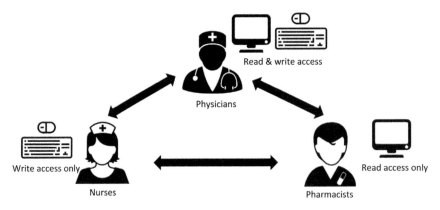

Figure 8.15
Staff access model in healthcare systems (Sahi et al., 2018).

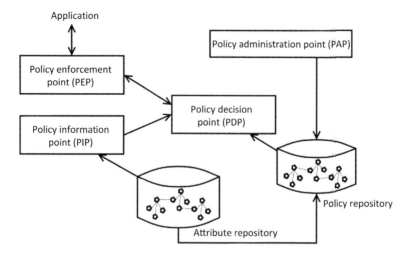

Figure 8.16
Sematic-extended XACML framework.

and semantic rules (Lu & Sinnott, 2018). In addition to deciding the access rights, an obligation component was built on a semantic rule set to infer the level of data disclosure.

8.3.2.3 Break-glass access control

Patient-centric access control is preferred to be used in smart healthcare applications; however, in the situations of emergency, data owners (patients) may not be able to grant access to any doctors for urgent needs. Towards the potential risk, break-glass solutions are introduced as a quick means for extending a person's access rights (Brucker & Petritsch, 2009). Usually, break-glass solutions need to distribute prestaged user accounts in advance. To secure end-to-end communication, Brucker, Petritsch, and Weber (2010) proposed a break-glass solution with ABE techniques being extended. To detect unknown conflicts, a novel break-glass model, Rumpole was formalized in a logic programming language and thus can be extended with reasoning capabilities (Marinovic, Craven, Ma, & Dulay, 2011). As shown in Fig. 8.17, a generic break-the-glass access control architecture (BTG-AC) was proposed within a normal authorization component, that is, policy enforcement point performing as an authentication service provider between users and sensors, and policy decision point making decisions. In the access control module, three types of policies are developed and executed (Maw, Xiao, Christianson, & Malcolm, 2016). Specifically, authorization policies are used to make access decisions, checking if user requests should be permitted or denied; BTG policies are used to perform emergent operations on targeted objects; Obligation policies are used along with authorization and BTG policies in certain situations. For instance, an obligation policy can allow the administrator to take emergent

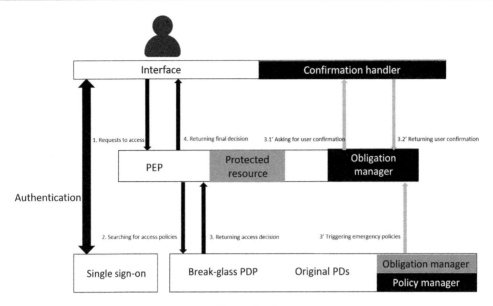

Figure 8.17
Break-glass architecture and message flows.

actions when the "glass is broken," while BTG policies can be defined for emergency situations where urgent access is required.

8.3.3 Anonymization

Privacy preservation is regarded as a personal right to be guaranteed. However, the implementation of monitoring systems may threaten patients' privacy due to unauthorized disclosures of attributes. Aside from patient demands, requirements defined in the ethical and legitimate regulations need to be satisfied in the process of data sharing. For instance, one of the most desirable cases is to ensure no one can be identified from health datasets released for research purposes (Harrelson & Falletta, 2007). When it involves health data analytics, it is necessary to focus on balancing preserving levels and information loss while modifying original values aiming for anonymization.

8.3.3.1 Statistical disclosure control

Statistical disclosure control (SDC) methods offer privacy protection by modifying (identifiable and non-identifiable) attributes at the cost of data utility (Shlomo, 2007). As shown in Fig. 8.18, a Risk-Utility map can be used to describe the trade-off exists between data utility and the privacy preservation: given a maximum tolerable risk level accepted by data custodians (e.g., hospitals) and data subjects (e.g., patients), the optimal SDC strategy should only incur the least information loss (Duncan, Keller-McNulty, & Stokes, 2004).

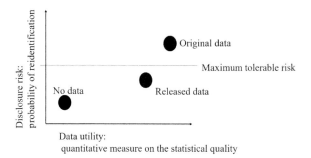

Figure 8.18
Risk-Utility map (Hundepool et al., 2012).

Age	Postcode	Reward
17	3001	1000
19	3002	1200
21	3003	1500
27	3005	5000
29	3117	45,000
34	3128	57,000
45	3159	31,000

Age	Postcode	Reward	
17,27	300*	1000	
17,27	300*	1200	Group 1
17,27	300*	1500	
17,27	300*	5000	
29,45	31**	45,000	
29,45	31**	57,000	Group 2
29,45	31**	31,000	

Figure 8.19
Group privacy in the k-anonymized dataset ($k = 3$).

Under such statistical requirements, k-anonymity and its variants are designed to deliver privacy protection by mitigating reidentification chance. Based on a set of predefined quasi-identifiers, k-anonymity requires any target individuals are obscured with $k-1$ other individuals (Sweeney, 2002). For instance, Fig. 8.19 describes an example scenario where a company payroll implements 3-anonymity. After generalizing atomic items, the original records will be released in two (equivalent) groups. On this basis, sensitive values in the *Reward* column can be hidden from illegal access requests.

While considering threats incurred by homogeneity attacks, methods such as l-diversity were designed to prevent sensitive knowledge disclosure from each equivalence group (Machanavajjhala, Johannes, Daniel, & Muthuramakrishnan, 2007). In other words, sanitized data should ensure that there is "diversity" across the sensitive attributes. This requires each group contains at least "l sensitive attribute types." If the target individual is known falling in the second group, his/her salary level can be inferred relatively high. Furthermore, t-closeness provides finer-grained deidentification by controlling the "closeness" among sensitive attributes within each group (Li, Li, & Venkatasubramanian, 2007). Apart from the protection based on mathematic models, SDC methods can be designed in case anyone collects deidentified information and seek out private information in an on-going "requesting and releasing" scenario. To address this issue, the *m*-invariance model was designed to disallow sensitive attributes updates during a time span (Xiao & Tao, 2007). By tracking the "historical release," τ-safety scheme was designed to adjust attribute combinations in case any disclosure may take place (Anjum & Raschia, 2013).

8.3.3.2 Privacy-preserving big data

Smart healthcare mostly represents a complex system. As a result, the involved activities rely on the integrated analysis on social, economic, political, and cultural information in the healthcare domain. For instance, Marco and Miltiadis (2018) designed an adaptive component by incorporating knowledge discovery into the science research framework. The prototype shows their method empowers the development of patient-centric healthcare with advanced applications, such as personalized medication. In addition, record linkage as a data integration technique has been applied in population-based studies. By comparing individual attributes, records about the same patients can be found and combined as record linkage (or linked records). A typical probabilistic record linkage (PRL) process is shown in Fig. 8.20: by evaluating record pairs against a pre-agreed "threshold", pairwise records can be classified as *Matched*, *Nonmatched*, and *Possibly matched*. In addition, data privacy needs attention to the linkage process (Christen, 2012). Correspondingly,

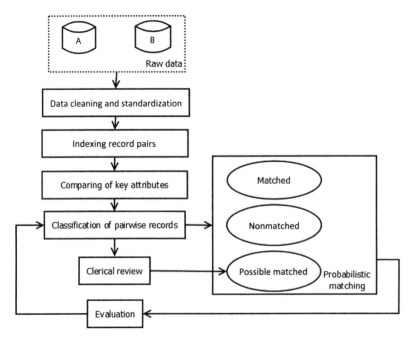

Figure 8.20
Probabilistic record linkage (Schmidlin, Clough-Gorr, & Spoerri, 2015).

privacy-preserving data linkage techniques are developed to match records across databases without revealing confidential information to any external stakeholders (Vatsalan, Sehili, Christen, & Rahm, 2017). Through the implementation of encoding methods on identifiers, high-quality linkage services can be delivered without relying on a "trusted third party" to conduct linkage. Fig. 8.21 depicts the practical model, secure multiparty computation (SMC), which disallows researchers to request the raw data but processed values (Dibben, Elliot, Gowans, Lightfoot, & Data Linkage Centres, 2015). Instead, statistical summaries can be shared among data holders (dashed lines) based on the linkage made with the submitted identifiers (solid lines). In the two-party secure computation protocol, a bloom filter can be used to compare strings and then records (Vatsalan, Christen, & Verykios, 2013). As shown in Fig. 8.22, through exchanging the resultant matrix, it enables similarity calculation based on the "number of edits" (Grannis, Overhage, & McDonald, 2004). To guarantee the privacy and security in results, certain disclosure policies can be added as an extra layer of protection to support SMC models (Durham et al., 2014).

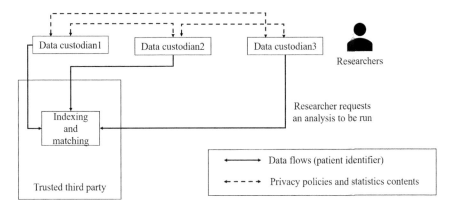

Figure 8.21
Secure multiparty computation linkage (Dibben et al., 2015).

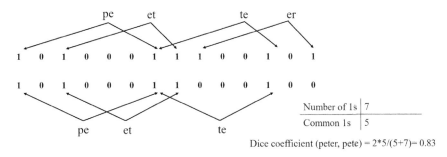

Figure 8.22
An example of bloom filter-based similarity calculation.

8.4 Discussion

Table 8.1 shows a systematic evaluation of selected security and privacy solutions in s-health systems. Specially, all of the key characteristics are identified from the earlier studies on security and privacy protection, as well as techniques implemented in the smart

Table 8.1: Characterization of selected solutions for security and privacy preservation.

	Research issues	Sources	C	A	I	Novelty	Mobility	Complexity	Richness
Authentication	IoT authentication	Rahman et al. (2017)	✓	✓		✓✓	✓✓✓	✓✓	✓
	User authentication	De Luca et al. (2015)	✓	✓		✓✓	✓✓✓	✓	✓
		Murillo-Escobar et al. (2015)	✓	✓	✓	✓✓	✓✓	✓✓	✓✓
		Hejazi et al. (2016)	✓	✓		✓✓✓	✓	✓✓✓	✓✓✓
		Zhang et al. (2018)	✓	✓		✓✓✓	✓	✓	✓
	Distributed authentication	Perlman (1999)	✓		✓	✓	✓	✓	✓
		Pashalidis and Mitchell (2003)	✓		✓	✓	✓✓	✓	✓
		Aberer et al. (2005)	✓		✓	✓	✓	✓	✓
		Goyal et al. (2006)	✓		✓	✓✓	✓	✓✓	✓✓
		Bethencourt et al. (2007)	✓		✓	✓✓	✓	✓✓	✓✓
		Watt and Sinnott (2011)	✓	✓	✓	✓	✓	✓	✓
		Chadwick and Fatema (2012)	✓	✓		✓	✓	✓✓	✓
		Ambrosin et al. (2016)	✓		✓	✓	✓	✓	✓
Privacy-aware access control	Patient-centric access control	O'Keefe et al. (2005)	✓	✓		✓✓	✓✓	✓	✓
		Gupta et al. (2016)	✓	✓		✓✓	✓✓	✓✓	✓
		Kunneman and Montori (2017)	✓	✓	✓	✓✓✓	✓✓✓	✓	✓
	Staff access control	Sicuranza and Esposito (2013)	✓	✓		✓	✓	✓	✓
		Brown et al. (2010)	✓	✓		✓	✓	✓	✓
		Sahi et al. (2018)	✓	✓		✓	✓	✓	✓
		Lu, Sinnott & Verspoor (2018)	✓	✓		✓✓	✓	✓✓	✓✓✓
	Break-glass access control	Brucker et al. (2010)	✓	✓		✓✓	✓✓	✓	✓
		Marinovic et al. (2011)	✓	✓		✓✓	✓✓	✓✓	✓
		Maw et al. (2016)	✓	✓		✓✓	✓✓	✓✓	✓✓
Anonymization	Statistical disclosure control	Sweeney (2002)	✓			✓	✓	✓✓	✓
		Machanavajjhala et al. (2007)	✓			✓	✓	✓✓	✓✓
		Xiao and Tao (2007)	✓			✓	✓	✓✓	✓✓
		Anjum & Raschia (2013)	✓			✓	✓	✓✓✓	✓✓
	Privacy-preserving big data	Grannis et al. (2004)	✓			✓	✓	✓✓	✓
		Durham et al. (2014)	✓			✓✓	✓	✓✓	✓✓✓
		Dibben et al. (2015)	✓			✓	✓	✓	✓

cities. The CIA concepts on the left side stand for the general security and privacy requirements. As for the compliance with s-health services, we select *Novelty, Mobility, Complexity,* and *Richness* as the indicators of assessing related solutions. Depending on the requirements such as "less utility but strong security," stakeholders can decide to configure which solutions in the system for security risk mitigation. A reliable solution (combination) should cover all three aspects—*Authentication, Access control, Anonymization,* and jointly satisfy the CIA requirements. For each solution, more ✓ showing in one cell means better performance in one certain aspect. As the study continues, Table 8.1 can be certainly enriched within multiple dimensions, such as considering patients' social awareness (e.g., *Immersion* and *Interaction*) and the *Smartness* of methods, depending on to what extents services can be enhanced by using machine learning technologies. Individuals' privacy concerns may cause different expectations. As a result, we suggest it should be considered while assessing the method *Effectiveness.*

8.5 Conclusions and open research issues in future

The adoption of sensors and mobile technologies leads to the provision of healthcare services in a pervasive manner. Through analyzing related concepts of smart city, electronic health (e-health), and mobile health (m-health), it is clear to see smart health (s-health) as a subfield of smart cities, keeping certain characteristics of e-health and m-health frameworks. As health-related activities emerge with ICT applications, it is essential to design the security and privacy solutions accordingly. Existing studies on authentication, access control, and anonymization can generally secure the access to and use of health records while special considerations on "smart features" should be addressed as well. Considering customer trust is intertwined with service quality and privacy concerns, this chapter selectively reviews security and privacy-preserving solutions developed in s-health contexts, and evaluates the potentials of satisfying privacy requirements as well as the assurance of service quality in a data-rich world. Future studies are still necessary for improving current solutions:

1. Processing a huge amount of data about home facilities, traffic, medical cares, and human information, data analytical methods need to be lightweight so as to provide seamless, real-time services. In terms of security and privacy, a highly efficient cryptographic algorithm would be rather desired while exchanging patients' information among platforms—it can guarantee the confidentiality and integrity at a minimal computation cost.
2. Making policies to restrict data collection by sensors and other IoT devices is always seen as a security procedure in smart cities. Sensors are widely deployed to collect patient information, which is then used for performing online data analysis. However, the majority of such data contains personal information and sensitive attributes, which could cause serious privacy issues. In addition to anonymizing personal records, government policies defined for increasing transparency can help strike a balance between benefits and security risks (Visvizi, Lytras, Damiani, & Mathkour, 2018).

3. The establishment of smart health systems relies on the sensing devices usually deployed in the open environment where numerous security risks exist. Therefore, it is essential to design a framework to assess and mitigate potential threats. This can benefit a great number of patients who choose the provided services. However, due to the heterogeneity of information collected by sensors, it is challenging to conceptualize such a knowledge model defining all possible risks and factors that are relevant to the evaluation. Besides, developing techniques for mitigating each treat model is not efficient. Ideally, techniques can be used in combinations to ensure security and privacy preservation in s-health applications (Lytras & Visvizi, 2018).

4. People are always in the center of smart cities (Visvizi & Lytras, 2018). When it comes to health data, patients should be given the rights of deciding with whom their data are shared and how it will be used. Their decisions will impact the quality of s-health services, and in return, their experience may continuously affect their choices. Therefore, the first step of designing security and privacy solutions is to understand individuals' privacy concerns about data exchange and services in smart health systems. The incorporation of these subjective factors to the model (suggested in the last point) can guarantee the correctness of solution formation.

8.6 Teaching assignments

- Q1: In addition to the privacy issues mentioned, what potential risks have you found in existing SHSs? Please discuss in groups and list three to five examples.
- Q2: Based on the answer of Q1, please rank the issues according to their potential impacts and explain why.
- Q3: To the issue ranked at the first place, is there any solutions have been developed can deal with it? If so, please discuss. If not, can you suggest a possible solution?
- Q4: Can you distinguish the concepts "Mobile Health (m-health)", "Smart Health (s-health)" and "Electronic Health (e-health)"? Explain their similarities and differences in your words.
- Q5: Can you summarize the security and privacy requirements in each of fields mentioned in Q4?

References

Aberer, K., Datta, A., & Hauswirth, M. (2005). A decentralized public key infrastructure for customer-to-customer e-commerce. *International Journal of Business Process Integration and Management, 1*, 26–33. (LSIR-ARTICLE-2005-001).

Ambhati, R. K., Kota, V. K., Chaudhari, S. Y., & Jain, M. (March 2017). *E-IoT: Context-oriented mote prioritization for emergency IoT networks. International conference on wireless communications, signal processing and networking (WiSPNET)* (pp. 1897–1903). IEEE.

Ambrosin, M., Anzanpour, A., Conti, M., Dargahi, T., Moosavi, S. R., Rahmani, A. M., & Liljeberg, P. (2016). On the feasibility of attribute-based encryption on internet of things devices. *IEEE Micro, 36*(6), 25−35.

Amendola, S., Lodato, R., Manzari, S., Occhiuzzi, C., & Marrocco, G. (2014). RFID technology for IoT-based personal healthcare in smart spaces. *IEEE Internet of Things Journal, 1*(2), 144−152.

Amrutha, K. R., Haritha, S. M., Haritha Vasu, M., Jensy, A. J., & Charly, J. K. (2017). IOT based medical home. *Network, 1*, 6.

Anjum, A., & Raschia, G. (March 2013). *Anonymizing sequential releases under arbitrary updates. Proceedings of the joint EDBT/ICDT 2013 workshops* (pp. 145−154). ACM.

Baig, M. M., & Gholamhosseini, H. (2013). Smart health monitoring systems: An overview of design and modeling. *Journal of Medical Systems, 37*(2), 9898.

Bertino, E., Bonatti, P. A., & Ferrari, E. (2001). TRBAC: A temporal role-based access control model. *ACM Transactions on Information and System Security (TISSEC), 4*(3), 191−233.

Bethencourt, J., Sahai, A., & Waters, B. (May 2007). *Ciphertext-policy attribute-based encryption. IEEE symposium on security and privacy 2007 (SP'07)* (pp. 321−334). IEEE.

Brown, I., Brown, L., & Korff, D. (2010). Using NHS patient data for research without consent. *Law, Innovation and Technology, 2*(2), 219−258.

Brucker, A. D., & Petritsch, H. (June 2009). *Extending access control models with break-glass. Proceedings of the 14th ACM symposium on access control models and technologies* (pp. 197−206). ACM.

Brucker, A. D., Petritsch, H., & Weber, S. G. (April 2010). *Attribute-based encryption with break-glass. IFIP international workshop on information security theory and practices* (pp. 237−244). Berlin, Heidelberg: Springer.

Catarinucci, L., De Donno, D., Mainetti, L., Palano, L., Patrono, L., Stefanizzi, M. L., & Tarricone, L. (2015). An IoT-aware architecture for smart healthcare systems. *IEEE Internet of Things Journal, 2*(6), 515−526.

Chadwick, D. W., & Fatema, K. (2012). A privacy preserving authorization system for the cloud. *Journal of Computer and System Sciences, 78*(5), 1359−1373.

Cherdantseva, Y., & Hilton, J. (2013). *A reference model of information assurance and security. 8th international conference on availability, reliability and security (ARES)* (pp. 546−555). IEEE.

Christen, P. (2012). *Data matching: Concepts and techniques for record linkage, entity resolution, and duplicate detection*. Springer Science & Business Media.

Cody-Allen, E., & Kishore, R. (April 2006). *An extension of the UTAUT model with e-quality, trust, and satisfaction constructs. Proceedings of the 2006 ACM SIGMIS CPR conference on computer personnel research: Forty-four years of computer personnel research: achievements, challenges & the future* (pp. 82−89). ACM.

Dafa-Alla, A. F., Kim, E. H., Ryu, K. H., & Heo, Y. J. (2005). *PRBAC: An extended role based access control for privacy preserving data mining. Fourth annual ACIS international conference on computer and information science* (pp. 68−73). IEEE.

De Luca, A., Hang, A., Von Zezschwitz, E., & Hussmann, H. (April 2015). *I feel like I'm taking selfies all day: Towards understanding biometric authentication on smartphones. Proceedings of the 33rd annual ACM conference on human factors in computing systems* (pp. 1411−1414). ACM.

Demirkan, H. (2013). A smart healthcare systems framework. *It Professional, 15*(5), 38−45.

Dibben, C., Elliot, M., Gowans, H., Lightfoot, D., & Data Linkage Centres. (2015). The data linkage environment. *Methodological Developments in Data Linkage*, 36−62.

Domingue, J., Galis, A., Gavras, A., et al. (Eds.), (2011). *The future internet*. Berlin, Heidelberg: Springer. Available from https://doi.org/10.1007/978-3-642-20898-0.

Duncan, G. T., Keller-McNulty, S. A., & Stokes, S. L. (2004). Database security and confidentiality: Examining disclosure risk vs. data utility through the RU confidentiality map. National Institute of Statistical Sciences. *Technical Repor, 142*, 1−24.

Durham, E. A., Kantarcioglu, M., Xue, Y., Toth, C., Kuzu, M., & Malin, B. (2014). Composite bloom filters for secure record linkage. *IEEE Transactions on Knowledge and Data Engineering, 26*(12), 2956−2968.

Fairchild, A. L., Gable, L., Gostin, L. O., Bayer, R., Sweeney, P., & Janssen, R. S. (2007). Public goods, private data: HIV and the history, ethics, and uses of identifiable public health information. *Public Health Reports, 122*(1_suppl), 7−15.

Firth-Cozens, J. (2004). Organisational trust: The keystone to patient safety. *BMJ Quality & Safety*, *13*(1), 56−61.

Ghamari, M., Janko, B., Sherratt, R. S., Harwin, W., Piechockic, R., & Soltanpur, C. (2016). A survey on wireless body area networks for ehealthcare systems in residential environments. *Sensors*, *16*(6), 831.

Gilbert, M. D. M. (1995). *An examination of federal and commercial access control policy needs. National computer security conference, 1993 (16th) Proceedings: Information systems security: User choices* (p. 107) DIANE Publishing.

Gope, P., & Hwang, T. (2016). BSN-Care: A secure IoT-based modern healthcare system using body sensor network. *IEEE Sensors Journal*, *16*(5), 1368−1376.

Goyal, V., Pandey, O., Sahai, A., & Waters, B. (October 2006). *Attribute-based encryption for fine-grained access control of encrypted data. Proceedings of the 13th ACM conference on Computer and communications security* (pp. 89−98). ACM.

Grannis, S. J., Overhage, J. M., & McDonald, C. J. (2004). Real world performance of approximate string comparators for use in patient matching. *In Medinfo*, 43−47.

Grossman, R. L., Heath, A. P., Ferretti, V., Varmus, H. E., Lowy, D. R., Kibbe, W. A., & Staudt, L. M. (2016). Toward a shared vision for cancer genomic data. *New England Journal of Medicine*, *375*(12), 1109−1112.

Gupta, P., Agrawal, D., Chhabra, J., & Dhir, P. K. (March 2016). *IoT based smart healthcare kit. International conference on computational techniques in information and communication technologies (ICCTICT)* (pp. 237−242). IEEE.

Hansen, F., & Oleshchuk, V. (2003). SRBAC: A spatial role-based access control model for mobile systems. In *Proceedings of the 7th nordic workshop on secure IT systems (NORDSEC'03)* (pp. 129−141).

Hardt, D. (2012). *The OAuth 2.0 authorisation framework*. Technical Report.

Harrelson, J. M., & Falletta, J. M. (2007). *The privacy rule (HIPAA) as it relates to clinical research. Cancer clinical trials: Proactive strategies* (pp. 199−207). Boston, MA: Springer.

Hejazi, M., Al-Haddad, S. A. R., Singh, Y. P., Hashim, S. J., & Aziz, A. F. A. (2016). ECG biometric authentication based on non-fiducial approach using kernel methods. *Digital Signal Processing*, *52*, 72−86.

Hu, V. C., Ferraiolo, D., Kuhn, R., Friedman, A. R., Lang, A. J., Cogdell, M. M., & Scarfone, K. (2013). *Guide to attribute-based access control (ABAC) definition and considerations*. NIST Special Publication, 800(162).

Hundepool, A., Domingo-Ferrer, J., Franconi, L., Giessing, S., Nordholt, E. S., Spicer, K., & De Wolf, P. P. (2012). *Statistical disclosure control*. John Wiley & Sons.

Khan, M., Jilani, M. T., Khan, M. K., & Ahmed, M. B. (2017). *A security framework for wireless body area network based smart healthcare system. International conference for young researchers in informatics* (pp. 80−85). Kaunas, Lithuania: Mathematics and Engineering (ICYRIME).

Kostadinovska, A., de Vries, G. J., Geleijnse, G., & Zdravkova, K. (2015). *Employing personal health records for population health management. ICT innovations 2014* (pp. 65−74). Cham: Springer.

Kumar, R. S., & Saxena, A. (January 2011). *Data integrity proofs in cloud storage. 3rd international conference on communication systems and networks (COMSNETS)* (pp. 1−4). IEEE.

Kunneman, M., & Montori, V. M. (2017). When patient-centred care is worth doing well: Informed consent or shared decision-making. *BMJ Quality & Safety*, *26*, 522−524.

Leiba, B. (2012). Oauth web authorization protocol. *IEEE Internet Computing*, *16*(1), 74−77.

Li, N., Li, T., & Venkatasubramanian, S. (April 2007). *t-closeness: Privacy beyond k-anonymity and l-diversity. IEEE 23rd international conference on data engineering 2007 (ICDE 2007)* (pp. 106−115). IEEE.

Lohr, S. (August 14, 2007). Google and Microsoft Look to Change Health CareWater aerobics. Retrieved from http://www.buzzle.comhttps://www.nytimes.com/2007/08/14/technology/14healthnet.html.

Lowrance, W. (2003). Learning from experience: Privacy and the secondary use of data in health research. *Journal of Health Services Research & Policy*, *8*(1_suppl), 2−7.

Lu, Y., & Sinnott, R. O. (2015). *Semantic security for e-Health: A case study in enhanced access control. Ubiquitous intelligence and computing and 2015 IEEE 12th international conference on autonomic and trusted computing and 2015 IEEE 15th international conference on scalable computing and communications and its associated workshops (UIC-ATC-ScalCom)* (pp. 407−414). IEEE.

Lu, Y., & Sinnott, R. O. (August 2016). *Semantic-based privacy protection of electronic health records for collaborative research. IEEE trustcom/BigDataSE/ISPA* (pp. 519−526). IEEE.

Lu, Y., & Sinnott, R. O. (2018). Semantic privacy-preserving framework for electronic health record linkage. *Telematics and Informatics, 35*(4), 737−752.

Lu, Y., Sinnott, R. O., & Verspoor, K. (2018). *Semantic-based policy composition for privacy-demanding data linkage. 2018 17th IEEE international conference on trust, security and privacy in computing and communications/12th IEEE international conference on big data science and engineering (TrustCom/BigDataSE)* (pp. 348−359). IEEE.

Lu, Y., Sinnott, R. O., Verspoor, K., & Parampalli, U. (2018). *Privacy-preserving access control in electronic health record linkage. 2018 17th IEEE international conference on trust, security and privacy in computing and communications* (pp. 1079−1090). IEEE.

Lytras, M., & Visvizi, A. (2018). Who uses smart city services and what to make of it: Toward interdisciplinary smart cities research. *Sustainability, 10*(6), 1998.

Machanavajjhala, A., Johannes G., Daniel K., & Muthuramakrishnan V. (2007). l-Diversity: Privacy beyond k-anonymity. In *ACM transactions on knowledge discovery from data (TKDD) 1.1* (p. 3).

Malik, S., & Park, S.-H. (2008). Integrated service platform for personalized exercise & nutrition management. In 10th international conference on advanced communication technology 2008 (ICACT 2008) (Vol. 3, pp. 2144−2148). IEEE.

Marco, S., & Miltiadis, L. (2018). Applied data science in patient-centric healthcare: Adaptive analytic systems for empowering physicians and patients. *Telematics and Informatics, 35*(4), 643−653. Available from https://doi.org/10.1016/j.tele.2018.04.002.

Marinovic, S., Craven, R., Ma, J., & Dulay, N. (June 2011). *Rumpole: A flexible break-glass access control model. Proceedings of the 16th ACM symposium on access control models and technologies* (pp. 73−82). ACM.

Maw, H. A., Xiao, H., Christianson, B., & Malcolm, J. A. (2016). BTG-AC: Break-the-glass access control model for medical data in wireless sensor networks. *IEEE Journal of Biomedical and Health Informatics, 20*(3), 763−774.

Murillo-Escobar, M. A., Cruz-Hernández, C., Abundiz-Pérez, F., & López-Gutiérrez, R. M. (2015). A robust embedded biometric authentication system based on fingerprint and chaotic encryption. *Expert Systems with Applications, 42*(21), 8198−8211.

Nguyen, L., Bellucci, E., & Nguyen, L. T. (2014). Electronic health records implementation: An evaluation of information system impact and contingency factors. *International Journal of Medical Informatics, 83*(11), 779−796.

O'Keefe, C. M., & Connolly, C. J. (2010). Privacy and the use of health data for research. *Medical Journal of Australia, 193*(9), 537−541.

O'Keefe, C. M., Greenfield, P., & Goodchild, A. (2005). A decentralized approach to electronic consent and health information access control. *Journal of Research and Practice in Information Technology, 37*(2), 161.

Pashalidis, A., & Mitchell, C. J. (October 2003). *Single sign-on using trusted platforms. International conference on information security* (pp. 54−68). Berlin, Heidelberg: Springer.

Prakash, R., & Balaji Ganesh, A. (2019). *Internet of Things (IoT) enabled wireless sensor network for physiological data acquisition. International conference on intelligent computing and applications* (pp. 163−170). Singapore: Springer.

Prasser, F., Kohlmayer, F., Spengler, H., & Kuhn, K. A. (2018). A scalable and pragmatic method for the safe sharing of high-quality health data. *IEEE Journal of Biomedical and Health Informatics, 22*(2), 611−622.

Provost, F., & Fawcett, T. (2013). *Data science for business: What you need to know about data mining and data-analytic thinking.* O'Reilly Media.

Perlman, R. (1999). An overview of PKI trust models. *IEEE Network, 13*(6), 38−43.

Rahman, F., Bhuiyan, M. Z. A., & Ahamed, S. I. (2017). A privacy preserving framework for RFID based healthcare systems. *Future Generation Computer Systems, 72*, 339−352.

Recordon, D., & Reed, D. (November 2006). *OpenID 2.0: A platform for user-centric identity management. Proceedings of the 2nd ACM workshop on digital identity management* (pp. 11−16). ACM.

Sahi, M. A., Abbas, H., Saleem, K., Yang, X., Derhab, A., Orgun, M. A., & Yaseen, A. (2018). Privacy preservation in e-healthcare environments: State of the art and future directions. *IEEE Access*, *6*, 464−478.

Sakr, S., & Elgammal, A. (2016). Towards a comprehensive data analytics framework for smart healthcare services. *Big Data Research*, *4*, 44−58.

Samonas, S., & Coss, D. (2014). The CIA strikes back: Redefining confidentiality, integrity and availability in security. *Journal of Information System Security*, *10*(3).

Schmidlin, K., Clough-Gorr, K. M., & Spoerri, A. (2015). Privacy preserving probabilistic record linkage (P3RL): A novel method for linking existing health-related data and maintaining participant confidentiality. *BMC Medical Research Methodology*, *15*(1), 46.

Shlomo, N. (2007). Statistical disclosure control methods for census frequency tables. *International Statistical Review*, *75*(2), 199−217.

Sicuranza, M., & Esposito, A. (December 2013). *An access control model for easy management of patient privacy in EHR systems. 8th international conference for Internet technology and secured transactions (ICITST)* (pp. 463−470). IEEE.

Solanas, A., Patsakis, C., Conti, M., Vlachos, I. S., Ramos, V., Falcone, F., & Martinez-Balleste, A. (2014). Smart health: A context-aware health paradigm within smart cities. *IEEE Communications Magazine*, *52*(8), 74−81.

Sweeney, L. (2002). k-Anonymity: A model for protecting privacy. *International Journal of Uncertainty, Fuzziness and Knowledge-Based Systems*, *10*(05), 557−570.

Takabi, H., Joshi, J. B., & Ahn, G. J. (2010). Security and privacy challenges in cloud computing environments. *IEEE Security & Privacy*, *6*, 24−31.

Vatsalan, D., Christen, P., & Verykios, V. S. (2013). A taxonomy of privacy-preserving record linkage techniques. *Information Systems*, *38*(6), 946−969.

Vatsalan, D., Sehili, Z., Christen, P., & Rahm, E. (2017). *Privacy-preserving record linkage for big data: Current approaches and research challenges. Handbook of Big Data technologies* (pp. 851−895). Cham: Springer.

Visvizi, A., & Lytras, M. D. (2018). Rescaling and refocusing smart cities research: From mega cities to smart villages. *Journal of Science and Technology Policy Management*, *9*(2), 134−145.

Visvizi, A., Lytras, M. D., Damiani, E., & Mathkour, H. (2018). Policy making for smart cities: Innovation and social inclusive economic growth for sustainability. *Journal of Science and Technology Policy Management*, *9*(2), 126−133.

Wang, H., Lee, M. K., & Wang, C. (1998). Consumer privacy concerns about Internet marketing. *Communications of the ACM*, *41*(3), 63−70.

Wang, X., Gui, Q., Liu, B., Jin, Z., & Chen, Y. (2014). Enabling smart personalized healthcare: A hybrid mobile-cloud approach for ECG telemonitoring. *IEEE Journal of Biomedical and Health Informatics*, *18* (3), 739−745.

Watt, J., & Sinnott, R. O. (May 2011). *Supporting federated multi-authority security models. Proceedings of the 2011 11th IEEE/ACM international symposium on cluster, cloud and grid computing* (pp. 620−621). IEEE Computer Society.

Xiao, X., & Tao, Y. (2007). *M-invariance: towards privacy preserving re-publication of dynamic datasets. Proceedings of the 2007 ACM SIGMOD international conference on Management of data* (pp. 689−700). ACM, June.

Zhang, Y., Gravina, R., Lu, H., Villari, M., & Fortino, G. (2018). PEA: Parallel electrocardiogram-based authentication for smart healthcare systems. *Journal of Network and Computer Applications*, *117*, 10−16.

Zhao, X., You, Z., Zhao, Z., Chen, D., & Peng, F. (2010). *Availability based trust model of clusters for MANET. 7th international conference on service systems and service management (ICSSSM)* (pp. 1−6). IEEE, June.

Further reading

Yue, C. (2013). *The devil is phishing: Rethinking web single sign-on systems security. Presented at 6th USENIX workshop on large-scale exploits and emergent threats.* Washington, DC: USENIX.

CHAPTER 9

Cloud-based health monitoring framework using smart sensors and smartphone

Abdulhamit Subasi[1], Lejla Bandic[2] and Saeed Mian Qaisar[3]

[1]Information Systems Department, College of Engineering, Effat University, Jeddah, Saudi Arabia, [2]International Burch University, Faculty of Engineering and Information Technologies, Francuske Revolucije bb. Ilidza, Sarajevo, Bosnia and Herzegovina, [3]Electrical and Computer Engineering Department, College of Engineering, Effat University, Jeddah, Saudi Arabia

9.1 Introduction

Advances in the smart device market including of smart sensors, smartphones, and tablets have widely began employing sensors to give the consumer an intuitive feeling of virtual environment. The role of wearable devices is influencing the smart sensor data for monitoring biomedical signals (Lytras et al., 2016). Within the last decade, clinically related wearables involved devices such as stethoscope, blood pressure monitors, Holter electrocardiogram (ECG) recorder, and wearable electroencephalogram (EEG) devices. Even though this trend remains even today, wearable design companies have created innovative devices and techniques for collecting and analyzing body signals without governing approvals. Hence, biomedical signals collected from wearable sensors empower the real-time implementation of mobile-monitoring of people with chronic diseases. Moreover, most of these biomedical signals have clinical implications from a disorder or disease supervision viewpoint (Athavale & Krishnan, 2017).

Although innovative biomedical signal recording devices are being employed in the hospitals and home-healthcare services, to help doctors in their decisions; modern wireless body sensors have opened a potential area for wearable devices that enable remote healthcare monitoring, especially for elderly citizens (Celler & Sparks, 2015; Mihajlović, Grundlehner, Vullers, & Penders, 2015). The successful implementation of wearable technologies has also encouraged other markets to locate themselves accordingly such as wearable sensor-based fabric design (Athavale & Krishnan, 2017).

In developed countries, the decreasing fertility and increasing long life rates contributed to elderly populations and accordingly increased medical needs (Anderson & Hussey, 2001). If healthcare can be provided remotely and the patient can be monitored regularly without

Innovation in Health Informatics.
DOI: https://doi.org/10.1016/B978-0-12-819043-2.00009-5

going to hospitals, costly medical cares can be eliminated. Furthermore, there is a big population which cannot take a better healthcare since they are living in rural communities, especially in developing countries. Their healthcare quality can be better quality if the doctor can be "brought" to their living environment through the assistance of information and communication technologies (ICT). In this way, researchers in biomedical engineering are dealing with to implement a cloud-based computing framework which is able to collect people's biomedical data and process them (Grand Challenges—14 Grand Challenges for Engineering, n.d.). Because of this purpose, new ideas and techniques are utilized, such as Body Area Network and cloud-based mobile healthcare (Xia, Asif, & Zhao, 2013).

Recently, there are several developments in biomedical equipment and healthcare technologies to accomplish the needs of current healthcare diagnosis and treatment. Although the innovative medical equipment in healthcare centers delivers quick and precise analysis, there is a need of continuous real-time patient monitoring and elderly people particularly for chronic diseases (Chiauzzi, Rodarte, & DasMahapatra, 2015). Cloud-based mobile healthcare monitoring (CBMHM) devices play a crucial role in the patient monitoring and analysis of the collected biomedical signals. Real-time patient monitoring framework collect the health feedback of persons continuously to investigate the risk associated with critical health circumstances (Pandey, Voorsluys, Niu, Khandoker, & Buyya, 2012). In recent years, sensor-based mobile patient monitoring has taken enormous popularity in personalized healthcare frameworks because of the connectivity of cloud server and sensing equipment (Catarinucci et al., 2015). CBMHM has evolved as a main

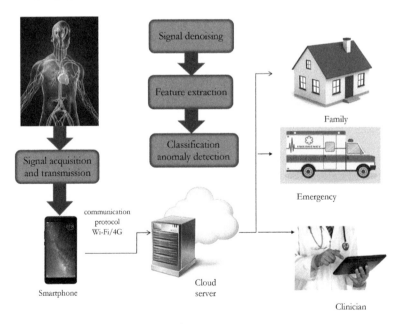

Figure 9.1
A framework for cloud-based mobile healthcare monitoring.

patient monitoring model in this era (Wang, Gui, Liu, Chen, & Jin, 2013). Fig. 9.1 shows the cloud-based mobile patient monitoring for medical diagnosis and treatment. In this framework, mobile devices collect the biomedical signals continuously from different smart sensors and acquiring devices to inform emergency, clinician and patient's family for any emergency cases through internet connection using mobile devices (Hsieh & Hsu, 2012). In CBMHM approach, mobile devices collect the biomedical signal such as ECG or EEG and send acquired data to the cloud. The cloud processing power is employed during the implementation of algorithms such as machine learning algorithms and data mining techniques (Wang, Gui, Liu, Jin, & Chen, 2014). Several signal processing and machine learning algorithms can be employed to analyze the biomedical signals for signal recognition. Shen et al. (2010) employed a cloud-based electroencephalograph (EEG) signal analysis, in which feature extraction and support vector machine (SVM) classifications are utilized to recognize brain disorders. An individual ECG monitoring system has been employed to carry out artificial intelligence-based ECG signal analysis and transmitting the data to the cloud (Atoui, Télisson, Fyan, & Rubel, 2008). Cloud-based congestive heart failure (CHF) recognition methods have become popular to monitor the patient with cardiac diseases (Melillo, Orrico, Scala, Crispino, & Pecchia, 2015; Venkatesan, Karthigaikumar, & Satheeskumaran, 2018). In this study, mobile cloud-based health monitoring framework is presented for the risk assessment chronic disorders such as CHF or epileptic seizure using ECG or EEG signals. CHF happens in subject because of the inadequate blood supply to heart muscles by the coronary arteries.

CBMHM system is supported by smart sensors, smartphones, personal digital assistants, and cloud computing (Kay, Santos, & Takane, 2011). The mobile health includes the utilization of a mobile phone's services, Bluetooth technology, global positioning system (GPS), general packet radio service, and 3G and 4G mobile telecommunications systems. Based on these capabilities, sensors can acquire biomedical signals but cannot process, analyze, and transmit these signals without using a mobile device and a relevant application (Guzik & Malik, 2016). Moreover, it turn out to be a prominent research area due to its noteworthy contributions in human-centered areas of a study aiming to improve the quality of life, contribute to the safety, transportation and health in smart cities and smart villages, and help policy-makers react effectively to improve the qualification of services (Mshali et al., 2018; Lytras & Visvizi, 2018; Spruit & Lytras, 2018).

Nowadays there is a significant growth of patients with chronic diseases such as brain disorders and CHF. Some disorders such as epileptic seizures occur randomly and are hard to predict at the medium and long run (Menshawy, Benharref, & Serhani, 2015). The appropriate method for detecting epileptic seizures is to monitor the patient continuously. To deal with the exponential rise in population suffering from life-long disorders such as epilepsy or CHF and their relevant costs, several countries decided to shift into cloud-based mobile health monitoring systems. In these frameworks, smart sensors and mobile devices are used as the main processing module. This permit long-term monitoring chronic disorders and decrease healthcare costs, as patients live in their custom environments and take professional healthcare services. The new trend of cloud-based mobile patient monitoring services has become possible, because of the magnificent developments in smart wearable sensors, mobile sensing devices, and smartphones alongside wireless and cellular communication networks. To collect different health-related biomedical signals, there are a huge number of precise, wireless, and smart sensors. These sensors can be integrated easily to a mobile smartphone to create a vital pillar for the adoption and development of an efficient cloud-based mobile health monitoring system. A smart sensor precisely acquires biomedical signals directly from the patient's body and transmits the acquired data to the mobile smartphone. Then the mobile smartphone sends the collected data to the cloud to continuously check the status of patient. In any emergency case, the application on cloud server sends information to the emergency department, clinician, and the family of the patient (Serhani, El Menshawy, & Benharref, 2016).

This chapter is focused on the employment of market-ready devices for biomedical signal monitoring in a cloud-based mobile environment. Typical biomedical signals taken from wearables include ECG and EEG. The presented framework is shown in Fig. 9.1 composed of front-end part (sensors and smartphone) and back-end part (cloud). The front-end part composed of two modules: (1) signal acquisition and (2) transmission module. The back-end part contains three modules: (1) preprocessing module; (2) feature extraction module; and (3) classification module. The smartphone is connected to the cloud via appropriate communication protocols.

9.2 Background and literature review

Continuous recording and monitoring of chronic disorders such as heart failure and epileptic seizure can be done easily with sophisticated mobile sensors when wirelessly connected to smartphones anywhere and anytime. The smart health approaches which are utilizing both vital signs and electrical activities acquired by ECG and EEG devices can be justified by the definite requirements when monitoring these vital signs (Serhani et al., 2016). The cloud healthcare monitoring has several imperative features. First, it can be retrieved employing any mobile device from anywhere. Second, the cost of cloud computing is significantly dropped based on the pay-per-usage scheme. Third, computing resources are utilized in an elastic way so that additional resources can be utilized once they are required. Furthermore, the cloud-computing system is geographically scalable. Fourth, maintenance and expansion of cloud software has become more reliable, easier, and safer (Xia et al., 2013). Numerous cloud-based healthcare systems have been proposed before. Hoang and Chen (2010) developed a mobile cloud for assistive healthcare framework for assistive healthcare. McGregor, Heath, and Wei (2005) implemented a web service architecture that enables real-time physical data transmission for local and remote Neonatal Intensive Care. They implemented a cloud-based Software-as-a-Service and Data-as-a-Service approach for remote real-time patient monitoring to help clinical research. Eren, Subasi, and Coskun (2008) developed a telemedicine application using mobile device to collect, analyze, distribute, and use medical diagnostics information from multiple knowledge sources and areas of expertise. In this medical decision support system, a JAVA-based application is created as a prototype using mobile device was implemented. Literature review is divided into two sections that are ECG in mobile healthcare services and EEG in mobile healthcare services.

9.2.1 Electrocardiogram in cloud-based mobile healthcare

The ECG represents the recording of electrical activities originated from heart on the body surface. ECG includes acquisition of electrical signals produced by heart muscles throughout its beating activity, by utilizing electrodes located over specific areas on the human chest (Athavale & Krishnan, 2017). The numerous concepts including the classification of a variety of waves, defining a number of the standard recording sites using the arms and legs, and creating the initial theoretical assemble through which the heart is modeled as a single time varying dipole, were introduced by Einthoven (1903). To trace an ECG waveform, a differential recording among two points on the body surface is performed. By convention, each differential recording is called as a lead (Berbari, 2000).

The ECG signal is the most vital tool of every day clinical practice. The scientific improvements in electrocardiography have been considerably accelerated with the contribution of computers, integrated circuits, and the internet. Moreover, the improvement in the ECG turn out to be possible with the involvement of wireless technologies for communication and networking of mobile and internet-based cloud computing and of a diversity of innovative materials for ECG sensors. Currently, there exist different tiny devices that can acquire, record, monitor, and transmit ECG signals to a cloud. These new devices permit to noninvasively acquire and store ECG signals over a much longer period when compared to standard Holter recorders. Notably, these devices can collect other vital signals or information, such as respiration rate, activity level, body position, skin temperature, or geolocation, besides the ECG (Guzik & Malik, 2016).

Clinical biomedical signals are always thought as a gold standard for diagnosing diseases and disorders. Clinical biomedical signals are artifact and noise free and during the signal acquisition, they are filtered and analyzed by experienced technicians before sending it to the consulting physician. To achieve a more general viewpoint about a patient's vital signals in more complex biomedical signal monitoring applications, it is needed to utilize wearable sensors and mobile devices for the continuous analysis and assessment of chronic disorders with long-term electrical activity of heart and brain. But this might lose out on doctor's existence and judgment that is required in disease prognosis. This can be eliminated by employing cloud services and computing by establishing a monitoring framework between patients and physicians. Furthermore, though some of the currently existing wearable devices can acquire biomedical signals from subjects, their utilization by physicians is rather limited since the quality of the data acquired is not confident. Besides, the data produced from these devices provide less interpretation to the users. Different start-ups research institutions have realized these gaps and started to develop vital signals monitoring applications. Some prominent wearables in the market already exist such as Muse (MUSE TM | Meditation Made Easy, n.d.), Epoc + + (Homepage—Emotiv, n.d.), Myo Controller (Myo Gesture Control Armband, n.d.), and GE's Holter ECG (GE Healthcare | Home | GE Healthcare, n.d.) to monitor biomedical signals. For instance, a sleep monitoring application for Apnea patients can be implemented using the 14-channel Epoc + + headset (Athavale & Krishnan, 2017).

In the literature of smart health monitoring systems, there are many exciting studies that led to the emergence of several architectures, solutions, and frameworks. In smart health monitoring systems, smart sensors, mobile devices, and ICT essentially offer solutions to provide healthcare services to remote patients. Salvador et al. (2005) developed a framework where cardiac patients were provided with portable acquisition device and cellular phone which support data transmission. But the framework only takes into consideration of patients in a steady condition and emergency conditions were intentionally excluded. Herscovici et al. (2007) surveyed existing technologies for building smart healthcare systems, such as HygeiaNet, that is employed to transmit 12-lead ECG to provide ambulance and rural health center emergencies for a mobile Tele-Echography that is a completely combined with mobile Tele-Echography system. Shih, Chiang, Lin, and Lin (2010) developed an embedded smart ECG framework to recognize and monitor elderly patients utilizing mobile devices. Ren, Werner, Pazzi, and Boukerche (2010) offered a smart healthcare system for monitoring patients with the emphasis on the security of the system and the wireless communications supporting it.

Jones et al. (2006) proposed a sensor-based chronic disorder detection of health emergencies. The system includes a mobile base unit and a set of wearable devices including sensors, actuators, etc. The system is able to communicate with remote servers. The system is tested to remotely monitor patients with high-risk pregnancies and ventricular arrhythmia, etc. Pandey et al. (2012) proposed a cost-effective cloud-based healthcare system for analysis of ECG signals. ECG data are taken from mobile devices and then transmitted to remote servers for analysis. Xia et al. (2013) proposed a cloud-based healthcare system for real-time ECG monitoring and analysis for ECG quality evaluation, ECG enhancement, and ECG parameter extraction.

9.2.2 Electroencephalogram in cloud-based mobile healthcare

EEG is used to measure the potentials which reproduce the electrical activity of the human brain. Hans Berger introduced the first EEG recording machine in 1929. He proposed that brain signals change depending on the functional status of the brain. During the EEG test, number electrodes are located in different positions of the scalp. Each electrode is connected to an EEG recording machine via an amplifier. Lastly, the EEG signals are transformed into waves on a computer screen to analyze the records. EEG is popular in several applications and employed broadly in cognitive psychology, cognitive science, neuroscience, and psycho physiological research. Since EEG signals involve big amount of data, the computer-aided analysis of EEG signals should be developed for a better understanding of mental states of brain. To acquire EEG signals, an electrode cap is placed on the scalp. Computers analyze and recognize the EEG signal patterns for different states of the brain (Siuly, Li, & Zhang, 2016).

Epilepsy is a neurodegenerative disorder whose crucial sign is the incidence of epileptic seizures. A temporary electrical disturbance of the brain that interrupts the electrical communication between neurons causes the epileptic seizures. This might happen as a partial seizure or generalized seizures (Subasi & Ercelebi, 2005). Throughout the seizure, patient lose his/her consciousness and fall down on the ground during walking on the road or even driving a vehicle. This may achieve a serious injury or become fatal. The sudden unexpected death in epilepsy occurs because of drowning and accidents (Bellon, Panelli, & Rillotta, 2015). Such patients need to be alerted before the onset of a seizure or emergency action when a seizure happen to improve the quality of life and safety significantly. One of the most crucial steps to protect the life of an epileptic patient is the seizure prediction which can assist patients to take preventive measures and avoid accidents. To realize the transition from a normal state to ictal state, to detect a seizure, the brain activity of a patient needs to be acquired and processed continuously. EEG is the usually employed method to measure brain activities for the prediction of epileptic seizure. In this direction, wireless body sensor networks (WBSNs) technology is the most promising system which enables real-time and continuous monitoring of patients remotely by minimizing the requirement for caregivers. WBSNs acquire the biomedical signals of a patient such as heart rate, ECG, and EEG. These wearable sensors are located on the human body and mobility is the crucial benefit of such sensors which enable the patients to move easily at home or outside home (Alemdar & Ersoy, 2010). Numerous wearable body sensor devices such as watch type blood pressure device and h-shirt for measuring heart rate were developed by the research specialists (Sareen, Sood, & Gupta, 2016; Zheng et al., 2014).

EEG signals usually utilized in wearable device design are the Delta, Theta, Alpha, and Beta waves that are mostly employed in designing simple brain—computer interfaces. For instance, Interaxon's Muse (MUSE TM | Meditation Made Easy, n.d.) is designed for EEG signals and employed for controlling applications on smart devices such as mind-games. From a vital signal evaluation perspective, EEG signal analysis has important since it can be utilized for detecting and diagnosing disorders such as epilepsy, Parkinson's disease, Alzheimer's disease, Huntington's disease, sleep Apnea, Restless Leg Syndrome, and the detection of brain death in coma patients. Actually, a wearable such as Muse can be suitable for healthy subjects in monitoring mental activity and stress levels, as notified by Athavale and Krishnan (2017) and Mihajlović et al. (2015). Cloud-based healthcare system play a crucial role in the development of mobile health services, combining mobile applications, huge storage capacity, and scalability of resources. Cloud-based mobile healthcare system offers the rapid analysis of produced sensor data in real time from sensors of different patients living in diverse geographic locations. The cloud-based mobile healthcare system integrated with WBSNs offers an infrastructure to monitor and analyze the sensor data of epileptic patients resourcefully in real time (Zheng et al., 2014). To achieve these goals, a model based on WBSNs, mobile phone, and cloud infrastructure is presented. This model composed of two different interoperable modules: front-end module and back-end module. The front-end module is utilized for acquiring the EEG signal from the patient's scalp via body sensors and transmitting EEG data to the cloud. This task is done by module: acquisition and transmission. On the other hand, the back-end module employed for the analysis of EEG signals of epileptic patients through five main modules: preprocessing and data management, GPS-based alert, feature extraction, feature selection, and feature classification (Sareen et al., 2016).

In terms of characteristic of brain signals, neurological disorder monitoring is the most challenging. Because the sensors used for acquiring brain signals with multiple contact points produce a substantial amount of data and the monitoring requires to run over long period of time. Lee, Lee, and Chung (2014) developed a mobile EEG which can help in noticing cars' driving lousiness produced by fatigue to avoid potential traffic accidents. On a similar research area, Lin et al. (2008) developed a framework which can utilize a dry wireless EEG sensor with mobile devices to help drivers take safe decisions. While Askamp and van Putten (2014) presented the usage of mobile EEG monitoring, but they criticize the absence of software that can support and assist in creating the smart patient monitoring system. Honda and Kudoh (2013) developed a portable EEG monitoring system, called "Air Brain System" utilizing smartphones. Stopczynski, Stahlhut, Larsen, Petersen, and Hansen (2014) developed a framework, called "Smartphone Brain Scanner" in which raw EEG signals are extracted from the sensor and processed on a smartphone (Serhani et al., 2016). Sareen et al. (2016) proposed a system which is composed of mobile phone and cloud computing/processing. The mobile phone includes data acquisition and transmission module. The mobile phone is connected to the cloud server via appropriate communication protocols. The cloud computing/processing includes preprocessing and data management, feature extraction, feature selection, signal classification, and GPS-based alert. Ranganathan, Chinnadurai, Samivel, Kesavamurthy, and Mehndiratta (2015) reviewed many articles in the field of epileptology by analyzing the current and existing applications of mobile phones in care of the epileptic patients worldwide.

Serhani et al. (2016) developed an innovative smart mobile end-to-end monitoring architecture for the monitoring of life-long diseases. They also implemented a user interaction system which is crucial for the accuracy and suitability of the monitoring process and for taking the benefits of employing the proposed remote monitoring system. Furthermore, they presented a scenario that can be applied to monitor epileptic seizures. An intervention system could be designed such a way that it warns the patient of approaching seizure in advance so that patient can be away from risky places such as swimming pools and streets and take prevention drug. Moreover, this enable patients to take as little amount of medicine as possible rather than taking it constantly (Li & Yao, 2005). Recently, researchers implemented EpiCare framework which permits the continuous monitoring of the patient, collecting EEG recordings, detecting epileptic events, and storing data to be reviewed by a clinician. This automated cloud-based mobile healthcare system for long-term remote epileptic patient monitoring essentially characterizes the aim of research which improves smart platform and build processing server which can predict epileptic seizure based on the signals received from the headset (Callegari et al., 2014). On the other hand, the system will not be based on spike detection that in many cases is not indication of the upcoming seizure (Džaferović et al., 2016).

9.3 Signal acquisition, segmentation, and denoising methods

The biomedical signals contain many types of artifacts such as eye-blinking, muscle, and other internal or external interfering noises and these artifacts should be cleaned. These artifacts can be removed by using several techniques. The hardware filters existing in the biomedical equipment can filter out most of the artifacts and noise (Sanei, 2013). The biomedical signals are acquired and processed to distinguish different user intention patterns. The biomedical signal analysis and processing are realized in three main steps: preprocessing/denoising, feature extraction/dimension reduction, and detection/ classification. The main goal of preprocessing is to simplify succeeding procedures without losing-related information and to enhance the signal quality by increasing the signal-to-noise ratio (SNR). A lower SNR means the biomedical signal patterns are suppressed in the rest of the signal and related patterns cannot be detected easily. But a higher SNR make the classification task simpler. Researchers employ different methods to eliminate or at least reduce the unwanted signal components by transforming the signals. These methods might improve the SNR (Graimann, Allison, & Pfurtscheller, 2009).

9.3.1 Adaptive rate acquisition

The classical biomedical signal processing systems are based on classical A/D conversion and processing approaches. Therefore they are time-invariant in nature, which results in a worst-case system parameterization (Duan, Zhang, Zhang, & Mosca, 2006; Noh & Katsianos, 2018; Qaisar, Fesquet, & Renaudin, 2007b). The system computational load and processing activity remain fixed irrespective of the input signal temporal discrepancies. Consequently, they are constrained especially in the case of time varying and intermittent biomedical signals such as ECG, EEG, and EMG. They capture and process a significant number of redundant samples. Consequently, it increases the overall system computational load, processing activity, and the power consumption (Akopyan, Manohar, & Apsel, 2006; Allier, Sicard, Fesquet, & Renaudin, 2003; Hou et al., 2018; Jin, Li, Li, & Wang, 2017; Marisa et al., 2017; Qaisar, Fesquet, & Renaudin, 2007a; Qaisar, Yahiaoui, & Gharbi, 2013; Sayiner, Sorensen, & Viswanathan, 1996). It confirms the interest of adapting the system acquisition and processing rate as a function of the incoming signal temporal variations. It assures a drastic computational gain of the proposed technique compared to the classical ones (Hou et al., 2018; Jin et al., 2017; Marisa et al., 2017; Miskowicz, 2006; Otanez, Moyne, & Tilbury, 2002; Qaisar et al., 2007a, 2007b, 2013; Vetterli, 1987).

In this context, the incoming analog biomedical signals are acquired with appropriate event driven A/D converters (EDADCs). The Nyquist sampling and processing theory governs the functionality of classical ADCs. The signal acquisition is performed at a constant rate irrespective of its sporadic nature, that is, without exploiting the signal local variations. Therefore classical ADCs are parameterized for the worst case (Kester & Engineeri, 2005; Qaisar et al., 2013). Thus they can be extremely ineffective particularly in the case of random biomedical signals. In Qaisar, Fesquet, and Renaudin (2006), Qaisar et al. (2007a, 2007b, 2013), Qaisar, Fesquet, and Renaudin (2008), and Qaisar, Fesquet, and Renaudin (2014), this shortcoming is addressed up to a certain extent by employing the EDADCs. They are based on the Level Crossing Sampling Scheme (LCSS). The LCSS is also known as the event-driven and opportunistic sampling scheme (Bilinskis, 2007; Greitans, 2007; Guan & Singer, 2007). The nonuniformity in the sampling process represents the signal temporal variations. In the case of LCSS, a sample is captured only when the input analog signal crosses one of the predefined thresholds. Samples are not uniformly spaced in time because they depend on the incoming signal variations (Allier et al., 2003; Qaisar et al., 2013; Sayiner et al., 1996). In this framework, an EDADC is employed to digitize the band-limited ECG and EEG signals.

9.3.2 Adaptive rate segmentation

The event-driven ADC output can be employed for further nonuniform digital processing. However, the practical system realization necessitates the finite time segmentation of the acquired data (Ifeachor & Jervis, 2002; Kester & Engineeri, 2005; Oppenheim, 1999). For this purpose, the activity selection algorithm (ASA) is employed (Qaisar et al., 2006, 2007a, 2007b). It exploits the sampling process nonuniformity to window only the relevant parts of signal. One shortfall of EDADCs is that the relevant signal parts can be locally sampled at higher rates compared to the classical case (Qaisar et al., 2007a, 2007b, 2013). In the proposed approach, this drawback is treated by using the ASA. It analyses each selected signal segment to extract its local features. Later on, these extracted features are used to adjust the suggested system parameters such as sampling frequency, shape and length of smoothening window, time-frequency resolution, and filter order (Qaisar et al., 2007a, 2008, 2014). It adapts the system computational complexity and processing activity in accordance with the signal temporal variations and results into a noticeable processing efficiency as compare to the counter solutions.

9.3.3 Adaptive rate interpolation

The resampling process requires interpolation, which introduces artifacts in the resampled signal compared to the original one (De Waele & Broersen, 1999). The resampling error depends on the interpolation technique used to resample the data (De Waele & Broersen, 1999). In the suggested system, for a given EDADC amplitude dynamics, the resampling error is a function of the used interpolation technique and the EDADC resolution, M (Qaisar, Akbar, Beyrouthy, Al-Habib, & Asmatulah, 2016). The employed EDADC thresholds are distributed uniformly within the range of FS.

9.3.4 Adaptive rate filtering

The digital filters are frequently used for the biomedical signals denoising (Kohler, Hennig, & Orglmeister, 2002). The classical filtering techniques are time-invariant in nature. The system is designed for the worst case. The signal is acquired at a fixed sampling frequency and is later on processed by a fixed order filter (Cuomo & Oppenheim, 1993; Ifeachor & Jervis, 2002). It can result into a noticeably useless increase in the system computational load and processing activity. The multirate processing techniques are proposed in this framework (Duan et al., 2006; Noh & Katsianos, 2018; Vetterli, 1987). Inspiring from the multirate processing approaches, an adaptive rate filtering techniques are devised (Qaisar et al., 2006, 2008, 2014).

The reference filter bank is designed with appropriate specifications for a set of reference sampling frequencies $Fref$. Then, upper bound on $Fref$ is selected as F_r. F_r is a chosen frequency for the system, which satisfies the Nyquist sampling criterion. Whereas, to assure a proper digital filtering operation, the lower bound on $Fref$ is chosen as $Fs_{min} \geq 2F_{Cmax}$.

During the online computation, an appropriate reference filter is chosen. The reference filter choice is made on the basis of *Fref* and the effective value of Fs^i. The Fs^i can be specific, therefore an appropriate reference filter is chosen. If $Fs^i \geq F_r$, then the reference filter which is offline designed for F_r is employed for W^i. Otherwise, if $Fs^i < F_r$, then the reference filter whose corresponding value of $Fref_c$ is closest to Fs^i is chosen for W^i. Here, *c* is the index notation which makes a distinction between the chosen reference frequency and the frequencies available in the reference filter bank.

This adaptation of *Frsi* makes to resample *Wi* closer to the Nyquist rates or at sub-Nyquist rates (Qaisar et al., 2006, 2008, 2014). Therefore it avoids unnecessary interpolations and filtering operations during the data resampling and denoising processes. As a result, it improves the proposed approach computational complexity and power efficiency.

In the proposed techniques, the adaptation process requires extra operations for each selected window. The first step is the choice of a reference filter. The data resampling operation is online performed by employing an appropriate interpolator. The choice of interpolator is application dependent. Therefore the interpolator computational complexity should be taken into account. The choice of interpolation technique should be intelligently made so that it provides an appealing tradeoff between the computational complexity and resampling precision for the intended application. Finally, the uniformly resampled signal is denoised. It promises that an effective integration of the suggested adaptive rate signal acquisition and denoising techniques will significantly improve the performance of modern cloud-based health monitoring systems in terms of the computational efficiency and power consumption.

9.4 Feature extraction methods

One of the critical stages in the classification of biomedical signals is the feature extraction. Accordingly, the biomedical signals consist of numerous data points, and distinctive and informative features can be extracted by using different feature extraction methods. These distinctive and informative parameters characterize the behavior of the signal waveform that might indicate a specific action. Emphasizing distinctive and informative features can characterize biomedical signals. The signal patterns can be represented by frequencies and amplitudes. These features can be extracted using different feature extraction algorithms which is another step in signal processing to simplify the succeeding stage for classification (Graimann et al., 2009; Sanei, 2013).

It is essential to deal with less number of values that define appropriate features of the signals to achieve better performance. Features are usually accumulated into a feature vector by transforming signals into a relevant feature vector known as feature extraction. Distinctive features of a signal are analyzed by a signal classification framework, and depending on those distinctive features class of the signal is decided (Siuly et al., 2016). In this study, autoregressive (AR) Burg method is utilized for feature extraction.

9.4.1 Autoregressive Burg model for spectral estimation

The model-based (parametric) feature extraction methods are employed for modeling the time series data $x(n)$ as the output of a linear system characterized by the spectrum estimation process composed of two steps. In the first step, the model-based parameters are estimated from a given data sequence $x(n)$, $0 \leq n \leq N - 1$. Then power spectral density (PSD) estimate is found from these estimations. The AR model is widely utilized parametric method where the signal can be modeled as an output of a causal, all-pole, discrete filter whose input is white noise. The AR model of order p can be expressed as:

$$x(n) = - \sum_{k=1}^{p} a(k)x(n - k) + w(n), \tag{9.1}$$

where $a(k)$ are the AR coefficients and $w(n)$ is white noise of variance equal to σ^2. The PSD is

$$P_{AR}(f) = \frac{\sigma^2}{\left|A(f)\right|^2}, \tag{9.2}$$

where $A(f) = 1 + a_1 e^{-j2\pi f} + \cdots + a_p e^{-j2\pi fp}$.

To find appropriate AR model, several aspects must be taken into consideration such as the signal length, the model order selection, and the level of stationarity of the signal (Muthuswamy & Thakor, 1998; Kay, 1993; Pardey, Roberts, & Tarassenko, 1996).

The AR Burg model employ the minimization of the forward and backward prediction errors and estimation of the reflection coefficient. The forward and backward prediction errors for a pth-order model is defined as:

$$\hat{e}_{f,p}(n) = x(n) + \sum_{i=1}^{p} \hat{a}_{p,i} x(n - i), \quad n = p + 1, \ldots, N, \tag{9.3}$$

$$\hat{e}_{b,p}(n) = x(n - p) + \sum_{i=1}^{p} \hat{a}_{p,i}^* x(n - p + i), \quad n = p + 1, \ldots, N. \tag{9.4}$$

The AR parameters are related to the reflection coefficient $\hat{k}_p$ can be denoted as

$$\hat{a}_{p,i} = \begin{cases} \hat{a}_{p-1,i} + \hat{k}_p \hat{a}_{p-1,p-i}^*, & i = 1, \ldots, p - 1 \\ \hat{k}_p, & i = p \end{cases}. \tag{9.5}$$

The Burg method reflects the recursive-in-order estimation of $\hat{k}_p$ given that the AR coefficients for order $p - 1$ have been computed. The reflection coefficient estimate is given by

$$\hat{k}_p = \frac{-2 \sum_{n=p+1}^{N} \hat{e}_{f,p-1}(n)\hat{e}_{b,p-1}^*(n-1)}{\sum_{n=p+1}^{N} \left[\left| \hat{e}_{f,p-1}(n) \right|^2 + \left| \hat{e}_{b,p-1}(n-1) \right|^2 \right]}. \tag{9.6}$$

The prediction errors satisfy the following recursive-in-order expressions,

$$\hat{e}_{f,p}(n) = \hat{e}_{f,p-1}(n) + \hat{k}_p \hat{e}_{b,p-1}(n-1), \tag{9.7}$$

$$\hat{e}_{b,p}(n) = \hat{e}_{b,p-1}(n-1) + \hat{k}_p^* \hat{e}_{f,p-1}(n), \tag{9.8}$$

and these expressions are utilized to yield a recursive-in-order algorithm for estimating the AR coefficients. From the estimates of the AR parameters, PSD estimation is formed as (Kay & Marple, 1981; Proakis & Manolakis, 2007; Stoica & Moses, 1997):

$$\hat{P}_{BURG}(f) = \frac{\hat{e}_p}{\left| 1 + \sum_{k=1}^{p} \hat{a}_p(k)e^{-j2\pi fk} \right|^2}, \tag{9.9}$$

where $\hat{e}_p = \hat{e}_{f,p} + \hat{e}_{b,p}$ is the total least squares error (Subasi, 2007).

9.5 Machine learning methods

A great deal current interest is inside the research community in the purpose of machine learning techniques for recognition, classification, and diagnosis of biomedical signals. Several examples include the diagnosis of heart attacks, cardiac hypertrophy, myocardial ischemia, epileptic seizure prediction, and detection generally lead to life-threatening situations. Early and correct diagnoses and identifications are of main implication so that required preventive measures or treatment can be administered. Doctors presently employ numerous diagnostic methods ranging from invasive techniques to noninvasive methods such as computerized tomography (CT) scans, MRI, EEG, and ECGs (Begg, Lai, & Palaniswami, 2007).

The analysis of biomedical signals is really important for monitoring anomalies in the human body since they are rapid, and monitoring must be continuous. The diagnostic procedure contains elimination of attributes from biomedical signals and succeeding assessments with known diseases to determine any difference from normal characteristic waveforms. Such a monitoring system ought to have the ability of finding abnormalities characterized by wave shape changes within the signal. Even though medical employees must be compulsory to be familiar with any variation in the biomedical signal, this is still time-consuming and very tedious for studying long-term checking the signals (Begg et al., 2007).

Machine learning techniques can automate the process of biomedical signal analysis and the classification among normal and pathological patterns by generating decision surfaces to classify these patterns. Automatic detection and classification of biomedical signals using different signal processing techniques have developed into a critical aspect of clinical monitoring (Begg et al., 2007). Since biomedical signals include a big amount of data, the key problem for classification is how to characterize the biomedical signal recordings. First, significant features must be extracted from the acquired biomedical signals, then dimension of these features must be reduced and in the last step, the reduced features are used for classification. In the classification, class labels are assigned to the extracted features of a set of data. An algorithm which implements classification is called as a classifier. Classifier learns how to categorize the class of a feature vector using training sets. The algorithms employed in classification process for predicting categorical labels are k-nearest-neighbor (k-NN), artificial neural networks (ANN), SVM, decision tree algorithms, Random Tree, Random Forest, Rotation Forest, etc. (Siuly et al., 2016).

9.6 Results

To obtain a reliable assessment of the quality of the model's predictive performance, the evaluation of the classification model is used. It is of great importance to differentiate between value of a particular dataset performance, training performance, and its predictable performance on the whole domain. Performance measures of classifiers are obtained by comparing the true class labels of the instances from dataset and the predictions generated by the classifier on the same dataset. This subset is usually separated into the training set, the validation set, or test set. For the evaluation that is performed to make some decisions that may affect the final model by adjusting its parameters called intermediate evaluation which use validation set. Then the performance of the ultimately created model should be evaluated by employing test set (Cichosz, 2014).

k-Fold cross validation is a good evaluation procedure if there is not enough number of samples. It randomly splits the available dataset into k subsets of the same size and then iterates over these subsets. Once all k iterations are completed, the model built without specific instance in the training set is used to generate a predicted class label for each instance in the dataset. The resulting predictions are compared to the true class labels employing one or more chosen performance measures. The k-fold cross-validation technique successfully virtualizes the training and validation or test sets. All available instances from the set can be employed for both model creation and evaluation, but not simultaneously (Cichosz, 2014).

Accuracy, precision, recall, F-measure, ROC area, and Kappa value are the measures used evaluation of the performance of classifiers. Accuracy is given as the ratio of correctly classified instances to all instances:

$$\text{Accuracy} = \frac{TP + TN}{TP + FP + FN + TN} \qquad (9.10)$$

Precision is the ratio of instances correctly classified as positive to all instances classified as positive. Recall is represented in the same way as the true positive rate. In order to make satisfactory measure of the performance of the classifier based on its confusion matrix, a complete pair of complementary indicators must be used. On this way model selection process is much harder, as there is no single criterion to rank candidate models from which the best could be chosen. Some measures have tried to fold two complementary indicators into a single one, to facilitate this task. One well-known example is the F-measure which is defined as the harmonic mean of the precision and recall indicators (Cichosz, 2014).

$$F\text{-measure} = 2 \times \frac{\text{Precision} \times \text{Recall}}{\text{Precision} + \text{Recall}} = \frac{2 \times TP}{2 \times TP + FP + FN} \qquad (9.11)$$

Receiver operating characteristic (ROC) analysis is one of the convenient tools which enables classifier performance evaluation in multiple operating points, operating point selection and operating point comparison. ROC curve shows the whole range of different operating points, with the corresponding different levels of the trade-off of the true positives and false positives, in a single plot. In the case when there are a variety of models, produced using different algorithms or parameter settings, the quick and easy way of ranking them with respect to their predictive utility without considering any particular operating points is needed. Such commonly used criterion is the area under the ROC curve (AUC) (Cichosz, 2014).

Kappa statistic is a measure that takes expected figure into account by deducting it from the predictor's successes. It expresses the result as a proportion of the total for a perfect predictor. The measurement of the agreement between predicted and observed categorizations of a dataset and correcting the agreement that occurs by chance is done by the Kappa statistic. Similarly to the plain success rate, it does not take into account the costs (Hall, Witten, & Frank, 2011).

In the studied case, the ECG and EEG signals are acquired with a 5-Bit resolution EDADC. The EDADC focuses only on the relevant signal parts and adapt the sampling rate as a function of the signal temporal variations (Akopyan et al., 2006; Allier et al., 2003; Qaisar et al., 2013; Sayiner et al., 1996). Its performance is studied in terms of the compression gain, the reduction in acquired number of samples as compared to the classical ADCs-based solution. The ASA adapts the window function length according to the characteristics of nonuniformly time repartitioned ECG and EEG signal. It also adapts the resampling frequency for each W^i. Therefore its performance is studied in terms of adapting the window length and the number of samples per window as compared to the time-invariant classical windowing approach. The segmented signal is resampled uniformly by employing the adaptive rate interpolation technique. The Spline interpolation is used for the data resampling. The resampled signal is denoised by using the *ARFIR* technique. Its performance is compared with the classical filtering in terms of the computational complexity.

The denoised signal discriminative parameters are extracted by using the AR Burg method. These extracted parameters are employed by several robust classification algorithms to make the classification decisions. The performance of *AR Burg* and classifiers is collectively studied in terms of the classification precision. It also reflects the performance of proposed system in terms of precision.

9.6.1 Experimental results for electrocardiogram

To demonstrate the interesting features of the proposed solution, its performance is studied for acquiring, processing, and classifying the ECG signals, obtained from the MIT-BIH Arrhythmia Database (Moody & Mark, 2001). Each ECG signal is segmented for a time length of 0.94 seconds. Therefore, for a given time length of 0.94 seconds and sampling frequency of 320 Hz, each digitized segment is composed of 300 samples. In this study, five different types of ECG signals are considered. These are normal signals (N), Right Bundle Branch Block (RBBB), Left Bundle Branch Block (LBBB), Atrial Premature Contraction (APC), and Premature Ventricular Contraction (PVC).

In the studied case, ECG signals are acquired with a 5-Bit resolution EDADC. They belong to five different classes of N, RBBB, LBBB, APC, and PVC. In the studied case, a more than two times compression gain is achieved for each intended ECG signal. It shows a noticeable reduction in the postprocessing modules computational load. In addition, the signal is digitized with a 5-Bit resolution EDADC. It confirms a simpler circuit level A/D conversion realization as compared to the counter classical 12-Bit resolution A/D conversion (Moody & Mark, 2001).

The EDADC output is segmented by using the ASA. To apply the ASA, the reference window length L_{ref} is chosen equal to 1 second. The ASA adapts the window function length, L^i, according to the characteristics of nonuniformly time repartitioned ECG signal, obtained at the EDADC output. It allows focusing only on the interesting signal parts and contributes in augmenting the system computational efficiency.

The output of ASA is uniformly resampled by employing the Spline Interpolation. The resampled signal is denoised by using an enhanced *ARFIR* filtering technique (Qaisar et al., 2014). In this context, a filters bank is offline designed by employing the Parks-McClellan algorithm. Each band-pass filter is designed for the cut-off frequencies of [$F_{Cmin} = 0.5$; $F_{Cmax} = 30$] Hz. This choice of pass band allows focusing on the ECG QRS complex while attenuating the P and T waveforms and noise (Sahoo, Kanungo, Behera, & Sabut, 2017). Therefore it improves the performance of post features extraction and classification modules. The filters bank is designed for a range of sampling frequencies, *Fref*, between 76.25 Hz > $2.F_{Cmax}$ and $F_r = 320$ Hz. In this case, $\Delta = 16.25$ Hz is chosen. It results into a bank of $Q = 16$ band-pass FIR filters. This filtering process improves the intended signal SNR and results into a reasonable classification accuracy.

The online filter selection and order adaption for each selected window allows achieving the intended signal denoising with a lesser computational complexity compared to the counter time invariant classical solutions (Alickovic & Subasi, 2015). The computational gains of the proposed *ARFIR* are computed over the classical one. The overall computational gains for each considered class of ECG signals is more than two times. It shows that the proposed *ARFIR* technique achieves noticeable computational gains over the counter classical approach.

The discriminative features of the denoised signal are extracted with the AR Burg. Afterwards, these features are used by the robust classifiers to automatically diagnose the cardiac arrhythmia. A summary of results obtained by using different classifiers for the five-class MIT-BIH ECG signals are presented in Table 9.1.

Table 9.1 shows that for the case of proposed approach, the best classification accuracy of 93.2% is achieved with the Rotation Forest. The SVM is the second one with 93.13% accuracy. The LADTree achieves the lowest accuracy of 77.13%. The best accuracy, achieved for the counter classical ADC, windowing- and filtering-based approach, is of 96%. It is achieved with the Random Forest. The SVM and the Rotation Forest are the second one with 95.27% accuracy. The LADTree achieves the lowest accuracy of 84.33%.

For the case of proposed approach, the best *F*-measure value of 0.932 is achieved with the Rotation Forest and the SVM. The Random Forest is the second one with 0.927 *F*-measure

Table 9.1: The summary of classification results obtained for the ECG dataset.

	Accuracy		F-measure		ROC area		Kappa	
	Classical	Spline	Classical	Spline	Classical	Spline	Classical	Spline
SVM	95.27%	93.13%	0.953	0.932	0.986	0.977	0.9408	0.9142
k-NN	93.67%	91.80%	0.937	0.917	0.981	0.975	0.9208	0.8975
ANN	92.47%	91.07%	0.925	0.91	0.991	0.987	0.9058	0.8883
Random Forest	96.00%	92.67%	0.96	0.927	0.997	0.993	0.95	0.9083
CART	89.40%	87.73%	0.894	0.877	0.959	0.936	0.8675	0.8467
C4.5	89.80%	87.13%	0.898	0.871	0.96	0.937	0.8725	0.8392
Rotation Forest	95.27%	93.20%	0.953	0.932	0.996	0.993	0.9408	0.915
REPTree	88.60%	86.13%	0.886	0.862	0.966	0.957	0.8575	0.8267
Random Tree	88.40%	87.93%	0.884	0.879	0.928	0.925	0.855	0.8492
LADTree	84.33%	77.13%	0.843	0.773	0.967	0.944	0.8042	0.7142

value. The LADTree achieves the lowest *F*-measure value of 0.792. The best *F*-measure value is achieved by the Random Forest for the counter classical approach is of 0.96. The SVM and the Rotation Forest are the second one with 0.953 *F*-measure. The LADTree achieves the lowest *F*-measure value of 0.843%.

The best AUC value of 0.993 is achieved with the Rotation Forest and the Random Forest for the proposed approach. The SVM is the second one with 0.977 AUC value. The Random Tree achieves the lowest AUC value of 0.925. The best AUC value achieved for the counter classical approach is of 0.997. It is achieved with the Random Forest. The Rotation Forest is the second one with 0.996 AUC. The Random Tree achieves the lowest AUC value of 0.928.

The best Kappa value of 0.915 is achieved with the Rotation Forest for the proposed approach. The SVM is the second one with 0.914 Kappa value. The LADTree achieves the lowest Kappa value of 0.7142. The best Kappa value is achieved by Random Forest for the counter classical approach is of 0.95. The SVM and the Rotation Forest are the second one with 0.9408 Kappa value. The LADTree achieves the lowest Kappa value of 0.8042.

9.6.2 Experimental results for electroencephalogram

In this study, the employed EEG signals are obtained from the dataset of epileptic seizure signals. It is composed of five different classes of normal eyes-open, normal eyes-close, epileptic ictal, epileptic interictal, and nonepileptic interictal. Each EEG signal is segmented for a time length of 1 second and with a 12-Bit resolution ADC. Therefore, for a given time length of 1 seconds and sampling frequency of 1024 Hz, each digitized segment is composed of 1024 samples.

In the studied case, EEG signals are acquired with a 5-bit resolution EDADC. In the studied case, a more than four times compression gain is achieved for each intended ECG class. It shows a noticeable reduction in the postprocessing modules computational load. In addition, the signal is digitized with a 5-Bit resolution EDADC. It confirms a simpler circuit level A/D conversion realization as compared to the counter classical 12-Bit resolution A/D conversion.

The EDADC output is segmented by using the ASA. To apply the ASA, the reference window length L_{ref} is chosen equal to 1 second. The ASA adapts the window function length, L^i, according to the characteristics of nonuniformly time repartitioned ECG signal, obtained at the EDADC output. It allows focusing only on the interesting signal parts and contributes in augmenting the system computational efficiency.

The output of ASA is uniformly resampled by employing the Spline Interpolation. The resampled signal is denoised by using an enhanced *ARFIR* filtering technique. In this context, a filters bank is offline designed by employing the Parks-McClellan algorithm. Each band-pass filter is designed for the cut-off frequencies of $[F_{Cmin} = 0.5; F_{Cmax} = 35]$ Hz. This choice of pass band allows focusing on the EEG intended components while attenuating the unwanted components and noise. Therefore it improves the performance of post features extraction and classification modules. The filters bank is designed for a range of sampling frequencies, *Fref*, between 79 Hz $> 2.F_{Cmax}$ and $F_r = 1024$ Hz. In this case, $\Delta = 15$ Hz is chosen. It results into a bank of $Q = 64$ band-pass FIR filters.

The online filter selection and order adaption for each selected window allows achieving the intended signal denoising with a lesser computational complexity compared to the counter time invariant classical solutions. The overall computational gains for each considered class of EEG signals is more than four times. It shows that the proposed *ARFIR* technique achieves noticeable computational gains over the counter classical approach.

The discriminative features of the denoised signal are extracted with the AR Burg. Afterwards, these features are used by the robust classifiers to automatically detect the epileptic seizure. A summary of results obtained by using different classifiers is presented in Table 9.2.

Table 9.2 shows that for the case of proposed approach the best classification accuracy of 96.25% is achieved with the Rotation Forest. The Random Forest is the second one with 96.08% accuracy. The SVM achieves the lowest accuracy of 89.58%. The best accuracy is achieved by the Rotation Forest for the counter classical ADC, windowing and filtering based approach, is of 98.5%. The *k*-NN is the second one with 98.42% accuracy. The REPTree achieves the lowest accuracy of 94.42%.

The best *F*-measure value of 0.963 is achieved by the Rotation Forest and the SVM with proposed approach. The Random Forest is the second one with 0.961 *F*-measure value.

Table 9.2: The summary of classification results obtained for the EEG dataset.

	Accuracy		F-measure		ROC area		Kappa	
	Classical	Spline	Classical	Spline	Classical	Spline	Classical	Spline
SVM	98.25	89.58	0.982	0.895	0.991	0.94	0.9737	0.8437
k-NN	98.42	90.25	0.984	0.903	0.988	0.963	0.9762	0.8537
ANN	98.33	95.00	0.983	0.95	0.997	0.987	0.975	0.925
Random Forest	98.33	96.08	0.983	0.961	0.999	0.996	0.975	0.9412
CART	95.50	92.67	0.955	0.926	0.978	0.955	0.9325	0.89
C4.5	96.50	93.58	0.965	0.936	0.98	0.959	0.9475	0.9037
Rotation Forest	98.50	96.25	0.985	0.963	0.999	0.996	0.9775	0.9437
REPTree	94.42	91.67	0.944	0.916	0.978	0.958	0.9162	0.875
Random Tree	95.75	91.00	0.958	0.91	0.968	0.933	0.9363	0.865
LADTree	95.67	93.00	0.957	0.93	0.993	0.985	0.935	0.895

The SVM achieves the lowest *F*-measure value of 0.895. The best *F*-measure value is achieved by the Rotation Forest for the counter classical approach is of 0.985. The *k*-NN and the Rotation Forest are the second one with 0.984 *F*-measure. The REPTree achieves the lowest *F*-measure value of 0.944%.

The best AUC value of 0.996 is achieved with the Rotation Forest and the Random Forest for the proposed approach. The ANN is the second one with 0.987 AUC value. The Random Tree achieves the lowest AUC value of 0.933. The best AUC value is achieved for the counter classical approach is of 0.999. It is achieved with the Random Forest and the Rotation Forest. The ANN is the second one with 0.997 AUC. The Random Tree achieves the lowest AUC value of 0.968.

The best Kappa value of 0.9437 is achieved with the Rotation Forest for the proposed approach. The Random Forest is the second one with 0.9412 Kappa value. The SVM achieves the lowest Kappa value of 0.8437. The best Kappa value is achieved by the Rotation Forest for the counter classical approach is of 0.977. The *k*-NN is the second one with 0.976 Kappa value. The REPTree achieves the lowest Kappa value of 0.916.

9.7 Discussion and conclusion

Future trends in smart sensor devices are making a flourishing in the wearable market, where scientists can improve wearable models for several applications. Cloud-based mobile health monitoring is a developing area of research and has attracted many attentions from diverse areas of healthcare technology. One of the goals of this chapter is to represent many of these advances and also identify some imperative research problems. A framework for cloud-based mobile health is presented with patients, healthcare professionals, IT, and m-health applications. Based on this kind of improvements, the increasing awareness in cloud-based mobile health monitoring in different areas claim that spreading the use of wearable devices into the clinical applications and medical home monitoring will be attractive. Biomedical signal monitoring for abnormal situation detection is a new direction and can play a crucial role in healthcare systems. The aim is to detect any crucial situation such as heart attack or epileptic seizure by utilizing cloud-based mobile healthcare system.

Continuous and precise remote monitoring of patients with chronic disorders such as CHF and epilepsy is a crucial task. In this chapter, we have presented a CBMHM system for the prediction and detection of chronic disorders (epileptic seizures from the EEG signal and heart arrhythmia from the ECG signals). The main aim of this chapter is to present how to implement an automatic, intelligent, and scalable CBMHM system to predict and detect the chronic disorders in a real time using wearable biomedical sensors. The biomedical data produced by wearable sensors are collected by a smartphone using Bluetooth technology and send it to a cloud for further analysis. Moreover, the GPS system of the smartphone can be utilized to determine the location of the patient and nearby hospital to deliver urgent assistance to the patient. Furthermore, such a framework helps healthcare agencies and hospitals to punctually intervene in the case of an emergency situation and protect the patients from accidents (Sareen et al., 2016).

In this chapter, we have analyzed a cloud-based mobile healthcare system for real-time biomedical signals. The aim is to present the usability of cloud-based mobile healthcare system for the detection of chronic disorders such as heart attack and epileptic seizure. The framework employs ECG and EEG data which can be send to a cloud server from a mobile phone at a certain frequency and signal analysis is completed in real time. The system has been confirmed to be practical, precise, and effective in monitoring and analyzing the biomedical signals. The improvements in mobile devices and sensor technology offer innovative solutions to improve the quality of healthcare for patients with chronic disorders. The devised solution is realized by combining the adaptive rate signal acquisition, segmentation, and denoising to decrease the signal transmission rate. Feature extraction is carried out by AR Burg model and assessment of biomedical signals is realized by employing different machine learning models. It results into a significant computational gain of the proposed approach compared to the classical ones. The overall computational gains, respectively, achieved per class for the considered ECG and EEG signals are more than two times and more than four times. It assures that the proposed adaptive rate acquisition, segmentation, and denoising-based solution achieves a comparable classification accuracy compared to the counter classical fixed rate acquisition, segmentation, and denoising solution while attaining a significant computational gain over it.

This chapter contributes to the cloud-based mobile healthcare system through the exploration of different biomedical signals for the detection of chronic disorders such as heart attack and epileptic seizure. The suggested approach is original and has a potential to contribute in the development of future generation medical systems and healthcare innovations. The system performance is a function of the employed resampling interpolator, denoising stage, parameters extraction module, and the classification algorithm. A study on the performance of system, in terms of accuracy and computational complexity, while using the higher order interpolators is a future work. Another future work is to explore other features extraction techniques such as Discrete Wavelet Transform, Wavelet Packet Decomposition, Tuneable Q Wavelet Transform, and Dual Tree Complex Wavelet Transform and study their impact on the system performance. The miniaturization, optimization, and embedded implementations of the suggested solutions are other prospects. Moreover, the proposed framework can be utilized for blood sugar level checking, blood pressure checking, and heart rate checking as well.

9.8 Teaching assignments

- Describe your reflection and highlights on the ECG and EEG signals usage for the patient health monitoring.
- Cite key differences between the classical and the adaptive rate signal acquisition and processing approaches.
- Describe the effect of signal conditioning stage on the performance of a post features extraction stage.
- Describe your reflection and highlights on the ECG classification techniques, employed in this chapter.
- Describe your reflection and highlights on the EEG classification techniques, employed in this chapter.

References

Akopyan, F., Manohar, R., & Apsel, A. B. (2006). A level-crossing flash asynchronous analog-to-digital converter. *Presented at the 12th IEEE international symposium on asynchronous circuits and systems.* IEEE.

Alemdar, H., & Ersoy, C. (2010). Wireless sensor networks for healthcare: A survey. *Computer Networks, 54* (15), 2688−2710.

Alickovic, E., & Subasi, A. (2015). Effect of multiscale PCA de-noising in ECG beat classification for diagnosis of cardiovascular diseases. *Circuits, Systems, and Signal Processing, 34*(2), 513−533.

Allier, E., Sicard, G., Fesquet, L., & Renaudin, M. (2003). A new class of asynchronous A/D converters based on time quantization. *Presented at the 9th international symposium on asynchronous circuits and systems* (pp. 196−205). IEEE.

Anderson, G., & Hussey, P. S. (2001). Comparing health system performance in OECD countries. *Health Affairs, 20*(3), 219−232.

Askamp, J., & van Putten, M. J. (2014). Mobile EEG in epilepsy. *International Journal of Psychophysiology, 91* (1), 30−35.

Athavale, Y., & Krishnan, S. (2017). Biosignal monitoring using wearables: Observations and opportunities. *Biomedical Signal Processing and Control, 38*, 22−33.

Atoui, H., Télisson, D., Fyan, J., & Rubel, P. (2008). Ambient intelligence and pervasive architecture designed within the EPI-MEDICS personal ECG monitor. *International Journal of Healthcare Information Systems and Informatics (IJHISI), 3*(4), 68−80.

Begg, R., Lai, D. T., & Palaniswami, M. (2007). *Computational intelligence in biomedical engineering.* CRC Press.

Bellon, M., Panelli, R. J., & Rillotta, F. (2015). Epilepsy-related deaths: An Australian survey of the experiences and needs of people bereaved by epilepsy. *Seizure, 29*, 162−168.

Berbari, E. J. (2000). Principles of electrocardiography. In: Joseph D. Bronzino (Ed.), *The biomedical engineering handbook* (1), 13−11.

Bilinskis, I. (2007). *Digital alias-free signal processing.* John Wiley & Sons.

Callegari, D., Conte, E., Ferreto, T., Fernandes, D., Moraes, F., Burmeister, F., & Severino, R. (2014). EpiCare—A home care platform based on mobile cloud computing to assist epilepsy diagnosis. *Presented at the EAI 4th international conference on wireless mobile communication and healthcare (Mobihealth)* (pp. 148−151). Citeseer.

Catarinucci, L., De Donno, D., Mainetti, L., Palano, L., Patrono, L., Stefanizzi, M. L., & Tarricone, L. (2015). An IoT-aware architecture for smart healthcare systems. *IEEE Internet of Things Journal, 2*(6), 515−526.

Celler, B. G., & Sparks, R. S. (2015). Home telemonitoring of vital signs—Technical challenges and future directions. *IEEE Journal of Biomedical and Health Informatics, 19*(1), 82−91.

Chiauzzi, E., Rodarte, C., & DasMahapatra, P. (2015). Patient-centered activity monitoring in the self-management of chronic health conditions. *BMC Medicine, 13*(1), 77.

Cichosz, P. (2014). *Data mining algorithms: Explained using R.* John Wiley & Sons.

Cuomo, K. M., & Oppenheim, A. V. (1993). Circuit implementation of synchronized chaos with applications to communications. *Physical Review Letters, 71*(1), 65.

De Waele, S., & Broersen, P. (1999). A time domain error measure for resampled irregular data. *Presented at the IEEE instrumentation and measurement technology conference proceedings* (Vol. 2, pp. 1172−1177). Institute of Electical Engineers Inc (IEEE).

Duan, Z., Zhang, J., Zhang, C., & Mosca, E. (2006). A simple design method of reduced-order filters and its applications to multirate filter bank design. *Signal Processing, 86*(5), 1061−1075.

Džaferović, E., Vrtagić, S., Bandić, L., Kevric, J., Subasi, A., & Qaisar, S.M. (2016). Cloud-based mobile platform for EEG signal analysis. *Presented at the 5th international conference on electronic devices, systems and applications (ICEDSA)* (pp. 1−4). IEEE.

Einthoven, W. (1903). The string galvanometer and the human electrocardiogram. *Presented at the KNAW proceedings* (Vol. 6, pp. 107−115).

Eren, A., Subasi, A., & Coskun, O. (2008). A decision support system for telemedicine through the mobile telecommunications platform. *Journal of Medical Systems, 32*(1), 31−35.

GE Healthcare | Home | GE Healthcare. (n.d.). Diagnostic Cardiology. <https://www.gehealthcare.co.uk/> Retrieved 19.10.18.

Graimann, B., Allison, B., & Pfurtscheller, G. (2009). *Brain−computer interfaces: A gentle introduction. Brain-computer interfaces* (pp. 1−27). Springer.

Grand Challenges—14 Grand Challenges for Engineering. (n.d.). Introduction to the Grand Challenges for Engineering. <http://www.engineeringchallenges.org/cms/8996.aspx> Retrieved 19.10.18.

Greitans, M. (2007). Time-frequency representation based chirp-like signal analysis using multiple level crossings. *Presented at the 15th European signal processing conference* (pp. 2254−2258). IEEE.

Guan, K. M., & Singer, A. C. (2007). Opportunistic sampling by level-crossing. *Presented at the IEEE international conference on acoustics, speech and signal processing (ICASSP 2007)* (Vol. 3, pp. III−1513). IEEE.

Guzik, P., & Malik, M. (2016). ECG by mobile technologies. *Journal of Electrocardiology, 49*(6), 894−901.

Hall, M., Witten, I., & Frank, E. (2011). *Data mining: Practical machine learning tools and techniques.* Burlington: Kaufmann.

Herscovici, N., Christodoulou, C., Kyriacou, E., Pattichis, M., Pattichis, C., Panayides, A., & Pitsillides, A. (2007). m-Health e-emergency systems: Current status and future directions [Wireless corner]. *IEEE Antennas and Propagation Magazine, 49*(1), 216−231.

Hoang, D. B., & Chen, L. (2010). Mobile cloud for assistive healthcare (MoCAsH). *Presented at the IEEE Asia-Pacific services computing conference (APSCC)* (pp. 325−332). IEEE.

Homepage − Emotiv. (n.d.). Brain Controlled Technology. <https://www.emotiv.com/> Retrieved 19.10.18.

Honda, K., & Kudoh, S. N. (2013). Air brain: the easy telemetric system with smartphone for eeg signal and human behavior. *Presented at the proceedings of the 8th international conference on body area networks* (pp. 343−346). ICST (Institute for Computer Sciences, Social-Informatics and Telecommunications Engineering).

Hou, Y., Qu, J., Tian, Z., Atef, M., Yousef, K., Lian, Y., & Wang, G. (2018). A 61-nW level-crossing ADC with adaptive sampling for biomedical applications. *IEEE Transactions on Circuits and Systems II: Express Briefs.*

Hsieh, J., & Hsu, M.-W. (2012). A cloud computing based 12-lead ECG telemedicine service. *BMC Medical Informatics and Decision Making, 12*(1), 77.

Ifeachor, E. C., & Jervis, B. W. (2002). *Digital signal processing: A practical approach.* Pearson Education.

Jin, S.-W., Li, J.-J., Li, Z.-N., & Wang, A.-X. (2017). A hysteresis comparator for level-crossing ADC. *Presented at the 29th Chinese control and decision conference (CCDC)* (pp. 7753−7757). IEEE.

Jones, V., Van Halteren, A., Dokovsky, N., Koprinkov, G., Bults, R., Konstantas, D., & Herzog, R. (2006). *Mobihealth: Mobile health services based on body area networks. M-Health* (pp. 219−236). Springer.

Kay, M., Santos, J., & Takane, M. (2011). mHealth: New horizons for health through mobile technologies. *World Health Organization, 64*(7), 66−71.

Kay, S. M. (1993). *Fundamentals of statistical signal processing, volume I: estimation theory*. Upper Saddle River, NJ: Prentice hall.

Kay, S. M., & Marple, S. L. (1981). Spectrum analysis—A modern perspective. *Proceedings of the IEEE, 69* (11), 1380−1419.

Kester, W. A., & Engineeri, A. D. I. (2005). *Data conversion handbook*. Newnes.

Kohler, B.-U., Hennig, C., & Orglmeister, R. (2002). The principles of software QRS detection. *IEEE Engineering in Medicine and Biology Magazine, 21*(1), 42−57.

Lee, B.-G., Lee, B.-L., & Chung, W.-Y. (2014). Mobile healthcare for automatic driving sleep-onset detection using wavelet-based EEG and respiration signals. *Sensors, 14*(10), 17915−17936.

Li, X., & Yao, X. (2005). *Application of fuzzy similarity to prediction of epileptic seizures using EEG signals. Presented at the international conference on fuzzy systems and knowledge discovery* (pp. 645−652). Springer.

Lin, C.-C., Lin, P.-Y., Lu, P.-K., Hsieh, G.-Y., Lee, W.-L., & Lee, R.-G. (2008). A healthcare integration system for disease assessment and safety monitoring of dementia patients. *IEEE Transactions on Information Technology in Biomedicine, 12*(5), 579−586.

Lytras, M., & Visvizi, A. (2018). Who uses smart city services and what to make of it: Toward interdisciplinary smart cities research. *Sustainability, 10*(6), 1998.

Lytras, M. D., Mathkour, H., & Torres-Ruiz, M. (2016). Innovative Mobile Information Systems: Insights from Gulf Cooperation Countries and All Over the World. *Mobile Information Systems, 2016*, Article ID 2439389, 5 pages. Available from https://doi.org/10.1155/2016/2439389.

Marisa, T., Niederhauser, T., Haeberlin, A., Wildhaber, R. A., Vogel, R., Goette, J., & Jacomet, M. (2017). Pseudo asynchronous level crossing ADC for ECG signal acquisition. *IEEE Transactions on Biomedical Circuits and Systems, 11*(2), 267−278.

McGregor, C., Heath, J., & Wei, M. (2005). A Web services based framework for the transmission of physiological data for local and remote neonatal intensive care. *Presented at the IEEE international conference on e-Technology, e-Commerce and e-Service, 2005 (EEE'05)* (pp. 496−501). IEEE.

Melillo, P., Orrico, A., Scala, P., Crispino, F., & Pecchia, L. (2015). Cloud-based smart health monitoring system for automatic cardiovascular and fall risk assessment in hypertensive patients. *Journal of Medical Systems, 39*(10), 109.

Menshawy, M. E., Benharref, A., & Serhani, M. (2015). An automatic mobile-health based approach for EEG epileptic seizures detection. *Expert Systems with Applications, 42*(20), 7157−7174.

Mihajlović, V., Grundlehner, B., Vullers, R., & Penders, J. (2015). Wearable, wireless EEG solutions in daily life applications: what are we missing? *IEEE Journal of Biomedical and Health Informatics, 19*(1), 6−21.

Miskowicz, M. (2006). Send-on-delta concept: an event-based data reporting strategy. *Sensors, 6*(1), 49−63.

Moody, G. B., & Mark, R. G. (2001). The impact of the MIT-BIH arrhythmia database. *IEEE Engineering in Medicine and Biology Magazine, 20*(3), 45−50.

Mshali, H., Lemlouma, T., Moloney, M., & Magoni, D. (2018). A survey on health monitoring systems for health smart homes. *International Journal of Industrial Ergonomics, 66*, 26−56.

MUSE TM | Meditation Made Easy.(n.d.). <http://www.choosemuse.com/> Retrieved 19.10.18.

Muthuswamy, J., & Thakor, N. V. (1998). Spectral analysis methods for neurological signals. *Journal of Neuroscience Methods, 83*(1), 1−14.

Myo Gesture Control Armband. (n.d.). <https://www.myo.com/> Retrieved 19.10.18.

Noh, D., & Katsianos, T. (2018). Multi-rate system for audio processing. US Patent Application No. 10/008,217.

Oppenheim, A. V. (1999). *Discrete-time signal processing*. Pearson Education India.

Otanez, P. G., Moyne, J. R., & Tilbury, D. M. (2002). Using deadbands to reduce communication in networked control systems. *Presented at the Proceedings of the American control conference* (Vol. 4, pp. 3015−3020). IEEE.

Pandey, S., Voorsluys, W., Niu, S., Khandoker, A., & Buyya, R. (2012). An autonomic cloud environment for hosting ECG data analysis services. *Future Generation Computer Systems, 28*(1), 147−154.

Pardey, J., Roberts, S., & Tarassenko, L. (1996). A review of parametric modelling techniques for EEG analysis. *Medical Engineering & Physics, 18*(1), 2−11.

Proakis, John G., & Manolakis, Dimitris G. (2007). *Digital signal processing: Principles, algorithms, and applications*. Pearson Prentice Hall.

Qaisar, S. M., Akbar, M., Beyrouthy, T., Al-Habib, W., & Asmatulah, M. (2016). An error measurement for resampled level crossing signal. *Presented at the 2nd international conference on event-based control, communication, and signal processing (EBCCSP)* (pp. 1−4). IEEE.

Qaisar, S. M., Fesquet, L., & Renaudin, M. (2006). Spectral analysis of a signal driven sampling scheme. *Presented at the 14th European signal processing conference* (pp. 1−5). IEEE.

Qaisar, S. M., Fesquet, L., & Renaudin, M. (2007a). Adaptive rate filtering fora signal driven sampling scheme. *Presented at the IEEE international conference on acoustics, speech and signal processing (ICASSP 2007)* (Vol. 3, pp. III−1465). IEEE.

Qaisar, S. M., Fesquet, L., & Renaudin, M. (2007b). Computationally efficient adaptive rate sampling and filtering. *Presented at the 15th European signal processing conference* (pp. 2139−2143). IEEE.

Qaisar, S. M., Fesquet, L., & Renaudin, M. (2008). An adaptive resolution computationally efficient short-time Fourier transform. *Journal of Electrical and Computer Engineering, 2008*, Article ID 932068.

Qaisar, S. M., Fesquet, L., & Renaudin, M. (2014). Adaptive rate filtering a computationally efficient signal processing approach. *Signal Processing, 94*, 620−630.

Qaisar, S. M., Yahiaoui, R., & Gharbi, T. (2013). An efficient signal acquisition with an adaptive rate A/D conversion. *Presented at the IEEE international conference on circuits and systems (ICCAS)* (pp. 124−129). IEEE.

Ranganathan, L. N., Chinnadurai, S. A., Samivel, B., Kesavamurthy, B., & Mehndiratta, M. M. (2015). Application of mobile phones in epilepsy care. *International Journal of Epilepsy, 2*(1), 28−37.

Ren, Y., Werner, R., Pazzi, N., & Boukerche, A. (2010). Monitoring patients via a secure and mobile healthcare system. *IEEE Wireless Communications, 17*(1), 59−65.

Sahoo, S., Kanungo, B., Behera, S., & Sabut, S. (2017). Multiresolution wavelet transform based feature extraction and ECG classification to detect cardiac abnormalities. *Measurement, 108*, 55−66.

Salvador, C. H., Carrasco, M. P., De Mingo, M. G., Carrero, A. M., Montes, J. M., Martin, L. S., & Monteagudo, J. L. (2005). Airmed-cardio: A GSM and Internet services-based system for out-of-hospital follow-up of cardiac patients. *IEEE Transactions on Information Technology in Biomedicine, 9*(1), 73−85.

Sanei, S. (2013). *Adaptive processing of brain signals*. John Wiley & Sons.

Sareen, S., Sood, S. K., & Gupta, S. K. (2016). An automatic prediction of epileptic seizures using cloud computing and wireless sensor networks. *Journal of Medical Systems, 40*(11), 226.

Sayiner, N., Sorensen, H. V., & Viswanathan, T. R. (1996). A level-crossing sampling scheme for A/D conversion. *IEEE Transactions on Circuits and Systems II: Analog and Digital Signal Processing, 43*(4), 335−339.

Serhani, M. A., El Menshawy, M., & Benharref, A. (2016). SME2EM: Smart mobile end-to-end monitoring architecture for life-long diseases. *Computers in Biology and Medicine, 68*, 137−154.

Shen, C.-P., Chen, W.-H., Chen, J.-M., Hsu, K.-P., Lin, J.-W., Chiu, M.-J., ... Lai, F. (2010). Bio-signal analysis system design with support vector machines based on cloud computing service architecture. *Presented at the annual international conference of the IEEE engineering in medicine and biology society (EMBC)* (pp. 1421−1424). IEEE.

Shih, D.-H., Chiang, H.-S., Lin, B., & Lin, S.-B. (2010). An embedded mobile ECG reasoning system for elderly patients. *IEEE Transactions on Information Technology in Biomedicine, 14*(3), 854−865.

Siuly, S., Li, Y., & Zhang, Y. (2016). *EEG signal analysis and classification*. Springer.

Spruit, M., & Lytras, M. (2018). Applied data science in patient-centric healthcare: Adaptive analytic systems for empowering physicians and patients. *Telematics and Informatics*, *35*(4), 643−653.

Stoica, P., & Moses, R. L. (1997). *Introduction to spectral analysis* (Vol. 1). Upper Saddle River, NJ: Prentice Hall.

Stopczynski, A., Stahlhut, C., Larsen, J. E., Petersen, M. K., & Hansen, L. K. (2014). The smartphone brain scanner: A portable real-time neuroimaging system. *PLoS One*, *9*(2), e86733.

Subasi, A. (2007). Selection of optimal AR spectral estimation method for EEG signals using Cramer−Rao bound. *Computers in Biology and Medicine*, *37*(2), 183−194.

Subasi, A., & Ercelebi, E. (2005). Classification of EEG signals using neural network and logistic regression. *Computer Methods and Programs in Biomedicine*, *78*(2), 87−99.

Venkatesan, C., Karthigaikumar, P., & Satheeskumaran, S. (2018). Mobile cloud computing for ECG telemonitoring and real-time coronary heart disease risk detection. *Biomedical Signal Processing and Control*, *44*, 138−145.

Vetterli, M. (1987). A theory of multirate filter banks. *IEEE Transactions on Acoustics, Speech, and Signal Processing*, *35*(3), 356−372.

Wang, X., Gui, Q., Liu, B., Chen, Y., & Jin, Z. (2013). Leveraging mobile cloud for telemedicine: A performance study in medical monitoring. *Presented at the 39th annual northeast bioengineering conference (NEBEC)* (pp. 49−50). IEEE.

Wang, X., Gui, Q., Liu, B., Jin, Z., & Chen, Y. (2014). Enabling smart personalized healthcare: A hybrid mobile-cloud approach for ECG telemonitoring. *IEEE Journal of Biomedical and Health Informatics*, *18*(3), 739−745.

Xia, H., Asif, I., & Zhao, X. (2013). Cloud-ECG for real time ECG monitoring and analysis. *Computer Methods and Programs in Biomedicine*, *110*(3), 253−259.

Zheng, Y.-L., Ding, X.-R., Poon, C. C. Y., Lo, B. P. L., Zhang, H., Zhou, X.-L., & Zhang, Y.-T. (2014). Unobtrusive sensing and wearable devices for health informatics. *IEEE Transactions on Biomedical Engineering*, *61*(5), 1538−1554.

CHAPTER 10

Mobile Partogram—m-Health technology in the promotion of parturient's health in the delivery room

Karla Maria Carneiro Rolim[1], Mírian Calíope Dantas Pinheiro[2], Plácido Rogério Pinheiro[3], Mirna Albuquerque Frota[4], José Eurico de Vasconcelos Filho[5], Izabela de Sousa Martins[6], Maria Solange Nogueira dos Santos[7] and Firmina Hermelinda Saldanha Albuquerque[8]

[1]DSc in Nursing from the Federal University of Ceará (UFC), Brazil. Full Professor of the Undergraduate Nursing Course of the University of Fortaleza (UNIFOR). Professor of the Graduate Program in Collective Health (PPGSC/UNIFOR). Coordinator of the Professional Master's Degree in Technology and Innovation in Nursing (MPTIE/UNIFOR), University of Fortaleza (UNIFOR), Fortaleza, Brazil, [2]DSc in Nursing from the Federal University of Rio de Janeiro (UFRJ), Brazil. Full Professor of the Undergraduate Nursing Course of the University of Fortaleza (UNIFOR). Professor of the Professional Master's Degree in Technology and Innovation in Nursing (MPTIE/UNIFOR), University of Fortaleza (UNIFOR), Fortaleza, Brazil, [3]DSc in Systems Engineering and Computing from the Federal University of Rio de Janeiro (UFRJ). Coordinator of the Graduate Program in Applied Informatics of the University of Fortaleza (PPGIA/UNIFOR), Fortaleza, Brazil, [4]DSc in Nursing from the Federal University of Ceará (UFC), Brazil. Full Professor of the Undergraduate Nursing Course of the University of Fortaleza (UNIFOR). Coordinator of the Graduate Program in Collective Health (PPGSC/UNIFOR). Professor of the Professional Master's Degree in Technology and Innovation in Nursing (MPTIE/UNIFOR), University of Fortaleza (UNIFOR), Fortaleza, Brazil, [5]DSc in Computer Science from the Pontifical Catholic University of Rio de Janeiro (PUC/RJ). Coordinator of the Laboratory of Innovation in ICT of the University of Fortaleza (NATI/UNIFOR). Professor of Computer Engineering at UNIFOR. Professor of the Professional Master's Degree in Technology and Innovation in Nursing (MPTIE/UNIFOR). Director of Citizenship and Digital Culture of the Coordination of Science Technology and Innovation of the Municipality of Fortaleza (CITINOVA/PMF), University of Fortaleza (UNIFOR), Fortaleza, Brazil, [6]MSc. in Technology and Innovation in Nursing, University of Fortaleza, Brazil (MPTIE/UNIFOR), Fortaleza, Brazil, [7]MSc. in Technology and Innovation in Nursing, University of Fortaleza, Brazil (MPTIE/UNIFOR), Fortaleza, Brazil, [8]MSc. in Nursing from the Graduate Program in Collective Health of the University of Fortaleza (PPGSC/UNIFOR), Fortaleza, Brazil

10.1 Introduction

Mobile technology is a growing reality in our society, influencing a new profile of information delivery, services, and interactivity for its users. According to a survey by Business Insider, the forecast is 1.4 billion smartphones in the world by the end of 2014, with a ratio of two handsets per nine people in the world. Health systems must meet the diverse needs of the population, thus promoting high-quality services even in distant environments with scarce resources, as well as training and supporting health workers (Kovach, 2014).

Health systems must meet the diverse needs of the population, thus promoting high-quality services even in distant environments with scarce resources, in addition to training and supporting health workers (Piette et al., 2012).

There are many difficulties in achieving the health goals proposed in the Millennium Development Goals, and the demand of consumers in health services is growing and has led managers to seek innovative ways to improve healthcare outcomes. With the advances of smartphones and tablets, there has been a transformation in mobile communication, commerce, the financial and entertainment sector, among other industries (Ammenwerth, Buchauer, Bludau, & Haux, 2000).

International Technical Organizations such as the World Health Organization (WHO) and the International Telecommunication Union are encouraging the adoption of m-Health technology—considered as the use of mobile computing in promoting healthcare and other Information Communication and Technology (ICT) in health systems, aiming to reduce geographical barriers and improvements in the provision of health information (Masika et al., 2015).

m-Health technology can be widely diffused in low- and middle-income countries and therefore with little infrastructure, since it has great potential to support health projects that are economically viable and sustainable (Piette et al., 2012). The definition of m-Health by the Global Health Observatory is like a public healthcare practice anchored by mobile devices such as mobile phones, patient monitoring devices, personal digital assistants, and other wireless devices (World Health Organization, 2015).

Advances in knowledge and technology in recent times have improved the quality of maternal and child health. However, the last few decades have been marked by even modest progress in reducing maternal mortality coefficients and an almost stagnation of the coefficients of infant mortality due to the difficulties in reducing the neonatal component.

m-Health tools are designed to improve health education and surveillance, systems management, and clinical decision-making, as well as support management-related behavior

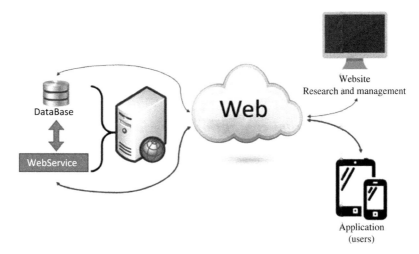

Figure 10.1
Architecture illustration: typical m-Health services.

changes, facilitating communication between clients and health professionals (World Health Organization, 2015).

The use of the architecture of m-Health services, the internet and web services, a real interaction between the health service provider and the patient is achieved. In this way, the patient's medical record can be accessed at any time or place through a computer, tablet, or smartphone (Silva & Lopes, 2015), as shown in Fig. 10.1.

On the other hand, m-Health strategies are user-centered, offering a means for acquiring new knowledge, modifying their attitudes or changing behavior. These strategies are focused on health education in a timely manner, self-monitoring and the dissemination of information related to health (Free et al., 2013). Particularly among low education populations (Labrique et al., 2017).

Moreover, there are barriers to the implementation of solutions in the area of m-Health, the main ones are related to the lack of information on the efficacy and cost benefit of m-Health applications, conflict of priorities in the health systems, absence of a policy of support and legal issues (World Health Organization, 2015). The m-Health area has an enormous potential for transforming health and clinical interventions in the community. Studies indicate the use of mobile phones to support public health interventions, such as studies that highlight successful mobile phone usage.

Although still are in the process of evaluation, many m-Health interventions, using smartphones that can promote changes in behavior through empowerment and incentives in education (Gurman, Rubin, & Roess, 2012).

Currently, healthcare, the technologies present themselves as proposed paradigm shift that allows you to meet the current reality regarding the relationship between health staff and users of the services such as significant elements of rearticulation between professional practice and population health needs.

10.2 The Mobile Partogram conception—m-Health technology in parturient care in the delivery room

The development of new technologies is intended to ensure safe care during labor and increase the survival of the binomial. Consider the main reason for monitoring labor to provide safety and to identify the deviation early enough for intervention (Berglund, Lefevre-Cholay, Bacci, Blyumina, & Lindmark, 2010). In addition, a great difficulty is to achieve a correct use of the Partogram, including appropriate and timely interventions (Downe, Gyte, Dahlen, & Singata, 2013). In this context, one of the most important observations is the difficulty in recognizing the warning signs and taking affirmative action. This leads to delays and is often associated with maternal mortality (Berglund et al., 2010).

In a large multicenter study sponsored by World Health Organization (1994), management and labor were evaluated in patients who used the Partogram, found a reduction in prolonged labor, a decrease in the need for oxytocic use, and a significant decrease in fetal deaths, concluding that the Partogram is a valid and acceptable method in the surveillance of labor (World Health Organization, 1994).

The Partogram brings quality of care benefits in terms of ease of registration, providing an overview of the progress of Labor, care auditing, clinical training, and care transfer. However, women progress in Labor in different rhythms, and the use of the Partogram can have adverse effects such as increased artificial rupture rates of membranes, increase of oxytocin and use of analgesia, resulting in a more negative work experience (Lavender, Hart, & Smyth, 2013).

It is observed, however, in practice that the Partogram, when it is completed, is not performed correctly or in its entirety. An example is the difficulty of these professionals in turning intuitive behaviors into numbers, that is, they evaluate the Labor of Delivery or they define medical interventions using as reference their professional experiences, without any scientific evidence.

Within the delivery room environment, it is important to provide safe care, as the WHO has launched the World Alliance for Patient Safety and in partnership with the Joint Commission International (JCI) comes encouraging the adoption of the International Patient Safety Goals (IPSGs) as a strategy to guide good practices for reducing risks and adverse events in health services. The first six IPSGs are directed at preventing adverse events of patient identification, communication failures, adverse drug events, adverse events in surgical procedures, care-associated infections, patient falls, and pressure ulcer prevention (Brasil. Ministério da Saúde. Secretaria de Políticos de Saúde, 2001).

The nurse is based on the nursing process, using the clinical judgment for the applicability of its interventions, strengthening the actions performed in an efficient and effective way for the decision-making about the care (Matos & Cruz, 2016). It should be emphasized that the challenge to address the reduction of risks and damages in healthcare depends on new technologies and the assistance provided by professionals. In line with the millennium goals, ensure a healthy life and promote well-being for all, at all ages (Pett & Harper, 2011).

Despite the documented benefits and recommendations, the use of the partograph is poor, inconsistent, or misused (Wakgari, Tessema, & Amano, 2015). The most important barriers to using the partograph are low resource settings, lack of human resources, poor competence, lack of continuous facilitative supervision, tool acceptability, and lack of functional referral mechanisms present a major challenge for the effective use of the partogram (Pett & Harper, 2011).

Such facts led to the need to implement a technological tool that helps and reduces errors in filling out the Partogram. The limiting factor for the use of the Partogram is the clinical difficulty for the accurate diagnosis of the beginning of Labor and its active phase (Hofmeyr, 2005).

In this context, one of the most important observations is the difficulty in recognizing the warning signs and taking affirmative action. This leads to delays and is often associated with maternal mortality (Hoogenboom et al., 2015).

In general, rigid routines are adopted without critical evaluation on a case-by-case basis. At the same time, adequate practices for a good follow-up of labor, such as the use of the Partogram, are not performed (Brasil. Ministério da Saúde. Secretaria de Políticos de Saúde, 2001). The evaluation of the quality of actions and health services is of fundamental importance for the progressive consolidation of a health system that is desirable and economically accessible to the country (Pereira, 2002).

New technologies of care are developed daily, resulting in a process based on daily experience and research, for the development of a set of ordered, organized, and articulated knowledge/know-how for employment in the process of conception, elaboration, planning, execution/operationalization and the maintenance of material, symbolic goods and services produced and controlled by human beings with a practical and specific purpose (Lavender et al., 2013).

Reassuring the need for technology use emphasize that to face challenges, nursing professionals, nurses, and technicians need to become agents of transformation and change, abandoning old informational and unilinear communication strategies (Brasil. Ministério da

Saúde. AGÊNCIA Nacional de Vigilância Sanitária, 2013; Matos & Cruz, 2016). Therefore adopting a practice with more dialogue and sensitivity, sharing with the "other" a new path and new senses. In keeping with the millennium goals, ensuring a healthy life and promoting well-being for all, at all ages (Organização das Nações Unidas, 2015).

Daily, new care technologies are developed, resulting in a process based on daily experience and research, for the development of a set of ordered, organized, and articulated knowledge/ knowledge for employment in the process of conception, elaboration, planning, execution/ operationalization and maintenance of material and symbolic goods and services produced and controlled by human beings, with a practical and specific purpose (Nietsche et al., 2012).

However, digital technologies make it possible to create educational materials that can motivate the team, making them complicit in the process of care and engaging them throughout the technology development process. To this end, new technologies such as the Internet, which stimulate adaptation to the social environment and the health professional, become the link of knowledge of these technologies and may facilitate the process of awareness and accreditation of neonatal nursing care (Schimith et al., 2011).

Therefore it is possible to observe that the concepts transmitted by the media influence decision, by making it a mediator, the promotion of obstetrical assistance through mobile devices is believable. Mobile Health (m-Health) is the term used to designate applications that support medicine and health services through mobile devices (Vital Wave Consulting, 2009). In Brazil, the supply and use of these applications tend to grow along with the popularization of smartphones, especially those operating on the Android platform (Android Developers Guide, 2015).

In this way, a m-Health technology was conceived, more specifically an application supported by web service and tablet device, with a focus on the evolution of Labor, on the complete and correct registration and on the interaction with the professionals. This tool aims for reliable and safe care and will sensitize doctors and nurses for a holistic view of the parturient. It will also provide interaction with professionals through the provision of clinical guidelines through warning signs, at the time of the recording of clinical findings with changes. This will motivate them to use the tool and a sharing of shared care and responsibility in the follow-up of the pregnant woman, providing a humanized and singular care to ensure a safe and harmless delivery.

10.3 Participatory user-centered interaction design to support and understand the conception of partograma mobile

In recent years, new publications have appeared on technologies, which facilitate and encourage the promotion of health and the prevention of diseases, since it expands the

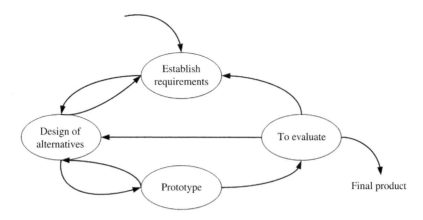

Figure 10.2
User-centered participatory interaction design, Fortaleza, Ceará, 2017.

scientific scenario, in which ICTs have been used as a communication strategy in health (Aguiar & Mendes, 2016). Thus this research counted in its development phase with the contribution of an own methodology for the development of the artifact—the user-centered interaction design (Rogers, Sharp, & Preece, 2013).

This methodology is characterized by the continuous participation of the researcher in its phases and by taking into account the needs, desires, and limitations of the users in all phases of the design and development of the project, since the objective of this process is to make the user interaction with the tool as simple and efficient as possible. In user-centered interaction design, the process of creating technological resources contemplates four iterative and strongly related activities, as shown in Fig. 10.2.

10.4 Identifying needs and defining requirements

Identifying user needs means to know as much about them as possible, their work, and the context in which they are involved to define how the developing system can support them in achieving their goals.

The needs of users should be the main focus in the development process of information systems, in order to promote effective satisfaction through the high degree of usability, accessibility, and quality of the tool. When conducting a research on the participatory design in the creation of information systems, these authors obtained the participation of the users in several ways, such as testimonials, workshops, models, scenario description, card-sorting, social network analysis, braindraw, and prototyping (Camargo & Fazani, 2014).

The activity of identifying needs (of users—nurses and obstetricians) and establishing requirements (of the technological artifact) occurred in the first stage (bibliographical survey and integrative review) of this research and was complemented by brainstorming meetings team of the Nucleus of Application in Information Technology with the researcher. Thus a technical document with the system requirements was recorded to guide the NATI team as to what should be developed and tested. In the next step, the low interface prototypes (where the concept and the initial idea of the system are shown) and high (which will look as close as possible to the final system) are designed.

Thus a technical document with the requirements of the system that is subsidy for the subsequent steps of the process was recorded, serving mainly to guide the Nucleus of Application in Information Technology team on what should be designed, developed, and tested.

To know the technologies involved in delivery support, a bibliographical survey of the main publications in Brazil and in the world was carried out on parturient care and the participation of professionals in completing the Partogram. From the study, information relevant to the process was identified (Table 10.1).

For this phase of the research, the brainstorming technique was adopted for the team's decision-making, with the purpose of collecting ideas and suggestions for solutions for the construction of the application. Brainstorming is a technique used in groups to submit to

Table 10.1: Example of important functions identified for Partogram record support, Fortaleza, Ceará, Brazil, 2017.

FUNCTION 1	Suggestions of Good Practices according to delivery period and characteristics
FUNCTION 2	Suggestions for possible diagnoses and interventions
FUNCTION 3	Anamnesis: Name, number of records, date of birth, ultimate rule of menstruation, gestation/delivery/abortion, childbirth/cesarean/delivery by forceps, children living, blood group and Rh factor, prenatal, intercurrences
FUNCTION 4	Calculation of probable birth and gestational age
FUNCTION 5	Broken or whole bag
FUNCTION 6	Characteristics of amniotic fluid
FUNCTION 7	Dilation of the uterine cervix
FUNCTION 8	Presentation height and position variety
FUNCTION 9	Exam time by system
FUNCTION 10	Blood pressure and pulse
FUNCTION 11	Maternal temperature
FUNCTION 12	Fetal heart rate
FUNCTION 13	Uterine dynamics
FUNCTION 14	Medications and fluids
FUNCTION 15	Signature and registration of the professional
FUNCTION 16	Alerts for revaluation
FUNCTION 17	Alert for signs of abnormalities
FUNCTION 18	Registry modification
FUNCTION 19	Postpartum
FUNCTION 20	Care indicators

productivity and the generation of ideas, mainly for the scenario of the present project that counts on a multidisciplinary team of the areas of computer engineering, design, and nursing (Treffinger & Isaksen, 2005).

Associated with the brainstorming, a benchmark research was carried out regarding the software products already developed to support the monitoring of Labor assistance. Also for the Benchmark—process of product comparison can be observed in Table 10.2 that some technological artifacts were found in virtual stores of applications, directed to the area of obstetrics, some free others not.

The applications found were Digital Partogram, Partogram, Partogram (system of a company), and Management of Childbirth, the descriptions of the same are as follows:

- Digital Partogram: Provides the partogram graph vitally for real-time filling. Allows for previous registrations and does not allow control of the duration of contractions. The application does not issue alerts or pipeline suggestions regarding the findings. It's a free app.
- Partogram: Assists in completing the Partogram by guiding the next examination. It allows to choose the time of the registry, thus allowing the tampering of the data. It

Table 10.2: Research conducted in applications aimed at monitoring the evolution: Play store, Apple store, Google play (keywords: Partogram; Partogram; Partograph; Labor of Delivery; Obstetrics), Fortaleza, February 2017.

Function	Digital Partogram	Partogram	Partogram/company	Delivery management
FUNCTION 1	Does not attend	Does not attend	Does not attend	Does not attend
FUNCTION 2	Does not attend	Meets	Meets	Does not attend
FUNCTION 3	Meets	Partially attends	Partially attends	Partially attends
FUNCTION 4	Does not attend	Does not attend	Does not attend	Does not attend
FUNCTION 5	Meets	Meets	Meets	Meets
FUNCTION 6	Meets	Meets	Does not attend	Meets
FUNCTION 7	Meets	Meets	Meets	Meets
FUNCTION 8	Meets	Does not attend	Meets	Meets
FUNCTION 9	Does not attend	Does not attend	Meets	Does not attend
FUNCTION 10	Meets	Does not attend	Meets	Does not attend
FUNCTION 11	Meets	Does not attend	Does not attend	Does not attend
FUNCTION 12	Meets	Does not attend	Meets	Does not attend
FUNCTION 13	Meets	Does not attend	Meets	Partially attends
FUNCTION 14	Meets	Meets	Does not attend	Partially attends
FUNCTION 15	Does not attend	Does not attend	Meets	Does not attend
FUNCTION 16	Does not attend	Does not attend	Meets	Does not attend
FUNCTION 17	Does not attend	Does not attend	Meets	Does not attend
FUNCTION 18	Meets	Meets	Does not attend	Meets
FUNCTION 19	Does not attend	Meets	Does not attend	Partially attends
FUNCTION 20	Does not attend	Does not attend	Does not attend	Does not attend

provides an option of which professionals can follow the induction of TP. You have no data regarding postpartum. It's a free app.

- Partogram Company: Help in completing the Partogram, generating the trace through the system. Generates alert as vital parameters are out of normal range. It does not generate care indicators. It's a private system.
- Childbirth Management: Displays the Partogram graph virtually to the fill in real time, generating the trace through the system. There is no control of the BCFs and vital signs of the parturient. It allows changing the data already recorded, as well as choosing the time the exam is being recorded. It does not generate care indicators. It's a free app.

The development of a mobile technology, to support the operation of the Partogram—the Mobile Partogram will allow the monitoring and evaluation of the TP in real time, with security and usability and that will provide subsidy for the health professionals in the decision-making, contributing of an important way in reducing maternal and perinatal mortality and morbidity, which characterizes the technological artifact in an innovative way in health informatics.

10.4.1 Design of alternatives

With regard to the design of alternatives of the artifact, prototype drawings were initially generated based on the identification of requirements and the establishment of requirements, color palette, typography and visual elements. This prototype of low fidelity, as it is already a reflection of the solution, allowed the discussion and revision of the design of alternatives by the team before beginning the codification of the artifact. The interfaces produced in this step.

There is a great need to consider the pedagogical and cultural aspects (re)design—design of alternatives, as well as the interaction of educational software, evaluating how the technical–pedagogical–cultural relationship influences the participatory design process of this type of tool, in the case of them a Virtual Learning Environment, which facilitates the expansion of the interaction between students and teachers, in face-to-face or distance learning courses. This same approach applies to the development of other technologies, including m-Health (Rosa & Matos, 2015).

10.5 Building an interactive version (high-fidelity prototype)

Structured in the high-fidelity interface prototypes developed as final product of the previous stage, the development (codification) of an interactive version of the application begins. This step included knowledge of software engineering, such as best practices and programming standards, generating a prototype with tablet applications (centered on the delivery room) and a web application developed using Ruby on Rails, HTML5, CSS3, and Bootstrap.

The design process is characterized by the possibility of iteration between stages, since each activity may reveal the need to return to previous functionality to redefine or enlarge the artifact produced. This iteration between activities occurs whenever it is deemed necessary and is limited only by the budget, time, and available resources.

At the end of this step, the application and its support service have been developed, allowing to advance to the evaluation stage.

10.6 Evaluation (usability)

Human computer interaction (HCI) has been the subject of research and development interdisciplinarily work that are in high expansion. Areas of knowledge such as experimental psychology, educational psychology, design, ergonomics, and even anthropology and sociology are examples of areas studied in HCI (Silva & Lopes, 2015).

After the first version of the technological artifact was made, the usability test was performed with medical professionals and nurses. The application of this empirical evaluation methodology, coming from the HCI area, aims to better understand the dynamism between the user and the proposed product. In this phase of evaluation, we sought recognition of the possibilities and limitations of the technological service. Thus the test was performed in a controlled environment so that the evaluator may had a greater control over the activities of the users during the test.

This allowed us to identify usability and system problems (Barbosa & Silva, 2010). At this point, the approach used allowed us to understand better the importance of technology for health, given that the application has reached its effectiveness as a tool to support professionals and management.

The Mobile Partogram, so will reach target audience with success, since all its items related to presentation and structure have been assessed very positively by the specialists.

10.7 Final considerations

Although it has been little used in maternity and normal delivery centers intra- and extra-hospital, the Partogram is a guiding strategy for adopting interventions, besides being a teaching tool in school hospitals, as it favors the professionals who are entering the Obstetrics can easily perceive the possibilities of conducts for each case in which this instrument is used (Barros & Veríssimo, 2011).

The prototype Mobile Partogram is the result of a multidisciplinary project of research and development of a technological application focused on the support and monitoring of the evolution of Labor. Such a project presented challenges especially in the HCI, being necessary a study of an interaction model compatible with the hospital environment. This foundation allowed the definition of the tooling and methodology for the design and development of the technological solution.

Possible reasons for the lack of documentation of the partograph may be the lack of health professionals, the complexity of the chart, the knowledge, and the difference of abilities among health professionals about how to use the partograph and limited knowledge about the importance of the tool (Mandiwa & Zamawe, 2017).

The development and evaluation of this innovation technology is designed for medical professionals and nurses working in obstetrics to facilitate their direct care with the woman patient and will also serve as a tool to aid in the practice of learning as well as support the management of the indicators of the assistance provided.

During the construction period of the app, interfaces and functionalities based on the scientific theoretical knowledge and the actions and interpretations about the care of pregnant women were inserted. In the first stage, the design and development of the application in the laboratory was carried out, with applications for smartphone with 18 screens, tablet applications with 21 screens, and the web applications with 15 screens, which composed of main menu—access, about the application.

At this stage, Participatory Interaction Design, especially in the design phase, provided the development of the screens and interfaces, with a special concern with its structure, content, and facilitation of use, and how it would occur inside the Delivery Room.

In the second phase, the application's usability test was applied by experts, who were nurses and doctors who contributed with their opinions on the physical structure of the app, its applications regarding appearance and content. From the reports of the participants, it was evidenced the need for adjustments in some screens with their respective functions of the tool.

The application proposal has emerged to reach the target audience in question, so that a change of routine is not perceivable, since the application will be used through tablets that should be made available in the Labor Delivery Room. Therefore they will facilitate the search of information, since they can be accessed in any space of time. In this way, the research developed and will qualify an innovative technology to support the follow-up to Labor.

Finally, through a virtual network of professionals, we believe in the possibility of broadening communication and interaction, creating a greater bond and consequent accreditation to the nursing institution and professionals.

With the positive evaluation by the specialists in obstetrics about the development of the Mobile Partogram and the findings made during the process of development and evaluation of the tool, it was felt the need to reorganize the content and make the clinical validation with the professionals in the delivery room, being the next stage of the study.

10.8 Teaching assignments

- Can a mobile digital technology (m-Health) support the implementation and use of the Partogram be considered a healthcare technology for parturients?
- Can this technology be considered adequate for monitoring labor? What are the stages of elaboration and validation regarding the content, appearance, and usability of a mobile health technology?
- Would computerizing usability and mobility and automating part of the Partogram fill make its use more effective and efficient?

References

Aguiar, F. C., & Mendes, V. L. P. S. (2016). Comunicação organizacional e tecnologias da informação e comunicação (TICs) na gestão hospitalar. *Perspectivas em Ciência da Informação*, *21*(4), 138−155. [S.l.], dez. ISSN 19815344. Disponível em:<http://portaldeperiodicos.eci.ufmg.br/index.php/pci/article/view/2690/1818>. Acesso em: 29 jan. 2019.

Ammenwerth, E., Buchauer, A., Bludau, B., & Haux, R. (2000). Mobile information and communication tools in the hospital. *International Journal of Medical Informatics*, *2*(57), 21−28.

Android Developers Guide. (2015). API guides. Disponível em: <http://developer.android.com/guide/index.html>. Acesso em: 02 ago. 2017.

Barbosa, S. D. J., & Silva, B. S. (2010). *Interação humano-computador*. Série SBC, Editora Campus-Elsevier.

Barros, L. A., & Veríssimo, R. C. S. S. (2011). Uso do Partograma em Maternidades Escola de Alagoas. *Rev Rene, Fortaleza*, *12*(3), 555−560. Disponível em: <http://www.revistarene.ufc.br/vol12n3_pdf/a15v12n3.pdf>. Acesso em: 13 dez. 2016.

Berglund, A., Lefevre-Cholay, H., Bacci, A., Blyumina, A., & Lindmark, G. (2010). Successful implementation of evidence-based routines in Ukrainian maternities. *Acta Obstetricia et Gynecologica Scandinavica*, *89*(2), 230−237.

Brasil. Ministério da Saúde. Secretaria de Políticos de Saúde. (2001). Área Técnica de Saúde da Mulher, Parto, aborto e puerpério: assistência humanizada à mulher. Brasília: Ministério da Saúde.

Brasil. Ministério da Saúde. AGÊNCIA Nacional de Vigilância Sanitária. (2013). Portaria no 529, de 1 de Abril de 2013 − Institui o Programa Nacional de Segurança do Paciente (PNSP). Brasília: MS.

Camargo, L. S. A., & Fazani, A. J. (2014). Explorando o Design Participativo como Prática de Desenvolvimento de Sistemas de Informação. *InCID: Revista de Ciência da Informação e Documentação*, *5*(1), 138−150. Ribeirão Preto, mar./ago. 2014. Disponível em: <https://doi.org/10.11606/issn.2178-2075.v5i1p138-150>. Acesso em: 04 ago. 2014.

Downe, S., Gyte, G. M. L., Dahlen, H. G., & Singata, M. (2013). Routine vaginal examinations for assessing progress of labour to improve outcomes for women and babies at term. *Cochrane Database of Systematic Reviews* (7). Available from https://doi.org/10.1002/14651858.CD010088.pub2Figueiredo, Art. No.: CD010088.

Figueiredo, C. M. S., & Nakamura, E. (2013). Computação móvel: novas oportunidades e desafios. *Rev T&C Amazônia*, *1*(2), 16−28.

Free, C., et al. (2013). Innovations and possibilities in connected health. *PLoS Medicine*, *18*(2), 1–26. Disponível em: <https://www.ncbi.nlm.nih.gov/pubmed/26415969>. Acesso em: 02 ago. 2016.

Gurman, T. A., Rubin, S. A., & Roess, A. (2012). Attitude of families of patients with genetic diseases to use m-Health technologies. *Journal of Health Communication*, *17*(1), 82–104.

Hofmeyr, G. J. (2005). Evidence-based intrapartum care. *Best Practice & Research Clinical Obstetrics & Gynaecology*, *19*(1), 103–115. Disponível em:<http://www.sciencedirect.com/science/article/pii/S1521693404001518>. Acesso em: 14 mar. 2017.

Hoogenboom, G., Thwin, M. M., Velink, K., Baaijens, M., Charrunwatthana, P., Nosten, F., & Mcgready, R. (2015). Quality of intrapartum care by skilled birth attendants in a refugee clinic on the Thai-Myanmar border: A survey using WHO Safe Motherhood Needs Assessment. *BMC Pregnancy Childbirth.*, *15*, 17. Available from https://doi.org/10.1186/s12884-015-0444-0.

Kovach, S. (2014). Will be a monster year for smartphone shipments. Disponível em: <http://www.businessinsider.com/1-billion-smartphones-shipped-2014-1#ixzz2tmtDOYcQ>. Acesso em: 15 de ago. de 2017.

Labrique, A. B., et al. (2017). How core competencies are taught during clinical supervision: Participatory action research in Family medicine. *Global Health: Science and Practice*, *1*(2), 160–171. Disponível em:<http://onlinelibrary.wiley.com/doi/10.1111/medu.12017/abstract>. Acesso em: 15 de ago. de 2017.

Lavender, T., Hart, A., & Smyth, R. M. D. (2013). Effect of partogram use on outcomes for women in spontaneous labour at term. *Cochrane Database of Systematic Reviews*. [Internet] Disponível em:<http://onlinelibrary.wiley.com/doi/10.1002/14651858.CD005461.pub4/epdf>. Acesso em: 22 mar. 2016.

Mandiwa, C., & Zamawe, C. (2017). Documentação do partograma na avaliação do progresso do trabalho por prestadores de cuidados de saúde na zona sudoeste do Malawi. *Reproductive Health*, *14*, 134. Available from https://doi.org/10.1186/s12978-017-0401-7, Publicado em linha2017 23 de outubro.

Masika, M. M., et al. (2015). Data acquisition in a wireless diabetic and cardiac monitoring system. *Pan African Medical Journal*, *12*(17), 1–12. Disponível em: <https://www.ncbi.nlm.nih.gov/pubmed/22255009>. Acesso em: 23 set 2017.

Matos, F. G. O. A., & Cruz, D. A. L. M. (2016). Development of an instrument to evaluate diagnosis accuracy. *Revista da Escola de Enfermagem da U S P*, *2*(43), 1088–1097. USP. Disponível em:<http://www.scielo.br/pdf/reeusp/v43nspe/en_a13v43ns.pdf>. Acesso em: 23 set. 2017.

Nietsche, E. A., et al. (2012). Tecnologias inovadoras do cuidado em Enfermagem. *Revista de Enfermagem da UFSM*, *2*(1), 182–189.

Organização das Nações Unidas. (2015). 17 Objetivos para transformar o mundo. Disponível em: <https://nacoesunidas.org/pos2015/ods3/>. Acesso em: 11 mar. 2017.

Pereira, M. G. (2002). *Qualidade dos Serviços de Saúde. Epidemiologia Teoria e Prática*. (pp. 538–560). Rio de Janeiro: Guanabara Koogan.

Pett, C., & Harper, P. (2011). Revitalizing the Partograph: Does the evidence support a global call to action? (Fistula Care Report of an expert meeting). Desmond tutu Center, New York, NY, November 15–16.

Piette, J. D., et al. (2012). Monitoring progress and adherence with positive airway pressure therapy for obstructive sleep apnea: The roles of telemedicine and mobile health applications. *Bull World Health Organization*, *90*(5), 365–372.

Rosa, J. C. S., & Matos, E. S. (2015). Considerando aspectos culturais no (re)design da interação de Ambientes Virtuais de Aprendizagem. In *Anais do XXIII Simpósio Brasileiro de Informática na Educação*.

Rogers, Y., Sharp, H., & Preece, J. (2013). *Design de Interação: muito além da interação humano-computador* (3rd ed.). Porto Alegre: Bookman.

Schimith, M. D., et al. (2011). Relações entre profissionais de saúde e usuários durante as práticas em saúde. *Trabalho, Educação e Saúde*, *9*(3), 479–503. Disponível em: <http://www.scielo.br/scielo.php?script = sci_arttext&pid = S1981-77462011000300008&lng = en&nrm = iso>. Acesso em: 22 out. 2017.

Silva, F., & Lopes, D. (2015). Estudo da Interação Humano-Computador em portfolios coletivos online. In *Proceedings of the 7th information design international conference*, [s.l.], pp. 1–4, set. Editora Edgard Blücher. Disponível em:<https://doi.org/10.5151/designpro-cidi2015-congic_45>. Acesso em: 12 fev 2017.

Treffinger, D. J., & Isaksen, S. G. (2005). Creative problem solving: The history, development, and implications for gifted education and talent development. *The Gifted Child Quarterly, 49*(4), 342–353, Disponível em: Acesso em: 08 set 2016.

Vital Wave Consulting. (2009). mHealth for development: The opportunity of mobile technology for healthcare in the developing world (p. 9). United Nations Foundation, Vodafone Foundation.Disponível em:<http://www.globalproblems-globalsolutionsfiles.org/unf_website/assets/publications/technology/mhealth/mHealth_for_Development_full.pdf>. Acesso em: 11 de ago. 2017.

Wakgari, N., Tessema, G. A., & Amano, A. (2015). Knowledge of partograph and its associated factors among health professionals in North Shoa Zone, Central Ethiop: A cross sectional study. *BMC Research Notes., 407*(8). Available from https://doi.org/10.1186/s13104-015-1363-x.

World Health Organization. (2015). m-Health: New horizons for health through mobile technologies. Disponível em: <http://www.who.int/goe/publications/goe_mhealth_web.pdf>. Acesso em: 24 ago. 2017.

World Health Organization. (1994). Partograph in management of labour. World Health Organization Maternal Health and Safe Motherhood Programme. *Lancet, 343*(8910), 1399–1404.

CHAPTER 11

Artificial intelligence—assisted detection of diabetic retinopathy on digital fundus images: concepts and applications in the National Health Service

Michael Kouroupis[1], Nikolaos Korfiatis[2] and James Cornford[2]

[1]Department of Ophthalmology, The Queen Elizabeth Hospital NHS Foundation Trust, King's Lynn, United Kingdom, [2]Norwich Business School, University of East Anglia, Norwich, United Kingdom

11.1 Introduction

According to the World Health Organization, diabetes has caused approximately 1.5 million deaths (Zaki et al., 2016). Diabetic retinopathy (DR) represents one of the most severe ocular complications of diabetes and is the leading cause of preventable blindness in working-age populations (Mohamed, Gillies, & Wong, 2007). Yau et al. (2012), on a pooled analysis of 35 studies, report an estimate of 34.6% for any form of DR, with more severe forms such as proliferative DR (6.96%), diabetic macular edema (DME; 6.81%), and vision threatening DR to show high prevalence (10.2%).

In the particular case of the United Kingdom, the prevalence of DR in patients with Type-I and Type-II diabetes was 48.4% and 28.3%, respectively (Mathur et al., 2017). In England, there are 1,280 new cases of blindness caused by DR every year (Judah et al., 2016). More than 2.5 million people (aged ≥ 12 years) with diabetes are offered DR screening (DRS) at least annually by the Diabetic Eye Screening Program (DESP), carried out by the National Health Service (NHS).

Whether diet, tablets, or insulin is used to control diabetic symptoms, risk factors for DR may include the length of time the person has had diabetes, poor control of blood sugar and high blood pressure. The current vision of NHS is to innovate in the context of smart healthcare solutions, and as such, DESP aims to reduce the risk of sight loss among patients with diabetes by timely diagnosis and effective treatment of sight-threatening DR at the appropriate stage of the disease process. To achieve that goal, innovation in medical

Innovation in Health Informatics.
DOI: https://doi.org/10.1016/B978-0-12-819043-2.00011-3

technology (*MedTech*) and smart healthcare solutions are needed (Lytras & Visvizi, 2018). This has profound economic and performance significance for the level of health services provided both in community services as well as hospital eye services (HES). However, introducing a smart healthcare solution to tackle such a quality of life degrading condition has its own challenges and risks. These obstacles are manifested both at the detection and the prevention stages of the health services provision.

This chapter discusses the current advances and challenges in introducing automated diagnostic processes for DR, utilizing recent advances in artificial intelligence (AI) for automated DR classification in the context of the DESP program. The initial discussion focuses on how procedural integration of DESP with AI-assisted DR can improve diagnostic efficacy and patient outcomes. To this end, this chapter is structured as follows: Section 11.2 describes the status quo and provides the background to the problem statement and in particular the challenges involved in the development of automated tools for diagnostic retinopathy. Sections 11.3 and 11.4 discuss the issues anticipated during the introduction of automated systems in clinical DR classification from the perspective of smart healthcare and predictive analytics. The primary argument is that automated DR classification can enhance the role of human graders and function in a supportive, rather than replacing them with technology. An outline of ethical and organizational challenges is provided in Section 11.5. The chapter concludes in Section 11.6 with considerations and the broader implications of AI implementation.

11.2 Diabetic retinopathy in the National Health Service

Retinal screening in England is overseen by the NHS DESP (NDESP) and delivered by more than 80 local programs. England has over 2.5 million people aged 12 and over with diabetes with a 5% projected increase every year (The Royal College of Ophthalmologists, 2012).

Most screening programs strive to attain a balance between three organizational objectives: (1) accept referrals of patients with diabetes, (2) provide long-term clinical care, and (3) facilitate feedback to service commissioners. Each local program uses technicians to provide screening in the community using digital photography. Patients with retinal abnormalities are referred to local HES. The primary operational challenge that needs to be addressed is the lack of resources to meet the demand of an increasing number of patients requiring screening. Standard performance metrics require at least 95% of the patients to be seen within 2 weeks for urgent referrals by the DRS to reach HES and specialist retinal clinicians to grade the images and advise next steps to the patient.[1]

---

[1] NHS diabetic eye screening program: pathway standards, https://www.gov.uk/government/publications/diabetic-eye-screening-standards-and-performance-objectives.

Local screening programs are contractually obliged to achieve key performance indicators (KPIs), dictating that routine referrals must be seen in HES within certain number of weeks (between 2 and 6 weeks). As such, HES are challenged by several factors such as (1) the rising prevalence of diabetes (Wild, Roglic, Green, Sicree, & King, 2004), (2) the costs of screening implementation (James, Turner, Broadbent, Vora, & Harding, 2000), (3) the maintenance of an effective quality assurance system (Scanlon, 2017), and (4) the high volume of referrals and the monotonous nature of grading which may lead to high attrition rates and other staffing issues.

Consequently, since the establishment of the DR screening program, most NHS eye departments exhibit significant deviations from these KPIs. This has resulted in longer patient waiting times (Graham-Rowe et al., 2018), which often lead to life-changing degradation of patient outcomes.

The major challenge of screening pathways can be characterized by (1) long waiting times, (2) false positive referrals, and (3) significant variations in the quality of grading provided, which hinders the efficiency of the screening process. The existing DR screening program is handicapped by the high volume of patients with diabetes, high variability of data handling, and limited hospital resources. Moreover, the screening process is time consuming. The delay in delivering results can lead to lost follow-ups, miscommunication and missed or postponed treatments all of which may increase the probability of vision loss (Hautala et al., 2014).

As a result, there is an urgent requirement to improve the above aspects of the present service performance to achieve tangible (e.g., reduced waiting times, lower number of false positive referrals, and better utilization of scarce hospital resources) as well as intangible benefits (e.g., improved patient experience). Patient data along with retinal fundus images are obtained through digital photography at the data acquisition stage. Graders (experts tasked with evaluating the condition of DR) assess both the quality and the information encapsulated on the image. If the image doesn't contain information that will allow the grading of the DR status due to issues associated with reduced mobility, inadequate patient cooperation, or pathological conditions (small pupil, media opacities, cataracts, vitreous haze, asteroid hyalosis, etc.), then a new referral outcome is staged in order to evaluate DR at hospitalized services. A typical grading task involves the evaluation of the existence of retinopathy (either in stage R1 or R2) or maculopathy (M1) or the evaluation of other non-DR lesions. In case non-DR lesions are found in the fundus image, internal quality assurance is performed which is done at a secondary grading stage. Fig. 11.1 provides an overview of the grader consensus pathway regarding the classification of the information contained in the fundus image.

The referral workflow dictates that patients with non-DR conditions (R0M0) will be recalled for annual screening at a later stage. For those that have DR conditions diagnosed

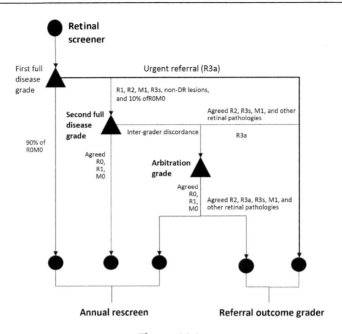

Figure 11.1

Grading pathway (stages involved in specification no. 22 of the NHS Diabetic Eye Screening Programme).

by the grader (R1, R2, M1, and previously treated stable proliferative DR—R3S) or exhibit other lesions which are not of diabetic nature, such as age-related macular degeneration, naevi of the choroid, suspicion of glaucoma, retinal vascular occlusions, a review of a second grader is involved. If there is an agreement between a primary and secondary grading (in the case of R0, R1, M0), referral outcomes are established or members of this cohort are invited for annual screening.

In addition, it is essential to minimize patients' anxiety associated with screening due to inappropriate referral. Therefore false positive referral rate should be monitored to ensure it is not more than 25% of all referrals and ideally 20% or fewer. This constitutes a significant portion of false positives, taking valuable time regarding referrals to specialists (National Diabetic Retinopathy Screening Programme, 2009). Further, graders must grade a minimum required numbers of image sets per year to maintain their expertise.

If a disagreement occurs, then an arbitration stage is involved where a senior grader is assigned to evaluate the case. Patients with either no-DR condition or mild nonproliferative DR are assigned to the annual digital screening program. All other patients labeled in a secondary or arbitration grade with maculopathy (M1), preproliferative DR (R2), active proliferative DR (R3S), or sight-threatening retinal condition such as neovascular age-related macular generation (wet AMD) are referred to the HES.

The workflow depicted in Fig. 11.1 provides a useful overview of the current DR diagnostic processes utilized in NHS. Nonetheless, these diagnostic assessments face a considerable challenge stemming from the continuous prevalence of DR and budgetary constraints that the NHS has as regard to diagnosis. A direct outcome of these challenges is the recruitment of graders and optimization of the referral pathway, with both been highly dependent on the grading quality. The management of grading quality is dictated by imposing good practice in the current skills of graders, requiring their continuous involvement in DR screening and participation in training programs.[2] This makes the system highly dependent on human input and faces the challenges related to staffing and training of new graders. We argue that the current established DR screening workflow can be substantially supported by the use of automated methods.

11.3 Predictive analytics in diabetic retinopathy screening

In the context of healthcare, the use of analytics has enabled substantial efficiencies (Davenport & Harris, 2007), ranging from extracting information from existing sources such as electronic health records to utilizing new forms such as genetic and genomic data. The development of diagnostic tools aiming to improve care quality and patient safety through *precision delivery* (Parikh, Kakad, & Bates, 2016) has been the cornerstone of smart healthcare solutions built using AI techniques.[3] Considering the nature of the data sources involved in DR screening, the application of conventional tools and methodologies is challenged by several properties of the data at hand. The consensus is that such analyses cannot be done with traditional approaches, but increasingly, as in the case of diabetic retina screening, involve the use of large and incongruent datasets, which move into the territory of *big data*.

Healthcare organizations optimize image analysis workflows and improve access to services by informing policy decisions around expansion and distribution of services and resource utilization using, for example, sensor technologies (Bates, Heitmueller, Kakad, & Saria, 2018). The primary data unit in this context is retinal fundus images. Fundus images are obtained by retinal fundus photography, which involves getting a digital image of the back of the eye (i.e., retina). The images are captured via specialized cameras consisting of an intricate microscope attached to a flash enabled DSLR. The ocular structures, which can be visualized on a fundus photo, are the retina (temporal, nasal, superior, inferior), the central macula, and the optic disk. The storage of these images and the associated metadata provide a promising data source which can be exploited by automated tools. In the subsequent section, we provide an overview of the properties of fundus images as regard to big data and discuss the possibilities for predictive analytics in that context.

---

[2] Diabetic eye screening: assuring the quality of grading. Public Health England. Available at: https://www.gov.uk/government/publications/diabetic-eye-screening-assuring-the-quality-of-grading

[3] See Topol (2019) for an overview of comparative performance of doctors vesrus AI in healthcare.

11.3.1 Big data in the context of diabetic retinopathy screening

Data emerging following the acquisition and organization of retinal imaging exhibit characteristics requiring expert input for all functions involved in the diagnostic process. As such their characteristics can be seen in the context of big data which are commonly characterized as "data that are so large or complex that traditional data processing applications are inadequate" (Bates et al., 2018). A common framework to describe the dimensions and challenges of big data management is the three Vs namely: volume, variety, and velocity (Chen, Chiang, & Storey, 2012; Kwon, Lee, & Shin, 2014; Laney, 2001). We discuss these dimensions in the context of DR screening data as follows:

- *Volume*: Every data record carries an average of approximately 16 MB of data. These include identification information, demographics, open text comments, and annotations by the screeners and eight 2 MB high-resolution tagged image file format retinal images from both eyes. The amount of data accumulated by more than three million diabetic patients in England every year is well within the Big Data territory.
- *Variety*: This refers to the structural heterogeneity in the data. The DRS database amalgamates structured data such as tabular fields and unstructured data in a binary form such as retinal images as shown in Fig. 11.2. Apart from variations in the data source, there also exist variations in metadata fields, depending on the actual characteristic of the grading task. One way to handle such an issue is with the use of

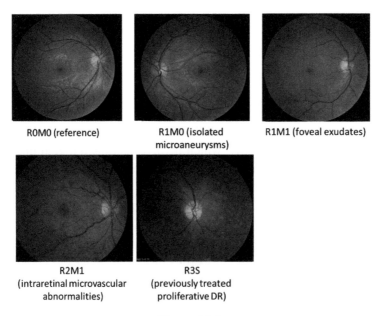

R0M0 (reference)   R1M0 (isolated microaneurysms)   R1M1 (foveal exudates)

R2M1 (intraretinal microvascular abnormalities)   R3S (previously treated proliferative DR)

Figure 11.2

DRS gradings on example fundus images. Source: *Authors' own work.*

structured schemas for diabetic retina records (Kimball & Ross, 2011). Other important information such as camera properties encapsulated in image metadata (e.g., through EXIF information encapsulated on the image file itself), also needs to be captured. Another level of variation concerns the technical differences in data capture which are often apparent even within the same provider. For example, as Scanlon (2017) reports, within NHS, there are several differences concerning image size, compression, and image capture requirements across providers (e.g., NHS England vs. Scotland) and even within commissioning groups depending on the appointed contractor.

- *Velocity*: This refers to the rate at which data are generated and the speed at which it should be analyzed and acted upon. The KPIs set by NHS England dictate a prompt initial classification of the severity of DR by the screeners and an urgent less than 6 weeks referral to HES for sight-threatening cases. As illustrated in Fig. 11.2, the continuous addition of information on initial images leads to an unprecedented rate of data creation. Generating high-frequency data drives a growing need for real-time analytics and evidence-based planning.

An additional challenge that DR-related datasets need to address is the concept of *Veracity* which represents the unreliability inherent in some sources of data. For example, retinopathy classification and disease severity grading by DRS technicians is uncertain, since it requires human judgment. However, it also contains valuable information that can be exploited with machine learning. Thus the need to deal with imprecise and uncertain data is another facet of these datasets from the perspective of big data, which is addressed using tools and analytics developed for management and mining of uncertain data (Gandomi and Haider, 2015).

11.3.2 Predictive analytics in diagnostic retina screening

In the last decade, the evolution of computation power has allowed the exploitation of large sources of clinical data, which can be analyzed by computerized algorithms. These algorithms exist along a continuum from fully human-guided to fully machine-guided data analysis at the high end of the machine learning spectrum (Beam & Kohane, 2018; Gulshan et al., 2016). Machine learning tasks are typically classified into (1) supervised learning, in which the system infers a function from labeled training data, (2) unsupervised learning, in which the learning system tries to deduce the structure of unlabeled data, and (3) reinforcement learning, in which the system interacts with a dynamic environment (Russell and Norvig, 2016).

Engineering features for machine learning can be challenging. Achieving accuracy in prediction and classification tasks is challenging due to the contextual relevance of the data in question, as well as the complexity of pairing the right feature with the response variable. While several use cases exist for applying machine learning techniques in various settings such as performance improvement, care quality monitoring, operational efficiency, and coordinated team-based care, the biases associated with insufficient availability and quality of data are a significant challenge for adoption of automated AI-driven approaches.

For the particular context of retinal screening, despite the richness and potential of available data, scaling the development of predictive models is difficult because, for traditional predictive modeling techniques, each outcome to be predicted requires the creation of a custom dataset with specific variables (Goldstein, Navar, Pencina, & Ioannidis, 2017). This creates a set of three specific challenges:

- *Dataset availability*: To train machine learning classifiers require annotated representative data from a varied set of fundus cameras and various locations.
- *Retinal image analysis*: Image analysis with computer vision is challenging due to the large and varied set of fundus images with different patterns and color variations.
- *Retinal images from multiple cameras*: Another primary challenge is handling retinal images from different types of fundus cameras.

11.3.3 Evaluation and performance measures

For automated detection of microaneurysms, two measures are mostly used: sensitivity and specificity. This considers the use of a confusion matrix (Table 11.1) for measuring the sensitivity (precision) and specificity (recall) of the diagnostic accuracy considering both true and false positives and negatives. More specifically: true positives (TP) are correctly identified retinopathy cases while false positives (FP) are misidentified. Similarly, true negatives (TN) are correctly identified negatives, and false negatives (FN) wrongly identified negatives.

Sensitivity is the probability of a positive classification of DR given that the patient has DR. It is defined as follows:

$$\text{Sensitivity} = \frac{TP}{P} = \frac{TP}{TP + FN} \tag{11.1}$$

Table 11.1: Confusion matrix for positive and negative classes in a DR diagnostic setting.

Predicted class		Actual class	
		C1 (Yes)	C2 (No)
	C1 (Yes)	True positives (TP)	False positives (FP)
	C2 (No)	False negatives (FN)	True negatives (TN)
		Sensitivity	Specificity

Specificity is the probability of a negative diagnosis of DR given that the patient has no DR. It is defined as follows:

$$\text{Specificity} = \frac{TN}{N} = \frac{TN}{FP + TN} \tag{11.2}$$

Automatic detection of DR abnormalities presents many challenges. The size and color of retinal hemorrhages are similar to blood vessels. Their size is variable and small so that the machine can potentially misinterpret it due to noise present in the image. In the human retina, there is variation in pigmentation, texture, size, and location of features from person to person (Agrawal, Bhatnagar, & Jalal, 2013). More false positives occur when the blood vessels are overlapping or adjacent with microvascular abnormalities.

A general specification of accuracy considers the combination of sensitivity and specificity as follows.

$$\text{ACC} = \frac{TP + TN}{FP + FN + TP + TN} \tag{11.3}$$

Several research groups have developed computer-aided diagnostic systems (CAD) for DR. The algorithms for detection of DR following studies are heterogeneous. Therefore it is not possible to make a direct comparison of their performance. In this regard, the British Diabetic Association estimates the accuracy rates of any screening program for DR should achieve sensitivity of 80% and specificity of 95% (Mead, Burnett, & Davey, 2001). This should be an essential criterion for comparing the automated screening options.

As can be seen in Table 11.2, the highest accuracy is observed in the study of Sánchez, García, Mayo, López, and Hornero (2009) by using Hard exudates and Fischer Linear discriminant analysis. The results from this study echo a well-known observation in forecasting, related with the forecasting effectiveness of simpler algorithms coupled with features of high informational value (Makridakis & Hibon, 1979). Nonetheless, this is a pathognomonic feature of sight-threatening DR which is easily spotted by a technician. Therefore this could act as an additional step together with more robust approaches which require less information such as the image pixel and color information reported by Noronha and Nayak (2013).

The evidence suggests that automated DR classification is feasible and can be done with minimal annotation input (with the assumption that the acquisition source is stable, e.g., CMOS camera settings). We outline the implementation challenges in the section that follows.

Table 11.2: Summary of studies on automated DRS ranked by accuracy.

Authors	Feature detected	Features and classifiers	Accuracy (%)
Zhang, Karray, Li, and Zhang (2012)	Microaneurysms and blood vessel detection	Dictionary learning and sparse representation classifier	84.67
García, Sánchez, López, Abásolo, and Hornero (2009)	Red lesions	Image and shape features using neural networks	86
Quellec et al. (2012)	Abnormal patterns in fundus images	Multiple-instance learning	88.1
Köse, ŞEvik, İKibaş, and Erdöl (2012)	Image pixel information	Inverse segmentation using region growing, adaptive region growing and Bayesian approaches	90
Giancardo et al. (2012)	Exudates in fundus images	Exudate probability map and wavelet analysis	94
Sánchez et al. (2009)	Hard exudates	Edge detection and mixture models	95
Qureshi et al. (2012)	Identifying macula optic disk	Ensemble combined algorithm of edge detectors, hough transform and pyramidal decomposition	95.33
Noronha and Nayak (2013)	Image pixel and color information	Wavelet transforms and support vector machine (SVM) kernels	99
Ganesan et al. (2014)	Trace transform functionals	SVM kernels, probabilistic neural network-genetic algorithm	99.12
Akram, Khalid, and Khan (2013)	Image shape and statistics	Gaussian mixture models and support vector machine	99.53
Sánchez et al. (2008)	Hard exudates	Color information and Fisher's linear discriminant analysis	100

Source: *Adapted from Ganesan, K., Martis, R., Acharya, U., Chua, C., Min, L., Ng, E., & Laude, A. (2014). Computer-aided diabetic retinopathy detection using trace transforms on digital fundus images.* Medical & Biological Engineering & Computing, 52(8), *663–672.*

11.4 Implementation in a smart healthcare setting

11.4.1 Upskilling the workforce

The potential of automated DR screening can be used to address the heterogeneity in skillsets and background knowledge required for the grading tasks that were discussed in Section 11.2. An overview of the different qualifications and professional categories involved in the diagnostic evaluation of DR is presented in Fig. 11.4. Critical decisions that affect complex cases are handled by arbitration graders who are often Retinal Specialists, Consultant Diabetologists/Ophthalmologists. Such specialties have limited capacity due to budget constraints. Reducing the values of the diagonal columns (false positives, false negatives) in the confusion matrix is necessary to create efficiencies in the time allotments that these experts get to review and arbitrate cases that are complex and often difficult to judge without experience.

On the other hand, as can be seen in Fig. 11.3, for all graders who are not physicians (medical retina specialists) or optometrists, qualification standards (e.g., City and Guilds)

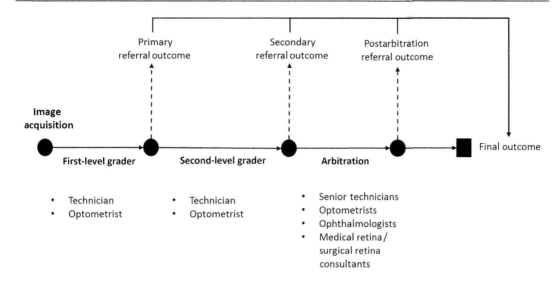

Figure 11.3

Profiles of graders involved in DR screening (see analytical pathway for profile description[4]).

are imposed before starting grading assignments. Such a training process is comprehensive, time consuming and has strict criteria for continuous training every year to revalidate the qualification and increase quality assurance in grading classification tasks.

Automated classification when is deployed alongside human graders can lead to reduced arbitration requirements and improve the efficiency of the existing DRS workflows. The primary need is to enable multimodal input both from automated DR *and* grader-based DR. This can lead to a significant reduction in false positives (which results to higher efficiencies in screening time) as well the elimination of false negatives (which reduces detrimental effects in patient safety).

A significant application of automated DR screening is training where the requirements for grader quality assurance impose a minimum number of DR evaluations to take place at each diagnostic period (usually a year). First-level graders may lack skills and experience in diagnosing complex cases and the incorporation of AI-driven DR evaluations can boost grader confidence and allow greater accuracy in the identification of DR lesions in fundus photography. Experience in handling these cases can often provide better diagnostic results in the first level of grading when high-level graders are involved in that task (Scanlon et al., 2003). Nonetheless, using only retinal fundus images as diagnostic inputs can increase diagnostic complexity before and as such new features may be needed to complement and enhance the ground truth for automated DR.

---

[4] Diabetic eye screening: assuring the quality of grading. Public Health England. Available at: https://www.gov.uk/government/publications/diabetic-eye-screening-assuring-the-quality-of-grading

The proposed reassignment of the DR grading from *humans* to *machines* will invariably generate a sense of anxiety and fear of financial loss to HI which is the private company currently obtaining and grading the retinal images. Understandably there is generalized anguish regarding jobs being lost to automation. People have come to believe that their jobs, their communities and the social contract that binds them to work, place and each other are under threat (Alexander, 2018). There is mounting evidence that machine-learning algorithms, like all previous technologies, bear the imprint of their designers and culture (Wajcman, 2017). Therefore one should be optimistic about the jobs that will be created as a result of the digital revolution (Brynjolfsson and McAfee, 2014).

The employees of HI should be reassured regarding the safety of their jobs. While HI will continue performing digital screening in the community, resources previously utilized for human grading of retinopathy could be repurposed to undertake other tasks. These tasks include (1) patients' awareness and training programs, (2) safeguarding vulnerable patients with diabetes, (3) dealing with the multifactorial public health phenomenon of high *Did Not Attend Appointment* rates amongst diabetic patients (Dervan, Lillis, Flynn, Staines, & O'Shea, 2008; Dyer, Lloyd, Lancashire, Bain, & Barnett, 1998; Le et al., 2017), (4) extending digital screening to more distant rural communities, (5) providing a higher volume image acquisition, and (6) *undertaking* additional administrative support duties.

11.4.2 Multimodal imaging in diabetic retinopathy: integrating optical coherent tomography

The main limitation of color fundus photography for diabetic retinal screening purposes lies in the inability of the examination to provide additional information on retinal layer structure and morphology. Features such as retinal thickness, presence of macular edema, intraretinal fluid associated with the microaneurysms, integrity of the retinal layers, and the retinal pigment epithelium are invariably undetected by the traditional fundus imaging (Hee et al., 1995). Furthermore, the computational complexity involved with feature extraction and analysis of medical images can be reduced by incorporating other modalities and data layers. Such an additional data layer can be sourced by advances in optical coherent tomography (OCT) screening.

OCT screening operates by capturing three-dimensional retinal images and can be considered as a three-dimensional DR screening tool. The guiding principle behind OCT is measurement of the intensity and the echo-time delay of light scattered from the retina layers. Scattered light produces two data sources, which act as reference and sample signals (or arms). The detection of the discrepancy between the reference and sample can be analyzed either by time domain detection or Fourier Domain detection (in either Spectral or Swept Source).

Fig. 11.4 provides an example of a false-negative characterization of a fundus image in a DR screening scenario. As can be seen in the left panel, the image shows subtle nonproliferative DR consisting of isolated microaneurysms. This referral outcome from the grader was R1M0 suggesting no evidence of DME. However, OCT demonstrates diffuse parafoveal DME, which is evident by the thickness profile shown in the thickness profile map under the right panel.

This example shows the limit of optical inspection from graders as to the diagnostic value of the fundus image and the pattern recognition capabilities of the grader himself. While arguably an experienced grader would come to a different decision in the initial referral, the particularity of the case could lead to a negative outcome for the patient. OCT can be used as a complementary layer for diagnostic accuracy, either by enabling the upskilling of first-level graders or by helping resolve arbitration tasks by reducing the involvement of highly experienced graders.

As aforementioned, graders need to undergo vigorous training in annotating DR cases, enabling them to complement the grading task with OCT modalities can help them improve their diagnostic accuracy. Furthermore, the relatively structured nature of OCT data can be used as an alternative feature in DR classification tasks.

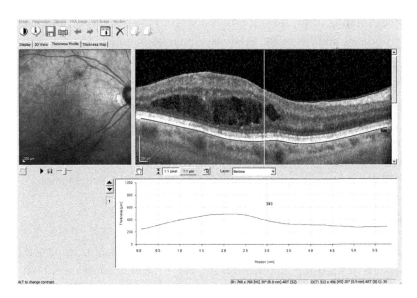

Figure 11.4

An example of false-negative fundus image (left panel), examined through OCT. The chart depicts the thickness profile of the retina by subtracting the locations of internal limited membrane and the basement membrane. As it is evident from the chart and the image above, there is a moderate central diabetic macular edema. Source: *Authors' own work.*

11.5 Challenges

11.5.1 Adoption and clinical governance

It is essential to achieve joint accountability for issues that cannot be decided by IT alone. In other words, the new centrally appointed CIO (Chief Information Officer) should participate with senior managers and retinal clinicians of the individual Trust to participate in visioning and strategy making, promoting an understanding of future (technology-enabled) possibilities (McLoughlin, Garrety, & Wilson, 2017). The rules of engagement between various stakeholders, the dynamics of influencing power and the frequency of interactions between CIO, CEOs (Chief Executive Officers), IT managers, and Clinical Leads of the hospitals should be formally articulated to achieve a satisfactory degree of collaboration and project outcomes (Zicari et al., 2016). The board of directors and the Trust, under the guidance of the local CCG (Clinical Commissioning Group), should engage in the process. This can only be achieved by demonstrating the appropriate levels of transparency and clarity for the nontechnical managers to be accountable for the project.

Key stakeholders represent a wide variety of departments. The primary contact will usually be someone from Purchasing/Supply Chain Management, with input from departments such as Legal and IT plus the main users from other departments. A collaborative engagement with clinicians is imperative to ensure a unanimous approval of the chosen diagnostic software. Further training of healthcare professionals in the context of familiarization of the system, future updates, and firmware versions should be negotiated and established.

This can be informed by the incorporation and understanding of the dynamic elements of such processes, considering that the introduction of AI-assisted grading is a complex intervention. Normalization process theory (May & Finch, 2009) can inform the adoption process of such interventions considering the input of multiple agents (e.g., the different classes of agents involved), contexts (e.g., various HES), and objects of intervention (graders/patients). As such, the adoption of AI-assisted grading, in the context of diabetic retinal screening needs to acknowledge the critical organizational aspects of a successful implementation.

11.5.2 Ethical and legal compliance

The use of data in diagnostic processes carries ethical issues such as informed consent, privacy, ownership/stewardship, anonymization, etc. Processes must meet both epistemological standards (e.g., of truth) and moral standards (e.g., of fairness or justice) (Mittelstadt & Floridi, 2016). The recently introduced General Data Protection Regulations (Iyengar, Kundu, & Pallis, 2018) cover a wide range of ethical issues including appropriation of data use and consent in using patient data for diagnostic purposes.

What is important to highlight here is that "*data concerning health*" and "*biometric data*" such as DRS databases will be subject to a higher standard of protection than personal data in general. Applications of DRS in other fields, such as cardiovascular diseases (Poplin et al., 2018), may pose additional challenges as regard to data governance. Aggregating and repurposing data for other pathologies than originally planned in the initial or *"historic"* consent agreement (such as cardiovascular diseases) may result in new public health and life-insurance implications, both positive and negative for the various parties.

11.6 Conclusion

The need for accurate retinal examination at the time of diagnosis of diabetes is widely accepted (Cheung, Mitchell, & Wong, 2010). The implementation of automated learning can contribute to enhanced clinical decision-making pathways with good diagnostic accuracy. A significant amount of research has recently resulted in the development of the first novice commercial predictive algorithms for the automated diagnosis of DR and its complications. However, most of these models have not been adopted by the NHS, and the clinical impact has not been widely investigated. Although evidence from implementation is lacking, this chapter supports the potential of automated diagnostics to transform the way healthcare providers use sophisticated technologies (Cichosz, Johansen, & Hejlesen, 2016).

In the future, as more smart healthcare solutions will become available in the ophthalmic practice, additional insight will be gained to improve decision-making, utilizing a large amount of electronically stored clinical data (Spruit & Lytras, 2018). Further research is necessary to evaluate the applicability of machine learning in healthcare settings and the utility of the automated screening processes to improve long-term vision outcomes. Currently the adoption of OCT for DR screening purposes by the national diabetic retinal screening programs is at its infancy and as such developing automated classifications of DR to enable the upskilling of human graders can result in higher standards of accuracy both from a manual and automated point of view. As such we echo the suggestions of Raman et al. (2018) as regard to the synergies arising from AI-supported medical imaging in an auxiliary approach to save healthcare resources and enable universal access to DR screening. It should benefit the NHS to enable the amalgamation of multiple modalities both at the annotation (AI-assisted grading) as well as the data acquisition (OCT input) layer to address the diagnostic dilemmas of graders and better stratify patients and optimize referral pathways.

References

Agrawal, A., Bhatnagar, C., & Jalal, A. S. (2013). *A survey on automated microaneurysm detection in diabetic retinopathy retinal images. Proceedings of the 2013 international conference on information systems and computer networks (ISCON)* (pp. 24−29). IEEE.

Akram, M. U., Khalid, S., & Khan, S. A. (2013). Identification and classification of microaneurysms for early detection of diabetic retinopathy. *Pattern Recognition, 46*(1), 107−116.

Alexander, B. (2018). The politics of angst in Robot City, USA. *MIT Technology Review, 121*(4), 20−25.

Bates, D. W., Heitmueller, A., Kakad, M., & Saria, S. (2018). Why policymakers should care about "big data" in healthcare. *Health Policy and Technology, 7*(2), 211−216.

Beam, A. L., & Kohane, I. S. (2018). Big data and machine learning in health care. *Journal of the American Medical Association, 319*(13), 1317−1318.

Brynjolfsson, E., & McAfee, A. (2014). *The second machine age: Work, progress, and prosperity in a time of brilliant technologies.* WW Norton & Company.

Chen, H., Chiang, R. H., & Storey, V. C. (2012). Business intelligence and analytics: From big data to big impact. *MIS Quarterly,* 1165−1188.

Cheung, N., Mitchell, P., & Wong, T. Y. (2010). Diabetic retinopathy. *Lancet, 376*(9735), 124−136.

Cichosz, S. L., Johansen, M. D., & Hejlesen, O. (2016). Toward big data analytics: Review of predictive models in management of diabetes and its complications. *Journal of Diabetes Science and Technology, 10*(1), 27−34.

Davenport, T. H., & Harris, J. G. (2007). *Competing on analytics: The new science of winning.* Harvard Business Press.

Dervan, E., Lillis, D., Flynn, L., Staines, A., & O'Shea, D. (2008). Factors that influence the patient uptake of diabetic retinopathy screening. *Irish Journal of Medical Science, 177*(4), 303.

Dyer, P., Lloyd, C., Lancashire, R., Bain, S., & Barnett, A. (1998). Factors associated with clinic non-attendance in adults with Type 1 diabetes mellitus. *Diabetic Medicine, 15*(4), 339−343.

Gandomi, A., & Haider, M. (2015). Beyond the hype: Big data concepts, methods, and analytics. *International Journal of Information Management, 35*(2), 137−144. Available from https://doi.org/10.1016/j.ijinfomgt.2014.10.007.

Ganesan, K., Martis, R., Acharya, U., Chua, C., Min, L., Ng, E., & Laude, A. (2014). Computer-aided diabetic retinopathy detection using trace transforms on digital fundus images. *Medical & Biological Engineering & Computing, 52*(8), 663−672.

García, M., Sánchez, C. I., López, M. I., Abásolo, D., & Hornero, R. (2009). Neural network based detection of hard exudates in retinal images. *Computer Methods and Programs in Biomedicine, 93*(1), 9−19.

Giancardo, L., Meriaudeau, F., Karnowski, T. P., Li, Y., Garg, S., Tobin, K. W., Jr, & Chaum, E. (2012). Exudate-based diabetic macular edema detection in fundus images using publicly available datasets. *Medical Image Analysis, 16*(1), 216−226.

Goldstein, B. A., Navar, A. M., Pencina, M. J., & Ioannidis, J. (2017). Opportunities and challenges in developing risk prediction models with electronic health records data: A systematic review. *Journal of the American Medical Informatics Association, 24*(1), 198−208.

Graham-Rowe, E., Lorencatto, F., Lawrenson, J. G., Burr, J. M., Grimshaw, J. M., Ivers, N. M., & Francis, J. J. (2018). Barriers to and enablers of diabetic retinopathy screening attendance: A systematic review of published and grey literature. *Diabetic Medicine, 35*(10), 1308−1319.

Gulshan, V., Peng, L., Coram, M., Stumpe, M. C., Wu, D., Narayanaswamy, A., & Cuadros, J. (2016). Development and validation of a deep learning algorithm for detection of diabetic retinopathy in retinal fundus photographs. *Journal of the American Medical Association, 316*(22), 2402−2410.

Hautala, N., Aikkila, R., Korpelainen, J., Keskitalo, A., Kurikka, A., Falck, A., & Alanko, H. (2014). Marked reductions in visual impairment due to diabetic retinopathy achieved by efficient screening and timely treatment. *Acta Ophthalmologica, 92*(6), 582−587.

Hee, M. R., Puliafito, C. A., Wong, C., Duker, J. S., Reichel, E., Rutledge, B., & Fujimoto, J. G. (1995). Quantitative assessment of macular edema with optical coherence tomography. *Archives of Ophthalmology, 113*(8), 1019−1029.

Iyengar, A., Kundu, A., & Pallis, G. (2018). Healthcare informatics and privacy. *IEEE Internet Computing, 22* (2), 29−31.

James, M., Turner, D. A., Broadbent, D. M., Vora, J., & Harding, S. P. (2000). Cost effectiveness analysis of screening for sight threatening diabetic eye disease. *British Medical Journal, 320*(7250), 1627−1631.

Judah, G., Vlaev, I., Gunn, L., King, D., King, D., Valabhji, J., & Bicknell, C. (2016). Incentives in Diabetic Eye Assessment by Screening (IDEAS): Study protocol of a three-arm randomized controlled trial using financial incentives to increase screening uptake in London. *BMC Ophthalmology, 16*(1), 28.

Kimball, R., & Ross, M. (2011). *The data warehouse toolkit: The complete guide to dimensional modeling*. John Wiley & Sons.

Köse, C., ŞEvik, U., İKibaş, C., & Erdöl, H. (2012). Simple methods for segmentation and measurement of diabetic retinopathy lesions in retinal fundus images. *Computer Methods and Programs in Biomedicine*, *107*(2), 274−293.

Kwon, O., Lee, N., & Shin, B. (2014). Data quality management, data usage experience and acquisition intention of big data analytics. *International Journal of Information Management*, *34*(3), 387−394.

Laney, D. (2001). 3D data management: Controlling data volume, velocity and variety. *META Group Research Note*, *6*(70), 1.

Le, J. T., Hutfless, S., Li, T., Bressler, N. M., Heyward, J., Bittner, A. K., & Dickersin, K. (2017). Setting priorities for diabetic retinopathy clinical research and identifying evidence gaps. *Ophthalmology Retina*, *1* (2), 94−102.

Lytras, M., & Visvizi, A. (2018). Who uses smart city services and what to make of it: Toward interdisciplinary smart cities research. *Sustainability*, *10*(6), 1998.

Makridakis, S., & Hibon, M. (1979). Accuracy of forecasting: An empirical investigation. *Journal of the Royal Statistical Society. Series A (General)*, *142*(Part 2), 97−145.

Mathur, R., Bhaskaran, K., Edwards, E., Lee, H., Chaturvedi, N., Smeeth, L., & Douglas, I. (2017). Population trends in the 10-year incidence and prevalence of diabetic retinopathy in the UK: A cohort study in the Clinical Practice Research Datalink 2004−2014. *BMJ Open*, *7*(2), e014444.

May, C., & Finch, T. (2009). Implementing, embedding, and integrating practices: An outline of normalization process theory. *Sociology*, *43*(3), 535−554.

McLoughlin, I. P., Garrety, K., & Wilson, R. (2017). *The digitalization of healthcare: Electronic records and the disruption of moral orders*. Oxford University Press.

Mead, A., Burnett, S., & Davey, C. (2001). Diabetic retinal screening in the UK. *Journal of the Royal Society of Medicine*, *94*(3), 127−129.

Mittelstadt, B. D., & Floridi, L. (2016). The ethics of big data: Current and foreseeable issues in biomedical contexts. *Science and Engineering Ethics*, *22*(2), 303−341.

Mohamed, Q., Gillies, M. C., & Wong, T. Y. (2007). Management of diabetic retinopathy: A systematic review. *Journal of the American Medical Association*, *298*(8), 902−916.

National Diabetic Retinopathy Screening Programme. *National diabetic retinopathy screening programme principles, processes and protocols*. (2009). <https://www.loc-net.org.uk/media/1479/unit_001_help_nov09.pdf> Retrieved 19.01.19.

Noronha, K., & Nayak, K. P. (2013). Automated diagnosis of diabetes maculopathy: A survey. *Journal of Medical Imaging and Health Informatics*, *3*(2), 280−287.

Parikh, R. B., Kakad, M., & Bates, D. W. (2016). Integrating predictive analytics into high-value care: The dawn of precision delivery. *Journal of the American Medical Association*, *315*(7), 651−652.

Poplin, R., Varadarajan, A. V., Blumer, K., Liu, Y., McConnell, M. V., Corrado, G. S., & Webster, D. R. (2018). Prediction of cardiovascular risk factors from retinal fundus photographs via deep learning. *Nature Biomedical Engineering*, *2*(3), 158−164. Available from https://doi.org/10.1038/s41551-018-0195-0.

Quellec, G., Lamard, M., Abràmoff, M. D., Decencière, E., Lay, B., Erginay, A., & Cazuguel, G. (2012). A multiple-instance learning framework for diabetic retinopathy screening. *Medical Image Analysis*, *16*(6), 1228−1240.

Qureshi, R. J., Kovacs, L., Harangi, B., Nagy, B., Peto, T., & Hajdu, A. (2012). Combining algorithms for automatic detection of optic disc and macula in fundus images. *Computer Vision and Image Understanding*, *116*(1), 138−145.

Raman, R., Srinivasan, S., Virmani, S., Sivaprasad, S., Rao, C., & Rajalakshmi, R. (2018). Fundus photograph-based deep learning algorithms in detecting diabetic retinopathy. *Eye*, *33*(1), 97−109.

Russell, S. J., & Norvig, P. (2016). *Artificial intelligence: A modern approach*. Malaysia: Pearson Education Limited.

Sánchez, C. I., García, M., Mayo, A., López, M. I., & Hornero, R. (2009). Retinal image analysis based on mixture models to detect hard exudates. *Medical Image Analysis*, *13*(4), 650−658.

Sánchez, C. I., Hornero, R., López, M. I., Aboy, M., Poza, J., & Abásolo, D. (2008). A novel automatic image processing algorithm for detection of hard exudates based on retinal image analysis. *Medical Engineering & Physics*, *30*(3), 350−357.

Scanlon, P. H. (2017). The English national screening programme for diabetic retinopathy 2003−2016. *Acta Diabetologica*, *54*(6), 515−525.

Scanlon, P. H., Malhotra, R., Greenwood, R., Aldington, S., Foy, C., Flatman, M., & Downes, S. (2003). Comparison of two reference standards in validating two field mydriatic digital photography as a method of screening for diabetic retinopathy. *British Journal of Ophthalmology*, *87*(10), 1258−1263.

Spruit, M., & Lytras, M. (2018). Applied Data Science in Patient-centric Healthcare: Adaptive Analytic Systems for Empowering Physicians and Patients. *Telematics and Informatics*, *35*(4), Special Issue: Patient Centric Healthcare, 643−653. [ISI impact factor: 3.398] [pdf] [online].

The Royal College of Ophthalmologists. *The NHS diabetic eye screening programme: New common pathway*. (2012). <https://www.rcophth.ac.uk/wp-content/uploads/2014/08/Focus-Winter-2012.pdf> Retrieved 02.11.18.

Topol, E. J. (2019). High-performance medicine: The convergence of human and artificial intelligence. *Nature Medicine*, *25*(1), 44.

Wajcman, J. (2017). Automation: Is it really different this time? *The British Journal of Sociology*, *68*(1), 119−127. Available from https://doi.org/10.1111/1468-4446.12239.

Wild, S., Roglic, G., Green, A., Sicree, R., & King, H. (2004). Global prevalence of diabetes: Estimates for the year 2000 and projections for 2030. *Diabetes Care*, *27*(5), 1047−1053.

Yau, J. W. Y., Rogers, S. L., Kawasaki, R., Lamoureux, E. L., Kowalski, J. W., Bek, T., . . . Meta-Analysis for Eye Disease (META-EYE) Study Group. (2012). Global prevalence and major risk factors of diabetic retinopathy. *Diabetes Care*, *35*(3), 556−564.

Zaki, W. M. D. W., Zulkifley, M. A., Hussain, A., Halim, W. H. W. A., Mustafa, N. B. A., & Ting, L. S. (2016). Diabetic retinopathy assessment: Towards an automated system. *Biomedical Signal Processing and Control*, *24*, 72−82.

Zhang, B., Karray, F., Li, Q., & Zhang, L. (2012). Sparse representation classifier for microaneurysm detection and retinal blood vessel extraction. *Information Sciences*, *200*, 78−90.

Zicari, R. V., Rosselli, M., Ivanov, T., Korfiatis, N., Tolle, K., Niemann, R., & Reichenbach, C. (2016). *Setting up a big data project: Challenges, opportunities, technologies and optimization. Big Data optimization: Recent developments and challenges* (Vol. 18, pp. 17−47). Springer.

CHAPTER 12

Virtual reality and sensors for the next generation medical systems

Félix Mata, Miguel Torres-Ruiz, Roberto Zagal-Flores and Marco Moreno-Ibarra

Instituto Politécnico Nacional, UPALM Zacatenco, Mexico City, Mexico

12.1 Introduction

Virtual reality (VR) is an environment of scenes or objects of real appearance. It is generated by software, and it produces in the user the feeling of being immersed inside it. This environment is contemplated by the user through display graphics on the screen, or through a device like glasses or helmet of VR. Moreover, it can be accompanied by other devices, such as gloves or special suits, which allow a greater interaction with the environment as well as the perception of different stimuli that intensify the sensation of reality (Hoffman et al., 2006). VR has been used as innovation in many treatments related with phobias (Meyerbröker & Emmelkamp, 2010; Opriş et al., 2012; Turner & Casey, 2014). An example, the spider phobia case is used in multiple contexts; thus, VR improved the outcome of exposure treatment by reducing the fear sensation (Shiban, Schelhorn, Pauli, & Mühlberger, 2015).

In other fields, mobile health technologies integrate VR, and those applications are increasingly becoming more accessible and affordable, providing a potential avenue to deploy outpatient behavioral therapy, an example is described in Kim, Schwartz, Catacora, and Vaughn-Cooke (2016).

VR has also been used to address issues related to prevention, diagnosis, and healthcare (Jacobus & Griffin, 1998). Moreover, a systematic review of the state of the art about the effectiveness of VR in the psychological treatment for mental health problems is presented in Nicholson, Chalk, Funnell, and Daniel (2006), and another comprehensive review is described in Eichenberg and Wolters (2012).

Therefore VR has been used in clinical settings to treat a range of cognitive, emotional, and motor problems in various psychological and psychiatric disorders and according to a recent poll of 70 psychotherapy experts, VR and other computerized intervention are ranked at the top of interventions, which are predicted to increase its use in the next 10 years (Norcross, Pfund, & Prochaska, 2013).

Innovation in Health Informatics.
DOI: https://doi.org/10.1016/B978-0-12-819043-2.00012-5

On the other hand, the overweight and obesity are considered the biggest problem of public health in Mexico. According to above, it is necessary to find solutions that support the design of policies for treatments, and apply technologies such as virtual or augmented reality. In this case, Mexico is the first place in the world with overweight and obesity in children and the second in diseases with respect to adults (Alcántara-Bumbiedro, Flórez-García, Echávarri-Pérez, & García-Pérez, 2006). These conditions increase the risk of chronic diseases, such as those occurring in the lower back, which is an area of high vulnerability in the human body, being subjected to stress, poor posture, trauma, misuse, hereditary defects, etc. The most risk factors include bad postural habits, low physical fitness, sedentary lifestyle, lack of strength, and resistance of the spine muscles. Others can be a trauma or previous accidents, heavy physical work, driving (e.g., machines or vehicles), repetitive tasks, advanced age, congenital pathologies, overweight, scoliosis, osteoporosis, and among others (Tate, Detamore, Capadona, Woolley, & Knothe, 2016).

So important actions are necessary to provide the knowledge to people about the adverse effects that obesity and overweight cause in the human body, such as the chronical back pain, high pressure, stomach, and heart diseases. This alertness and concentration can be achieved through the use of devices and technologies such as VR, in which it is possible to graphically show the present effects and future tendencies that can occur particularly on the back, in people who are overweight or obese.

On the other hand, Big Data Analytics Strategies are required to smart healthcare, an example in this field is the adaptive analytic systems, which are presented as a research perspective of the three intertwining aspects within the knowledge discovery process in healthcare. Spruit and Lytras (2018) pointed out that the adaptive component in healthcare system prototypes may translate to data-driven personalization including aspects of personalized medicine. Regarding the policy-making and the smart healthcare and analytics integration, there is a scientific debate related to a new generation of policy-aware smart cities research geared toward innovation and socially inclusive economic growth for sustainability. The integration of sophisticated technology platforms and advanced policies requires a new managerial paradigm at all levels of decision-making across and beyond continents and local boundaries. So in Visvizi, Lytras, Damiani, and Mathkour (2018) the socially aware policy-making process as an inevitable part of smart cities' research is deeply discussed.

In the context of smart cities and smart healthcare, there is research debate about the smart cities from the perspectives of, on the one hand, citizens' awareness of applications and solutions that are considered "smart" and, on the other hand, their ability to use these applications and solutions. Lytras and Visvizi (2018) showed that even the most educated users of smart city services, that is, those arguably most aware of and equipped with skills to use these services effectively, express very serious concerns regarding the utility, safety, accessibility, and efficiency of those services.

Meanwhile, in other research studies, a normative bias of smart cities research is introduced the nested clusters model. By advocating the inclusion of policy-making and strategy considerations in the smart cities debate, a case is made for a holistic, scalable, and human-centered smart cities agenda focused (Visvizi & Lytras, 2018).

Summing up, in this research chapter, a system that allows the user to have a prediagnostic (evaluation) of their posture, determining their current state of physical health was developed. In addition, the goal is to generate information recommendations about the negative effects of overweight in the lumbar spine, as well as other possible consequences on the health. Thus the use of human interfaces and augmented VR technologies was taken into consideration in the implementation of the system. The data obtained can better record the clinical status of patients and can be used to measure the quality and efficiency of healthcare professionals, primary care in the health of back; therefore, the use of human interfaces combined with VR represents an important innovation in the field of Health Informatics. Fig. 12.1 depicts a general framework based on a VR-semantic data gathering with an analysis model oriented toward treating the chronical back pain.

The chapter is organized as follows: Section 12.2 presents the state of the art related to the work in this field. Section 12.3 describes the proposed methodology to perform recommendations, in which a mobile application senses the physical performance of a person. Section 12.4 depicts the experimental results, applying the proposed methodology. The conclusion and future works are outlined in Section 12.5. Finally, Section 12.6 presents some teaching assignments related to the main topics and focus of this chapter.

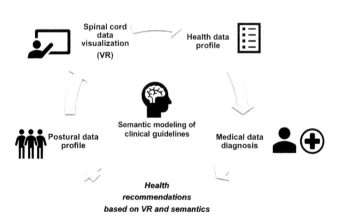

Figure 12.1

VR-semantic data gathering and analysis model for the treatment of chronical back pain.

12.2 Related work

Today, the usefulness of the VR in the health domain has been well identified. For example, VR-based simulators offer numerous benefits and are very important in assessing and training surgical skills. Although these are standards in some surgical subspecialties, their current use in spine surgery is still in progress. Thus there are technical reviews of VR based on simulators that are available for spinal surgery (Pfandler, Lazarovici, Stefan, Wucherer, & Weigl, 2017). However, those reviews are not working with human interfaces devices (Tate et al., 2016), and they are not oriented to physical evaluation and prediagnostics. The human interface device refers to a type of user interface for computers that interact directly with inputs from humans and can deliver outputs to humans. In Valmaggia, Latif, Kempton, and Rus-Calafell (2016), a general view of computational applications in the health field, highlighting the use of VR technology resources in Brazil and other countries is presented. From this initial survey, suggestions for improvements in this area were presented along with the relevant research needed to make these improvements and overcome the current obstacles.

The process to determine if a person is prone to suffer a disease of the back, caused by the overweight and the obesity is made by evaluating the posture of a patient. A typical procedure for evaluation is obtained by applying the sagittal plane. It consists of a vertical reference that theoretically crosses the body by means of the middle and intermediate, dividing into the human body the left and right halves. Next, the planes that are perpendicular to the ground, and form a right angle with the frontal planes, must be oscillated with full margins. When these margins are exceeded by excess or defect, those are considered deformations of the column. Such deformations are presented by the increase or decrease of pressure, abolition, and even inversion of the physiological curves (Riva et al., 2011). Fig. 12.2 illustrates the sagittal plane to evaluate postures of human beings.

The third wave of VR began in 2015, with several commercial consumer products and devices such as Oculus. It generates new works focused on VR experiences, including researches oriented toward treatment in the health (DeFanti et al., 2009). Moreover, the use of devices and sensors with VR has offered the characteristics of immersion (Ryan, 2001). In our research experience, the immersion approach fits well in the case of back examinations, where patients can experiment and watch in animations, what are the effects of a bad posture or possible diseases in the back, and which are caused by bad habits or costumes.

Some healthcare applications based on VR are addressed to back treatments, caused by overweight and obesity, the IMSS Clinical Practice Guideline in Mexico have presented evidences with respect to this issue (de Salubridad General, 2009). In other cases, patients

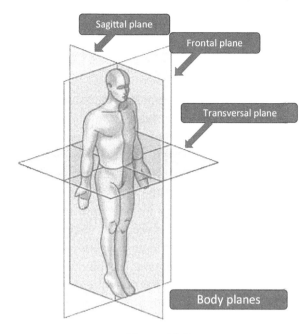

Figure 12.2
Sagittal plane to evaluate posture.

with overweight and high values of body mass index represent a risk factor for low back pain, following the European guidelines (Airaksinen et al., 2006). In contrast, the University of Oxford conducted a study about the relationship between obesity and low back pain, in which people who were overweight and persons with adequate weight suffered low back pain. The outcome presented that obesity and overweight increase the risk of low back pain. They also found a strong association in seeking care for low back pain and chronic low back pain (Shiri, Karppinen, Leino-Arjas, Solovieva, & Viikari-Juntura, 2009).

In this sense, the VR technology has represented the most important increase with a significant impact in healthcare applications, clinical studios, and general medicine. Recently, VR technology is dramatically changing medical assessments, clinical care, preventive health, and wellness, and it will help to facilitate the shift of the place of medical care, from the clinic to the home (Greenleaf, 2016).

In Valmaggia et al. (2016), a review of controlled studies in the use of VR in psychological treatment (VRT) is described. In fact, only studies that compare immersive VR were also included. The search resulted in 1180 articles published between 2012 and 2015, of which 24 were controlled studies. They confirmed the effectiveness of VRT compared to the treatment as usual and showed similar effectiveness when VRT is compared to conventional therapies.

Other applications of VR simulators are increasingly becoming as an essential part of modern education. In Roy, Bakr, and George (2017), an overview of the VR dental simulators is presented, it also reviews the relationship between VR simulation and current pedagogical knowledge.

On the other hand, postural stability is an important measure for preventing many medical diseases such as Parkinson (Morris, Iansek, Smithson, & Huxham, 2000). In the last years, some researches have been focused on using inexpensive and portable devices to measure postural stability, while the visual targets were physical objects in the environment (Soffel, Zank, & Kunz, 2016). Sensing balancing boards were used to measure stance forces, while movements of the upper body were not taken into account. In Soffel et al. (2016), postural stability was measured using the HTC Vive. A variation of a virtual fixation point's distance was analyzed and compared with respect to a reference condition with closed eyes. It is shown that body sway in the VR conditions is increased in the anterior—posterior and decreased in the medial-lateral directions. In Jamali, Shiratuddin, Wong, and Oskam (2015), a mobile prototype for learning environment that uses mobile augmented reality is proposed. It consists of making the selection of learning topics related to the anatomy of the human skeletal structure and provides scenes in augmented reality. The primary objective is to aid students and potentially enhance their learning process.

There are proposals in VR that are focused on the field of dentistry, in which the benefits of VR are continually assessed as a method. Other applications are improving the fine motor skills, hand—eye coordination in preclinical settings. In the financial and intellectual domains, the VR application implies big challenges to involve this technology in security and training (Biocca & Levy, 2013).

In this chapter, the model of VR experiences is applied in the domain of healthcare, particularly in people with obesity and overweight problems. In addition, a paradigm for using VR to medical and patients in studies of the back pain is outlined. Moreover, in order to achieve the goal, a virtual world with avatars to display the possible problems in back for several situations of daily life was developed.

12.3 The proposed methodology

The methodology is oriented toward performing a prediagnosis of two types of back pains, in people with obesity or overweight such as scoliosis and low back pain. This methodology is focused on making recommendations and deploying in a virtual environment the ailments detected, and their possible consequences for the future. The stages of the proposed methodology are the follows:

- *Postural analysis.* It consists of performing an analysis based on a human interface device. The device adopted for this characterization is the Kinect sensor, which captures and verifies key points of the patient's posture. It is necessary to determine if there is some anomaly, then in the case that anomaly is detected, an alert is sent to the physician and the patient.

- *Virtual modeling.* This stage consists of designing and deploying a virtual model. It is composed of a human skeleton that shows an approximation of the current state of the patient spinal column (this state was obtained from the Postural Analysis stage). Moreover, an animation in a virtual world is displayed, to show the possible effects of the wrong posture when it is detected by the test.

- *Self-assessment.* It is in charged of asking the user to answer a supplementary questionnaire, which allows increasing the degree of certainty in the analysis that is made by using an application ontology. The conceptual representation contains the data represented by concepts that are related to the daily life and characteristics that describe the diseases in the back.

- *Analysis and presentation.* This stage shows to the doctor and patient what is the ideal postural state that patient should have, indicating if patient has or may suffer some diseases such as low back pain, or scoliosis caused by deformations in the lumbar spine. Moreover, a set of recommendations or possible treatments to prevent problems related to the back are presented.

Fig. 12.3 depicts the conceptual framework of the proposed methodology, in which VR technology is used to analyze and detect deformations in the curvatures of the spinal column. Thus the measurements obtained from the Kinect sensor and photos of the patients are employed to show in a VR model the current and ideal states of the back.

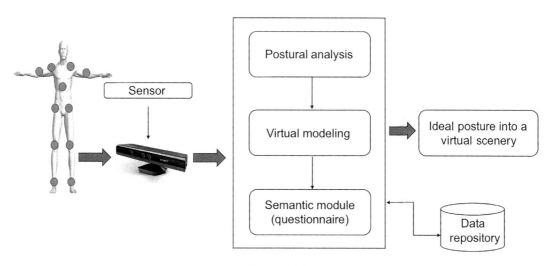

Figure 12.3
Virtual reality conceptual framework for back healthcare.

The modules that integrate the system are described as follows:

- *Identification module.* This is in charged of processing the person identification, as well as the calibration of the Kinect sensor, to recognize parts of the body of the detected person and the necessary gestures for interacting with the system.
- *Postural analysis module.* The measurements of the frontal and lateral displacements of the head are obtained by the Kinect sensor. So shoulders, hip, knees, and ankles, as well as a rotation of the head are shown to the user by means of the virtual model of the spinal column.
- *VR module.* It visually displays the virtual model of the spinal column, which is an approximation of the current posture of a person.
- *Information repository module.* This module stores the measurements that were obtained from the postural analysis stage of each user, as well as the outcomes of those analyses. The study consists of applying the Oswestry Low Back Pain Disability Questionnaire (Alcántara-Bumbiedro et al., 2006).
- *Configuration module.* In this module the standard measurements that the system takes to perform the lateral and frontal postural analyses are introduced. They can be adjusted by the specialist doctor, if necessary. In addition, it is possible to include other questionnaires to enrich the analysis.

12.3.1 Postural analysis stage

In this stage, the postural analysis is evaluated. The evaluation starts by asking the patient be placed in front of the Kinect sensor, to perform the evaluation in two phases: (1) *Postural frontal analysis*, it is identified by using a set of selected points in the patient such as head, shoulders, hip, knees, and ankles. (2) *Postural side analysis*, it is made by taking the following key points: head, shoulder, hip, knee, and ankle. Those points are depicted in Fig. 12.4.

The postural analysis is made in an area of 2.00 m $\times$ 4.90 m, and a white background to reduce the noise and facilitate the identification is used. In this, the patient is situated in 1.5 m, away from the Kinect sensor. This procedure is depicted in Fig. 12.5.

In Fig. 12.6, an area marked with a cross for indicating to the user in which position should be stand to start the calibration process is shown. Later, the postural analysis test is applied. This method is similar to use in photography, which is also a noninvasive technique to analyze the curvatures of the static posture column as described in Shiri et al. (2009). It has a low to moderate validity and reliability when it is compared to an X-ray. Moreover, this analysis is applied to the lateral and frontal, to obtain a quantitative measure, considering the following points: alignment of shoulders, hip, knees, head, and ankles. In addition, Fig. 12.6 depicts the frontal and lateral postural analyses, which were performed on the

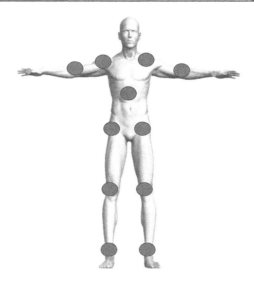

Figure 12.4
Key points for postural identification.

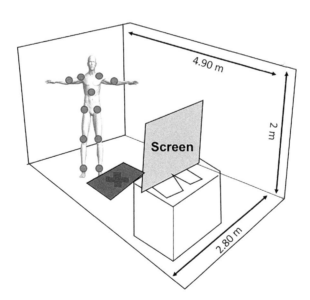

Figure 12.5
Procedure for the postural analysis area.

patient, by using the voice commands: "Front analysis" and "Lateral analysis" (previously programmed in the Kinect sensor), with the goal of beginning the measurements.

Moreover, Fig. 12.7 shows a virtual model of the skeleton with the measured approximations of the current postural state. The process is described as follows: it starts by

(A)   (B)

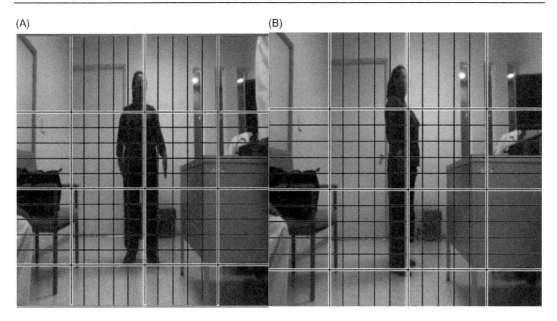

Figure 12.6
(A) *Left side*: Frontal postural analysis. (B) *Right side*: Lateral postural analysis.

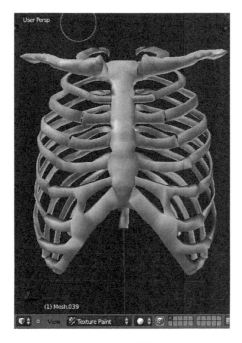

Figure 12.7
Modeling the patient's rib cage.

capturing the position values of a person measured by the Kinect sensor. The displacement of the anatomical points is computed by extracting the coordinates "*x*" from the anatomical location to be analyzed (e.g., left shoulder and right shoulder).

Then, an algebraic sum is made, since the body is centered in the (0, 0) coordinate on the Cartesian plane of the Kinect sensor. So it is possible to know the direction of the displacement of some point (left side, if the negative value predominates, and right side, if the positive value prevails). For computing the rotation of the anatomical points, it is necessary to obtain the angle between two lines, applying Eq. (12.1).

$$\theta = \cos^{-1}\left(\frac{|U{\cdot}V|}{|U|{\cdot}|V|}\right) \tag{12.1}$$

The interpretation of the obtained results is displayed when all measurement has finished. So the different alerts will be emitted as green, yellow, and red. If the person has a posture within the normal range, a green alert will be activated; the yellow warning refers that an asymmetry was detected and it must be corrected. Finally, the red alert indicates that a visit to a specialist is recommended, because the measurement shows that a deeper and more accurate assessment must be carried out.

12.3.2 Virtual modeling stage

The VR system was designed by taking into account the principles of immersion: to abstract the person from the real world and to induce him in the virtual world. It means to increase the stimuli of the virtual world and diminish the stimuli of the real world. So the interactivity consists of generating a change in the virtual world, including the feasibility, based on congruence with the laws of the virtual world, interactivity, and immersion. In Figs. 12.7 and 12.8, the models of spinal column designated from different angles are presented.

In the case of the person model, the goal is to build an avatar that is situated in a virtual scenery. It will display the avatar walking according to the posture detected in the examine of a person. The animation shows the possible damage that patient can suffer in the future, if the individual is not submitted to a doctor revision, the relationships between the spinal mobility and the assessments were taken into consideration for the diagnosis (Grönblad, Hurri, & Kouri, 1997). Fig. 12.9 depicts the avatar that corresponds to the person model.

The developed avatar is based on the "Character Sheet" sketch for rendering (Bates, 1992). The construction of the model was made by using the Level of Detail technique. This method allows several representations for the same object, according to the zoom level, to reduce the degree of computer processing. Moreover, the clipping technique was implemented in the tool. It consists of "trimming" everything that path does not allow to watch, and it makes the rendering faster.

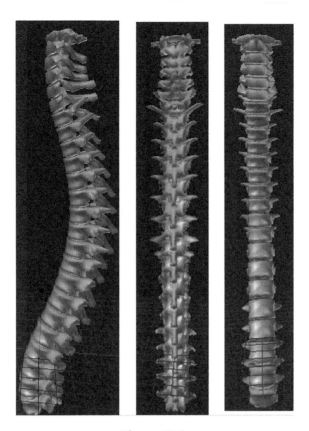

Figure 12.8
The front, back, and side views of the spinal column.

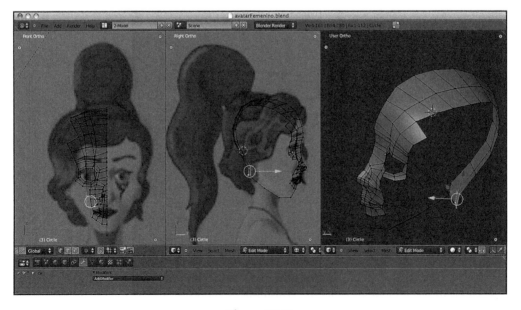

Figure 12.9
Representation and modeling of the skull and face.

12.3.3 Self-assessment stage

In the self-evaluation phase, health questionnaires are proposed to carried out the task. The phase is mainly based on the Oswestry questionnaire (Alcántara-Bumbiedro et al., 2006), which were applied in two public health institutions in Mexico, they are Mexican Social Security Institute (IMSS) and National Institute of Rehabilitation (INR). The questionnaire assesses how much it affects the low back pain in the life of the patient. It performs a complementary analysis to the postural, through an inquiry that measures the intensity of pain, personal image, mental health, and other parameters. The purpose of this inquiry is to improve the results obtained from the examination of the back by making some additional suggestions. Each patient should answer the questionnaire and the system will show to the patient and doctor the interpretation of the obtained results, from both the postural analysis and the questionnaire. The self-assessment is logically presented in Algorithm 1.

An application ontology was used to generate the recommendations that are necessary to make the patient aware of his/her current situation and inform him regarding to some repercussions that he/she should can suffer.

So the ontology construction was based on the IMSS Clinical Guidelines (de Salubridad General, 2009), which are represented in Algorithm 1; particularly, for adult patients with acute and chronic back pain. This ontology is explored by the algorithm *OntoRead* in order to extract the recommendations. This algorithm searches a match between the answer from the questionnaire and the results obtained from the sensors (Algorithm 2). The search is based on the binary tree procedure. It starts at the root node, and the nodes of the tree are traversed downwards, if the node matches, it contains the name, then the node is chosen, otherwise the exploring continues and chooses the subnode.

The results associated to the application of Algorithms 1 and 2 are presented in Table 12.1.

12.3.4 Analysis and presentation stage

This stage provides spinal column recommendations based on the IMSS Clinical Guidelines (Hoffman et al., 2006), as well as the implications of the Oswestry questionnaire. So the stage generates alerts to the patients, which receive recommendations of the treatment and health status.

The process of recommendation consists of exploring the ontology to find the adequate recommendation for each people. The algorithm *OntoReading* searches a match between the answer from the questionnaire and the results obtained from the sensors. In Fig. 12.10, a fragment of developed ontology is shown.

Algorithm 1 Evaluation and prediagnostic of acute and chronic back pain

Input: Clinic history, physical exploration

Output: *Diagnostics*

Begin

Perform clinical history and physical examination:

- *identify risk factors (physical, psychosocial, labor)*
- *differentiate inflammatory vs. mechanical type lumbar pain*
- *scientific complete neurological examination*
- *Indicates type of pain, location, duration, irradiation, triggering factor, associated neurological signs or symptoms*

IF alarm_signals

  Then

  *call **second_level()***

ELSE

  Non-pharmacological treatment

  -give triptych of education and orientation

  Avoid bed rest

  Foster early reincorporation into daily and work activities

  Column hygiene

  -recommending appropriate physical activity

  -First-line pharmacological treatment

  IF improvement <6 weeks

  Then

  Strengthen education and guidance

  Column hygiene

  Self-care

  Reincorporate daily activity and work

  Discharge

ELSE

  Re-examine and explore

  Identify chronicity data

  Identify risk factors

Value of radiographs

-search for neurological data

IF improve <12 weeks

Strengthen education and guidance

Column hygiene

Self-care

Reincorporate daily activity and work

Discharge

ELSE

Chronic back pain >12 weeks

Send_ algorithm2

function second_level (x)

Case 'Suspicion of fracture':

Get_history of trauma

if >50 years old

then

Minor trauma

Else

Evaluate osteoporosis

Review if taking asteroids

Severe trauma

Case 2: 'Suspicion of aortic aneurysm'

Pain not influenced by movements, postures or efforts

-cardiovascular risk factors

-Introduction of vascular disease

Case 'suspected infection':

Fever

Immunosupression

Penetrating wound

urinary infection

Skin infection

Case 'suspected infection':

  - suspected cauda equina / severe root compromise

  - Loss of control and sphincters

  Urinary retention

  -Anesthesia in chair d mount

  Sensory-Neuromotor Deficiency

  Pain in both legs

Case 'suspected inflammatory disease':

  < 40 years old

  Pain that improves with exercise

  Duration>3 months

  Morning stiffness>60 minutes

  Insidious onset type

  Rare neurological deficit

Case 'Suspicion of neoplasia':

  Antecedent of cancerhood >50 years

  Pain of more than 1 month of evolution

  Rest night pain

  Unexplained weight loss

The integration of human interfaces combined with VR represents a new study line, because the data generated can be integrated with data science approaches. It will improve not only the process to care about the health of back, and they can provide interesting insights for patients and medicals. This trend will be presented in the future generation of medical systems and healthcare innovations in the treatment and care of the back of patients.

12.4 Experimental results

The obtained results were compared against data from physical and radiography examinations, showing an average performance of 80% of effectiveness in a sample of 50 patients. In this sample, 20 are women and 30 are men, the groups of age are the following: 30—40 years, 40—50 years, and 50—60 years. Those outcomes are summarized in Table 12.2.

Algorithm 2 OntoRead—approach to read the content of an ontology

Input: Diagnostic Key

Output: *Recommendation*

Begin

Let q[i] **diagnostic key**

  Locate the root node.

  If contains key.

  extract nodes_children

  for each node_children

  retrieve treatment

  Else

    $N = 0$

    while $n < i$

    node.start()

    while node $! =$ null

    $j++, i++$

    if matching(concept_name, key)

a.   conVec[j]neighborhood_relations(node)
b.   node.next()

    Vector[k] = search(conVec[j])

    health_and_signal(conVec[j])

  $j++, k++, n++$

End

In Fig. 12.11, a graphical interface for the Kinect Sensor is depicted. This dashboard is used to interact with the application and display the values obtained from the sensors, in the postural examination.

Moreover, in the graphical interface, the functionality to observe a virtual scenery with the animation of the avatar and use the values obtained from the examination is offered. According to the tests, the statistics describes that people who are taller (up to 1.70 m) face more back problems, taking into consideration the questionnaire; thus, this detected that people who work in environments with furniture such as tables and chairs with different heights do not favor and force them to adopt bad postures.

Table 12.1: Interpretation of the Oswestry questionnaire.

Percentage	Disability	Implications
0–20	Minimal	The patient can perform most of the activities of his life. Often, the treatment is not indicated except for suggestions for weight lifting, posture, physical activity, and diet. Patients with sedentary occupations, for example, office workers may experience more problems than others.
21–40	Moderate	The patient may present more pain and difficulty lifting, sitting, or standing. Travel and social life are more difficult and may be unable to work. Personal care, sexual activity, and sleep are not affected. Conservative treatment may be sufficient.
41–60	Severe	Pain is the main problem in these patients, but they can also present significant difficulties in traveling, personal care, social life, sexual activity, and sleep. A detailed evaluation is appropriate.
61–80	Disability	Back pain has an impact on all aspects of daily life and work. Active treatment is required.
81–100	Maximum	These patients may be prostrate in bed. Careful evaluation is recommended.

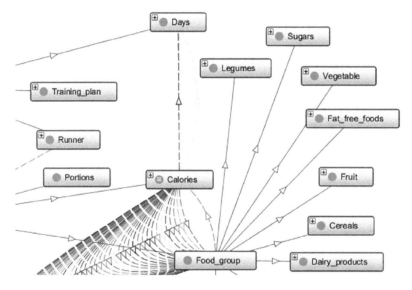

Figure 12.10
The application ontology for recommendations.

Other results are related to the activities; for example, the sitting time, people who said that sitting on an average from 5 to 6 hours per day, presented more back difficulties, such as pain from medium to high. Besides, people who said that do not practice exercise, showed several problems with respect to the posture and various levels of pain from low to high.

Typical positions, incorrect postures, as well as associated conditions or to which a person may be prone are depicted in Fig. 12.12. A virtual model that represents different postures and the spinal column is presented in the same figure.

Table 12.2: The statistics from the posture analysis.

Anomaly detected	Gender	Age	Detected by radiography	Detected by VR	% effectiveness for VR
1	M	25	2	1	79
2	F	34	3	2	84
3	M	42	4	3	82
4	M	54	4	4	91
4	M	41	4	4	86
2	M	45	2	2	90
1	M	60	1	1	80
3	F	35	3	3	83
2	M	18	2	2	94
2	M	19	3	1	74

Figure 12.11
Graphical interface of the postural analysis application.

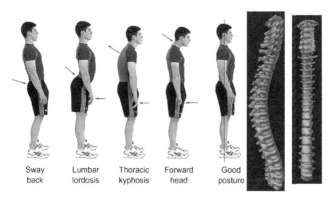

Figure 12.12
Graphical interface of the postural analysis.

Anomaly detected: ¶ ¶ *Thoracis kyphosis* ¤	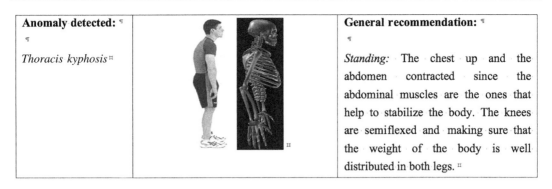 ¤	General recommendation: ¶ ¶ *Standing:* The chest up and the abdomen contracted since the abdominal muscles are the ones that help to stabilize the body. The knees are semiflexed and making sure that the weight of the body is well distributed in both legs. ¤

Figure 12.13
Results that correspond to the detection analysis.

Table 12.3: Activity and recommendations for patients.

Activity	Recommendation
Sitting	The back should be straight, shoulders back and down, and the soles of the feet resting on the floor. You should avoid the habit of crossing your legs, as it can alter the circulation and cause swollen legs, more tired and with varicose veins.
Walking	Keep your head up and neck erect and avoid looking at the floor, because it can cause severe neck pain.
Standing	The chest up and the abdomen contracted since the abdominal muscles are the ones that help to stabilize the body. The knees are semiflexed and making sure that the weight of the body is well distributed in both legs.
Running	The elbows should be bent at a right angle so that the movement of the arms is consistent with that of the legs. It should be avoided to receive the impact when stepping on the heel as it can cause injuries.
Sleeping	The best way to sleep and avoid ailments is on the side and with the legs cramped, as it is the best way to keep the spinal column in a proper position.
Stepping	The correct way to stepping is: first with the heel of the foot and then with the tip.

As illustrated in Fig. 12.12, the differences between the posture detected by the sensor and ideal position are appreciated. It is achieved by using an animation that generates a document with the recommendations, including if the person requires visiting a doctor (see Fig. 12.13).

The recommendations generated for a patient with a bad posture are indicated according to six activities of daily life, which are described in Table 12.3.

In addition, the corresponding virtual models are displayed, to show to the patient the possible detected anomalies (see Fig. 12.14).

Now, the tests include an animation that simulates to the patient walking, according to the detected posture; the virtual scenery is shown, and people can watch and interact with the animation by using the functions: pause, play, fast forwarding, and back forwarding (see Fig. 12.15).

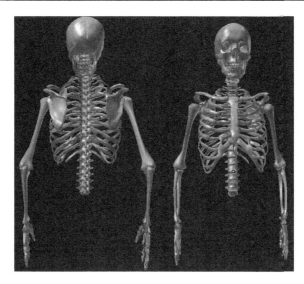

Figure 12.14
Rotation of column using values obtained from the postural analysis.

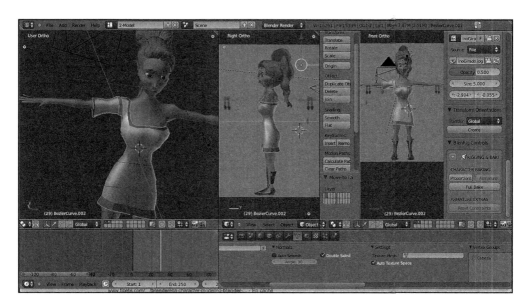

Figure 12.15
Animation performed to show the effects of posture over time.

The last step consists of showing the avatar into a virtual environment, where the patient can see the representation of movements and the effects of the ailments in the future. Three-dimensional modeling techniques were used and implemented to simulate height, width, and depth, as well as the *stop-motion technique*. It consists of moving an avatar or

Figure 12.16
Avatar into a virtual environment.

position model and recording it for a few moments and then change its position, it gives the sensation of movement (Fig. 12.16).

12.5 Conclusions and future work

This work is oriented toward enhancing the approach of VR on the health context, particularly in the treatment of the chronical back pain. In other cases, many researches are oriented to aid the patient in the treatment or specialists in the diagnosis, but the combination when people suffer obesity or overweight had not been treated.

The main contribution in this work is the approach in which the VR helps make awareness and assist doctors and patients in the quick identification of back low pain and the consequences.

In our work, the VR raises awareness with respect to the healthcare, offering not only the usual recommendations in text, but also through a VR simulation that allows the patient to observe what will happen in the future, in case that he does not attend or neglect his treatment, generally when patient has overweight or obesity.

The measurements obtained from the Kinect sensor were extracted in conjunction with the adaptation of the Oswestry questionnaire, and the assessment of low back pain. For the case of low back pain, the focus is to know how much it is affecting and the evolution time that it has. The cause is determined by studies and the physician's judgment, but according to the evaluation, the general recommendations of the IMSS Clinical Guidelines are deployed.

On the other hand, the approach has not been explored in the treatment follow-up to support the guidelines and cares showing for showing in the future the consequences if the required treatment is not carried out.

Future works are oriented toward including other diseases such as hyperlordosis or kyphosis in the display of results, by means of using the radiography approach. Other directions of this work are the combination with augmented reality, for didactical purposes in medicine and anatomy, to show how the diseases appear and how should be diagnosed. Other possible research is to integrate sensors, to sense in real time, the progress in the treatment or to know if the patient is applying in correct way the procedure.

On the other hand, VR is a technology that can assist doctors and patients to know the adverse effects of overweight and obesity on the spinal column and its health consequences.

Finally, the uses of human interfaces combined with VR represent a new data source. These data can be oriented toward Machine Learning applications or Data Science approaches. For example, data of many patients can be used to exploratory analysis to identify possible diseases or problems in the back of patients, and show in real time how will progress a possible disease.

Another possible application is the use of cloud systems based on Artificial Intelligence algorithms, where stored data can be explored to apply deep learning how a treatment is working in many patients (not only in one) and show with the assistance of VR how a population is affected by a problem in the back of patients. So the design of future recommender systems can be oriented toward giving recommendations-based to improve the health and generating statistics related to physical activity in a particular population.

12.6 Teaching assignments

- Explore how specialists in health make an examination of physical health, and analyze what of them can be improved using a sensor with human interfaces (e.g., cellular phones).
- Find a model composed of a set of points that represents a wrong posture in a patient, and use the model as an input for a virtual world. Finally, discuss if the process can be applied for cellular phone (instead of the Kinect sensor).
- Integrate a Machine Learning algorithm to cluster the model that is composed of a set of points (back of patient) from a set of patients. Discuss if the generated cluster shows new insights into healthcare.

Acknowledgments

This work was partially sponsored by the Instituto Politécnico Nacional (IPN), the Secretaría de Investigación y Posgrado (SIP) under grant 20196338, 20196251, and 20196263 as well as the Consejo Nacional de Ciencia y Tecnología (CONACYT) with the grant PN2015-1051. Additionally, we are thankful to the reviewers for their invaluable and constructive feedback that helped improve the quality of this chapter.

References

Airaksinen, O., Brox, J. I., Cedraschi, C., Hildebrandt, J., Klaber-Moffett, J., Kovacs, F., & Zanoli, G. (2006). European guidelines for the management of chronic nonspecific low back pain. *European Spine Journal*, *15*, s192−s300.

Alcántara-Bumbiedro, S., Flórez-García, M. T., Echávarri-Pérez, C., & García-Pérez, F. (2006). Escala de incapacidad por dolor lumbar de Oswestry. *Rehabilitación*, *40*(3), 150−158.

Bates, J. (1992). Virtual reality, art, and entertainment. *Presence: Teleoperators & virtual environments*, *1*(1), 133−138.

Biocca, F., & Levy, M. R. (Eds.), (2013). *Communication in the age of virtual reality*. Routledge.

de Salubridad General, C. (2009). Diagnóstico, tratamiento y prevención de lumbalgia aguda y crónica en el primer nivel de atención.México: Secretaría de Salud, CENETEC.

DeFanti, T. A., Dawe, G., Sandin, D. J., Schulze, J. P., Otto, P., Girado, J., & Rao, R. (2009). The StarCAVE, a third-generation CAVE and virtual reality OptIPortal. *Future Generation Computer Systems*, *25*(2), 169−178.

Eichenberg, C., & Wolters, C. (2012). *Virtual realities in the treatment of mental disorders: A review of the current state of research. Virtual reality in psychological, medical and pedagogical applications*. InTech.

Greenleaf, W. J. (July 2016). *How VR technology will transform healthcare*. In SIGGRAPH VR village, pp. 5:1−5:2.

Grönblad, M., Hurri, H., & Kouri, J. P. (1997). Relationships between spinal mobility, physical performance tests, pain intensity and disability assessments in chronic low back pain patients. *Scandinavian Journal of Rehabilitation Medicine*, *29*(1), 17−24.

Hoffman, H. G., Seibel, E. J., Richards, T. L., Furness, T. A., Patterson, D. R., & Sharar, S. R. (2006). Virtual reality helmet display quality influences the magnitude of virtual reality analgesia. *The Journal of Pain*, *7*(11), 843−850.

Jacobus, C. J., & Griffin, J. L. (1998). U.S. Patent No. 5,769,640. Washington, DC: U.S. Patent and Trademark Office.

Jamali, S. S., Shiratuddin, M. F., Wong, K. W., & Oskam, C. L. (2015). Utilising mobile-augmented reality for learning human anatomy. *Procedia-Social and Behavioral Sciences*, *197*, 659−668.

Kim, B., Schwartz, W., Catacora, D., & Vaughn-Cooke, M. (2016). *Virtual reality behavioral therapy. Proceedings of the human factors and ergonomics society annual meeting* (Vol. 60, pp. 356−360). Los Angeles, CA: Sage.

Lytras, M. D., & Visvizi, A. (2018). Who uses smart city services and what to make of them: Toward interdisciplinary smart cities research. *Sustainability*, *10*(6), 1−16.

Meyerbröker, K., & Emmelkamp, P. M. (2010). Virtual reality exposure therapy in anxiety disorders: A systematic review of process-and-outcome studies. *Depression and Anxiety*, *27*(10), 933−944.

Morris, M., Iansek, R., Smithson, F., & Huxham, F. (2000). Postural instability in Parkinson's disease: A comparison with and without a concurrent task. *Gait & Posture*, *12*(3), 205−216.

Nicholson, D. T., Chalk, C., Funnell, W. R. J., & Daniel, S. J. (2006). Can virtual reality improve anatomy education? A randomised controlled study of a computer-generated three-dimensional anatomical ear model. *Medical Education*, *40*(11), 1081−1087.

Norcross, J. C., Pfund, R. A., & Prochaska, J. O. (2013). Psychotherapy in 2022: A Delphi poll on its future. *Professional Psychology: Research and Practice*, *44*(5), 363.

Opriş, D., Pintea, S., García-Palacios, A., Botella, C., Szamosközi, Ş., & David, D. (2012). Virtual reality exposure therapy in anxiety disorders: A quantitative meta-analysis. *Depression and Anxiety*, *29*(2), 85−93.

Pfandler, M., Lazarovici, M., Stefan, P., Wucherer, P., & Weigl, M. (2017). Virtual reality based simulators for spine surgery: A systematic review. *The Spine Journal*, *17*(9), 1352−1363.

Riva, G., Gaggioli, A., Grassi, A., Raspelli, S., Cipresso, P., Pallavicini, F., & Donvito, G. (2011). NeuroVR 2-A free virtual reality platform for the assessment and treatment in behavioral health care. *MMVR*, 493−495.

Roy, E., Bakr, M. M., & George, R. (2017). The need for virtual reality simulators in dental education: A review. *The Saudi Dental Journal, 29*(2), 41−47.

Ryan, M. L. (2001). *Narrative as virtual reality: Immersion and interactivity in literature and electronic media.* Johns Hopkins University Press.

Shiban, Y., Schelhorn, I., Pauli, P., & Mühlberger, A. (2015). Effect of combined multiple contexts and multiple stimuli exposure in spider phobia: A randomized clinical trial in virtual reality. *Behaviour Research and Therapy, 71*, 45−53.

Shiri, R., Karppinen, J., Leino-Arjas, P., Solovieva, S., & Viikari-Juntura, E. (2009). The association between obesity and low back pain: A meta-analysis. *American Journal of Epidemiology, 171*(2), 135−154.

Soffel, F., Zank, M., & Kunz, A. (November 2016). *Postural stability analysis in virtual reality using the HTC vive. Proceedings of the 22nd ACM conference on virtual reality software and technology* (pp. 351−352). ACM.

Spruit, M., & Lytras, M. (2018). Applied data science in patient-centric healthcare: Adaptive analytic systems for empowering physicians and patients. *Telematics and Informatics, 35*(4), 643−653.

Tate, M. L. K., Detamore, M., Capadona, J. R., Woolley, A., & Knothe, U. (2016). Engineering and commercialization of human-device interfaces, from bone to brain. *Biomaterials, 95*, 35−46.

Turner, W. A., & Casey, L. M. (2014). Outcomes associated with virtual reality in psychological interventions: Where are we now? *Clinical Psychology Review, 34*(8), 634−644.

Valmaggia, L. R., Latif, L., Kempton, M. J., & Rus-Calafell, M. (2016). Virtual reality in the psychological treatment for mental health problems: An systematic review of recent evidence. *Psychiatry Research, 236*, 189−195.

Visvizi, A., & Lytras, M. D. (2018). Rescaling and refocusing smart cities research: From mega cities to smart villages. *Journal of Science and Technology Policy Management, 9*(2), 134−145.

Visvizi, A., Lytras, M. D., Damiani, E., & Mathkour, H. (2018). Policy making for smart cities: Innovation and social inclusive economic growth for sustainability. *Journal of Science and Technology Policy Management, 9*(2), 126−133.

CHAPTER 13

Portable smart healthcare solution to eye examination for diabetic retinopathy detection at an earlier stage

Nighat Mir, Mohammad A.U. Khan and Mome Gul Hussain
College of Engineering, Effat University, Jeddah, Saudi Arabia

13.1 Introduction

Human health is a global concern and various healthcare mechanisms are established to facilitate cure. Healthcare is undergoing a revolution and becoming smarter with the technological and communication advancements, becoming more preventive and personalized. Traditional healthcare setups are slow, involving regular visits toward treatment, which sometimes may lead to severity of disease where smart healthcare is intended to be efficient, high quality with lower cost.

Smart healthcare is not limited to the electronic and mobile health but has grown through the enterprise resource planning systems as reported by Spinellis (2017). Such systems work with data received from mobile and sensory devices and process it into a personalized healthcare information.

Smart healthcare is now under attention from academia, governments, industry, and the healthcare community in offering the affordable and effective solutions. It has the potential to revolutionize several aspects that end up involving many integrated technologies. Studies are currently made in proposing innovations in many areas such as smart cities, Big Data, next generation of networking and communication technologies, and security aspects as reported by Spruit and Lytras (2018) and Lytras and Visvizi (2018). Many issues pertaining to these developments need to be addressed with respect to the internetworking of smart healthcare technologies, portable solutions, communication of data, and many more. However, it has been envisioned that communication technologies are going to play a lot more significant role for the effective, faster, and of high quality for the stakeholder reported as by Hossain, Xu, Li, Bilbao, and El Saddik (2018).

Innovation in Health Informatics.
DOI: https://doi.org/10.1016/B978-0-12-819043-2.00013-7

There are several smart healthcare solutions already in practice over the world which shows the success factor and vision in contributing the devices and resources facilitating the needs. Park, Park, and Lee (2017) reported a remote monitoring system based on Internet of Things (IoT) in which patients can be monitored at their homes for any emergency condition. Rojas et al. (2017) also devised a model for emergency room (ER) for the benefits of patients. Kuang and Davison (2017) used twitter tweets to monitor healthcare information and Li, Huang, Zhou, and Zhong (2017) worked on the emotional part and presented a research which can detect human emotions from EEG signals. There is tremendous research available that shows the viability and need of technology with advancements and mobility.

Chen et al. (2018) presented a solution naming "5G-Smart Diabetes" for the diagnosis and treatment of diabetes. It requires communication for the monitoring remote patient's physical and physiological health. Smart healthcare solutions are highly desirable for widely spreading health concerns such as diabetes.

People with diabetes often develop complications pertaining to the eye such as corneal abnormalities, glaucoma, iris neovascularization, cataracts, and neuropathies. The most common and potentially most harmful of these complications, however, is diabetic retinopathy (DR), which is, in fact, the leading cause of vision loss among working-age adult in the United States. Diabetic retinopathy can damage the area of the retina called macula and the chances of this happening increase manifold with the progression of the disease. Clinically speaking, DR involves changes to retinal blood vessels that can cause them to bleed or leak fluid, distorting vision. Treatment is available to slow down the rate of damage and in some cases can prevent loss of vision. However, the treatment must be started at an early stage as once the total vision is lost, treatment is unlikely to restore it. DR often goes unnoticed until vision loss occurs; therefore, it is advisable for patients with diabetes to undergo regular dilated eye examinations. Early detection, timely treatment, and appropriate follow-ups are the hallmarks of guard against vision loss.

The statistics show that DR is one of the leading causes of the blindness which can be prevented (Mohamed, Gillies, & Wong, 2007). According to a UN report, DR is effecting (4.8%) of the world's population. Verma et al. (2003) reported that up to 50% of all patients having DR and not receiving the timely treatment tend to become blind within next 5 years. Whereas 98% of the DR patients can save their visual loss with the early detection and timely treatment as reported by Glasson, Crossland, and Larkins (2016). It is almost a general consensus among all researchers that vision loss is an irreversible process and once it progresses it becomes permanent. According to a recent survey, less than 50% Australian and American population have access to the appropriate diabetics screening which makes it worst for those living in rural communities with no or limited access to the proper ophthalmology services. McKay, McCart, and Taylor (2000) stated that 36% of the diabetic patients never went through eye examination process and Taylor et al. reported that only 20% of the diabetic patients had an annual eye examination.

In healthcare, technology is playing a major role in almost all stages, starting with patient registration to data monitoring. With an explosive growth in devices like smartphones and tablets, the conventional hospital patient monitoring is replaced with the option of undergoing consultation in the privacy of their own homes. Technological advancements in healthcare make it possible for the services to be taken out of the confines of hospital walls and integrating them with user-friendly, accessible devices. With rapid advances in new technology, we can now collect, store, retrieve, and transfer the patient's information electronically at much higher speed (Kioumars & Tang, 2011). This also provides a big hope for patients with DR, where the eye examinations can be made more comfortable with smartphones.

DR is the direct consequence of the vascular changes, and thus, the progression of the disease is associated with the change in width of the blood vessels. The blood vessels need to be monitored regularly. Instead of manual monitoring, the process of blood vessel extraction and examination can be automated. A number of methods are proposed in literature for the eye vessels detection and segmentation. Notable among them is the one suggested by Soares, Leandro, Cesar, Jelinek, and Cree (2006); who used Gabour wavelet and Gaussian model to categorize the image pixels as a vessel or nonvessel. One of the hardest part of the vessel extraction is to deal with minute and thin arteries which have low contrast. Another researcher, Usman Akram, Khalid, Tariq, and Younus Javed (2013) worked on DR images by using multivariable m-Mediod-based classifier to detect the resultant abnormal blood vessels.

This sight-threatening complication occurs among people with long-term diabetes. Blood vessels in the retina are damaged over time and these vessels leak blood and other fluids. This causes the retinal tissue to swell which affects vision. The early stages of DR do not have any visual symptoms. However, over time visual symptoms include cloudy or blurred vision, seeing spots, dark or empty spot in center of vision, or difficulty seeing at night. If left untreated, DR can cause glaucoma and blindness.

Since DR has no symptoms in its early stage, people with diabetes are recommended to have a yearly comprehensive dilated eye examination. Vision lost caused by DR is sometimes irreversible. However, according to the National Eye Institute, early detection and treatment can reduce risk of blindness by 95%. People with advanced DR and special cases such as pregnant women with DR are recommended to have more frequent examinations (NIH).

The International Diabetes Federation (IDF) has been measuring the global prevalence of diabetes since the year 2000. Their latest report estimates that there are 451 million (age 18−99 years) people with diabetes globally and by 2045 this number will increase to 693 million. Over two-thirds of people with diabetes live in urban areas and one-third live in rural areas. The IDF also reports that the high cost of diabetic care is from treatment of related complications.

As diabetes increases globally, it will also impact Saudi Arabia. It is an acknowledged fact that dietary habits followed by a sedentary life style has significantly increased diabetes in Saudi Arabia (el had, 2007). In 2017, the IDF reported 3,852,000 total cases of diabetes in Saudi Arabia. By 2045 this number is expected to be over 7.5 million people. Parrey et al. assessed 705 Saudi adults in Arar City for visual impairment. Among this group, DR was the third cause of visual impairment [22 cases (13.2%)]. The study concluded that a large number of visual impairment cases were treatable. Based on these findings, more eye care services were recommended for the region. Studies in other regions of Saudi Arabia have also shown DR to be a cause for visual impairment.

13.2 Fundus eye images: the fundus photography and its acquisition

First photographs of retina were published by Jackman and Webster in 1886 with a breakthrough of first commercial fundus camera created by Carl Zeiss in 1926. Fundus photography has a great impact on imaging and screening of retina toward protective measurements against blindness, especially for developing countries where there are limitations for healthcare (Panwar et al., 2016).

Fundus camera has an intricate microscope attached with a flash which is used to capture the photograph of the back of an eye. It can directly capture the eye retina and macula as the pupil is used as an entry and exit point for illuminating the light rays for imaging. Imaging can be done monochrome, using colored filters, using fluorescein, and indocyanine green as presented by Ophthalmic Photographers (2015).

Wong et al. (2008) presented that in addition to the DR, fundus images also help in determining the cardiovascular risk factors that can be checked based on measurement of retinal vessel properties.

Procedure for diagnosis for DR:

1. Eyes are dilated.
2. Patient sits at camera placing chin and forehead against the bar.
3. Focus and alignment is conducted.
4. Pictures are taken and analyzed for:
   a. Small blow-out swellings of blood vessels
   b. Small leaks of fluid from damaged blood vessels
   c. Small bleeds from damaged blood vessels
   d. Blood vessels may just become blocked
   e. New abnormal blood vessels may grow from damaged blood vessels
5. Photographs are used by ophthalmologists for diagnostic and treatment of eye diseases.

Patrick et al. explained that there are three different view angles for retina photography using fundus camera. 30 degrees is called normal angle which results into a 2.5 times larger images than life, where images taken between 45 degrees and 140 degrees normally provides proportionately less retinal magnification and then is 20 degrees or less which is called a narrow angle of view.

Fig. 13.1 shows the normal fundus photographs of right eye (left image) and left eye (right image) which are observed as without any disease. Macula is seen in the center of image, the left image (right eye) illustrates lighter areas close to the larger vessels, which is taken as a normal finding of younger people.

Fundus image in Fig. 13.2 shows the signs of DR (macular edema and microaneurysms). Retinal details are easier to visualize in fundus photographs then to directly examine a patient.

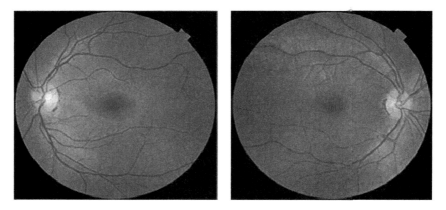

Figure 13.1
Fundus image normal left and right eye.

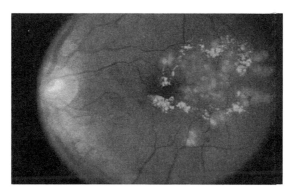

Figure 13.2
Fundus image for diabetic retinopathy.

13.3 Fundus eye imaging and problems

Loss of vision from DR can't be restored, but with early detection, treatment is mostly successful and can prevent one from losing the sight or getting worse.

Lee et al. (1993) and Chia and Yap (2004) compared the ophthalmoscope and fundus photographs using a nonmydriatic camera with dilated pupils, to diagnose retinopathy and found fundus photography better than the ophthalmoscopy.

Traditional fundus cameras though provides quality images but there are static, bulky, office based, technician dependent, and costly. Besides its features it is not convenient for remote places so to address this there are many technological advancements that radicalized retinal photography. Improvements in telecommunications and smartphones are two remarkable breakthroughs that have made ophthalmic screening in remote areas a realizable possibility (Panwar et al., 2016).

Traditional fundus cameras offer good-quality images but are bulky, office based, technician dependent, and costly. Besides access to the retinal imaging device, affordability is of paramount importance in screening programs, especially in the remotest of places. Recently, there have been significant technological advances that have radicalized retinal photography. Improvements in telecommunications and smartphones are two remarkable breakthroughs that have made ophthalmic screening in remote areas a realizable possibility.

However, besides these features there are many disadvantages noted in the research.

- Image produced is 2D, unlike 3D in binocular indirect binocular ophthalmoscopy
- Difficulty observing and assessing abnormalities (e.g., cotton wool spots) due to lack of depth appreciation on images
- Less magnification and image clarity than indirect ophthalmoscopy
- Conditions such as cataracts will reduce image clarity
- Artifact errors may produce unusual images
- Lack of portability
- High cost

Fundus photography plays a very important role in addressing the cause of preventive blindness especially in developing countries, where infrastructure and access to healthcare are limited.

However, these are static machines with restricted access to the office-based clinics with the limitations for tele-ophthalmology. There are massive developments in the field introducing portable cameras and smartphone-based fundus imaging systems have resulted in an exponential surge in available technologies for portable fundus photography. And there is a whole new change expected in the near future with cameras with low cost, portable with automated controls and digitalized images with web-based transfer.

13.4 Smartphone fundus cameras in the market

There are several smartphone-based fundus cameras available in market which can be used as an alternative to a more traditional ophthalmoscope. For the purposes of this research, we are concerned with development of a smartphone fundus camera that is easy to use and does not require eyes to be dilated. We looked at three different smartphone fundus cameras and selected the D-EYE camera. Early detection of DR generally requires eyes to be dilated. Literature does not report a camera that can detect early DR without dilated eyes. A comprehensive eye examination certainly requires dilated eyes.

13.4.1 Volk iNview

Volk optics has developed the iPhone Fundus Camera which can capture images automatically or manually. A user can master two imaging techniques—one is recommended for beginners and the other for advanced users. Both techniques require the pupils to be dilated. The iPhone app allows users to create a patient file and images are saved to each patient. Images can be shared, saved, and printed directly from the app or downloaded to a desktop computer.

13.4.2 Peek vision

Peek vision is a fundus camera that can fit several smartphones so it is not limited to the iPhone. Peek does not use an app to interface the lens with the smartphone. Instead, all pictures and videos are saved to the phone's photo gallery. It requires dilated pupils for best results.

13.4.3 D-EYE smartphone-based retinal imaging system

The D-EYE is a small rectangular camera that comes with an iPhone bumper that clips the camera on. This camera comes with an app to organize and save patient pictures. The camera works with both a dilated and undilated eye. A dilated eye gives a 20-degree field of view and an undilated eye gives a 6-degree field of view. Different diseases can be viewed with depending on the view used.

13.4.4 ODocs eye care

The founder of ODocs Dr. Hong Sheng Chiong provides a fully functioned 3D printable smartphone ophthalmoscope. Once assembled, the ophthalmoscope needs an ophthalmic lens and then can be fixed to a smartphone camera. The ophthalmoscope provides a 40-degree field of view of the retina.

Table 13.1: Portable devices comparison.

Portable devices	How long in the market	Cost	Target audience	Advantages	Disadvantages
Volk iNview	Well-established company Obtain a wide 50-degree field of view	$995	Medical	Easy to balance because of external cone	Expensive
Peek	New company Does not specify field of view Dilation not needed	$230	Medical Education Veterinary Rural	Can be used with any smartphone	Not released and tested yet! Still in development stage
D-EYE	Traditional old field view Dilation optional	$435	Doctors as a screening tool	Light weight Simple installation	Learning curve; need to know basic eye anatomy Not meant to replace traditional eye examination devices
ODocs Eye Care	Wide field of view (50-degree FOV) with dilation	$325	Medical Rural	Simple installation	Not available for shipping

Note: Peek and D-EYE show the retina in similar ways and have to be used in the same way. Close up pictures needed that both companies display are after cropping the external region of the eye. Neither camera can zoom in enough to only capture the retina.

Table 13.1 shows a comparative analysis of the portable eye devices used for scanning purposes.

13.5 What is the problem?

Longer diagnostic time

(30−60 minutes, as reported by Ophthalmologists)

Currently, it is time-consuming and tedious manual process involving a trained clinician to examine and evaluate eye that may take several days to come up with diagnosis. We need automated solution for fast and accurate diagnosis.

The main motto of the research presented here is a computerized solution that is related with faster detection and accurate diagnosis. For diabetics, it is vital that eyes are checked regularly by a trained ophthalmologist in their clinics. Damage to the retina at the back of the eye is a common complication with the advancement in diabetic disease. If left untreated, it can become worse and cause some loss of vision, or total loss of vision in some cases. The safeguard against the DR disease is its earlier detection through symptoms not too obvious at the early stage of the disease.

The regular eye examination at the specialized clinics takes place. First the eyes are dilated and pictures are taken with a specialized fundus camera. The fundus images are analyzed for:

- Small blow-out swellings of blood vessels.
- Small leaks of fluid from damaged blood vessels.
- Small bleeds from damaged blood vessels.
- Blood vessels may just become blocked.
- New abnormal blood vessels may grow from damaged blood vessels.

13.6 Impact of the problem

By the time human readers submit their reviews, the delayed results lead to lost follow up, miscommunication, and delayed treatment.

May result into:

- False diagnosis
- Missing early diagnosis
- Loss of vision

The management of diabetes primarily involves lowering of blood sugar, through diet, lifestyle changes, and antidiabetic drugs. If DR is present, the treatments options involve laser therapy, administration of antivascular growth factors, and steroids have been shown in large randomized clinical trials to prevent blindness and further visual loss.

Because the resulting imaging setup is technically challenging, fundus imaging historically involved relatively expensive equipment and highly trained ophthalmic photographers. Over the last 10 years or so, there has been a major effort to make fundus imaging more accessible, resulting in less dependence on such experience and expertise for requirement for population-based early detection of retinal diseases using fundus imaging. To ensure timely treatment, effective screening programs require the examination of the retina of diabetic patients at least once a year. The current practice of DR screening is based on manual examination of fundus photographs by human experts. It requires trained ophthalmologists to examine the retinal images, searching for retinal lesions. Screening programs are costly and time-consuming due to the high prevalence of diabetes and the shortage of specialists. These persons need to undergo retinal examinations resulting in a huge amount of images that need to be reviewed. This puts an enormous burden on ophthalmologists and increases waiting lists, compounding the quality of healthcare. Currently, it is time-consuming and manual process needing a trained clinician to examine and evaluate. By the time human readers submit their reviews, the delayed results lead to lost follow up, miss-communications, and delayed treatment. May result into false diagnosis, missing early diagnosis, and loss of vision.

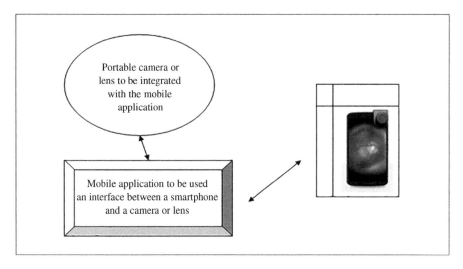

Figure 13.3
Suggested system.

13.7 Proposed solution

The proposed solution is automated DR detection system. Diminution of the necessary resources in terms of specialists, diminution of the examination time, improving accuracy as depicted in Fig. 13.3.

- Use of patented algorithm to extract vital information for vessels exudates, and other abnormalities and report to the doctor
- Using one of the available portable camera's for taking images
- Developing mobile application to connect the portable camera with a smartphone

•Making use of web to communicate the taken images with the physicians or technician for further screening purposes

13.8 Methodology and validation

Proposed solution has been verified with the practicing ophthalmologists and accumulated statistics show significance of system for *time* and *accuracy*.

Automatic blob detection comprises of an important processing step for the analysis of many images. Blobs may represent nuclei organization in a cultured colony reported by Yang and Parvin (2002); homogeneous regions in geophysical data showed by Kaspers (2011); tumor locations in MRI or CT data by Logeswari and Karnan (2010), hand gesture recognition presented by Cipolla, Battiato, and Farinella (2010). A blob is defined as a connected region linked with a local extremum, either a maximum for a brighter blob on a darker background or a minimum for a dark blob on brighter background. One intuitive way to detect blobs with this definition by employing a filtering function with large weights for the central pixels as compared with their surrounding region. This naturally comes with the Laplacian operator. However, it is rarely used in its basic form, for the reason its noise sensitivity. Usually a Gaussian smoothing employed first. This arrangement results in operator referred to as a Laplacian of Gaussian (LoG). LoG has been a method of choice for blob detection that achieves peak response at the center of the blob-like structures research reported by Blostein and Ahuja (1989) and Soomro et al. (2018).

The larger the eccentricity of the blob, the higher will be the discrepancy in detecting centers. Elliptical blobs can arise in many practical situations, such as the hand gesture recognition work proposed in Bretzner, Laptev, and Lindeberg (2002) where the aim is to track the number of well-defined, purposeful hand postures for communicating with electronic appliances. Also, in retinal vessel detection and fingerprint image enhancement (possessing ridge structure), a generalized elliptical blob detection strategy is absolutely essential to get the job of enhancement and segmentation being performed with reasonable accuracy.

Ridges in addition to edges are thought to be an important feature of an image researched by Khan, Bailey, Khan, and Kong (2017). Ridges are widely investigated in computer vision by Lindeberg (1998a,1998b), in tensor analysis by Schultz, Theisel, and Seidel (2010), and in combustion simulations by Frank and Kaiser (2008). According to Khan, Khan, Bailey, and Soomro (2018); ridge extraction can be divided into three main categories for segmentation purposes. The first refers to scale-normalized differential geometry-based descriptors proposed in Lindeberg (1998a,1998b). The differential descriptor outputs 1D ridge curve in a 2D image space. However, the descriptors generally capture the major axis of symmetry for an elongated object rather than a complete cross-section of the object. Furthermore, the differential descriptor response is severely limited by the local contrast of the ridges to be detected. In practical settings, due to uneven illumination and background noise, we rarely have high local contrast available for all regions of the image. The second category for ridge detection has to do with providing a measure that models the complete shape profile of the ridge under consideration. To achieve this, researchers propose measures that are product of regulated functions of many differential descriptors.

For ridge detection, another interesting approach is to first improve the contrast of an elongated object and then convert it to a binary output using a simple threshold. An elongated object, for this purpose, can be thought of a deformation of a circular object, which can be approximated around each point by an affine map using first-order Taylor formula. This principle led to affine shape adaptation technique. Mikolajczyk and Schmid (2004) propose a shape adaptation algorithm based on the previous work of Lindeberg and

Garding (1997). This algorithm estimates affine transformations in two steps, which are iteratively applied: the location detection and the affine deformation. Initially, applying a geometry-based scale-invariant detector a set of isotropic interest points (location + scale) are obtained. Then with an incremental refinement of estimated second-moment matrix, the image goes through various passes of anisotropic smoothness till convergence. Later on, Lakemond, Fookes, and Sridharan showed that substituting the second-moment matrix by the Hessian matrix the algorithm provides similar results. The proposed normalized second-order ridge detector is related and contrast with those of earlier differential ridge measure, affine-adapted ridge enhancement, and model-based ridge detection.

13.9 Popular ridge detectors for vessel segmentation

In this section, normalized GLoG detector is modified to produce a normalized second-order detector for finding ridges, considered as another important characteristic in an intensity image. Recently Lopez-Molina, de Ulzurrun, Baetens, den Bulcke, and Baets (2015) proposed the use of the second derivative of anisotropic Gaussian kernels for ridge detection. Such kernels, which have proven successful in edge and corner detection, offer interesting advantages over isotropic kernels. In the case of ridge detection, these advantages include the increased sensitivity at junction points. The computerized vessel detection is found useful for a set of eye diseases, referred to as DR by Soomro et al. (2017). DR is a progressive disease as there are no such signs of disease at its early stages but as the time passes the disease turns severe presented by Soomro et al. (2017). The regular screening of DR results in a large number of retinal images that need to be examined by the ophthalmologists. Here, first, some popular ridge models are described and then their performance is contrasted with the proposed ridge detector. For evaluation purposes, a publicly available DRIVE database is utilized.

The quality of acquired images present in DRIVE database is far from being used directly with ridge models, as the basic underlying assumption behind these models is the smoothness of the image surface. The acquired images contain unevenly illuminated, blurred, and noisy regions. It becomes pertinent to first smooth the image to an adequate acceptable level. A preprocessing module is deployed as front-end to the later stage of ridge model application. The module is described as follows.

13.10 Proposed method

Elliptical blobs can be used in an overlapping manner to cover long vessels. This shows that NGLoG can be used for vessel detection. However, a better alternative can be identified if we keep only the first term of the NGLoG expression that results in what we refer to as normalized second-order affine Gaussian derivative kernel.

The normalized SAGDK is used with the input retinal image in the following manner.

Step 1 The input image $f(x, y)$ is passed through a series of preprocessing steps, as explained in preprocessing module section, to produce a uniform smooth image $f_u(x, y)$.

Step 2 The uniform image $f_u(x, y)$ is passed through a normalized SAGDK filter bank.

Step 3 The normalized images can be combined into a single enhanced image by maximization over all possible combination.

13.11 Experimental results

For experimental purpose, two publicly available databases DRIVE and STARE are used. There are 40 images of DRIVE database and 20 images of STRIVE database. The databases are further categorized into two sets: the training set and the test set. Both databases have independent manually segmented images as ground truth. In literature, many researchers used only 20 test images of the DRIVE database for the experiment purpose. In this research, 20 test images of DRIVE database are used for measuring the performance of proposed algorithm with recently published methods. In both databases, the manual segmentation of the first observer is used as the ground truth for validation while the second observer performance is used as the benchmark for comparison.

The performance of the proposed retinal vessel segmentation is quantified by comparing a segmented output image with its corresponding ground truth image. In this research work, our algorithm was evaluated by measuring sensitivity (Se), specificity (Sp), and accuracy (Acc). Se and Sp give the information of well-classified vessels and nonvessels. Acc provides overall information of well-classified pixels.

First, we evaluated the performance of the proposed method with average Acc, Se, and Sp. The accuracy of the proposed method is slightly higher than the other ridge detection methods, but the sensitivity of this method is much better on the DRIVE database than the other ridge detection methods and some of the state of the art methods. It shows that our methods have the capability to detect smaller blood vessels.

We also analyzed the performance of our proposed method on the DRIVE database, as shown in Table 13.2. The analysis shows promise in favor of proposed method as compared to the other ridge detection methods for its improved accuracy and sensitivity.

Table 13.3 compares the performance of our method with most novel and recently implemented methods, on the DRIVE database. More important, the performance of human observer in Table 13.3 is shown in regard to Se, Sp, and Acc using manual segmentation

Table 13.2: Sensitivity, specificity, and accuracy of proposed modifications on DRIVE database.

		Sensitivity		Specificity		Accuracy	
Average		Dev.	Average	Dev.	Average	Dev.	
Ridge strength measure	0.7487	0.0652	0.9509	0.0662	0.9253	0.0667	
Affine shape adaption	0.7401	0.0640	0.9532	0.0666	0.9263	0.0663	
Frangi vesselness measure	0.7520	0.0651	0.9528	0.0598	0.9283	0.0556	
Proposed	0.7610	0.0621	0.9608	0.0538	0.9436	0.0556	

Table 13.3: Comparison of proposed method with published methods.

	Sensitivity		Specificity		Accuracy	
	Average	Dev.	Average	Dev.	Average	Dev.
Human observer	0.7761	0.0593	0.9725	0.0082	0.9473	0.0048
Chaudhuri	0.2716	0.2118	0.9794	0.0388	0.8894	0.0321
Jiang	0.6478	0.0642	0.9625	0.029	0.9222	0.0069
Zana	0.6696	0.0764	0.9769	0.0079	0.9377	0.0077
Perez	0.7086	0.1815	0.9496	0.0260	0.9181	0.239
Azzopardi symmetric	0.7526	0.0622	0.9707	0.0092	0.9427	0.0780
Azzopardi Asymmetric	0.7499	0.0522	0.9621	0.0192	0.9422	0.0710
Proposed	0.7610	0.0651	0.9608	0.0598	0.9436	0.0556

data observed from the second observer. The proposed method gives slightly better accuracy than the supervised methods.

13.12 Conclusion and future work

A generalized LoG function has been developed to test its capability in modeling vessels found in retinal fundus images. The developed detector is generalized in the sense that it can be used as a blob detector as well as a ridge detector, this behavior can be switched by tuning its σ parameter. For the purpose of this research project, it has been tested for its effectiveness as a ridge detector role and is compared with some of the existing popular ridge detectors. Experimental results show that the proposed Generalized LoG can function as a ridge detector providing superior performance than the currently existing many ridge detectors. Currently, a mobile application based on the proposed methodologies is under development which is intended to integrate all the needed technical and medical attributes and its communication.

Future of smart healthcare is not limited to one field and is encompassing the physical, emotional, and physiological health of a patient by developing and modeling various systems and applications. Smart healthcare is undergoing a wide transformation with the advancements in computing and communication technologies. It is no longer considered as a hospital-centered environment and significant developments are anticipated with decision support systems through Big Data integrating a deep communication of healthcare and technology professionals.

Technology has done significant developments in public health developing smart analysis applications for behavior, analyzing ER process (Rojas et al., 2017), remotely monitoring patients (Park et al., 2017), tracking malaria via mobile applications.

There is still a huge potential in developing efficient medical healthcare systems to monitor and track of performance. Existing systems have addressed the wide scope of area which shows the demand and need from various aspects. One of such kinds is presented by Cho, Lee, and Lee (2017) to monitor preterm delivery in a medical information system to enable efficient EMG data transmission. Peng, Wang, Guo, Wang, and Deng (2017) showed a fault tolerant system for the monitoring of healthcare systems in a wireless body area, Yuh, Chung, and Cheong (2017) presented a reformulation-linearization technique for efficient kidney exchange where Mahmood, Ning, Ullah, and Yao (2017) suggested a secure communication protocol between patients and caregivers remotely. Hence a vast area of healthcare is to be explored using the smart healthcare, IoT and Big Data, security and Artificial Intelligence in particular and computing in general.

13.13 Teaching assignments

1. Briefly describe DR and its impact on human eye.
2. Briefly describe the traditional way of eye examination and how is it different from Fundus Imaging?
3. What kinds of smart fundus cameras are available in the market?
4. Why can automatic blob detection be an alternative methodology?
5. What are the needs of mobile or smart devices for eye examinations?

References

Blostein, D., & Ahuja, N. (1989). A multiscale region detector. *Computer Vision, Graphics, and Image Processing, 45*, 22–41.

Bretzner, L., Laptev, I., & Lindeberg, T. (2002). *Hand gesture recognition using multi-scale colour features, hierarchical models and particle filtering. Fifth IEEE International Conference on Automatic Face and Gesture Recognition* (pp. 423–428).

Chen, M., Yang, J., Zhou, J., Hao, Y., Zhang, J., & Youn, C.-H. (2018). 5G-smart diabetes: Toward personalized diabetes diagnosis with healthcare Big Data clouds. *IEEE Communications Magazine, 56*(4), 16–23.

Chia, D. S. Y., & Yap, E. Y. (2004). Comparison of the effectiveness of detecting diabetic eye disease:Diabetic retinal photography versus ophthalmic consultation. *Singapore Medical Journal, 45*(6), 276.

Cipolla, R., Battiato, S., & Farinella, G. M. (2010). *Computer vision: Detection, recognition and reconstruction.* Springer, ISSN 1860-949X.

Frank, J., & Kaiser, S. (2008). High-resolution imaging of dissipative structures in a turbulent jet flame with laser rayleigh scattering. *Experiments in Fluids, 44,* 221−233.

Glasson, N. M., Crossland, L. J., & Larkins, S. L. (2016). An innovative Australian outreach model of diabetic retinopathy screening in remote communities. *Journal of Diabetes Research, 2016,* Article ID 1267215.

Hossain, M. S., Xu, C., Li, Y., Bilbao, J., & El Saddik, A. (2018). Advances in next-generation technologies for smart healthcare. *IEEE Communication Magazine, 56,* 14−15.

Kaspers, A. (2011). *Blob Detection* (Master's thesis). Faculty of Medicine, Utrecht University Repository.

Khan, T. M., Bailey, D. G., Khan, M. A. U., & Kong, Y. (2017). Efficient hardware implementation for fingerprint image enhancement using anisotropic Gaussian filter. *IEEE Transactions on Image Processing, 26*(5), 2116−2126.

Khan, M. A. U., Khan, T. M., Bailey, D. G., & Soomro, T. A. (2018). A generalized multiscale line-detection method to boost retinal vessel segmentation sensitivity. *Pattern Analysis and Applications,* 1−20.

Khan, M. A. U., Soomro, T. A., Khan, T. M., Bailey, D. G., Gao, J., & Mir, N. (2016). *Automatic retinal vessel extraction algorithm based on contrast-sensitive schemes. International* conference on image and vision computing New Zealand (IVCNZ) (pp. 1−5).

Kioumars, H., & Tang, L. (2011). *Wireless network for health monitoring: heart rate and temperature sensor. 5th international conference on sensor technology* (pp. 362−369).

Kuang, S., & Davison, B. D. (2017). Learning word embeddings with chi-square weights for healthcare tweet classification. *Applied Sciences, 7,* 846.

Lee, V. S., Kingsley, R. M., Lee, E. T., Lu, M., Russell, D., Asal, N. R., . . . Wilkinson, C. P. (1993). The diagnosis of diabetic retinopathy: Ophthalmoscopy versus fundus photography. *Ophthalmology, 100*(10), 1504−1512.

Li, Y., Huang, J., Zhou, H., & Zhong, N. (2017). Human emotion recognition with electroencephalographic multidimensional features by hybrid deep neural networks. *Applied Sciences, 7,* 1060.

Lindeberg, T. (1998a). Edge detection and ridge detection with automatic scale selection. *International Journal of Computer Vision, 30,* 465−470.

Lindeberg, T. (1998b). Feature detection with automatic scale selection. *International Journal of Computer Vision, 30*(2), 77−116.

Lindeberg, T., & Garding, J. (1997). Shape-adapted smoothing in estimation of 3-D depth cues from affine distortions of local 2-D brightness structure. *Image and Vision Computing, 15*(6), 415−434.

Logeswari, T., & Karnan, M. (2010). *An improved implementation of brain tumor detection using soft computing. Second* international conference on communication software and networks (pp. 147−151).

Lopez-Molina, C., de Ulzurrun, G. V.-D., Baetens, J., den Bulcke, J. V., & Baets, B. D. (2015). Unsupervised ridge detection using second order anisotropic gaussian kernels. *Signal Processing, 116,* 55−67.

Lytras, Miltiadis D., & Visvizi, Anna (2018). Who uses smart city services and what to make of it: Toward interdisciplinary smart cities research. *Sustainability Journal, 10*(6), 1−16.

Mahmood, Z., Ning, H., Ullah, A., & Yao, X. (2017). Secure authentication and prescription safety protocol for telecare health services using ubiquitous IoT. *Applied Sciences, 7,* 1069.

McKay, R., McCart, C. A., & Taylor, H. R. (2000). *Diabetic retinopathy in Victoria, Australia: The visual impairment project, . British Journal of Ophthalmology* (84, pp. 865−870).

Mohamed, Q., Gillies, M. C., & Wong, T. Y. (2007). Management of diabetic retinopathy: A systematic review. *JAMA, 298*(8), 902−916.

Panwar, N., Huang, P., Lee, J., Keane, P. A., Chuan, T. S., Richhariya, A., . . . Agrawal, R. (2016). A review of recent technological advances and their implications for worldwide healthcare. *Telemed Journal of eHealth, 22*(3), 198−208.

Park, K., Park, J., & Lee, J. (2017). An IoT system for remote monitoring of patients at home. *Applied Sciences, 7,* 260.

Peng, Y., Wang, X., Guo, L., Wang, Y., & Deng, Q. (2017). An efficient network coding-based fault-tolerant mechanism in WBAN for smart healthcare monitoring systems. *Applied Sciences, 7,* 817.

Rojas, E., Sepúlveda, M., Munoz-Gama, J., Capurro, D., Traver, V., & Fernandez-Llatas, C. (2017). Question-driven methodology for analyzing emergency room processes using process mining. *Applied Sciences, 7,* 302.

Schultz, T., Theisel, H., & Seidel, H.-P. (2010). Crease surfaces: From theory to extraction and application to diffusion tensor MRI. *IEEE Transactions on Visualization and Computer Graphics, 16,* 109–119.

Soares, J. V. B., Leandro, J. J. G., Cesar, R. M., Jelinek, H. F., & Cree, M. J. (2006). Retinal vessel segmentation using the 2-D gabor wavelet and supervised classification. *IEEE Transactions on Medical Imaging, 25*(9), 1214–1222.

Soomro, T. A., Gao, J., Khan, T., Hani, A. F. M., Khan, M. A. U., & Paul, M. (2017). Computerised approaches for the detection of diabetic retinopathy using retinal fundus images: A survey. *Pattern Analysis and Applications, 20*(4), 927–961.

Soomro, T. A., Khan, T. M., Khan, M. A. U., Gao, J., Paul, M., & Zheng, L. (2018). Impact of ICA-based image enhancement technique on retinal blood vessels segmentation. *IEEE Access* (6), 3524–3538.

Spinellis, D. (2017). The elusiveness of smart healthcare. *IEEE Transactions on Conuters, 66*(9), 1547–1561.

Spruit, M., & Lytras, M. (2018). Applied data science in patient-centric healthcare: Adaptive analytic systems for empowering physicians and patients. *Telematics and Informatics, 35,* 643–653.

Usman Akram, M., Khalid, S., Tariq, A., & Younus Javed, M. (2013). *Detection of neovascularization in retinal images using multivariate m-Methods based classifier. Computerized Medical Imaging and Graphics.* Elsevier, CMIG-1196.

Verma, L., Prakash, G., Tewari, H. K., Gupta, S. K., Murthy, G. V., & Sharma, N. (2003). Screening for diabetic retinopathy by non-ophthalmologists: An effective public health tool. *Acta Ophthalmologica Scandinavica, 81*(4), 373–377.

Wong, T. Y., Cheung, N., Islam, F. M., Klein, R., Criqui, M. H., Cotch, M. F., . . . Sharrett, A. R. (2008). Relation of retinopathy to coronary artery calcification: The multi-ethnic study of atherosclerosis. *American Journal of Epidemiology, 167*(1), 51–58.

Yang, Q., & Parvin, B. (2002). *CHEF: Convex hull of elliptic features for 3D blob detection, 16th international conference on pattern recognition* (2, pp. 282–285).

Yuh, J., Chung, S., & Cheong, T. (2017). Reformulation-linearization technique approach for kidney exchange program IT healthcare platforms. *Applied Sciences, 7,* 847.

Further reading

Arnold, A. L., Dunn, R. A., Taylor, H. R., et al. (2009). National indigenous eye health survey: Minum Barreng *(Tracking Eyes)* (p. 217) .

Cho, G. Y., Lee, G. Y., & Lee, T. R. (2017). Efficient real-time lossless EMG data transmission to monitor pre-term delivery in a medical information system. *Applied Sciences, 7,* 366.

Frangi, F., Niessen, W. J., Hoogeveen, R. M., van Walsum, T., & Viergever, M. A. (1999). Model-based quantitation of 3-d magnetic resonance angiographic images. *IEEE Transactions on Medical Imaging, 18* (10), 946–956.

Fundus Photography. *Overview—Ophthalmic photographers' society.* (2015). <www.opsweb.org> Retrieved 17.09.17.

Häggström, M. (2014). Medical gallery of Mikael Häggström. *Wiki Journal of Medicine, 1*(2), 8, ISSN 2002-4436.

Hoover, A., Kouznetsova, V., & Goldbaum, M. (2000). Locating blood vessels in retinal images by piece-wise threshold probing of a matched filter response. *IEEE Transactions on Medical Imaging, 19*(3), 203–210.

Hoover, A., & Goldbaum, M. (2003). Locating the optic nerve in a retinal image using the fuzzy convergence of the blood vessels. *IEEE Transactions on Medical Imaging, 22*(8), 951–958.

Jackman, W. T., & Webster, J. D. (1886). On photographing the retina of the living human eye. *The Philadelphia Photographer, 23,* 340–341.

Khan, M. A. U., & Khan, T. M. (2017). Calibrating second-moment matrix for better shape adaptation with bias term from directional filter bank. *Signal, Image and Video Processing*, *11*(8), 1453−1460.

Lalkhen, G., & McCluske, A. (2008). Clinical tests: Sensitivity and specificity. *Continuing Education in Anaesthesia*, *8*(6), 221−223.

Liu, X., Wu, Q., Zhao, W., & Luo, X. (2017). Technology-facilitated diagnosis and treatment of individuals with autism spectrum disorder: An engineering perspective. *Applied Sciences*, *7*, 1051.

Mendonca, M., & Campilho, A. (2006). Segmentation of retinal blood vessels by combining the detection of centerlines and morphological reconstruction. *IEEE Transactions on Medical Imaging*, *25*(9), 1200−1213.

Mikolajczyk, K., & Schmid, C. (2004). Scale and affine invariant interest point detectors. *International Journal of Computer Vision*, *60*, 63−86.

Soomro, T. A., Khan, M. A. U., Gao, J., Khan, T. M., & Paul, M. (2017). Contrast normalization steps for increased sensitivity of a retinal image segmentation method. *Signal, Image and Video Processing*, 1509−1517.

Staal, J. J., Abramoff, M. D., Niemeijer, M., Viergever, M. A., & van Ginneken, B. (2004). Ridge based vessel segmentation in color images of the retina. *IEEE Transactions on Medical Imaging*, *23*, 501−509.

Yannuzzi L.A. (2010). *The Retinal Atlas*. (Vol. 149, Issue 3). New York, NY: Elsevier, 361−363.e1.

CHAPTER 14

Improved nodule detection in chest X-rays using principal component analysis filters

Mohammad A.U. Khan, Nighat Mir and Fahad Hameed Ahmad

College of Engineering, Effat University, Jeddah, Saudi Arabia

14.1 Introduction

Transformation of healthcare through technology-based smart solutions is increasing reducing the gaps between automated and manual diagnosis. Informatics in smart healthcare applies the concepts and practices prevalent in the computing world in providing better and efficient health outcomes. With the cities and villages turning smarter with the sustainability agenda, health is the primary focus where stakeholders are relying heavily on smart healthcare systems presented by Visvizi, Lytras, Damiani, and Mathkour (2018) and focuses a great attention toward embedding emerging technologies within the realm of conventional healthcare practices.

In the last decade, computer technology has greatly improved in processing power with an extent that computerized models for smart healthcare systems and applications are now routinely developed and incorporated to automate some of the challenging decision-making work for disease diagnosis, for improved quality of healthcare and even management in some health-related complications. One possible avenue for health informatics innovation is the field of radiological imaging. The lack of necessary radiological services and expertise in the rural areas suggests the utility of computers to perform the screening. The research effort presented here focuses on developing software methods to automatically screen for signs of disease in the X-ray images. The specific goal is to develop algorithms to automatically separate the lung region, detect and remove ribs, and then detect texture features characteristic of a pulmonary disease.

Lung cancer has been declared one of the most common cancer-related death in both men and women according to American Cancer Society (2003). Early detection of lung cancer is the most promising strategy to enhance a potential patient's chances of survival as researched over decades (Florack, ter Haar Romeny, Koenderink, & Viergever, 1992; Hyvarinen, Karhunen, & Oja, 2001; Koenderink, 1984; Lindeberg, 1990; Smith et al., 2018).

Innovation in Health Informatics.
DOI: https://doi.org/10.1016/B978-0-12-819043-2.00014-9

Chest X-ray plays an important role in the diagnosis of lung cancer. According to the latest statistics provided by the American Institute of Cancer Research, lung cancer is found the most common cancer in the world estimating 15.5% increase.

The most common screening for lung cancer makes use of chest radiography. Chest radiography involves the exposure of chest to a small dose of ionizing radiation to display pictures of the internal organs. More advanced techniques such as computer tomography (CT) scans have been in use for quite some time in technologically advanced countries. CT is considered more beneficial than harm for screening under specific settings by Mazzone, Powell, Arenberg, and Bach (2014). However, the conventional chest radiography remains the default technique in larger parts of the under-developed world. Chest radiographs can be interpreted by involving a combination of systematic analysis to look for blob-like objects referred to as lung nodules (Shiraishi et al., 2006). Lung nodules that may happen to be a lung cancer, however, can be overlooked by the medical examiners in almost 16% of the cases in which nodules are visible in retrospect by Xu, Doi, Kobayashi, MacMahon, and Giger (1997) and Shiraishi et al. (2000). Therefore it has been a practice to employ computer-aided detection (CAD) scheme as a front end improving radiologist's detection accuracy reported by McLean (2004) and Lu and Rajapakse (2005). CAD for analysis of nodules is making the scanning process more efficient and cost effective (Ciompi et al., 2017).

Though chest X-ray provides an important diagnostic examination in clinical daily routine, they are complex in the sense that relevant diagnostic structures are superimposed by irrelevant bony objects. A major challenge, therefore, in current CAD schemes (Coppini, Diciotti, Falchini, Villari, & Valli, 2003; Giger, Doi, MacMahon, Metz, & Yin, 1990; de Koning et al., 2013; Lange, Pratt, & Inbar, 1997) for chest radiographs is the detection of nodules overlapping with ribs, rib crossings, and clavicles as shown in Fig. 14.1. These bony structures results in large number of false positives by Keserci and Yoshida (2002) and

(A)   (B)   (C)

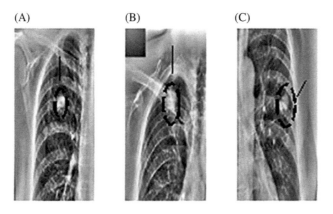

Figure 14.1
Some instances of obscured nodules with rib structures.

Shiraishi, Abe, Engelmann, and Doi (2003), and Cui, Li, Han, and Liu (2015). As far as visual inspection is concerned, nodules overlapping with ribs and clavicles are reported to be most difficult for radiologists to detect by Paumier and Le Péchoux (2010) and Carreira, Cabello, Penedo, and Mosquera (1998). Therefore it can be claimed that a given CAD system is made more accurate by suppressing ribs and clavicles in a chest radiographs.

In clinical practice, this separation is made by employing a technique referred to as dual-energy imaging. Dual-energy imaging works on the principle of different amount of X-ray energy absorption pattern for bones (having calcium) and soft tissue. This is a two shot acquisition process. Although several commercial X-ray units available nowadays do possess dual-energy imaging capability at some negligible additional radiation, it is not routinely performed unless and until specifically asked for it. The work presented here looks for ways and means to provide the abovementioned capability for conventional single shot chest radiography by software means where a patient don't need to go through high dose of radiation. The research literature reports on three different approaches to deal with the problem of rib suppression in chest radiograph.

One possible way to deal with ribs is to describe them mathematically by a suitable model. This approach has been advocated by Park, Jin, and Wilson (2003) and Kim, Pyo, Lee, Lee, and Park (2000). The authors argue that ribs can be suitably modeled by a set of geometrical structures called parabola. The standard parabola equation has been initially fitted to the rib borders using Hough transform. Later on, these parabolas are adopted for a given rib structure in an iterative manner to achieve a locally optimized solution. The solution provided, in some subtle cases, may stay away from the actual ribs, where a further postprocessing in the shape of reducing energy between the calculated ribs and the corresponding snakes of the model. In addition, the final solution is manually tuned to come up with a reasonable practical model.

The second approach is to use a training based nonlinear neural network technique. The candidates advocating this approach are Suzuki, Abe, MacmMahon, and Doi (2006) and Idit Diamant et al. (2017). Here, contrast of ribs and clavicles in chest radiograph is suppressed by means of a multiresolution massive training artificial neural network (MTANN). An MTANN is a nonlinear filter whose coefficients are being trained by a number of chest radiographs. After training, the nonlinear neural network can be applied to a given chest radiograph for extracting the bone-like images containing exclusively ribs and clavicles. The extraction leaves behind a chest radiographs containing low contrast rib structure. However, in general, for neural networks, it is hard to trace the actual process taking place. Mostly it is treated as a black box having complex nonlinear structure.

Therefore it is hard to alter or improve a neural network once it is converged. Moreover, a neural network needs training with random weights and its convergence is not guaranteed. More often, multiple runs of the training session are employed before deciding the final solution.

Another method similar to what we propose is that of Loog et al. In this work, a nonlinear filter is developed based on regression technique. The regression technique takes advantage of the relationships between input image pixels and output image pixels and learns mappings from a set of dual-energy images. The main issue with this data-driven filter is the handling of large dimensional data. Once the data are reduced in lower dimensions, the algorithm runs in iteration to extract certain parameters. The iterations are closely watched for their convergence. The authors suggested to incorporate predictors in the test phase in addition to training phase to get better results. The need for those predictors arose due to a certain mismatch between test and training examples. Here dimensionality reduction is a critical step that affects the overall accuracy of the system. Moreover, the local as well as global parameter adjustment is an issue. On the contrary in our work we derive data-driven filters from the given input image as a preprocessing step in a straight forward manner without the need for iteration.

The third approach looks at the rib suppression in a chest radiograph as a blind source separation (BSS) problem. It considers an X-ray chest radiograph composed of anatomically two images, one that contains the bone structure and the other, made of background tissue image, both linearly mixed. The independent component analysis (ICA) which performs a BSS for a linear mixing of sources has been used for separating rib image from rest of the soft-tissue image. This statistical approach for rib suppression is described in Ahmed, Rasheed, Khan, Rashid, and Ahmed (2007) and Ahmed, Rasheed, Khan, Cho, et al. (2007). The ICA basis filters are derived for a given chest radiograph and found to be combination of Gabor filters and step functions (depicting sharp transition of intensity values). These basis are given the name of edge filters (Bell & Sejnowski, 1997). In the final image reconstruction process, we leave out those basis filters that contain information about rib and other bony structure edges. The image thus reconstructed provides a rib suppressed chest radiograph. The major positive for this approach is that it is neither training based nor fitting an already assumed model, rather it is a data driven highly adaptive technique.

However, the ICA algorithm includes a step where the given input data are whitened that removes the variance preference of one particular feature over the other. In case of chest radiograph, it can be seen that the bony structure like ribs and clavicles contributes large variance as compared to the soft tissue. Thus the advantage of separating ribs is lost in an ICA approach. So it is proposed that if a data-driven but sensitive to the variance contents technique is developed, this research may come up with filters that represent ribs more appropriately. The principal component analysis (PCA) is one such data-driven algorithm (Li, Luo, Hu, Li, & Wang, 2015; Lopez-Alonso & Alda, 2004) that sorts an image into its principle components based on the superiority of second-order statistics like variance. In this research, the use of PCA filtering is investigated in suppressing ribs and clavicles, with enhancing the capability of subsequent CAD performance (Hancock, Roland, & Smith, 1992; Heidemann, 2006).

(A)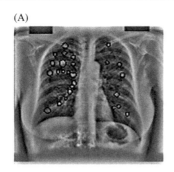   (B)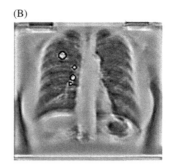

Figure 14.2
Improvement in nodule detection with PCA: Blob detector output without PCA filtering (A) and with PCA filtering (B).

The results of rib suppression using PCA filter are shown in Fig. 14.2B. A standard Gaussian detector Laplacian of Gaussian (LOG) mask has been used to find peaks where a potential nodule may exist. The application of mask resulted in large number of false positives in the original chest x-ray image as shown in Fig. 14.2A and many of them happen to be on the ribs. However, after the rib suppression using PCA filtering operation, the mask was able to detect the true nodule in addition to quite a limited number of false positives. It is believed that this reduction in number of false positive can be attributed largely to the effective suppression of ribs.

It is important to note here that the PCA filtering framework is not limited to just rib suppression. In the process of deriving rib-sensitive filters, couple of filters associated with thermal noise of the acquisition device are also identified. Since PCA filters can be sorted in terms of their variance energy, the noise level can be conveniently suppressed in output X-ray images by invoking these noise-associative filters.

This chapter is organized as follows: in Section 14.2 different techniques for rib suppression are discussed. In this section justification for the use of PCA filters for rib suppression is presented. In Section 14.3 discussion about data acquisition and the selection of an appropriate X-ray database for the given experiment is presented. In the next section proposed system for Cancer Nodule detection is discussed. In Section 14.5 experimental setup is presented and Section 14.6 provides results, and final section presents the conclusion.

14.2 Looking at rib structure from signal processing point-of-view

Let us investigate the rib suppression problem from signal processing point-of-view. The chest X-ray is a two-dimensional signal $L(x, y)$ having a size of 256×256 pixels with 256 brightness values. A single vertical scan line at $y = 71$ was extracted from the image yielding the one-dimensional signal $L(x) = L(x, 71)$, plotted in Fig. 14.3. The position in the image from which $L(x)$ was extracted is shown as a black line in Fig. 14.4. If the one-dimensional plot to the gray levels in the region around the line is compared, it is observed that light regions in the image have large values (near 255), and dark regions have low values (near zero).

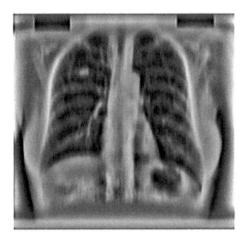

Figure 14.3
Some instances of obscured nodules with rib structures.

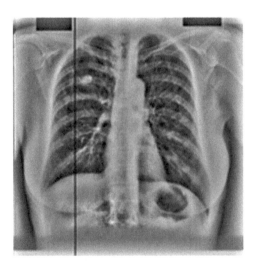

Figure 14.4
One vertical scan of the chest X-ray image (JPCLN006) at column 71 of the Japanese Society of Radiological Technology (JSRT) database. The x-ray image displayed here is taken from a Japanese Radiology Database with permission. Source: Shiraishi et al., 2000..

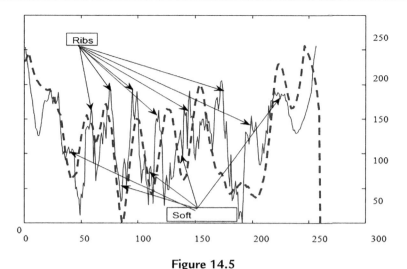

Figure 14.5

Rib suppression using running average filter on locally normalized X-ray image (JPCLN006).

From the one-dimensional plot shown in Fig. 14.3, it can be seen that ribs being represented by peaks repeated at regular interval with a dominating spatial frequency. The repetition interval is estimated to be 11 points long. Therefore one immediate solution is to apply an 11-point running average FIR filter whose coefficients are predetermined and fixed, which is done similarly and the result $M(x)$ was plotted on the same graph with dotted line (Fig. 14.3). It is noticed that output $M(x)$ is a smoother version with ribs depressed. The smoothness is the result of the relative attenuation of the high frequencies in the signal that corresponds to ribs edges in the image. However, to get a visual assessment of the 11-point average, the filter was applied over all the columns of the image. The result is shown in Fig. 14.5, where it is obvious that the FIR filter has blurred the soft tissues present in the chest image and may in fact blur the shape of a possible nodule. This image if fed to a nodule detection mechanism will result in the detection of the nodule at a larger radius.

Therefore it can be safely assumed that a fixed linear filtering is not appropriate for suppressing ribs while keeping intact the rest of the data.

FIR filter is needed whose spatial response is well-matched to the ever changing rib direction that should selectively do a job of rib suppression without distorting nodules. In the past, such data-dependent orientation−based linear filters were derived using statistical data analysis technique such as ICA and PCA by Alonso et al. (2004), Veelen, Nijhuis, and Spaanenburg (1999), and Bell and Sejnowski (1997).

The ICA has been used previously with natural images to derive filters in Hancock et al. (1992). It was found that the resultant filters are dominantly oriented edge filters with strong local character. If such oriented edge filters are applied to a chest X-ray image, the image will be decomposed into a set of edge images. However, none of these edge images provides basis for developing a filter toward the goal of rib suppression.

First 100 basis vectors of a set of training images from JSRT database representing different structures present in the X-ray image. The starting basis vectors are of low frequency, while the mid-basis vectors represent medium frequencies while from last basis vectors it can be clearly observed that it presents high-frequency contents.

On the other hand, the PCA filters obtained with natural images are oriented bar-detectors that correspond to the low-frequency structure present in an image (Field, 1994). The data-driven PCA filters have already been successfully utilized in speech recognition by Minh and Lee (2004). For the natural images, the principal component or filters as commonly referred to resemble derivatives of Gaussian operators. However, the important finding reported was the fact that while filter of natural images do not depend on scale, those from text images are found to be highly scale dependent. More amazingly, convolution of one of the filters from text images with an original image showed that it is sensitive to inter-word gaps. The findings reported for text images provided the basis of proposed motivation where filters that matches in their spatial frequency to the inter-rib distance of a given X-ray image are been checked.

The PCA is mostly used as a tool for data analysis and for predictive models. PCA makes use of eigenvalue decomposition of a data covariance matrix of a given data, usually after subtracting the mean for each attribute. From image analysis perspective, the image patches are examined as compared with the whole image. This is done due to the reason that rib can be well-represented in an image patch. If image patches are visualized as n-dimensional vector, it can create n-dimensional space having points representing image patches. Once PCA is applied to this n-dimensional data space, will rotate the coordinate axes in such a manner to maximize the variance along each axis. The new axes will emerge and will be grouped in descending order of their variance contents. These axes are also referred to as filters, as the data being reconstructed with few of these axes may happen to wipe out or retain some spatial features.

In our scheme, the PCA filtering step is employed as a preprocessing step for each incoming X-ray image. Square patches of size $m \times m$ are extracted by choosing an area within an image at random. The mean gray level, as estimated over all patches, is subtracted from each pixel value of a given patch. The patch is then masked by a Gaussian window whose standard deviation is chosen in such a manner that borders of the patch are more than three standard deviations from the center, far enough to avoid edge effects. The patch is then normalized to unit length.

This column vector can be viewed as one possible realization of a random vector X, representing the source generating all these image patches. By collecting many such realizations, a training set for developing PCA filters can be assembled. The average vector of the training set is defined by:

$$\bar{x} = \frac{1}{M} \sum_{i=1}^{M} x(i)$$

Each $X(i)$ differs from the average by the vector $D(i) = X(i) - X$.

Let $B = [D(1) \ D(2) \ \cdot \ \cdot \ D(M)]$ be the representation of that training set. Next the vectors μ and scalars λ are found which are the eigenvectors and eigenvalues, respectively, of the covariance matrix shown in the following equation:

$$C = B.B^{\mathrm{T}} \tag{14.1}$$

Let A be a matrix formed by eigenvectors of C. The first row of A corresponds to the largest eigenvalue and the last row represents the smallest value in a descending order. These eigenvectors of C are referred to as basis function conventionally. In this case, as PCA filters are been referred. The matrix A obtained by PCA training process of a given chest X-ray image patches is visually displayed in Fig. 14.6.

The starting two rows shown in Fig. 14.7 corresponds to low frequency that catches the big structure present in an image. These rows resemble to a larger extent with Gaussian derivative operators of first- and second-order. The middle few rows provide filters having medium frequency and the last couple of rows are undoubtedly high-frequency filters and their proximity to higher order Gaussian derivative operators is evident. It can be seen clearly that there exists an ordering of the filters in terms of their frequency contents. By taking a given X-ray image and convolving with each of these FIR filters, it will end up in principal components of the image, referred to as principal image as shown in Fig. 14.7. By casting a look over these principal images, it is observed that fourth principal image contains rib structure as a dominant feature.

In other words, to obtain a rib suppressed image, the principal image corresponding to rib structure is subtracted from the original image during the reconstruction process. In our case, the principal image corresponding to rib structure is based on the fourth PCA filter. The above description is expressed in the following equation:

$$L_{\mathrm{ribsup}} = L - \alpha L_{\mathrm{ribstruct}} \tag{14.2}$$

where L_{ribsup} is the rib suppressed image, L is the original image, and $L_{\mathrm{ribstruct}}$ is the image formed as a result of the fourth basis containing prominent rib structure. Here α is the scaling factor having a range of $0-1$, this research typically used $\alpha = 0.4$ for the given experimentation purpose.

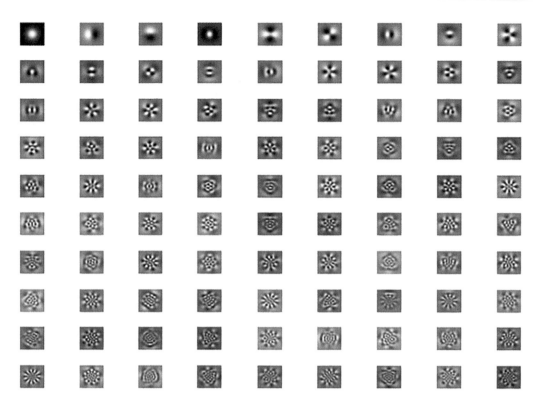

Figure 14.6
The black solid line represents the original column 70 of the locally normalized X-ray image (JPCLN006) in which the peaked edges are ribs and the rest are soft tissues. The dotted line represents the effect for running average filter on the overall column. It can be seen clearly that not only ribs have been affected by the running average filter but also the soft tissues are damaged.

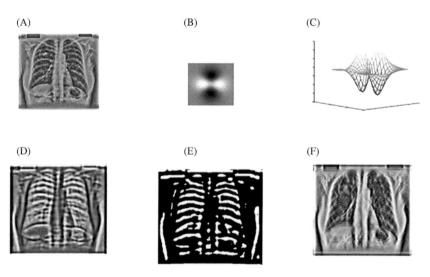

(A) (B) (C)

(D) (E) (F)

Figure 14.7
(A) Locally normalized image, (B) PCA data-driven filter, (C) 3D plot of (B) showing beaks and valley corresponding to second-order difference.

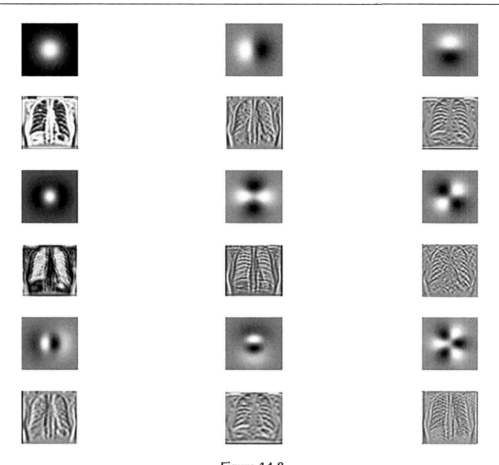

Figure 14.8
The PCA filters extracted from the image (JPCLN006) along with their associated principal images right beneath them.

The image retrieved after the subtraction process is the desired rib suppressed image where the nodule affected due to rib overlap is better exposed.

The image obtained after applying PCA filtering is shown in Fig. 14.8 that shows that the soft tissues are less damaged as compared with the results extracted with the average filter shown in Fig. 14.5.

To assess the scaling effect on the resulting PCA filters, PCA technique is used to extract filters for chest X-ray image with a range of scales. The purpose of the experiment was to figure out the appropriate image patch size to be used with a given X-ray input image (JPCLN009 from JSRT database). Four different chest X-ray images subsampled in descending order to lower spatial resolution, while keeping the image patch size constant. The image patches extracted are shown in Fig. 14.9 on the left-hand side. The results,

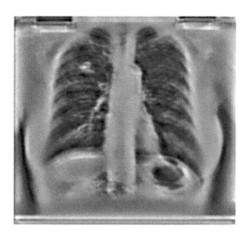

Figure 14.9
Image (JPCLN006) retrieved after PCA filtering. The image retrieved is a rib suppressed image
where the nodule affected due to rib overlap is better highlighted.

Fig. 14.9, now show a very marked scale dependence for the filters extracted. Note that the sign differences are not significant rather it is the absolute value that marked their variance. In this figure, the fifth column filters are matched in spatial frequency to the inter-rib spacing. Especially this trend can be seen in the fourth row of Fig. 14.9. It can also be observed from the fourth row that the filter gained in the seventh column had orientation matched to the rising edge of the ribs. Fig. 14.9 also describes the fact that the horizontal boundaries corresponding to the first-order Gaussian derivative are stronger in terms of their variance than those at the rib boundaries. It is concluded from this experiment that the image patch size (Fig. 14.9). Effect of patch size on the PCA filters extracted: each row contains the original image patch along with the first eight PCA filters. The first two rows confirms the extraction of filters sensitive to the ribs, while the last two rows shows filters that are sensitive to inter-rib gaps chosen to find appropriate PCA filters for rib suppression does matter and should be of size such that contains only one rib going right in the middle of the patch.

14.3 Data acquisition

The improvement shown by the proposed rib suppression scheme need to be quantitatively assessed. The assessment and then subsequent comparison with earlier schemes is only possible if the database employed to obtain these results is identical. Large X-ray databases are yet not been made public to test CAD systems, but smaller X-ray databases are available. These databases can be used to test different CAD schemes, provided that they contain a large enough variation in their data set to represent the different real world variations in blob size and shape. The validity of our results will be highly dependent on the database chosen.

For the experiment of this research, the JSRT database has been selected which was developed by the Japanese Society of Radiological Technology (JSRT) in cooperation with the Japanese Radiological Society (Shiraishi et al., 2003). It is found that two previous CAD schemes tested on this database by Coppini et al. (2003) and Wei, Hagihara, Shimizu, and Kobatake (2002). Furthermore, the database has large enough variations to justify its use as a standard database for comparison. The details of the database are as follows:

The JSRT database comprises 247 digitized images of poster anterior chest films (14 $\times$ 14 in.) collected from 13 medical centers in Japan and one institution in the United States. Digitized images had a size of 2048 $\times$ 2048 matrix, 0.175 mm pixel size, and 12-bit gray levels corresponding to a 0.0 $-$ 3.5 optical density range. Of the 247 images, 154 X-ray images contain a nodule and 93 images are without a nodule. Of the 154 images that contained a nodule, 100 images contain a cancerous and 54 contain a benign nodule. The location of all nodules was confirmed by three chest radiologists which constitutes the ground truth. X-ray images with multiple nodules have been discarded in the database. The nodules present in the database were of variable size, 31 nodules were 0–10 mm, 52 were 11 $-$ 15 mm, 36 were 16 $-$ 20 mm, 14 were 21 $-$ 25 mm, 17 were 26 $-$ 30 mm, and 4 that were 31 $-$ 60 mm in diameter. The average size of all nodules included in the database was 17.3 mm.

14.4 System design

The system architecture is shown in Fig. 14.10. The various blocks representing the processing steps are explained as follows. The first task was to down sample the images from their spatial resolution of 2048 $\times$ 2048 down to 512 $\times$ 512. This was done to facilitate experimentation as it allows for a considerable decrease in computation time. The loss of spatial resolution does not cast a significant influence on the results obtained and the method developed here also works on the original data as was previously claimed by Loog et al. The process of down sampling for 2D images is performed by employing a prefilter to reduce the high-frequency data and then the required number of rows and columns are removed. Thus the original image undergoes a process of low pass filtering before being subsampled so that the down-sampled image approximates the original image optimally even if it has high-frequency contents. However, the final judge is the radiologist sitting on the other end. It has been verified that blob detection is least affected by this amount of spatial resolution deduction from the radiologist's point-of-view and algorithmic accuracy by Lindeberg (1993).

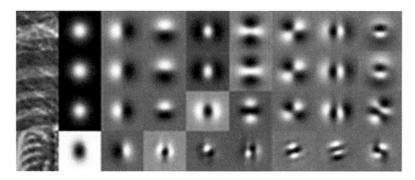

Figure 14.10
Effects of patch size on the PCA filters extracted.

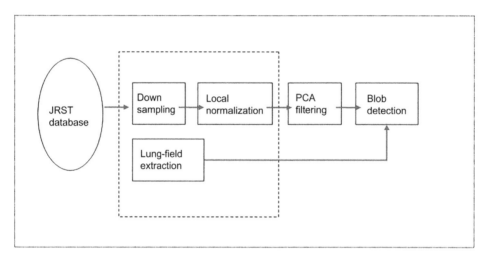

Figure 14.11
Block diagram for local normalization of X-ray images.

14.4.1 Local normalization

Since nodules are small, hard to distinguish objects in the lung field, hence it is required to enhance nodule contrast with respect to its background to make nodules more visible. A technique called Local Normalization is used to obtain a globally equalized contrast throughout the X-ray image. Locally normalized image is shown in Fig. 14.11. Locally normalizing an image is done as shown in Fig. 14.12. The process is explained as follows.

A Gaussian low pass filtered image is subtracted from our original image. Gaussian low pass filter provides local mean of our X-ray image. The mean subtracted image is then divided by the corresponding local standard deviation. Here σ_1 and σ_2 are standard deviation used for the Gaussian smoothing functions, which control the estimation of the

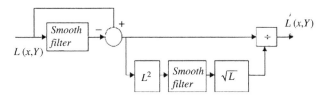

Figure 14.12
Multiscale computer-aided detection system with PCA filtering as a preprocessing step.

local mean and local variance. In this case σ_1 and σ_2 equal to 10 which approximately equals the width of a rib are used. This would lead to better contrast enhancement for nodules as rib contrast would be diminished to some extent. The next task is lung field segmentation.

Any nodule detected outside the lung field will be counted as a false positive. Lung field segmentation is a necessity if it is to restrict the nodule detector outputs to the lung field. In this case, it is described the lung field as those parts of the lung that are not obscured by the heart, mediastinum, and structures below the diaphragm. This step will significantly reduce the number of false positives and will lead to an improvement in our results. On the other hand, a significant part of the lung field will not be analyzed that does not fulfill our definition above. Nodules present in those areas will be missed by the system and will not be detected at a later stage. A trade off exists between reducing false positives on the one hand and reducing true positives on the other. In this research, lung field segmentation is implemented to significantly reduce the number of false positives detected outside the lung field defined earlier. The decrease in system sensitivity due to missed true positives is not significant and the trade-off is acceptable. To segment the lung field an active shape model (ASM; Freedman et al., 2002) is used. The settings for our ASM are obtained from the report of Lu and Rajapakse (2005) and lung field segmentation is trained using X-ray images from the JSRT database.

14.4.2 Multiscale nodule detection

Nodules in this database show considerable variation in size ranging from 6 to 60 mm. Nodule detection is therefore inherently a multiscale problem which requires multiscale representation of our image data. Multiscale techniques are widely used for the purpose of nodule detection. Though there are other blob detectors such as the difference of Gaussian, the determinant of Hessian, we focus here on the most widely-used LoG detector.

The detector works by taking an input image $L(x, y)$ and convolving it by a Gaussian Kernel.

$$G(x, y; s) = \frac{1}{2\pi s} e - (x^2 + y^2)/2s \tag{14.3}$$

At a certain scale s to provide a scale-space representation.

$$L(x, y; s) = G(x, y; s) \times L(x, y) \tag{14.4}$$

The semicolon between the spatial and scale parameters is conventionally put there to make the difference between these parameters explicit.

Then the Laplacian operator

$$L_{xx} + L_{yy} \tag{14.5}$$

is computed for each image in the family. This results in strong positive responses for dark blob of size $\sqrt{s}$. After applying Laplacian operator, it needs to compare the images among the whole family on a pixel-by-pixel basis. To do a fairer comparison, it is required to consider scale-normalized Laplacian operator

$$q^2 L(x, y; s) = s\left(L_{xx} + L_{yy}\right) \tag{14.6}$$

and then to detect pixels that are simultaneously local maxima/minima of $q^2 L$ with respect to both space and scale. Thus, it can be said that, in discrete case given a two-dimensional input image $L(x, y)$, a three-dimensional discrete scale-space family $L(x, y; s)$ is constructed and a pixel is declared as a blob if the at this pixel is greater than the value in all its 26 neighbors.

14.4.3 Detection of nodules in discrete X-ray images

Nodule detection in X-ray images after the rib suppression using PCA filter is carried out using the abovementioned scale-space framework discrete implementation for our LOG filter. In summary, the implementation of the abovementioned work has been performed as follows:

- Given a discrete locally normalized and rib suppressed X-ray image (here of size 512×512 pixels), select a scale range for the analysis (here: $s_{min} = 1$ to $s_{max} = 16$). Within this range, a set of scale levels s_k ($k = 1, 2, 9$) are distributed such that the ratio between successive scale levels is approximately constant.
- For each scale, s_k compute the scale-space representation of the X-ray image L using normalized Laplacian. Fig. 14.13 shows the output of this step. It can be seen that the true nodules can be detected correctly at $\sigma = 4.6661$. However, it is observed that a large number of false positive appeared. It needs to find ways to reduce false positives (Fig. 14.14). Results of nodule detection at different scales superimposed. Note that blobs are generally detected at a number of contiguous scales. For each scale image, a

(A) 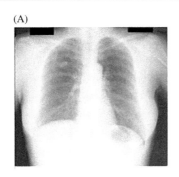 (B)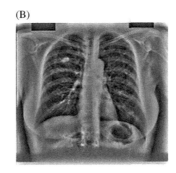

Figure 14.13
X-ray image (JPCLN006) before and after nodule contrast enhancement using local normalization (A) before local normalization and (B) after local normalization.

threshold is defined and detected spatial location and their corresponding responses for greater than threshold pixels.
- These locations and their corresponding responses are noted in an array. Then each nodule strength at each location is compared with all these locations that come under the support region of the largest radius blob. The overlapping blobs with lower strength are eliminated.

14.5 Experiment

The first part of our experiment consists of Rib Suppression followed by multiscale blob detection. The next phase is appropriate features extraction followed by development of a classifier.

PCA filtering technique discussed earlier is implemented on the entire JSRT database. The resulting rib suppressed images are taken as input for the Multiscale Blob Detection step. The multiscale blob detector is first used to obtain the size and locations of the nodules in the X-ray images. The scale range for the detector covers $\sigma = 1-16$ pixels with nine exponential spacing. Thresholds are then applied to the output of this blob detector to determine the extremes after developing scale space representation. These thresholds are set taking into consideration the mean and standard deviation of the pixel values in the image. The threshold applied should allow maximum detection at this stage to ensure detection of all true positives, as any nodule missed at this stage will not be recovered at a later stage. The size of a nodule could be estimated by the scale at which it is detected.

The scale at which the normalized trace of the Laplacian is maximum is taken as the detection scale. The radius of the detected blob is approximately half the detection scale. These detected nodules consist of a large number of false positives depending on the

(A)   (B)   (C)

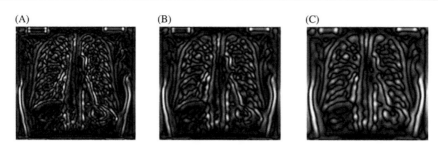

Figure 14.14
Locally normalized image after LOG filter at scale, (A) $\sigma = 2.5198$, (B) $\sigma = 3.4290$, and (C)
$\sigma = 4.6661$.

threshold set. Detector outputs are obtained for the whole JSRT database. This completes
the first step of our experiment.

Since blob detector output contains a large number of false positives; therefore, a false
positive reduction process is implemented to reduce the number of false positives. Our first
reduction step is implemented by noting the fact that some of these false positive occurs
outside the region of interest. In this case, researchers are interested in the detection of nodules
for the lung field area. Therefore lung field segmentation is carried out and all nodules
detected outside the lung field are subsequently removed. This is illustrated in Fig. 14.15.

Next step is to extract appropriate features to be used in a classifier. These features should
be carefully chosen to improve the separability between a nodule and non-nodule structures.
Blobs structures generally consists of bright circular regions surrounded embedded in a dark
region. A contrast box strategy has already been successfully used to detect blobs. It is
generalized that this contrast box strategy to include multiscale analysis. This results in
increasing or decreasing the size of the box according the given nodule size. An appropriate
feature set could be obtained by describing a blob in terms of its mean and standard
deviation within and outside this box. The contrast box consists of two regions. The inner
circular region could be marked by a circle with radius σ detected during our multiscale
analysis around the region of interest. Similarly, the outer region could be described by
another concentric circle with radius $1.5 \times \sigma$ around the inner region. Mean and standard
deviation of pixel values are calculated at the detected scale within and in a band outside
the region surrounding the detected point. These mean and standard deviation are calculated
by applying region growing algorithm to get the correct boundaries. These features are
extracted from X-ray images at a higher resolution (1024×1024) to reduce error in our
feature calculation.

Training features are taken from the feature extraction step. The JSRT database consists of
154 images. For each detected nodules, four features are collected, that is, m_1 (mean gray
level of the inner region), v_1 (standard deviation of gray values inside the inner region),

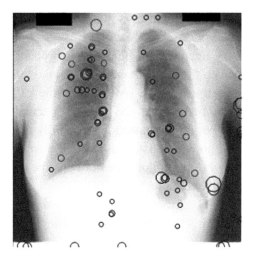

Figure 14.15 (A)
Segmented lung field obtained after active shape segmentation. (B) Blob detection results for
CAD scheme after lung field segmentation.

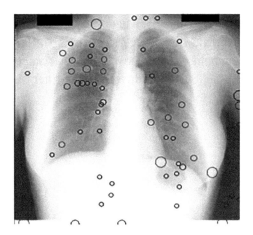

Figure 14.16
Detected nodules at scales where filter responses are maximum.

m_2 (mean gray level of the outer region), and v_2 (standard deviation of the gray values of
the outer region). To increase class separability, that is, nodules versus non-nodules, linear
discriminant analysis (LDA) is used. LDA easily handles the case where the within-class
frequencies are unequal, this method maximizes the ratio of between-class variance to the
within-class variance in any particular data set thereby guaranteeing maximal separability.
The class separability matrix was applied to the four extracted features and reduce them
into two highly discriminative features. The features are gained from LDA are $m_1 - m_2$ and
$v_1 - v_2$. The resulting two-dimensional feature space is depicted in Fig. 14.16.

A simple k-nearest neighbor (kNN) classifier is implemented to classify the detected nodules. The posterior probability of the kNN classifier gives us the probability estimate for the detected nodules after experimentation. The posterior probability is the conditional probability that is assigned when the relevant evidence is taken into account. The kNN classifier searches the n-dimensional feature space to find the kNN. The posterior probability of the classifier is n/k where n is the number of actual nodules in the k nearest neighbors. A threshold can be put on the posterior probability of the kNN classifier to reduce the number of detected nodules. ROC curves are drawn for different sensitivity of our blob detector. The sensitivity of the blob detector could be adjusted by changing the posterior probability for the kNN classifier.

14.6 Results

Multiscale blob detection system has been employed as a basic nodule detection scheme. Different post- and preprocessing steps are then implemented to reduce the number of false positives and increase CAD system sensitivity.

Blob detector takes X-ray images from JSRT database as input. The average number of nodules detected by our Multiscale Blob Detection system is 218 per image. Since any true positive missed at this stage would not be recovered at later stages, hence lower thresholds are set when obtaining local maximas in multiscale LOG filter outputs. Fig. 14.17 shows the output of our block detector for the Basic CAD scheme.

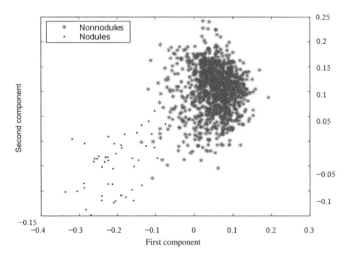

Figure 14.17

Blob detection results for the basic computer-aided detection scheme. The number of nodules detected is maximum in this scheme.

It is observed that 68% of these false positives are detected at the first few fine scales in our scale space images. A lot of high-frequency noise is present at these scales; therefore, they can be safely ignored when taking the best LOG filter responses from the detected multiscale outputs. This act as seed points for KNN classification as shown in Fig. 14.15. Only the strongest candidates are retained.

Output for our CAD scheme with PCA filtering as a preprocessing step (Fig. 14.19). PCA filtering suppresses ribs as a result false positives occurring on ribs are removed. PCA filtering also enhances nodules that are obstructed by ribs.

A first postprocessing step to our CAD scheme, as a result 142 false positives are removed. No candidate nodules are present at these scales in the JSRT database hence there is no reduction in true positives. Fig. 14.18 shows the output for our CAD scheme where the outputs from first few fine scales are ignored.

Lung field segmentation further reduces false positives by removing detected local maximas outside the lung field. The lung field is described as those parts of the lung that are not obstructed by the heart, the mediastinum and structure below the diaphragm. Thirteen of 154 candidate nodules lie in those parts of the lung that are hidden or obstructed. The loss of 13 true positives leads to a decrease in CAD system sensitivity. These true positives will not be recovered in later postprocessing steps. CAD system sensitivity drops by 8.4% after lung field segmentation. Twenty-five candidate nodules per image lying outside the lung field are removed as a result. Fig. 14.15 shows CAD system output after lung field segmentation.

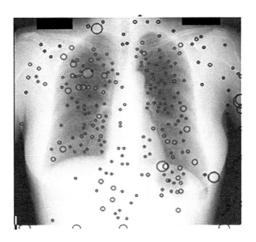

Figure 14.18
Blob detection results for the basic CAD scheme with fine scales eliminated. Noise detected at fine scales is eliminated.

kNN classification is added as a third postprocessing step which further reduces the number of detected nodules to 13 per image. Fig. 14.16 shows the feature space constructed for JSRT database with the chosen features defined earlier. Fig. 14.19 shows our CAD system output after kNN classification.

Our final and fourth strategy takes PCA filtered rib suppressed images as inputs to the CAD system. The effect of rib suppression is clearly visible in Fig. 14.20. The average number of candidate nodules retained with PCA filtering drops to three nodules per image. A large number of false positives are detected on rib edges and these false positives are removed when rib suppressed images are taken as inputs. PCA filtering also leads to an increase in our CAD system sensitivity as rib obstructed cancer nodules become more enhanced.

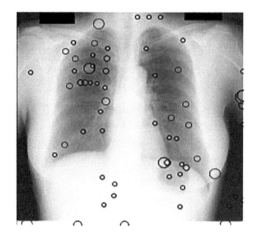

Figure 14.19
Blob detection result.

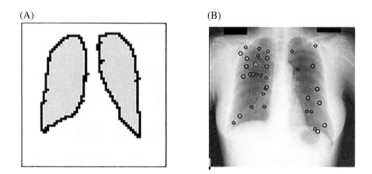

Figure 14.20
Output for our CAD scheme with PCA filtering as a preprocessing step. PCA filtering suppresses ribs as a result false positives occurring on ribs are removed. PCA filtering also enhances nodules that are obstructed by ribs.

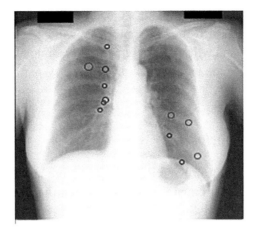

Figure 14.21
Linear discriminant analysis in developing two classes with minimum overlap.

Sensitivity of our blob detection system is adjusted by changing the posterior probability of our kNN classifier. Sensitivity for our system is defined as the number of true positives detected versus the total number of nodule candidates detected after the classification step. Fig. 14.21 is constructed by plotting sensitivity levels as a function of false positives detected per image.

14.7 Implication of automated lung nodules detection for future generation medical systems

The recent advances in chest X-ray acquisition technology has increased the rate of detection of small nodules that also include those of peripheral lung cancer (Ko, Rusinek, & Naidich, 2003). However, despite the increased higher spatial and contrast resolution of the newly built X-ray machines, nodule lesions are missed by radiologist while examining the chest X-ray. One of the major factor contributing to the difficulty of detecting nodules is their relatively small size less than 5 mm in diameter and the fact that most of these small nodules are partially occluded by the ribs and other bonny structure. The nodules with less than 5 mm in diameter are the most challenging due to their variable colorization, and an added complexity if they are hidden beneath the major rib. It was revealed in several studies that sensitivity of a CAD system did not differ significantly from that of radiologists. Radiologists were found to be more sensitive at detecting nodules attached to ribs, whereas CAD was better for finding isolated small nodules (Lee et al., 2004). The computer-assisted diagnostic system is lower in sensitivity score than that of radiologist is the inability of the computerized models to suppress the ribs. Detecting small nodules and especially those hidden by ribs is important because their volume-doubling time is the predictor of malignancy. With the method described in this chapter that explicitly talks about methodology to suppress ribs in an X-ray image will certainly boost the sensitivity of the computer-aided system and will make it surpass the radiologist detection. Thus a rib suppression add-on will raise the level of computer-aided system as to provide a second prospective on the X-ray scans.

14.8 Discussion and conclusion

The output achieved as a result of using PCA filters before applying multiscale CAD scheme are very efficient and promising. In this research the internationally available JSRT database of radiographs by Shiraishi et al. (2000) is used for the evaluation of proposed algorithm. The JSRT closely resembles a real world scenario for the size and location of lung cancer nodules. The size of these cancer nodules varies from 6 to 60 mm. Shiraishi et al. (2000) indicates that it is very difficult for the radiologist to detect the subtle nodules in the JSRT database. Only 50% of confident detection was observed out of which radiologists detected an average of 85% of practicable cases and 44% of the hard cases. On average of three false positives, our scheme correctly marks 46% of the hard cases and 84% of the practicable cases as shown in Fig. 14.21. This ensures that our method can be very useful for clinical assessments. Comparing our CAD scheme with others who have also worked using the same JSRT database shows that our work is more effective. The RS-2000 system has been tested on the same database by Freedman et al. (2002). It detected 66% of the nodules having an average of five false positives per image. However, RS-2000 has proven its worth in over 10,000 cases to obtain FDA approval. To reach that performance of Wei et al. (2002), 202 uncorrelated features were used; that is cause for some concern because it means that the system uses more features than the available number of false positive samples in the database, and as a result the risk of overtraining the system is high. At 5.4 false positives per image, our CAD scheme reaches 73% sensitivity, and uses less than 20 features. Coppini et al. (2003) also used the JRST database and found a sensitivity of only 60% at 4.3 false positives per image for their CAD system. Loog et al. also used JRST database and found a sensitivity of 41% at four false positives per image. It is claimed that proposed results provide better results than those reported by Wei and Loog.

The main drawback of proposed scheme is the failure to detect certain subtle nodules. In the future, researchers are working toward developing a multiscale enhancement technique that will work jointly with multiscale detection used here. For this purpose currently team is in the process of developing a multiscale IRIS filter (Hidefumi et al., 1996), which is aimed to detect the most subtle nodule once used in multiscale detection environment.

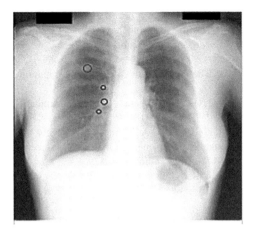

Figure 14.22
Results of nodule detection at different scales superimposed.

Innovations in smart healthcare with the advancements of technology have led many improvements in the medical system to make human life more comfortable. This area is developing fast with the help of several stakeholders from academics, policy makers, technologists, and healthcare specialists.

Today we live in the age of information and health informatics needs to embrace and capture as much as possible from the advanced developments of technology. There are several areas which deem research and integration of health with network and communication technology, smart and efficient decision support systems, with deeper and efficient data analysis and over all the security paradigms of these. The research presented here is one example that clearly shows the role played by computer technology in improving the diagnosis system while greatly reducing the risk of radiations to a patient.

14.9 Teaching assignments

- Justify why rib suppression is necessary for chest X-ray analysis.
- Describe various lung nodule detection techniques.
- Describe various rib suppression software-based methods.
- Describe in detail how a rib suppression technique is helpful in improving the sensitivity of a computer-aided design for chest X-ray screening process (Fig. 14.22).

References

Ahmed, B., Rasheed, T., Khan, M. A. U., Rashid, A., & Ahmed, S. (2007). Rib suppression in chest radiographs using ICA algorithm. *Information Technology Journal, 6*(7), 1085–1089.

Ahmed, B., Rasheed, T., Khan, M. A. U., Cho, S. J., Lee, S., & Kim, T.-S. (2007). Rib suppression for enhancing frontal chest radiographs using independent component analysis. *ICANNGA*, *2*, 300−308.

American Cancer Society. (2003). *Cancer facts and figures 2003. Technical reports.* Atlanta, GA: American Cancer Society, Inc.

Bell, A. J., & Sejnowski, T. J. (1997). The independent components' of natural scenes are edge filters. *Vision Research*, *37*(23), 3327−3338.

Carreira, M. J., Cabello, D., Penedo, M. G., & Mosquera, A. (1998). Computer-aided diagnoses: Automatic detection of lung nodules. *Medical Physics*, *25*(10), 1992−2006.

Ciompi, F., Chung, K., van Riel, S. J., Setio, A. A. A., Gerke, P. K., Jacobs, C., . . . van Ginneken, B. (2017). Towards automatic pulmonary nodule management in lung cancer screening with deep learning. *Nature Journal, Scientific Reports*, *7*(2017), Article number: 46479.

Coppini, G., Diciotti, S., Falchini, M., Villari, N., & Valli, G. (2003). Neural networks for computer-aided diagnosis: Detection of lung nodules in chest radiograms. *IEEE Transactions on Information Technology in Biomedicine*, *7*, 344−357.

Cui, J.-W., Li, W., Han, F.-J., & Liu, Y.-D. (2015). Screening for lung cancer using low-dose computed tomography: Concerns about the application in low-risk individual. *Translational Lung Cancer Research*, *4*(3), 275−286.

Diamant, I., Bar, Y., Geva, O., rWolf, L., Zimmerman, G., Lieberman, S., . . . Greenspan, H. (2017). Chest radiograph pathology categorization via transfer learning. *Deep Learning for Medical Image Analysis*, 299−320.

Field, D. J. (1994). What is the goal of sensory coding? *Neural Computation*, *6*, 559−601.

Florack, L. M. J., ter Haar Romeny, B. M., Koenderink, J. J., & Viergever, M. A. (1992). Scale and the differential structure of images. *Image and Vision Computing*, *10*(6), 376−388.

Freedman, M. T., Shih-Chung, B.-L., Osicka, T., Lure, F., Xu, W. X., Lin, J., . . . Zhang, R. (2002). Computer aided detection of lung cancer on chest radiographs: Effect of machine cad false positive locations on radiologists behavior. *Proceedings of the SPIE*, *4684*, 1311−1319.

Giger, M. L., Doi, K., MacMahon, H., Metz, C. E., & Yin, F. F. (1990). Pulmonary nodules: Computer-aided detection in digital chest images. *Radiographics*, *10*(1), 41−51.

Hancock, P. J. E., Roland, J. B., & Smith, L. S. (1992). The principal component of natural images. *Network*, *3*, 61−70.

Heidemann, G. (2006). The principal components of natural images revisited. *IEEE Transactions on Pattern Analysis and Machine Intelligence*, *28*(5), 822−826.

Hyvarinen, A., Karhunen, J., & Oja, E. (2001). *Independent component analysis.* Wiley Interscience.

Keserci, B., & Yoshida, H. (2002). Computerized detection of pulmonary nodules in chest radiographs based on morphological features and wavelet snake model. *Medical Image Analysis*, *6*(4), 431−447. (17).

Kim, S., Pyo, H.-B., Lee, S.-K., Lee, S., & Park, S. H. (2000). Digital image subtraction of temporally sequential chest images by rib image elimination. In: *Proceedings of the 22nd annual EMBS international conference* (pp. 1752−1755), Chicago, IL.

Ko, J. P., Rusinek, H., & Naidich, D. P. (2003). Wavelet compression of low-dose chest CT data: Effect on lung nodule detection. *Radiology*, *228*, 70−75.

Koenderink, J. J. (1984). The structure of image. *Biological Cybernetics*, *50*, 363−370.

de Koning, H. J., Meza, R., Plevritis, S. K., ten Haaf, K., Munshi, V. N., Jeon, J., , et al.McMahon, P. M. (2013). Benefits and harms of computed tomography lung cancer screening strategies: A comparative modeling study for the U.S. preventive services task force. *Annals of Internal Medicine*, *160*, 311−320.

Lange, D. H., Pratt, H., & Inbar, G. F. (1997). Modeling and estimation of single evoked brain potential components. *IEEE Transactions on BioMedical Engineering*, *44*, 791−799.

Lee, J. W., Goo, J. M., Lee, H. J., Kim, J. H., Kim, S., & Kim, Y. T. (2004). The potential contribution of a computer-aided detection system for lung nodule detection in multidetector row computer tomography. *Investigative Radiology*, *39*, 649−655.

Li, X., Luo, S., Hu, Q., Li, J., & Wang, D. (2015). *Rib suppression in chest radiographs for lung nodule enhancement. IEEE international conference on information and automation.* Lijiang, China: IEEE.

Lindeberg, T. (1990). Scale-space for discrete signal. *IEEE Transactions on Pattern Analysis and Machine Intelligence, 12*(3), 234−254.

Lindeberg, T. (1993). Detecting salient blob-like image structures and their scales with a scale-space primal sketch: A method for focus-of-attention. *International Journal of Computer Vision, 11*(3), 283−318.

Lopez-Alonso, J. M., & Alda, J. (2004). Characterization of artifacts in fully digital image-acquisition systems: Application to web cameras. *Society of Photo- Optical Instrumentation Engineers, 43*(1), 257−265.

Lu, Wei, & Rajapakse, C. J. (2005). Approach and applications of constrained ICA. *IEEE transactions on Neural Networks, 16*(1), 203−212.

Mazzone, P., Powell, C. A., Arenberg, D., Bach, P., Detterbeck, F., Gould, M. K., ... Silvestri, G. (2014). Components necessary for high-quality lung cancer screening: American college of chest physicians and american thoracic society policy statement. *Chest, 147*(2), 295−303.

McLean, R. T. (2004). Why do physicians who treat lung cancer get sued? *Chest, 126*, 1672−1679.

Minh, V. D., & Lee, S. (2004). *A PCA-Based human auditory filter bank for speech recognition. International conference on signal processing and communications (SPCOM '04)* (pp. 393−397). IEEE.

Park, M., Jin, J. S., & Wilson, L. S. (2003). Detection of abnormal texture in chest X-rays with reduction of ribs. *VIP2003*, 71−74.

Paumier, A., & Le Péchoux, C. (2010). Radiotherapy in small-cell lung cancer: Where should it go? *Lung Cancer, 69*(2), 133−140.

Shiraishi, J., Abe, H., Engelmann, R., & Doi, K. (2003). Effect of high sensitivity in a computerized scheme for detection extremely subtle solitary pulmonary nodules in chest radiographs: Observer performance study. *Academic Radiology, 10*, 1302−1311.

Shiraishi, J., Li, Q., Suzuki, K., Engelmann, R., & Doi, K. (2006). Computer-aided diagnostic scheme for the detection of lung nodules on chest radiographs: Localized search method based on anatomical classification. *Med Phys, 33*, 2642−2653.

Shiraishi, J., Katsuragawa, S., Ikezoe, J., Matsumoto, T., Kobayashi, T., Komatsu, K., ... Doi, K. (2000). Development of a digital image database for chest radiographs with and without a lung nodule: Receiver operating characteristic analysis of radiologists' detection of pulmonary nodules. *American Journal of Roentgenology, 174*, 71−74.

Smith, R. A., Andrews, K. S., Brooks, D., Fedewa, S. A., Manassaram-Baptiste, D., Saslow, D., ... Wender, R. C. (2018). Cancer screening in the United States, 2018: A review of current American Cancer Society guidelines and current issues in cancer screening. *CA: A Cancer Journal for Clinicians, 68*, 297−316.

Suzuki, K., Abe, H., MacmMahon, H., & Doi, K. (2006). Image-processing technique for suppressing ribs in chest radiographs by means of massive training artificial neural network (MTANN). *IEEE Transactions on Medical Imaging, 25*(4), 406−416.

Veelen, M. V., Nijhuis, J. A. G., & Spaanenburg, L. (1999). Estimation of linear filter banks for multi-variate time series prediction with temporal principal component analysis. *International Joint Conference on Neural Networks, 4*, 2624−2628.

Visvizi, Anna, Lytras, Miltiadis D., Damiani, Ernesto, & Mathkour, Hassan (2018). Policy making for smart cities: Innovation and social inclusive economic growth for sustainability. *Journal of Science and Technology Policy Management, 9*(2), 126−133.

Wei, J., Hagihara, Y., Shimizu, A., & Kobatake, H. (2002). *Optimal image feature set for detecting lung nodules on chest X-ray image. Computer assisted radiology and surgery (CARS 2002)* (pp. 706−711). Berlin: Springer.

Xu, X. W., Doi, K., Kobayashi, T., MacMahon, H., & Giger, M. L. (1997). Development of an improved CAD scheme for automated detection of lung nodules in digital chest images. *Medical Physics, 24*, 1395−1403.

Further reading

Babaud, J., Witkin, A. P., Baudin, M., & Duda, R. O. (1986). Uniqueness of the Gaussian Kernel for scale-space filtering. *IEEE Transactions on Pattern Analysis and Machine Intelligence, 8*(1), 26−33.

Blostein, D., & Ahuja, N. (1989). A multiscale region detector. *Computer Vision, Graphics, and Image Processing, 45*, 22–41.

Brown, M. S., Wilson, L. S., Doust, B. D., Gill, R. W., & Sun, C. (1998). Knowledge-based method for segmentation and analysis of lung boundaries in chest X-ray images. *Computerized Medical Imaging and Graphics, 22*, 463–477.

Cootes, T. F., Taylor, C. J., Cooper, D., & Graham, J. (1995). Active shape models their training and application. *Computer Vision and Image Understanding, 61*(1), 38–59.

Ergun, D. L., Mistrella, C. A., Brown, D. E., Bystrianyk, R. T., Sze, W. K., Kelc, F., & Naidich, D. P. (1990). Single-exposure dual-energy computed radiography: improved detection and processing. *Radiology, 174*(1), 243–249.

Florack, L. M. J., ter Haar Romeny, B. M., Koenderink, J. J., & Viergever, M. A. (1994). Linear scale-space. *Journal of Mathematical Imaging and Vision, 4*(4), 325–351.

Floyd, C. E., Jr., Patz, E. F., Jr., Lo, J. Y., Vittitoe, N. F., & Stambaugh, L. E. (1996). Diffuse nodular lung disease on chest radiographs: A pilot study of characterization by fractal dimension. *American Journal of Roentgenology, 167*(5), 1185–1187.

Fortuna, J., & Capson, D. (2004). *ICA filters for lighting invariant face recognition*, Proceedings of the 17th international conference on pattern recognition (ICPR'04) (I, pp. 334–337).

Frangi, A. F., Niessen, W. J., Vincken, K. L., & Viergever, M. A. (1998). *Multiscale vessel enhancement filtering, Medical imaging computing and computer-assisted intervention* (Vol. 1496, pp. 130–137). Berlin: Springer Verlag.

Van Ginneken, B., ter Haar Romeny, B. M., & Viergever, M. A. (2001). Computer-aided diagnosis in chest radiography: A survey. *IEEE Transactions on Medical Imaging, 20*, 1228–1241.

Grimson, W. E. L., & Hildreth, E. C. (1985). *On digital step edges from zero crossings of second directional derivatives, . IEEE transactions on pattern analysis and machine intelligence (PAMI-7)* (1, pp. 121–127).

Klcz, F., Zink, F. E., Peppler, W. W., Kruger, D. G., Ergun, D. L., & Mistrella, C. A. (1994). Conventional chest radiography vs dual-energy computed radiography in the detection and characterization of pulmonary nodules. *American Journal of Roentgenology, 162*(2), 271–278.

Kobatake, H., & Murakami, M. (1996). A adaptive filter to detect rounded convex regions: IRIS filter. In: *13th international conference on pattern recognition (ICPR'96)* (pp. 340–344).

Koenderink, J. J., & Richards, W. (1992). Generic neighborhood operators. *IEEE Transactions on Pattern Analysis and Machine Intelligence, 14*(6), 597–605.

Kwak, K.-C., & Pedrycs, W. (2007). Face recognition using an enhanced independent component analysis approach. *IEEE Transactions on Neural Networks, 18*, 1–12.

Lampeter, W. A., & Wandtke, J. C. (1986). Computerized search of chest radiographs for nodules. *Investigative Radiology, 21*(5), 384–390.

Lee, S.-M., Fang, S.-H., Hung, J.-W., & Lee, L.-S. (2001). Improved MFCC feature extraction by PCA-optimized filter-bank for speech recognition. *IEEE Workshop on Automatic Speech Recognition and Understanding*, 49–52.

Mao, F., Qian, W., Gaviria, J., & Clarke, L. P. (1998). Fragmentary window filtering for multiscale lung nodule detection: Preliminary study. *Academic Radiology, 5*(4), 306–311.

Pauwels, E. J., Fiddelaers, P., Moons, T., & van Gool, L. J. (1995). An extended class of scaleinvariant and recursive scale-space filters. *IEEE Transactions on Pattern Analysis and Machine Intelligence, 17*(7), 691–701, 1995.

Penedo, M. G., Carreira, M. J., Mosquera, A., & Cadello, D. (1998). Computer-aided diagnosis: A neural network-based approach to lung nodule detection. *IEEE Transaction on Medical Imaging, 17*(6), 872–880.

Sarkar, S., & Chaudhuri, S. (1997). Detection of rib shadows in digital chest radiographs. *CIAP97, II*, 356–363.

Schilham, A. M., van Ginneken, B., & Loog, M. (2006). A computer-aided diagnosis system for detection of lung nodules in chest radiographs with an evaluation on public database. *Medical Image Analysis, 10*, 246–258.

Takiguchi, T., & Ariki, Y. (2007). PCA-based speech enhancement for distorted speech recognition. *Journal of Multimedia*, 2(5), 13–18.

Vogelsan, F., Weiler, F., Dahmen, J., Kilbiner, M., Wein, W., & Gunther, R. W. (1998). *Detection and compensation of rib structures in chest radiographs for diagnose assistance, Proceedings of the International Symposium on Medical Imaging (SPIE)* (3338-1, pp. 774–785).

Voorhees, H., & Poggio, T. (1987). Detecting textons and texture boundaries in natural image, In: *Proceedings of 1st international conference on computer vision* (pp. 250–258). London, England.

Witkin, A. P. (1983). Scale space filtering. In: *Proceedings of 8th international joint conference on artificial intelligence* (pp. 1019–1022). Karlsruhe, West Germany.

Yen-Wei, C., Zeng, X. Y., & Hanqing, L. U. (2002). *Edge detection and texture segmentation based on independent component analysis, Proceedings of the 16th international conference on pattern recognition (ICPR'02)* (3, p. 30351).

Yuille, A. L., & Poggio, T. A. (1986). Scaling theorems for zero-crossings. *IEEE Transactions on Pattern Analysis and Machine Intelligence*, 8(1), 15–25.

CHAPTER 15

Characterizing internet of medical things/personal area networks landscape

Adil Rajput[1] and Tayeb Brahimi[2]

[1]Information Systems Department, Effat University An Nazlah Al Yamaniyyah, Jeddah, Saudi Arabia,
[2]Natural Sciences, Mathematics, and Technology Unit, College of Engineering, Effat University, Jeddah, Saudi Arabia

15.1 Introduction

Advances in the communication and technology realm have given rise to an interconnected world which has eliminated the need for human intervention (Lytras, Raghavan, & Damiani, 2017; Lytras, Aljohani, Hussain, Luo, & Zhang, 2018). While the fields of artificial intelligence (AI), decision support system, and machine learning have been advocating various techniques to enhance the decision-making and more importantly reduce the human-related errors, it is the inexpensive price of hardware that has made the Internet of Things (IoT) a reality. The term "Internet of Things" was first coined by Ashton (2009). Although many definitions exist for IoT, the IoT environment is characterized by a collection of "devices" connected together via a "network." Such devices need both a hardware and software component—a system known as Cyber-Physical System (CPS).

The term CPS refers to the intertwined system of hardware and software components that allows the software to control the hardware components minimizing or eliminating the use of the human intervention. The prerequisite for such systems to operate is the underlying ubiquitous network be it on a Local Area Network (LAN) or Wide Area Network (WAN). Such a network allows the various hardware components to communicate with the software component in real time (or near real time). Almost in all cases, the CPS systems strive to minimize or eliminate the human intervention thus increasing the demand on both CPU, memory and the network. Given that the size of the hardware components is usually small (e.g., a wearable device), the power and memory capacity cause serious challenges as the size of the components connected and the demands placed on such devices.

15.1.1 Internet of medical things and health informatics

The Internet of Medical Things (IoMT)—known as the healthcare IoT (Ashton, 2009) technology—ensures the availability and the analysis of healthcare data through smart

Innovation in Health Informatics.
DOI: https://doi.org/10.1016/B978-0-12-819043-2.00015-0

medical devices and the web (Dastjerdi & Buyya, 2016; Islam, Kwak, Kabir, Hussain, & Swak, 2015; Joyia et al., 2017; Singh, Tripathi, & Jara, 2014). IoMT builds upon the underlying architecture of the IoT as it has a multitude of interconnected devices sending data over a network (mostly the Internet) to the cloud that can be accessed by the medical practitioners (Deliotte, 2018; Díaz, Martín, & Rubio, 2016; Gatouillat, Badr, Massot, & Sejdic, 2018). Applications range from gathering data with remote monitoring systems to be analyzed in nonreal time (e.g., sleep monitoring) to emergency notification services (e.g., pacemaker monitoring).

Devices such as Fitbit, Garmin, Xiaomi, or Misfit wireless fitness tracker are used to monitor patients' vital signs. Given the battery and computation limitations, the majority of the data are transmitted via the network (LAN and possibly WAN) placing high requirements on the network. Furthermore, the real-time nature of IoMT coupled with the nascent stage of development has brought forth various challenges to the helm. Such challenges include (but not limited to) security/privacy of data, efficient data handling, transmission, and massive data volume (Joyia et al., 2016). Recent research and developments in advanced sensors, mobile applications, AI, Big Data, 3D printing, and mobility have created new opportunities for medical technology companies to design and manufacture a wide range of affordable smart medical devices (Deliotte, 2018; Dey, Hassanien, Bhatt, Ashour, & Satapathy, 2018; McDonald, Gossett, & Moore, 2018; Raghupathi & Raghupathi, 2014).

15.1.2 Personal area networks

The idea behind IoMT centers around the concept of Personal Area Networks (PANs). A PAN is a small network that centers around a sensor device (could be attached to a machine or a human). The basic premise behind PAN network is the following:

1. Various devices and/or human body will have sensors connected to them.
2. Such devices communicate the status of each device using a network.
3. The network formed is ad hoc and limited in range.
4. The devices have limited battery power and hence can be limited in terms of functionality.
5. Given the low power limitations, the network throughput can be low.
6. Depending on the nature of the information, the information needs to be secured.

The goal of this chapter is to describe the various components that form the underlying basis of PANs. The crux of this chapter is presented in the next section. First, we describe the two main components of IoT/IoMT namely the physical and network components. Then we delve deeper into the network component and explain the three standards that underly the network component of the PANs along with an overview of Body Area Networks (BANs). Section 15.3 discusses some of the prevalent applications in the IoMT world. Section 15.4 offers the concluding remarks along with future research directions.

15.2 Architectural landscape

Revisiting the CPS definition highlights the intertwined nature of the hardware and the software. Furthermore, the physical world we live in deals with information that is represented in an analog manner. Such information is encoded as part of waves that can take on values over a continuum. On the other hand, computers and software only deal with a discrete set of values that can be mapped onto 0s and 1s. Both the healthcare professionals along with the technology architects need to fully comprehend the underlying makeup of such systems to better address the implementation details along with the associated risks. Therefore, to delve into such details, we need to address the following:

1. physical components and
2. network components

The physical components allow the analog signals to be transferred from a device/body to a node that can process such information and receive instructions on steps to be performed. The network components actually allow the messages to be transferred between devices—both in asynchronous and synchronous mode.

15.2.1 Physical components

The IoT paradigm is made possible by both a physical and network component. The physical components make it possible for the devices to both follow changes on the physical level and take an action.

The physical level is composed of various microelectromechanical systems (MEMS) devices. In simple terms, MEMS systems are an amalgamation of both microelectronic and micromechanical components along with a microsensor and a microactuator referred to as sensors and actuators going forward. The success of MEMS along with low cost of hardware has also given rise to nanoelectromechanical systems which follows the same idea but the size of hardware is even smaller than MEMS. While the electronic and mechanical components are worked on by a small number of experts, it is the sensors and actuators components that practitioners in the IoT realm deal with.

15.2.1.1 Physical components

The sensors provide the ability to monitor physical stimuli such as temperature or humidity. This part is the job of the microelectronics components. Based on the certain changes in the stimuli, the actuators take certain actions underpinned by the micromechanical system. As an example, consider the time—temperature monitoring system which after detecting the temperature dropping past a certain temperature threshold would cause the heat to turn on. While such abilities used to be hardcoded into the hardware, the MEMS systems are characterized by a Central Processing Unit that would make programming such devices a reality.

The sensors can be both digital and analog. A digital signal has a finite set of values while an analog signal is a continuous change of a given parameter over a period of time—mostly voltage. The voltage can oscillate between a minimum and maximum range on a continuous basis. As an example, some digital sensors represent the "on"/"off" state by using the value of 3.3 V. In other words, the sensor can take on only two values (0 for off or 3.3 V). On the other hand, an analog sensor can take any value on the continuum between 0 and 3.3 V. The analog sensors need to provide a way to convert the analog signal to a digital one so that it can be processed by a software.

An actuator is a mechanical component that is responsible for performing a certain action based on the input from the sensor. The actuator needs a source of energy that can be provided via various means such as an electric signal, liquid compression, change in pressure, etc. In all cases the energy is received as a control signal which will then be converted into mechanical form causing the action to be performed.

15.2.2 Network component

The backbone of an IoT infrastructure is the network component. While a wired network can be used, wireless networks are now considered the norm. The hardware components describe in Section 15.2.1 are connected via a network—hence the term CPSs. The term Wireless Sensor Networks has become synonymous with the network component of the IoT systems. However, PANs more accurately describe the concept at hand.

While a LAN allows connectivity with a high rate of transmission, PANs specifically cater to devices that have limited power and bandwidth. While the narrow definition assumes that the components belong to a particular individual, in reality, PANs take on a bigger meaning, for example, when applied to industrial IoT. Recall that IoT is characterized by devices that are low on power and resources. The challenge, therefore, becomes as to how information can be transmitted with such constraints.

The IEEE 802.15 working group deals with defining the standards for wireless PANs. While the working group has defined 10 areas for research, we will discuss the following 4 standards as they are deemed essential for transmitting the data to other devices.

1. Bluetooth
2. IEEE 802.15.4 Low-rate WPAN
3. IEEE 802.15.3 High-rate WPAN
4. IEEE 802.15.6 Body Area Networks

15.2.2.1 Bluetooth

Historically the Bluetooth standard was termed as 802.15.1 but it is no longer maintained by IEEE. Rather the standard is now maintained by the Bluetooth SIG (https://www.bluetooth.com/specifications/bluetooth-core-specification). The Bluetooth technology is encapsulated in a chip that can be part of any particular device. The technology uses the master/slave concept which is referred to as host and controller. A Bluetooth host receives information from the device using a cable (or simulation of a cable) that is submitted to another mobile Bluetooth device using a special frequency.

15.2.2.1.1 Protocol stack

Consider a typical scenario for a Bluetooth application. A host device such as an automobile music system has the Bluetooth capability turned on. A user wants to user her smartphone to play an audio clip. The smartphone device is paired with the music system which allows the synchronous playing of the audio clip on the car's music system allowing the car system to control the smartphone device. What appears to be a seamless operation for an end user requires sending and receiving traffic over a set of protocols. The layers described in Fig. 15.1 present a typical Bluetooth Operation (note that the list is not exhaustive).

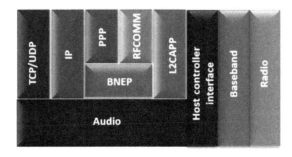

Figure 15.1
Bluetooth protocol stack.

The radio is responsible for receiving and transmitting the actual signal using a given radio frequency. The Link Management Protocol is mostly responsible for the connection at this level. The Low Energy Link Layer is also employed to minimize energy usage. The Baseband technology converts analog signals to digital signals that can be transmitted using various protocols.

The Baseband technology, in turn, is divided into physical and logical parts. The physical channel is the actual transmission of radio signals over a given frequency. Given the probability of clashes on such frequency, the physical channel has the ability to switch the frequencies over a given range. In addition, the physical layer can be either a synchronous connection oriented (SCO) or asynchronous connection less (ACL). As suggested by the names, SCO is used for appoint-to-point applications such as voice applications. ACL, on the other hand, allows a publish-subscribe model implementation between a master and one or more slaves.

The Bluetooth has been divided into five logical channels. Such logical channels transfer different types of information. The Control Channel carries low level control information such as error codes etc. The Link Manager provides a mechanism to transfer low level physical information to higher layers. The other three logical channels namely User Asynchronous (UA), Use Isochronous (UI) and User Synchronous (US) channels are used to relay asynchronous, isochronous and synchronous information respectively. All these channels happen at the link level. The link manager transmits the signal to the host controller interface (HCI) that is also responsible for setting various parameters such as security. Once the signal is passed to the HCI, it deals with the logical link control and adaptation protocol (L2CAP) whose sole purpose is to pass on the information from the Baseband Layers to higher protocols. In simpler terms, L2CAP serves a similar purpose to IP protocol when it comes to basic network connectivity as we know it. The L2CAP layer acts as the conduit to higher layers and hence is responsible for many important functions such as reassembling the packets, controlling synchronous and asynchronous communications etc. The importance of L2CAP mandates a detailed discussion which is beyond the scope of this chapter. The authors highly encourage users to explore this further to understand the intricacies of Bluetooth technology.

The L2CAP packets can be delivered between two devices using point-to-point protocol or in an asynchronous way. The RFCOMM protocol provides the serial line interface and hence the packets are transferred using a typical IP network. The Bluetooth Network Encapsulation Protocol on the other hand is used to encapsulate L2CAP packets that can be transferred over a typical IP network. Lastly, the Service Delivery Protocol allows various devices to negotiate a connection at the L2CAP layer as shown in Fig. 15.1.

15.2.2.1.2 Pico and scatter networks

Now that we have a basic comprehension of the various protocols that come into play, let us briefly discuss the types of networks Bluetooth technology allows. Recall that the

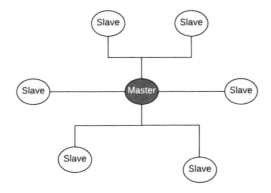

Figure 15.2
PicoNet.

WPAN formed using a Bluetooth technology is limited in distance in terms of range. We alluded to the concept of Master/Slave in the previous section but we will explain the concept further in the context of Bluetooth technology. The Master device relates to the host that is responsible for transmitting and receiving information from various devices— termed as slaves.

A Pico network is the basic unit in a Bluetooth network where a master device allows/ requests a connection from various slave devices. The ad hoc network formed once the devices come into contact is known as a Pico network, Fig. 15.2 depicts such a network (PicoNet). The concept is similar to the formation of a LAN/WLAN where many devices are connected to one switch/router.

The combination of two or Pico networks, shown in Fig. 15.3, is called a Scatter network. Note that a device can act as a slave in one Pico network while serving as a master in another one. This flexibility allows efficient dissemination of information using a Bluetooth network.

15.2.2.2 Low-rate WPAN

A low-rate WPAN (LR-WPAN) provides a cost-effective way for low-cost devices with limited battery/power capabilities to form an ad hoc network. Given the lack of power resources, the throughput is low and does not conform to many QoS requirements. The LR-WPAN details are published by the IEEE 802.15.4 standard and the strength of the protocol lies in its simplicity and flexibility (https://standards.ieee.org/standard/802_15_4-2011.html).

The protocol only defines the physical layer (PHY) and the MAC layer details and allows other protocols to operate on top of the MAC layer. The devices in an LR-WPAN network can operate either as a full-functional device (FFD) or a reduced-function device (RFD) (Fig. 15.4). An FFD can act as a PAN coordinator which roughly can be translated to as the master device in a master-Slave framework. An RFD, on the other hand, is a pure slave

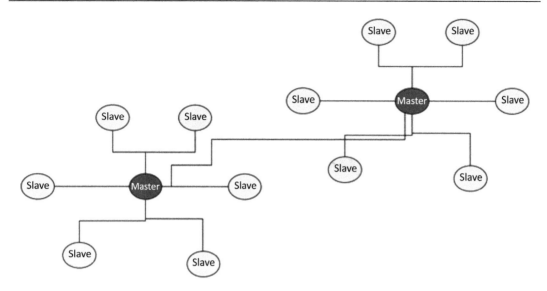

Figure 15.3
ScatterNet.

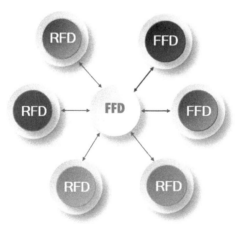

Figure 15.4
Star topology.

node. Such devices are intended for very simple tasks (e.g., turning on a light switch). An FFD device can handle a higher level of traffics and hence are characterized by stronger resources compared to an RFD.

The task of the PHY is similar to the one in OSI model, that is, physically manage the PHY to send the frames. In this case, the PHY consists of managing the radio signals. The MAC layer is responsible for channeling the packets from higher layers to the PHY layer.

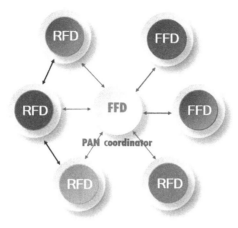

Figure 15.5
Mesh topology.

The devices can operate in one of two network topologies namely (1) star topology and (2) mesh topology. In a star network topology, devices choose a PAN coordinator whose job is to disseminate information to other devices. The star topology depicted in Fig. 15.4 follows a typical Master-Slave model.

A mesh topology, on the other hand, follows a peer-to-peer model. While the presence of PAN coordinator is still mandated, the nodes can contact each other directly as shown in Fig. 15.5. Note that unlike other mesh topologies, the PAN coordinator is not responsible for routing the messages to other devices but rather the devices can connect to each other directly.

The PAN coordinator is responsible for assigning unique short-term addresses to the devices operating within its own network. The devices can be part of more than one PAN network as each network operates on its own unique frequency. A star network is suitable for a home or industrial control environment. A mesh or peer-to-peer network provides the flexibility to span wider areas and applications.

As opposed to the Bluetooth, the 802.15.4 does not provide the complete OSI model support. Rather it is the platform upon which other protocols such as 6LoWPAN, Zigbee, WirelessHART, and ISA100.11a are built. The discussion of these protocols is beyond the scope of this chapter.

15.2.2.3 High-rate WPAN

A high-rate WPAN (HR-WPAN)—defined by the IEE standard 802.15.3—is an attempt to provide a similar capability to the LR-WPAN but increase the data transfer rate. The standard utilizes the millimeter-wave-based alternate PHY. This allows the throughput to increase anywhere from 11 to 55 Mbps (https://standards.ieee.org/standard/802_15_3-2016. html). Such technology is imperative in providing streaming abilities such as live video feed from the source to destination spanning huge distances.

While the idea is similar to 802.15.4, the HR-WPAN builds upon the concept of Piconets. The protocol defines the protocol adaptation layer (PAL) in addition to the PHY and MAC layer as shown in Fig. 15.6. The PAL layer allows the higher level protocols to communicate with the MAC and in turn the physical layer of the HR-WPAN.

Once the protocol layer is established, the protocol requires a Piconet coordinator (PNC) similar to the PAN coordinator in LR-WPAN. The PNC coordinator finds a channel through which it can communicate to the devices that are in its span. In addition to the Piconet capability discussed in the Bluetooth section, the standard allows for child Piconets and neighbor Piconets in case a particular Piconet cannot find a frequency channel to communicate. Both the child and neighbor Piconets can help the extend the range of a given Piconet.

The child Piconets use the same channel to communicate with devices in its own network or the parent network. Given that the frequency is the same, the networks utilize something called channel time allocation (CTA) with the help of a scheduler.

A neighbor Piconet on the other hand requests from a PNC to share the frequency to communicate with its members using the same frequency utilizing the CTA. As opposed to the child Piconet, a neighbor Piconet cannot communicate directly to the devices under the control of the PNC of the neighbor PNC.

If a PNC wishes to exit the Piconet, it will try to find a suitable device which can take over the PNC responsibilities. In case no such device exists, the PNC will send a message to all

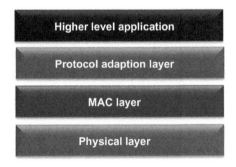

Figure 15.6
802.15.4 Protocol stack.

the devices informing them about the termination of Piconet. In case a child or neighbor Piconet exist, they will continue to operate without hindrance as the parent/neighbor channel frequency will be available to them.

15.2.2.4 Body area networks

The IEEE standard 802.15.6 defines the BANs. Given that the standard still falls under the 802.15 (PANs), it is safe to conclude that the concepts used in the other standards are in play. However, there is one more element that the standard introduces—human body communications that occur at the PHY. The communication happens using the electric field communications centered at 21 MHz. This layer allows the human body to send signals that are then converted to the MAC layer.

Once the above happens, the next question would be regarding the topology the network uses. As opposed to the LR-WPAN and HR-WPAN, the only network topology BANs use is that of star topology. Thus there needs to be a device that acts as the coordinator—called the Hub. The remaining devices connect to the Hub (the Hub-Spoke model is used synonymously with Master-Slave model).

The communication between the hub and the devices happens in terms of exchanging frames. Given the sensitivity of the information, the standard defines three security levels as follows:

> Level 0—Unsecured communication
> Level 1—Authentication
> Level 2—Authentication and Encryption

If the hub intends to communicate with the nodes in level 1 or level 2 mode, the nodes can be in any one of the following states.

1. Orphan—The device is not connected to the hub.
2. Connected—The device and hub are allowed to exchange secure frames with each other but not unsecured frames.
3. Associated—The device can transfer only information regarding connection and being in a secure state.
4. Secured—The device and hub can exchange information securely with each other.

On the other hand, insecure communication allows the nodes to be in one of the two following states.

1. Orphan—The device is not connected to the hub.
2. Connected—The device and hub are allowed to exchange secure frames with each other but not unsecured frames.

15.3 Prevalent internet of medical things applications

15.3.1 Internet of medical things services and applications

Two aspects of the IoMT can be found in the literature namely the services such as wearable devices and the applications such as ECG or blood pressure monitoring (Gatouillat et al., 2018; Islam et al., 2015; Magsi et al., 2018; UST, 2017). Fig. 15.7 illustrates an example of the main services and application in an IoMT. By examination of this figure, it is clear that services are used to develop IoMT application while applications are directly used by patients. Aside from their utility in supervising and managing daily health and normal well-being, IoMT devices have additionally been utilized for chronic disease (CD) management and prevention, remote assistant living and intervention, improved drug management, and wellness and preventive care in any remote location (Joyia, Liaqat, Farooq, & Rehman, 2017; Shelke & Sharma, 2018).

Different wearable devices exist in the market such activity monitors, automated external defibrillator, blood pressure monitor, blood glucose meter, fall detector, fitness and heart

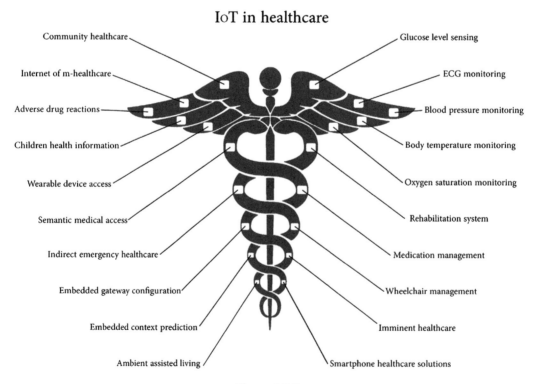

Figure 15.7
Main services and application in an internet of medical things (IoMT).

rate monitor, multiparameter monitor, programmable syringe pump, pulse oximeter, smart pill dispenser, smart watches, and wearable injector, to cite only few (Bayo-Monton et al., 2018; Cruz & Lousado, 2018; Krohn, Metcalf, & Salber, 2017; Metcalf, Khron, & Salber, 2016; Metcalf, Milliard, Gomez, & Schwartz, 2016). The application domain of IoMT may include CDs, health fitness management, home-based medical health, hospital monitoring, human activity recognition (HAR), medical nursing, patient physiological conditions, patients' wearable IoMT devices, pediatric and elderly care, remote patient monitoring (RPM), simultaneous reporting and monitoring, and tracking patient medication (TPM).

Besides these application domains, telemedicine monitoring remote consultation represents a new approach to medicine which can be defined as the utilization of medical history and information shared from one party to another via electronic communications to enhance, assist or maintain patients' health status (Field, 2002; Giorgio, 2011; Shams, Hanif Khan, Aamir, & Saleem, 2014; Xiao, Alexander, & Hu, 2008). For a border definition, telemedicine is associated with the term "Telehealth" which defines the remote healthcare (Lazarev, 2016; Higgs, 2014). There are many useful applications used to ease the medical process under this approach. According to a recent study and analysis by Deloitte Centre for Health Solutions (Deliotte, 2018), the market for connected medical devices is predicted to grow from $14.9 billion in 2017 to $52.2 billion in 2022. Today, there are more than 500,000 different types of medical devices including wearable external medical devices, implanted medical devices, and stationary medical devices as reported by Deliotte (2018). Fig. 15.8 shows the trend of the global wearable computing devices from 2017 to 2019 based on the data published by ABI Research (2018) and Dias and Paulo Silva Cunha (2018). According to this data, healthcare wearable devices show an increasing growth and

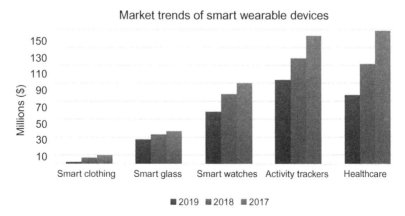

Figure 15.8

Trends of the global market value of wearable devices, 2017−19. Source: *Adapted from ABI Research. (2014).* Global wearable computing devices; world market, forecast: 2013 to 2019. *New York, NY: Author.*

even exceed wearable devices used in sport activities. In another study, the "Wearable Medical Devices—Global Market Outlook (2017−2026)" (Global Market Outlook, 2018) reported that in 2017 global wearable medical devices accounted for $6.05 billion, this trends will continue and it is expected to reach $29.53 billion in 2026.

Wearable IoMT devices are smart devices that can deliver efficient personal experience and services, and they are the heart of smart IoT healthcare solutions. These wearable devices, integrated with telemedicine, are used in continuous patient monitoring. They integrate into applications including measuring vital signs and exchange reliable and secure information through the IoT. The field of wearable health monitoring systems is advancing in minimizing the size of wearable devices and medical sensors (Haghi, Thurow, & Stoll, 2017). Another application related to healthcare is the HAR where IoT is used to remotely monitor vital human signs (Rodriguez et al., 2017). Human activity detection and analyzing is a challenging task because it requires considerable time-consuming and high-cost hardware. Accurate recognition of human activities could help in healthcare services for improved patient recovery training guidance, or an early indicator of emergency medical conditions that elder patients may encounter, such as falls and heart failures (Liu, Liu, Simske, & Liu, 2016).

In the case of tele patients with CDs, a home monitoring system is used to monitor multiple features such as weight scales, pulse oximeters, glucometers, and blood pressure cuffs. Readings are recorded in personal health records, and warnings are sent wirelessly to healthcare providers when readings fall beyond the normal range. Diabetes is one of the common CDs in which there are high blood glucose levels over a lengthy period. Managing this requires noninvasive glucose sensors to monitor the level patterns. An IoMT method to manage this is to have sensors from patients connected through IPv6 connectivity to healthcare providers. This device consists of a blood glucose collector, a mobile phone, and a background processor (Islam et al., 2015). Another crucial case is patients with heart disease, monitoring the electrical activity of the heart is an essential procedure for these patients. The early diagnosis of the arrhythmias can prevent a major risk. To prevent that, associating IoT in ECG monitoring give the potential to offer accurate features and information about the patient's signs remotely (Islam et al., 2015). For monitoring body temperature, the IoMT promises to develop practical solutions to the healthcare services by allowing monitoring temperature as it is a vital body parameter. The involvement of IoMT has integrated temperature sensor interface with wireless media. The sensor in smart temperature patch can detect the data and send it over Bluetooth or Wi-Fi connectivity to a specific cloud application where the concerned doctor can perform data-analysis for the patient.

For elderly care, it is important to note that supporting the independent life of elderly people in their living place safely can make them more confident by ensuring better

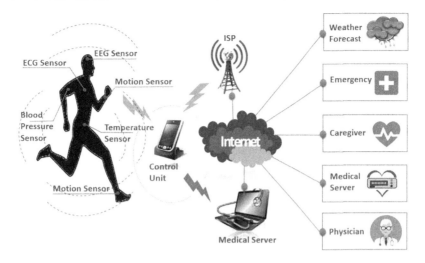

Figure 15.9
A typical wireless body sensor network.

autonomy and giving them real assistance. This is the main objective of the Ambient Assisted Living (AAL), an IoT platform powered by AI that uses the information and communication technologies to serve this objective. Activity recognition and behavior understanding are the desired results of using a variety of sensors in AAL (Bevilacqua et al., 2014; García, Meana-Llorián, & Lovelle, 2017; Monekosso, Revuelta, & Remagnino, 2015). This can be direct via wearable sensors or indirectly through environmental sensors and stream analysis. On TPM, it is becoming possible for patients to track their medication ingestion. Fig. 15.9 illustrates a typical wireless body sensor network where the information is received from multiple body sensors and transmitted remotely via a gateway to the central server for storage or decision. It is important; however, to danger with the noncompliance with medication schedule which can lead to serious complications for the patient's health (Kuzela, 2015). The revolutionary of intelligent smart pill technology provided a comprehensive solution to the patient's noncompliance in medications. The pill bottle, FDA approved (FDA, 2017), is embedded with an ingestible event marker (IEM) sensor that tracks the medication intake and reminds patients to take their medication at appropriate times. Once the patient swallows it, the IEM can detect the ingestion and communicates this data to a wearable sensor or mobile device through cloud infrastructure (Botta, De Donato, Persico, & Pescapé, 2014, 2016; Demeo & Morena, 2014).

15.3.2 Internet of medical things companies leading the way

With the overwhelming growth of healthcare electronic devices connected to each other to send and receive safely and effectively sensitive data and information, US Food and Drug

Administration (FDA) (2017) has examined cybersecurity risks and released on September 6, 2017, its final guidance on "Design Considerations and Premarket Submission Recommendations for Interoperable Medical Device." FDA identified six issues that medical device manufacturers should take into account: (1) identify the purpose of the electronic interface including the type and data exchanged, (2) determine the anticipated user, (3) consider risk management including risk that may arise from other users connecting through the interface, (4) verification and validation by maintaining and implementing appropriate verification and validation of the device functionality, (5) labeling considerations, and (6) use of consensus standards related to the interoperability of the medical device.

The key players in the IoMT market include Adheretech (https://www.adheretech.com/) patient support programs with its smart pill bottle and underlying software to detect compliance with medications and alerts patients in case they forget or miss a dose, or detect a serious problem in which case the patients' pharmacy is notified. AliveCor (https://www.alivecor.com) records patient EKG using KardiaMobile Smartphone. Bosch Healthcare (https://www.bosch-healthcare.com) developed a breath analysis device for asthma patients. Capsule Technologies (https://www.capsuletech.com) takes control of patient medical device data and provide powerful data configuration options. Cerner Corporation (https://cerner.com/), a supplier of health information technology, ranges from medical devices to electronic health records to hardware. Cisco Inc. (https://www.cisco.com) supports critical applications such as imaging and electronic medical records. DeepMind Health (https://deepmind.com) helps clinicians get patients from test to treatment. Diabetizer Ltd. (https://diabetizer.com), as indicated by its name, analyzes diabetes and generates an assessment of patient current health status. Ericsson, with the possibility of study people's behaviors and values, GE Healthcare (https://www.gehealthcare.com), a leading provider of medical imaging, monitoring, biomanufacturing, and cell and gene therapy technologies. Honeywell Life Care Solutions provides an RPM solution. IBM Watson for drug discovery, Medtronic Inc. (www.medtronic.com), a global leader in medical technology, services, and solutions. Microsoft (https://www.microsoft.com) allow patients to receive care at home, monitor medical assets, and track equipment usage. Proteus Digital Health (https://www.proteus.com/) measures the effectiveness of the medication treatment as well as helping physicians to improve clinical outcomes. Qualcomm Life Inc. (https://www.qualcomm.com) integrates healthcare data for access anywhere, anytime. Stanley Healthcare (https://www.stanleyhealthcare.com/) provides analytics solutions to ensure safety and security for senior living organizations, hospitals, and health systems. Vodafone integrates patient healthcare devices with their hardware, software and manages their connectivity. Zebra Technologies (https://www.zebra.com) connects medical providers with patient records for better care and better outcomes.

15.4 Conclusions and future directions

IoMT offers huge potential and a great set of challenges to researchers. PANs form the underlying basis of IoT and IoMT. In this chapter, we have focused on four standards, namely, Bluetooth, IEEE 802.15.3, 802.15.4, and 802.15.6. Furthermore, we have also briefly discussed BANs along with some of the prevalent IoMT applications and the vendors that provide such services. Any disruption in PANs would render the entire service unusable and hence deserves a lot of attention from researchers. Our work aims at introducing the readers to the intricacies of PANs and their importance to health informatics. PANs are characterized by very limited storage and hence rely heavily on transferring data to stable persistent storage via the underlying networking technologies. This chapter also introduces the reader to various types of networks that are in use and how the choice affects the type of applications built upon such networks.

15.4.1 Future research directions

PANs have limitations both in terms of functionality and the security aspect. The protocols used are relatively new and hence future work should look into the strengths of weaknesses of such protocols. In addition, the coexistence of such protocols presents an interoperability challenge that also needs to be explored.

Furthermore, researchers will also need to classify various applications in terms of the nature of the temporal aspects of the application being studied. Real-time applications have high throughput requirements and certain underlying networks will be unsuited for certain applications.

Lastly, the researchers need to look into the security and privacy aspect of such networks. Given the federal laws governing the privacy of patients' data, it remains to be seen the implications of widespread adoption of such technologies.

15.4.2 Recommended assignments

- What kind of security threats exist in terms of PANs?
- How the performance of BANs is affected by the security and encryption of packets?
- Can Bluetooth standard fulfill the security and performance requirements eliminating the need of low- and high-rate WPANs?

References

ABI Research. (2014). *Global wearable computing devices; world market, forecast: 2013 to 2019*. New York, NY: ABI Research.

Ashton, K. (2009). That 'internet of things' thing. *RFID Journal, 22*(7), 97–114.

Bayo-Monton, J., Martinez-Millana, A., Han, W., Fernandez-Llatas, C., Sun, Y., & Traver, V. (2018). Wearable sensors integrated with the internet of things for advancing eHealth care. *Sensors, 18*(6), 1851. Available from https://doi.org/10.3390/s18061851.

Bevilacqua, R., Ceccacci, S., Germani, M., Iualè, M., Mengoni, M., & Papetti, A. (2014). Smart object for AAL: A review. *Ambient Assisted Living*, 313–324. Available from https://doi.org/10.1007/978-3-319-01119-6_32.

Botta, A., De Donato, W., Persico, V., & Pescapé, A. (2014). On the integration of cloud computing and internet of things. In *2014 International conference on future internet of things and cloud (FiCloud)* (pp. 23–30). IEEE (sensor-cloud).

Botta, A., De Donato, W., Persico, V., & Pescapé, A. (2016). Integration of cloud computing and internet of things: A survey. *Future Generation Computer Systems, 56*, 684–700. (sensor-cloud).

Cruz, A., & Lousado, J. P. (2018). A survey on wearable health monitoring systems. In *2018 13th Iberian conference on information systems and technologies (CISTI)*. https://doi.org/10.23919/cisti.2018.8399422

Dastjerdi, A. V., & Buyya, R. (2016). *Internet of things: Principles and paradigms*. Cambridge, MA: Morgan Kaufmann.

Deliotte. (2018). *Medtech and the internet of medical things: How connected medical devices are transforming health care*. Center for Health Solutions.

Demeo, D., & Morena, M. (2014). Medication adherence using a smart pill bottle. In *2014 11th international conference & expo on emerging technologies for a smarter world (CEWIT)*. https://doi.org/10.1109/cewit.2014.7021149

Dey, N., Hassanien, A. E., Bhatt, C., Ashour, A. S., & Satapathy, S. C. (2018). *Internet of things and big data analytics toward next-generation intelligence*. Cham: Springer International Publishing.

Dias, D., & Paulo Silva Cunha, J. (2018). Wearable health devices-vital sign monitoring, systems and technologies. *Sensors (Basel, Switzerland), 18*(8), 2414. Available from https://doi.org/10.3390/s18082414.

Díaz, M., Martín, C., & Rubio, B. (2016). State-of-the-art, challenges, and open issues in the integration of Internet of things and cloud computing. *Journal of Network and Computer Applications, 67*, 99–117.

Field, M. J. (2002). Telemedicine and remote patient monitoring. *JAMA, 288*(4), 423. Available from https://doi.org/10.1001/jama.288.4.423.

García, C. G., Meana-Llorián, D., & Lovelle, J. M. C. (2017). A review about smart objects, sensors, and actuators. *International Journal of Interactive Multimedia & Artificial Intelligence, 4*(3), 7–10.

Gatouillat, A., Badr, Y., Massot, B., & Sejdic, E. (2018). Internet of medical things: A review of recent contributions dealing with cyber-physical systems in medicine. *IEEE Internet of Things Journal, 5*, 3810–3822. Available from https://doi.org/10.1109/jiot.2018.2849014.

Giorgio, A. (2011). Innovative medical devices for telemedicine applications. *Telemedicine Techniques and Applications*. Available from https://doi.org/10.5772/17966.

Global Market Outlook. (2018). *Wearable medical devices—Global market outlook (2017-2026)*. Research and Markets, Stratistics Market Research Consulting Pvt Ltd.

Haghi, M., Thurow, K., & Stoll, R. (2017). Wearable devices in medical internet of things: Scientific research and commercially available devices. *Healthcare Informatics Research, 23*(1), 4. Available from https://doi.org/10.4258/hir.2017.23.1.4.

Islam, S. R., Kwak, D., Kabir, M. H., Hussain, M., & Swak, K. S. (2015). The internet of things for health care: A comprehensive survey. *IEEE*. Available from https://doi.org/10.1109ACCESS.2015.2437951.

Joyia, G. J., Liaqat, R. M., Farooq, A., & Rehman, S. (2017). Internet of medical things (IOMT): Applications, benefits and future challenges in healthcare domain. *Journal of Communications*. Available from https://doi.org/10.12720/jcm.12.4.240-247.

Krohn, R., Metcalf, D., & Salber, P. (2017). *Connected health improving care, safety, and efficiency with wearables and IoT solution.* Milton: CRC Press.

Kuzela, C. (2015). *Smart drugs: Where IoT meets healthcare, a market snapshot.* Retrieved October 6, 2018, from <https://siliconangle.com/2015/06/30/smart-drugs-where-iot-meets-healthcare-a-market-snapshot/>.

Lazarev, K. (2016). *Internet of things for personal healthcare: Study of eHealth sector, smart wearable design* (p. 26). Retrieved October 6, 2018.

Liu, X., Liu, L., Simske, S. J., & Liu, J. (2016). Human daily activity recognition for healthcare using wearable and visual sensing data. In *2016 IEEE international conference on healthcare informatics (ICHI).* https://doi.org/10.1109/ichi.2016.100

Magsi, H., Sodhro, A. H., Chachar, F. A., Abro, S. A., Sodhro, G. H., & Pirbhulal, S. (2018). Evolution of 5G in Internet of medical things. In *2018 International conference on computing, mathematics and engineering technologies (iCoMET).* https://doi.org/10.1109/icomet.2018.8346428

McDonald, J. M., Gossett, C., & Moore, M. (2018). Moving to the cloud: The state of the art for cloud-based production pipelines. *Journal of Digital Media Management*, 6(3), 215−230.

Metcalf, D., Khron, R., & Salber, P. (2016). *Health-e everything: Wearables and the internet of things for health: Part One: Wearables for healthcare.* Orlando, FL: Moving Knowledge.

Metcalf, D., Milliard, S. T., Gomez, M., & Schwartz, M. (2016). Wearables and the internet of things for health: Wearable, interconnected devices promise more efficient and comprehensive health care. *IEEE Pulse*, 7(5), 35−39. Available from https://doi.org/10.1109/mpul.2016.2592260.

Monekosso, D., Revuelta, F. F., & Remagnino, P. (2015). Ambient assisted living. *IEEE computer society.* Retrieved July/August 2015, from <https://www.computer.org/intelligent>.

Raghupathi, W., & Raghupathi, V. (2014). Big data analytics in healthcare: Promise and potential. *Health Information Science and Systems*, 2(1), 3.

Rodriguez, C., Castro, D. M., Coral, W., Cabra, J. L., Velasquez, N., Colorado, J., . . . Trujillo, L. C. (2017). IoT system for human activity recognition using BioHarness 3 and smartphone. In *Proceedings of the international conference on future networks and distributed systems (ICFNDS'17).* https://doi.org/10.1145/3102304.3105828

Shams, R., Hanif Khan, F., Aamir, M., & Saleem, F. (2014). Internet of things in telemedicine: A discussion regarding to several implementation. *Journal of Computer Science of Newports Institute of Communications and Economics*, 5(2014), ISSN: 2226-3683.

Shelke, Y., & Sharma, A. (2018). Internet of medical things. Aranca, Technology Intelligence & IP Research. Retrieved September 18, 2018, from <https://www.aranca.com/assets/uploads/resources/special-reports/Internet-of-Medical-Things-IoMT_Aranca-Special-Report.pdf>.

Singh, D., Tripathi, G., & Jara, A. J. (2014, March). A survey of internet-of-things: Future vision, architecture, challenges, and services. In *2014 IEEE world forum on Internet of things (WF-IoT)* (pp. 287−292). IEEE.

US Food & Drug Administration (FDA). (2017). *Design considerations and pre-market submission recommendations for interoperable medical devices* (document issued on: September 6, 2017, pp. 1−18, Tech. No. 2017-18815-82 FR 42101). U.S. Department of Health and Human Services Food and Drug Administration. doi:FDA-2015-D-4852.

Xiao, Y., Alexander, Q., & Hu, F. (2008). Telemedicine for pervasive healthcare. *Mobile Telemedicine*, 389−404. Available from https://doi.org/10.1201/9781420060478.ch20.

Social Issues and policy making for smart healthcare

CHAPTER 16

Threats to patients' privacy in smart healthcare environment

Samara M. Ahmed[1] and Adil Rajput[2]

[1]*College of Medicine, King Abdulaziz University, Jeddah, Saudi Arabia,* [2]*Department of Computer Science, College of Engineering, Effat University, Jeddah, Saudi Arabia*

16.1 Introduction

The ubiquitous web technology gave way to web 2.0 where enterprises transformed from mere automation to managing business processes. The web 3.0 (Lassila & Hendler, 2007) promises to utilize artificial intelligence to not only help enterprises carry our effective (correct) and efficient business process but also transform processes to make them smarter. The healthcare field is no exception and the past 20 or so years have seen the clinicians educate themselves with the intricacies of personal health records (Ibraimi, Asim, & Petković, 2009) and electronic health records (Huang, Chu, Lien, Hsiao, & Kao, 2009; Wang, Wu, Qin, & Domingo-Ferrer, 2014). The researchers, however, have taken it a step further and familiarized themselves with and utilized artificial intelligence in the field of bioinformatics culling together various disciplines.

A smart healthcare environment aims at providing patients and practitioners a platform to provide healthcare services seamlessly. Patients can be monitored remotely while healthcare practitioners can share data in real-time about an emergency situation (Doukas et al., 2011; Hussain, Wenbi, da Silva, Nadher, & Mudhish, 2015). A smart healthcare environment necessitates the use of storage and network technologies. The use of such technologies adds to the risk of violating patients' data privacy. The Health Insurance and Portability Accountability Act (HIPAA) passed in 1996 (https://csrc.nist.gov/topics/laws-and-regulations/laws/fisma) outlined various regulations aimed at safeguarding patients' privacy. This initiative was further bolstered by the Federal Information Security Management Act of 2002 (FISMA) (https://csrc.nist.gov/topics/laws-and-regulations/laws/fisma). The act mandated the federal agencies of tracking the various information systems and putting appropriate security controls in place.

Innovation in Health Informatics.
DOI: https://doi.org/10.1016/B978-0-12-819043-2.00016-2

Since the adoption of the FISMA act, the field of healthcare has changed dramatically. The widespread use of mobile devices and integrating sensors in medical devices and human body allows for exchange of sensitive data through various media. Such exchange constitutes a challenge for preserving patients' data privacy. The Federal Government bolstered the FISMA initiative with Cyber Enhancement Act of 2014 (https://www.gpo.gov/fdsys/pkg/PLAW-113publ283/pdf/PLAW-113publ283.pdf) that continued to recognize the networked nature of the federal government systems and further refined the security controls that the federal agencies must put in place. The Food and Drug Administration (FDA) published nonbinding requirements for medical devices (https://www.fda.gov/downloads/MedicalDevices/DeviceRegulationandGuidance/GuidanceDocuments/UCM623529.pdf). In the same vein, FDA supported the Mitre corporation effort that addresses the cybersecurity for medical devices (https://www.mitre.org/publications/technical-papers/medical-device-cybersecurity-regional-incident-preparedness-and). However, medical devices are only one part of the equation when working in the smart healthcare environment.

The authors in Kang, Dabbish, Fruchter, and Kiesler (2015) conducted a study that measured the depth of understanding of human understanding of how Internet operates. The study underscored the depth of lack of understanding on part of common people and in turn how this gives people a false sense of security when conducting transactions on the net. Given the federal requirements outlined in HIPAA and FISMA, a smart healthcare environment needs to be monitored with higher scrutiny than many other domains. Note that while the requirements are specific to the United States, many countries have implemented similar legislative measures.

In addition to various systems implemented on a network, the growth of Internet of Things (IoT) paradigm (Ashton, 2009) allows various mobile devices and sensors to monitor heterogeneous systems and humans in real time. The IoT paradigm has brought forth many opportunities and challenges in the smart healthcare domain. Practitioners can now practice preventive medicine via routine checkups, etc., deliver critical medical care using the IoT platform or take a hybrid approach where the critical medical care is delivered in the traditional sense while maintain close monitoring of various vital signs via IoT (Doukas et al., 2011; Hussain et al., 2015; Piro, Cianci, Grieco, Boggia, & Camarda, 2014). Work done in Ashton (2009) and Rajput and Ahmed (2019a, 2019b) look at issues gathering data from social media and how it can be used to get a glimpse into patients' frame of mind. In addition to the challenges posed by such devices, the practitioners need to reckon that Personal Area Networks (PANs) have added another dimension of complexity to the Local Area Networks (LANs) and Wide Area Networks (WANs) complexities (Rajput & Brahimi, 2019).

The underlying architecture for such enabling technologies further complicates the comprehension of the vast landscape that underscores a smart healthcare environment. This chapter aims at educating the reader of various challenges that the smart healthcare environment poses to the security and privacy of patients' data. Specifically, we will address the following:

1. Provide various definitions specific to this field
2. Describe legislations and other efforts that put policies and procedures in place
3. Describe a typical smart healthcare architecture and its components
4. Provide a brief overview of various threats that exist in such an environment

16.2 Definitions

Authentication Authentication is the process of allowing a user to get on the corporate network

Authorization Authorization is the process through which a user is granted access to corporate digital and information assets

Information Assurance Information assurance refers to getting the managing risks related to the use, processing, storage, and transmission of information or data

Sensors Sensors are devices that measure the changes in the environment (usually through analog signals) such as changes in temperature and convey the information digitally to a processor

Actuators Actuators are the mechanical components that can move and perform an action given the input received from the sensors. Along with sensors, they form the basis of the IoT paradigm

Bluetooth Bluetooth is a standard that allows humans, sensors, and various devices to form a network within a small range

Personal Area Networks PANs are small range networks (usually 10–30 m) that are centered around a human or a device

Local Area Networks LANs are networks that are confined within an enterprise premises. They have higher throughput and can span few kilometers

Wide Area Networks WANs allow devices to connect across a great distance. Internet is an example of a WAN

Data Confidentiality Data confidentiality refers to the availability of data to authorized users only

Data Integrity Data integrity refers to the assurance that the data viewed has not been tampered with

Data Availability This property allows the data to be available to authorized users in a timely manner

Data Custodian Data custodians are individuals who are entrusted with safeguarding the data. The custodian usually should not have access to the data itself

Data Owner Data owners refer to business process owners who either produce and/or control the access to data

Encryption Encryption refers to the process of encoding a text in a way that only the intended recipient can decode (decrypt) the message

Public Key Infrastructure (PKI) PKI is an asymmetric encryption technique that uses both public and private key. The encryption technique helps avoid exchanging of secret keys and relies on a trusted third party to encrypt and decrypt messages

Analog Signals Analog signal refers to information encoded in forms of a continuous wave (signal) that is transmitted over a medium—air or copper

Digital Signals Digital signals represents information that is represented as a set of discrete values (mostly 0's and 1's)

Security Controls Security controls are set of actions that prevent unauthorized access to certain physical and/or digital asset. Security controls can be physical (e.g., a bolted door) and digital (e.g., id and password)

Hacking Hacking is the process to gain illegal access to corporate digital assets

Demilitarized Zones (DMZ) A DMZ allows various devices and their users to be visible and available to each other for performing tasks and providing services

16.3 Legislation and policy

The United States has enacted certain laws that affect the implementation of various systems in a smart healthcare environment. While the laws are implemented by the Congress of the United States at the federal level, the Congress has deferred the recommendation of various security controls to the National Institute of Science and Technology (NIST) (www.nist.gov). In this section we will provide a brief overview of various laws, regulations, and recommendations that are relevant to identifying various threats to security and privacy of such systems. Note that while such laws are enacted by federal government of the United States, they remain highly relevant and applicable in a global environment. In fact NIST specifically mentions that such standards can be adopted by any government or organization interested in applying security controls and risk management mechanisms.

16.3.1 Privacy rule in Health Insurance and Portability Accountability Act

The HIPAA law was enacted to protect the health insurance coverage and health data integrity, availability, and confidentiality (https://www.gpo.gov/fdsys/pkg/BILLS-104s1028is/pdf/BILLS-104s1028is.pdf). The HIPAA legislation aims at empowering the patient and gives various options to the patient. The salient features of these rules can be characterized as follows:

- The individual has the ability to choose how their health information is exchanged individually.
- The individual is provided all the necessary information specific to his/her health information.
- The individual is informed clearly regarding the context in which the information will be exchanged and more importantly the purpose for which it is being shared.
- The individual has the ability to choose the level of detail in terms of the patient information that can be exchanged.
- The individual is given the right to place certain restrictions on their records.

The HIPAA law places restrictions on both health practitioners and information systems that are in place. The health practitioners are given clear guidelines in terms of how such information should be handled or shared. This includes clear instructions on ensuring that individual credentials used to access the healthcare systems are not shared and intended for the sole purpose of the health practitioner only. However, the healthcare practitioners do not comprehend the nature of risks involved when storing information in a digital format and are usually lulled in a false sense of security given the authorization process put in place.

The information technology (IT) practitioners are responsible for ensuring how the data are stored and transmitted in a safe manner (referred to as data at rest and data in motion, respectively). Section 16.5 discusses various scenarios under which such data can be compromised.

16.3.2 Federal Information Security Management Act of 2002

The FISMA act (also known as the E-Government Act of 2002) officially recognized and encouraged the use of various E-Government services that were (or were planned to be in place) (https://csrc.nist.gov/topics/laws-and-regulations/laws/fisma). The act empowered the Federal Chief Information Officer's powers and required the person holding this position to collaborate with the CIOs of various government entities. The law also mandated the use of Enterprise Architecture across various federal agencies. Furthermore, the law recognized the networked nature of the various IT systems in place and the need to put security controls in place that will help the various agencies manage threats and risks to the organization.

While certain hospitals and healthcare entities might not fall under the umbrella of federal organizations, the FISMA act coupled with the HIPAA directive effectively forced all healthcare organizations to put measures in place to safeguard the privacy and security of patients' data. The FISMA act assigned specific responsibilities to both Office of the Management Budget (OMB) and National Institute of Science and Technology (NIST). OMB was delegated the responsibility to monitor the implementation of the FISMA act. NIST—a nonregulatory body under the US Department of Commerce—was assigned the task of developing various standards and policies that would help government agencies to put information security controls in place.

NIST publishes two set of documents that aim at ensuring the compliance with the FISMA act. These set of documents are called the Federal Information Processing Standards (FIPS) series and the Special Publications 800 (SP-800) series. The FIPS series is a list of standards that the federal agencies need to comply with. The SP-800 series recommends various controls that can be implemented on the basis of the risk profile of the information systems and the organization. The following table lists the important documents in the two series (https://csrc.nist.gov/publications/fips; https://csrc.nist.gov/publications/sp800).

Title	Description
FIPS-140	Security Requirements for Cryptography Modules
FIPS-199	Standards for Security Categorization of Federal Information and Information Systems
FIPS 200	Minimum Security Requirements for Federal Information and Information Systems
FIPS 201	Personal Identity Verification for Employees and Contractors
SP800-12	An Introduction to Information Security
SP800-18	Guide for Developing Security Plans for Federal Information Systems
SP800-30	Guide for Conducting Risk Assessments

(Continued)

(Continued)

Title	Description
SP800-32	Introduction to Public Key Technology and the Federal PKI
SP800-37	Risk Management Framework for Information Systems and Organizations: A System Life Cycle Approach for Security and Privacy
SP800-39	Managing Information Security Risk: Organization, Mission, and Information System View
SP800-46	Guide to Enterprise Telework, Remote Access, and Bring Your Own Device (BYOD) Security
SP800-53	Security and Privacy Controls for Federal Information Systems and Organizations
SP800-66	An Introductory Resource Guide for Implementing the Health Insurance Portability and Accountability Act (HIPAA) Security Rule
SP800-121	Guide to Bluetooth Security
SP800-183	Networks of "Things"
SP800-187	Guide to LTE Security

Specifically, the FISMA act focuses on the following:

1. Recognize the highly networked nature of the federal systems and the underlying security vulnerabilities.
2. Perform an inventory of all the information systems that are being utilized in the government agency.
3. Categorize the information systems according to the risks they are exposed to and in turn expose the organization to various vulnerabilities and threats.
4. Each federal organization has to put in a minimum set of security controls in place as specified in FIPS 200 (https://www.nist.gov/publications/minimum-security-requirements-federal-information-and-information-systems-federal).
5. After the categorization and putting the minimum set of security controls, the organization will perform a risk assessment to identify further risks to the information systems and the organization. Based on such assessment, the organization will choose additional controls per the NIST 800-53 standards (https://csrc.nist.gov/publications/detail/sp/800-53/rev-4/final).
6. Once the risk assessment is finalized, a system security plan is established per the NIST 800-18 standard (https://csrc.nist.gov/publications/detail/sp/800-12/rev-1/final).
7. The information system in question is certified once all the security controls are deemed functional.
8. Lastly, FISMA requires continuous monitoring to ensure that the security controls continue to function as required.

16.3.3 Cyber Enhancement Act 2014

The Cyber Enhancement Act (CEA) of 2014 (https://www.gpo.gov/fdsys/pkg/PLAW-113publ283/pdf/PLAW-113publ283.pdf) augments the FISMA 2002 Act (https://csrc.nist.

gov/topics/laws-and-regulations/laws/fisma) and emphasizes further areas of focus. The following list contains some of the salient features of this act (not all inclusive):

1. The critical infrastructure contains both the physical and the digital assets of the US government in alignment with the US Patriot Act (https://www.gpo.gov/fdsys/pkg/PLAW-107publ56/pdf/PLAW-107publ56.pdf).
2. Importance of the NIST standards that had been and continue to be published and the role it played in securing the federal systems.
3. Guidelines to conduct further research in cybersecurity that should include:
   a. Testing of complex software systems
   b. Testing of both hardware and software that meets the security requirements (this include both locally developed and acquired)
   c. Guarantee the privacy of the individuals
   d. Determine the origin of the message on the Internet
   e. Build new security-aware protocols
   f. Address the problem of insider-threat
   g. Protect information transmitted to and stored in the cloud
   h. Improve the consumer education.
4. Improve the cybersecurity education at all levels including school, college, and professional education.
5. Improve the cybersecurity awareness programs. This includes:
   a. Ensuring the wide spread dissemination of cybersecurity standards
   b. Ensuring that such standards are usable by various individuals
   c. Clear guidelines on how to act in case of security breaches.
6. Continue the advancement of technical standards.

16.3.4 NIST Cyber Security Framework

Recognizing the importance of the role that private organizations play in building federal information systems and the lack of interoperability and understanding globally, NIST published the Cyber Security Framework in 2014 (https://www.nist.gov/cyberframework/framework-version-10) and augmented in 2018 (https://www.nist.gov/cyberframework/new-framework), the guide divides the cybersecurity activities into the following broad categories—termed as the Framework Core.

1. Identify: The goal of this category is to identify various elements of the people, process, and technology framework that can add risk to the organization profile.
2. Protect: This category hones on the controls that are needed to minimize the risks identified.
3. Detect: This category focuses on various ways to detect the security breaches and incidents that do occur.

4.   Respond: Once a breach and an event does occur, there needs to be mechanisms to respond to such breaches to minimize the damage.
5.   Recover: After responding, isolating, and eliminating the threat vector, this category guides on how to recover and restore information, capabilities, and services that might have been lost.

Under each of the aforementioned categories, NIST defines subcategories that would further enumerate and refine the types of controls being put in place. Furthermore, the list is rounded off by providing references to various standards in literature from which the controls and recommendations are derived.

In addition, the NIST framework defines four tiers that help organizations recognize their implementation profiles. While these tiers are not considered similar to an SEI-CMM maturity levels (Weber, Curtis, & Chrissis, 1994), nevertheless they help the organizations move up the implementation ladder in a systematic manner. The tiers are defined as follows:

1.   Partial: Organizations falling in this tier do not have a formal risk management process and risks are managed in an ad hoc manner.
2.   Risk-informed: The management of organization falling under this tier reckons and emphasizes the effective risk management practices, but such practices are not adopted organization wide.
3.   Repeatable: The risk management practices are defined formally and adopted as a policy organization wide. The risk management is carried on an organization-wide level.
4.   Adaptive: In addition to the above, the organization adopts its cyber security policies and practices based on lessons learned from responding to various events and incidents.

16.4 Typical smart healthcare architecture

As mentioned in Kang et al. (2015), one of the biggest challenges when dealing with patients' data and the underlying privacy is the lack of understanding as to how the information is transmitted and stored via a network. Fig. 16.1 shows a typical smart healthcare environment.

16.4.1 Network layer

As FISMA reckons the networked nature of the prevalent operating environment, the key to a healthcare organization is the network layer. However, we need to distinguish the types of networks that a user is working with.

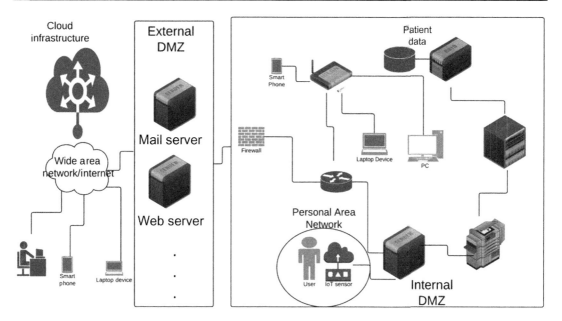

Figure 16.1
A typical smart healthcare architecture.

16.4.1.1 Local Area Network

The LAN environment is the internal network of an organization. People from outside are usually barred to reach the machines that are within a corporate network. A corporate LAN can be both wired and wireless as shown in Fig. 16.1 (the LAN includes both a physical router and WLAN router allowing staff to connect to the local network). A staff member can connect to the internal machines and hence access the resources.

An internal DMZ allows the corporate staff to access the corporate digital resources. Note that for the sake of simplicity, we have only one internal DMZ shown in the corporate LAN displayed in the figure. Thus anyone can access any corporate resource via the corporate network. However, usually more than one internal DMZ's exist on a corporate LAN segregating the type of users. Hence a hospital administrator might be able to access the database server hosting the personal files of all the physicians and nurses in a hospital, but such machine is not reachable for people with physicians' and nurses' credentials'. In this case, the personal files are placed in a DMZ entirely different from the one that the physicians' and nurses' access. Such limitations can be changed in a robust manner by the network administrators based on official authorization from the right person.

Lastly, note that while the access to a corporate LAN was traditionally limited to the enterprise's premises, the past few years allow certain staff members to access the corporate network via a Virtual Private Network (VPN). In simple terms, a link is created on the

Internet that is encrypted and allows the user to access the digital resources remotely. While VPNs are considered safe, we will see in the next section that they can be hacked putting the patients' data at risk.

In addition to the VPN, sometimes organizations allow staff members to connect to their email and access other resources via the Internet. Such services are placed in the external DMZ. The web server, which hosts the official website of the organization, is also placed in the external DMZ allowing any person to access the website globally. A staff member will reach the VPN server via the Internet and after providing their credentials is allowed to access the corporate resources using the VPN. NIST recognized the fact that telecommuting and remote access will be part and parcel of many organization's operating model and recommends various controls to such operations (https://csrc.nist.gov/publications/detail/sp/800-46/rev-2/final).

16.4.1.2 Personal Area Network

A PAN is a much smaller network in terms of range and is limited to within $10-20$ m of the person or device. Such networks have gained popularity recently due to the advances in technology such as Bluetooth. In such a network, a sensor is usually placed on a person or a device that will notice any changes in certain stimuli (e.g., heart rate of a person, temperature of a room) and once a certain threshold is crossed (e.g., heart rate becoming too low), a trigger is activated. Such a trigger would cause an actuator to move and convey the change via the network to the desired parties.

In Fig. 16.1, we have shown the PAN to be part of a corporate network, but it can easily be outside the corporate network. In both the cases, the presence of a network is considered paramount, so the relevant parties can be alerted to the scenario. In more advanced case, an actuator can also administer a certain dose to the patient. The more sophisticated the scenario, higher is the stake for the security and privacy of the data being transmitted.

16.4.1.3 Wide Area Network

Internet is considered a WAN where the users can access the resources globally. Internet is not the only type of WAN as corporations can choose to connect their global locations using a proprietary network. However, with the availability of VPN technology, the word WAN has become synonymous with Internet.

As mentioned in the previous sections, a staff member can be given access to internal resources using the VPN technology. Thus there is almost always a link between the external and internal DMZ (in rare cases, some organizations choose to keep their external and internal DMZs completely separate). Thus the compromising of the link between the WAN and corporate LAN (external and internal DMZs) can potentially become the cause of compromising the patients' data.

16.4.1.4 Public Key Infrastructure

The reader by now can surmise that the information transferred over the network (WAN and LAN) can be subject to compromise. The nature of the Internet and the network protocols is such that the information is transferred in plain text. Anyone using a sniffing tool (covered in next section) can steal the information. The PKI allows the sender to send the information in a secure encrypted manner. NIST publishes and maintains a special document pertaining to PKI security (https://csrc.nist.gov/publications/detail/sp/800-32/final). A PKI can be used both internally and externally and is also known as asymmetric key infrastructure as we will see later.

A PKI requires a third-party certificate authority that issues "certificates" to organizations. Such certificate consists the organization public key. Thus the browser of the user connecting to a website in a secure manner (using the https protocol) would encrypt the messages that are sent using the organization's public key. Once the message is encrypted, the only way to decrypt is to use the organization's private key which is known only to the organization (hence the name asymmetric).

In a healthcare environment, the PKI technology should be used both internally and externally. A physician annotating the patients' records anywhere in the hospital should be fully confident that the information transferred is being done in a secure and encrypted manner. While considered very safe, yet there have been cases where people have been able to break the PKI encryption as we shall see in the next section.

16.4.2 Technology layer

This layer comprises of various devices that make up the healthcare solution. This layer shows the servers, client devices, and the underlying Operating Systems upon which such solutions are offered. The employees connect to various services based on this layer. The devices that act as servers are hosted on the internal DMZ that is either located on premises or in the cloud. A person outside the organization can connect to such devices via servers that are placed on the external DMZ. The servers on the external DMZ after doing proper vetting pass on the request to the ones on the internal DMS. Therefore it is imperative that such devices have proper security controls that cannot be compromised easily.

16.4.3 Applications layer

The internal DMZ hosts various applications that provide services to both internal and external clients. These services can be either acquired as off the shelf or built in-house or a hybrid of both. Such solutions at times can introduce certain security threats that can be exploited by hackers. It is worth noting that a Database Management Software is acquired as part of technology but it is the application layer that populates the database. Needless to say, security controls at the application level need to be designed and implemented with extreme caution.

16.5 Typical security threats

Given the various components of a typical healthcare solution and the numerous layers, one can imagine the vulnerabilities patients' data are exposed too. In this section we will describe a typical hacking process and various security threats that exist. Note that this section describes a typical process and the most common threats that have been faced. This by no means should be considered an all-inclusive and exhaustive list.

16.5.1 Attacks' classification

Before we delve into the actual process of hacking and what it can entail, it would be a good idea to look at the type of attacks that an organization can be subject to. While it is very difficult to list all the attacks, the great majority of attacks can be grouped into the following five categories.

16.5.1.1 Social engineering attacks

The hackers in this category bank on the human psychology factor. The target could be the data of individual himself/herself or the data of the organization he/she works for. Such attacks can take various shapes or forms, for example, someone snooping while watching a victim type their password, asking for personal details such as spouse's name, and using this as the basis of hacking the victim's password (https://www.tripwire.com/state-of-security/security-awareness/5-social-engineering-attacks-to-watch-out-for/). Lists the following five most common attacks that fall under this category.

1. Phishing: A phishing attack involves the victim getting an email or a link that the victim might click. While some attacks are more sophisticated than others, the victim is lulled into thinking that the email comes from a genuine source and the victim accidentally clicks it. The end result could be the user giving their credentials to a particular site (e.g., bank login credentials) or worse allow the hackers to install malicious software (viruses, trojans, and worms) that exposes the victim and possibly their organization. Recall that the NIST standards along with HIPAA and FISMA require that the user should be made aware of the origin of the email.

2. Pretexting: This refers to a hacker who is well aware of the victim and its organization background. They can start off by providing the information that normally only a

genuine person would know (this can be in form of a phone or an email). The goal is to lull the victim into a false sense of security and divulge valuable information that can expose the victim and his/her organization.

3. Baiting: The hackers use this process to manipulate the user to think they are getting something for free. The service could include both physical or virtual media (USB, free movie access, etc.) Many document sharing software are included in this type of attack. Once the user uses the service, the hackers utilize this to install software on the user's end.

4. Quid Pro-Quo: Similar to baiting, this offers free services or benefits in return. An example could be an email promising a credit card with low interest rate. The user will once again fall into a false sense of security that would expose the victim along with their organization.

5. Tailgating: This mostly falls under the physical access to the premise where a hacker follows the victim into trusting the hacker and allow him access to the premises. NIST publishes the FIPS 201 standard that addresses the Personal Identification Verification cards (https://csrc.nist.gov/publications/detail/fips/201/2/final).

16.5.1.2 Insider threats

An insider threat refers to a person who is part of a particular organization and acts in a malicious manner. Such person either gains information that he/she is not authorized for or grants an outsider access to the digital assets of the organization. The Verizon Data Breaches published in 2018 (https://enterprise) reported that 28% of data breaches were a result of insiders divulging corporate information. The insider agent can install unwanted software, pass on valid login credentials, or allow physical access to the premises that will allow the hacker to gain access to the network, understand the solution architecture of the healthcare organization and gain access to patients' data.

16.5.1.3 Denial of Service

The Denial of Service attack involves a hacker overloading the system with so many requests that the service becomes unavailable. As an example, consider a hacker that overloads the network of a hospital with so many requests that the system becomes overloaded and eventually unavailable for the healthcare practitioners to use. The attack can come from both inside or outside of an organization. Such attacks would target the availability of the data and could prove costly to a particular organization that requires real-time access to data. With healthcare organizations depending on real-time alerts for critical-care patients, one can imagine that this could result in irrecoverable loss of life.

16.5.1.4 Viruses, trojans, and worms

A malicious software known as malware is written by hackers with the intention of the victims executing this software. The malwares are classified into three broad categories (https://www.cisco.com/c/en/us/about/security-center/virus-differences.html).

- Virus: Viruses are malicious software that is downloaded on the victim's computer and attaches itself to another program. Thus whenever the victim executes the program in question, the malicious software will execute putting the victim's data at risk.
- Worm: A worm is similar to virus in the sense that it is malicious software that the hacker somehow manages to install on the victim's machine. However, a worm need not attach itself to any other program and can run independently. In addition, it has the ability to replicate itself and spread to other devices that are present on the network.
- Trojan: A trojan is a software that will give access to outsiders once it is downloaded to a victim's computer. A staff member connected to a corporate network would inadvertently provide a window to the outside hacker who can gain unfettered access to the corporate resources.

16.5.1.5 Typical hacking process

As noted in Section 16.2, hacking is the process of disrupting or gaining illegal access to a service. The increased awareness of various security threats and the plethora of security controls put in place (most of the time such controls are mandated by legislation described in Section 16.3), the hackers need to have a masterclass understanding of various layers of typical solution put in place. Moreover, the hackers are quite well versed in psychology of humans when it comes to using systems and they can use this coupled with their technical understanding to gain illegal access to patients' data. Once they find a particular vulnerability, the hackers exploit it to expose and gain a foothold inside the organization's digital assets. The end goal can vary depending on the hacker(s) as some perform these types of attacks to disrupt operations while the rest are content to see this as a personal challenge.

A typical hacking attack usually goes through the following lifecycle.

1. Reconnaissance: In this step, the hacker would engage in active and passive information gathering regarding the target. The active information gathering involves scavenging information on the Internet where many blogs and social media sites might contain sensitive information posted by a staff member (grudgingly or by mistake). Once this is complete, the hacker would start gathering information that needs to be public because of the Internet infrastructure. One example of this is the Domain Name Service where the Internet Assigned Numbers Authority (IANA) maintains a list of the domain names coupled with the public IP addresses (https://www.iana.org/). A browser requesting a site (e.g., www.whitehouse.gov) would send a request to IANA who would translate the name to an IP address. The browser will in turn send the user request to the desired IP address. Note that this IP address is the same as the web server of the organization that is placed in the external DMZ of the victim organization. Such harvesting can also include list of emails of the employees of an organization that can be sent a Phishing request.

2. Enumeration/foot-printing: This step requires the hacker to scan for vulnerabilities in the victim's organization. Specifically, the vulnerabilities that need to be exploited exist at three layers namely (1) the network, (2) the devices, and (3) the applications. The end goal of such vulnerabilities is to reach the database server(s) that contain the patients' information. The communication is carried at the network level using "ports" which are a gateway to various devices. Thus a webserver would usually open port 80 that would allow the traffic to pass to and from the webserver. All the devices that communicate with each other do so using the same concept. A scanner allows the hacker to find out the ports open on the victim's organization infrastructure that can be used to exploit. Furthermore, the attacker would also try to gage the type of Commercial Off the Shelf Software (COTS) running on the victim's organization. The COTS usually have known vulnerabilities that can be a boon to a hacker.

3. Identifying vulnerabilities: Once the attacker has pinpointed the open ports and other relevant information, the hacker would look for vulnerabilities that they can exploit. Thus an organization running an older version of COTS expose itself to an opening that the hackers can use. The hacker would compile a list of possible vulnerabilities that they can use to gain unauthorized access to the organization's digital resources.

4. Carrying out the attack: The hacker would go through each vulnerability and choose an appropriate attack vector that can exploit that particular vulnerability. These can include weak passwords, unpatched software (software that is not updated to close any security loopholes), and lack of firewall to name a few. Listed below is a classification of common attacks that the hackers employ.

   a. Network attacks: These attacks are directed toward the vulnerabilities in the network. An attacker might discover a port that was left open by accident and can send malware that can reach the devices on the corporate network. Gaining access to the corporate network—entire or partial—will result in exposing the devices that are on the internal DMZ and were hidden from the world otherwise. The detailed discussion of this topic is beyond the scope of this work, but network attacks are considered the bread and butter of the hackers.

   b. Misconfiguration of devices: The devices on the network can be misconfigured thus exposing the digital assets to danger. A firewall that might not filter the traffic appropriately can pass on a malicious software to the internal DMZ thus exposing the corporate digital assets.

   c. Operating Systems attacks: Hackers who are well aware of the intricacies of the Operating Systems running on devices can exploit a known vulnerability that can allow them access to the corporate network and the corporate digital assets in turn. Note that the Operating System is the link between the software and the hardware and any inherent vulnerability can prove to be catastrophic.

   d. Application-specific attacks: These are attacks directed at various COTS product and their respective customization. For example, Microsoft's SharePoint product (https://products.office.com/en-us/sharepoint/collaboration) is used by many organizations to implement the external and internal portal capabilities. Such COTS products are customized by individual organizations to match their requirements and needs. In such cases, the COTS product might have an inherent vulnerability, or the customized version introduces one. The hackers attack such vulnerabilities to gain control of the software that they can either exploit directly or use as a channel to reach the Operating System and in turn the network.

e. IoT attacks: Given the nascent nature of PANs and the IoT devices, the security profile of these devices and network is not as mature as those on LANs and WANs. Hence a hacker outside a corporate network will focus on breaking an IoT device that would grant them access to the corporate network. It is worth noting that the protocols used for the PANs are different than the ones used in traditional networks and are bridged to the traditional network protocols such as Internet Protocol (IP), User Datagram Protocol (UDP), and Transmission Control Protocol (TCP).

f. Password hacking/sniffing: There are many tools available that can help a hacker break the passwords of various users. The compromising of user credentials opens the corporate network to the hacker. If the passwords are sent as clear text, the hacker can sniff the passwords using various tools and man in the middle attacks.

g. VPN and SSL hacking: While this task can be a bit difficult, both the VPN and SSL technologies can be hacked using certain tools that are available to the hacker.

The Open Web Application Security Project is a not-for-profit organization that lists the most common vulnerabilities and various resources to educate and remedy such vulnerabilities (http://owasp.org). Various organizations have made it a habit to employ ethical hackers who would perform penetration testing on corporate assets to expose the various vulnerabilities to the management. The management takes appropriate corrective actions to mitigate the risks that such vulnerabilities bring to an organization.

16.6 Conclusion

The challenges to preserving the patients' data security and privacy are quite a few. However, a thorough understanding of relevant legislation, policies and procedures coupled with the comprehension of various threats and tools a hacker can use is the first step to tackle such challenges. In this chapter, we have introduced the relevant laws and regulations that are in place. Furthermore, we described a typical smart healthcare environment and its various components. Finally, we provided an overview of a typical hacking process, common threat vectors and the types of attacks a hacker can use to expose the patients' data. A logical next step would be to provide an overview of different ways that can mitigate and minimize the risks posed by such attacks.

16.6.1 Future research directions

One of the areas that need exploration is the effect of IoT devices in healthcare. Patients' data are being transferred over various networks and they remain to be seen whether there could be potential for HIPAA violations.

Another area that should be explored is the discussion/sharing of patients' information on various social media sites by healthcare professionals. One example is discussion between physicians/healthcare professionals regarding patients' conditions on WhatsApp application. It will be an interesting exercise to gather data from Physicians' WhatsApp applications.

Lastly, Body Area Networks have been getting lot of attention in the medical domain especially with the focus on telemedicine. There is a need to see what are the privacy implications in such circumstances.

16.6.2 Teaching assignments

- Application of HIPAA laws to IoT devices
- WhatsApp use by healthcare professionals to discuss/exchange patients' data
- Suitability of PKI to IoT devices

References

Ashton, K. (2009). That 'internet of things' thing. *RFID Journal, 22*(7), 97−114.

Doukas, C., Metsis, V., Becker, E., Le, Z., Makedon, F., & Maglogiannis, I. (2011). Digital cities of the future: Extending @home assistive technologies for the elderly and the disabled. *Telematics and Informatics, 28* (3), 176−190.

Huang, L. C., Chu, H. C., Lien, C. Y., Hsiao, C. H., & Kao, T. (2009). Privacy preservation and information security protection for patients' portable electronic health records. *Computers in Biology and Medicine, 39* (9), 743−750.

Hussain, A., Wenbi, R., da Silva, A. L., Nadher, M., & Mudhish, M. (2015). Health and emergency-care platform for the elderly and disabled people in the Smart City. *Journal of Systems and Software, 110*, 253−263.

Ibraimi, L., Asim, M., & Petković, M. (2009). *Secure management of personal health records by applying attribute-based encryption.* 2009 6th international workshop on wearable micro and nano technologies for personalized health (pHealth) (pp. 71−74). IEEE.

Kang, R., Dabbish, L., Fruchter, N., & Kiesler, S. (2015). *My data just goes everywhere: User mental models of the internet and implications for privacy and security. Symposium on usable privacy and security (SOUPS)* (pp. 39−52). Berkeley, CA: USENIX Association.

Lassila, O., & Hendler, J. (2007). Embracing "Web 3.0". *IEEE Internet Computing, 11*(3), 90−93.

Piro, G., Cianci, I., Grieco, L. A., Boggia, G., & Camarda, P. (2014). Information centric services in smart cities. *Journal of Systems and Software, 88,* 169–188.

Rajput, A. E., & Ahmed, S. E. (2019a). Making a case for social media corpus for detecting depression. arXiv preprint arXiv:1902.00702.

Rajput, A. E., & Ahmed, S. M. (2019b) Big Data and social/medical sciences: State of the art and future trends. arXiv preprint arXiv:1902.00705.

Rajput, A., & Brahimi, T. (2019). Characterizing IOMT/personal area networks landscape. In M. Lytras, et al. (Eds.), *Innovation in health informatics: A smart healthcare primer.* Amsterdam, Netherlands: Elsevier. (earlier version available as arXiv preprint arXiv:1902.00675).

Wang, H., Wu, Q., Qin, B., & Domingo-Ferrer, J. (2014). FRR: Fair remote retrieval of outsourced private medical records in electronic health networks. *Journal of Biomedical Informatics, 50,* 226–233.

Weber, C., Curtis, B., & Chrissis, M. B. (1994). *The capability maturity model, guidelines for improving the software process. Harlow:* Addison Wesley.

Further reading

Acquisti, A., Brandimarte, L., & Loewenstein, G. (2015). Privacy and human behavior in the age of information. *Science, 347*(6221), 509–514.

Anwar, M., Joshi, J., & Tan, J. (2015). Anytime, anywhere access to secure, privacy-aware healthcare services: Issues, approaches and challenges. *Health Policy and Technology, 4*(4), 299–311.

Arias, O., Wurm, J., Hoang, K., & Jin, Y. (2015). Privacy and security in internet of things and wearable devices. *IEEE Transactions on Multi-Scale Computing Systems, 1*(2), 99–109.

Avelar, E., Marques, L., dos Passos, D., Macedo, R., Dias, K., & Nogueira, M. (2015). Interoperability issues on heterogeneous wireless communication for smart cities. *Computer Communications, 58,* 4–15.

Farooq, M. U., Waseem, M., Khairi, A., & Mazhar, S. (2015). A critical analysis on the security concerns of internet of things (IoT). *International Journal of Computer Applications, 111*(7), 1–6.

Fernández-Alemán, J. L., Señor, I. C., Lozoya, P. Á. O., & Toval, A. (2013). Security and privacy in electronic health records: A systematic literature review. *Journal of Biomedical Informatics, 46*(3), 541–562.

Furnell, S. M., Bryant, P., & Phippen, A. D. (2007). Assessing the security perceptions of personal Internet users. *Computers & Security, 26*(5), 410–417.

Guo, L., Zhang, C., Sun, J., & Fang, Y. (2014). A privacy-preserving attribute-based authentication system for mobile health networks. *IEEE Transactions on Mobile Computing, 13*(9), 1927–1941.

Haas, S., Wohlgemuth, S., Echizen, I., Sonehara, N., & Müller, G. (2011). Aspects of privacy for electronic health records. *International Journal of Medical Informatics, 80*(2), e26–e31.

Hargittai, E. (2010). Facebook privacy settings: Who cares? *First Monday, 15*(8).

Huang, L. C., Chu, H. C., Lien, C. Y., Hsiao, C. H., & Kao, T. (2009). Privacy preservation and information security protection for patients' portable electronic health records. *Computers in Biology and Medicine, 39* (9), 743–750.

Kargupta, H., Das, K., & Liu, K. (2007, September). *Multi-party, privacy-preserving distributed data mining using a game theoretic framework. European conference on principles of data mining and knowledge discovery* (pp. 523–531). Berlin, Heidelberg: Springer.

Nico, P. L., Turner, C. S., & Nico, K. K. (2004, November). Insecurity by contract. In: *IASTED conference on software engineering and applications* (pp. 269–274).

Rajput, A. (2019). Natural language processing, sentiment analysis and clinical analytics. In M. Lytras, et al. (Eds.), *Innovation in health informatics: A smart healthcare primer.* Amsterdam, Netherlands: Elsevier. (earlier version available as arXiv preprint arXiv:1902.00679).

Sadan, B. (2001). Patient data confidentiality and patient rights. *International Journal of Medical Informatics, 62*(1), 41–49.

Sahi, A., Lai, D., & Li, Y. (2016). Security and privacy preserving approaches in the eHealth clouds with disaster recovery plan. *Computers in Biology and Medicine, 78*, 1−8.

Sweeney, L. (2002). k-Anonymity: A model for protecting privacy. *International Journal of Uncertainty, Fuzziness and Knowledge-Based Systems, 10*(5), 557−570.

Williams, P. A., & Woodward, A. J. (2015). Cybersecurity vulnerabilities in medical devices: A complex environment and multifaceted problem. *Medical Devices (Auckland, NZ), 8*, 305.

Wu, R. (2012). *Secure sharing of electronic medical records in cloud computing.* Arizona State University.

Xu, L., Jiang, C., Wang, J., Yuan, J., & Ren, Y. (2014). Information security in big data: Privacy and data mining. *IEEE Access, 2*, 1149−1176.

Yüksel, B., Küpçü, A., & Özkasap, Ö. (2017). Research issues for privacy and security of electronic health services. *Future Generation Computer Systems, 68*, 1−13.

Ziegeldorf, J. H., Morchon, O. G., & Wehrle, K. (2014). Privacy in the Internet of Things: Threats and challenges. *Security and Communication Networks, 7*(12), 2728−2742.

CHAPTER 17

Policy implications for smart healthcare: the international collaboration dimension

Miltiadis D. Lytras[1,2], Akila Sarirete[2] and Vassilios Stasinopoulos[3]

[1]*Deree College—The American College of Greece, Athens, Greece,* [2]*Effat College of Engineering, Effat University, Jeddah, Saudi Arabia,* [3]*Frederick University, Limmasol, Cyprus*

17.1 Introduction

The recent evolution of information and communication technology (ICT) leads to a significant shift in the agenda and promise of medical informatics. Smart healthcare is promoted as a unified paradigm of novel insights for personalized medicine worldwide. In this era of early adoption, investments in medical informatics, especially in the context of research and development projects as well as in commercialized technologies, envision the ultimate objective: to facilitate a sociotechnological ecosystem of data, services, applications, and applied medical systems for the promotion of health and wellbeing. The purpose of this concluding chapter is to set up a context for further dialog related to the integration of innovation in medical systems and advanced policy making.

17.2 The smart healthcare utilization framework

The current debate on innovation in the context of smart healthcare (Meulendijk et al., 2016; Spruit & Lytras, 2018; Spruit, Vroon, & Batenburg, 2014) challenges the design of personalized medical systems, capable of materializing measurable goals to services, and highly performing applications (Agyeman & Ofori-Asenso, 2015). The governance of this complicated sociotechnical healthcare system requires sophisticated governance with well-defined key performance indicators, as well as analytics and control variables. Thus the policy implications for smart healthcare need a critical relevance to significant societal goals, toward wellbeing, health, and safety of citizens. The prelude of smart healthcare research and innovations in smart healthcare needs to be anchored in a thorough understanding of the new wave of technological innovations, together with a joint analysis of the latest challenges in healthcare systems.

Innovation in Health Informatics.
DOI: https://doi.org/10.1016/B978-0-12-819043-2.00017-4

In another critical dimension, the utilization of budget and resources spent for Health and Innovation in Smart Healthcare has to consider the international dimension. The creation of competence centers, the reusability of best practices, and the exploitation of a global-wide data-driven ecosystem of healthcare decision-making are just few of the new arrivals in the agenda of smart healthcare.

Thus the recently well-received discussion and research on Smart Cities and Sustainable Development has to promote the integration of smart healthcare within the social impact and global outreach context. Health is a social good and the beneficiaries of innovations in medical informatics have to promote the greatest inclusivity. From this perspective, any significant contribution in Innovations in Smart Helathcare requires inter- and multidisciplinary approaches (Visvizi & Lytras, 2018).

In Fig. 17.1, we summarize what we call "The smart healthcare utilization framework." The policy-making quest for the promotion of smart healthcare serves as a holistic quality and control layer that utilizes all the resources available.

This concluding chapter sets the basis for the dialog, we intend to promote in this book series. From a policy-making perspective, we interpret healthcare as a synergetic and collaborative system of systems. Within this sytem eight different types of resources are cooperating and synchronized toward high effective personalized medicine and healthcare:

- Patients: The Human factor and the focus of innovative solutions and medical innovation
- Medicine: The new ideas for personalized medicine, as a combination and value carrier of advanced sophisticated research, treatment, and decision-making capabilities
- Human resources: Including doctors, medical staff, and managers as well as policy makers and experts
- Medical education: As a technology-driven and applied research-led mechanism and strategy for the diffusion of novel knowledge and its application to relevant medical contexts

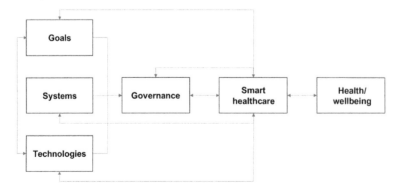

Figure 17.1
The utilization framework for smart healthcare.

- Infrastructures: The required investment-led establishments, architectural designs, buildings, systems, and global-wide interconnections.
- Technology: The constitutional technological parts, of medical innovations, including numerous emerging and streamline technologies:
  - Data warehouses
  - Robotics
  - Big Data Analytics
  - Cloud Computing
  - 5G networks
  - Anticipatory Computing
  - Cognitive Computing and Artificial Intelligence (AI)
  - Virtual reality
  - Blockchain
  - Data Privacy and Security
  - Interoperability
- Governance: Includes the applied management of the utilization framework, as shown in Fig. 17.1. It is one of the most sophisticated factors in healthcare. We plan to dedicate one of the forthcoming books in our series to Healthcare Innovation Management and Governance.
- Research: This is the high-impact factor of the entire ecosystem. The promotion, conduct, facilitation, and exploitation of medical research in our times need to be seen at a global scale. The bold solution and treatment to major diseases needs a worldwide collaboration framework and support environment.
- Innovation: Medical innovation is as sophisticated as the entire ecosystem. We have to understand that technology is only an enabler of innovation, and the integration of multi- and interdisciplinary research in all the other dimensions of factors that appear in Fig. 17.2 is a key challenge towards smart healthcare evolution.

The ultimate vision of this book series is to set an evolutionary process for resilient smart healthcare (Fig. 17.3). Two key dimensions define an evolutionary process: Resilient Policy Focus and Evolution/Sustainability. We plan to analyze further this process in a forthcoming edition but the main idea is that ICT beyond their radical innovation character, continuously support a digital transformation of healthcare process. Within this process, some maturity stages justify the depth and breadth of the integration of technology, governance, and health sophistication and performance. It is extremely important to understand that in our days the international dimension and collaboration is one of the most critical factors for resilient smart healthcare.

In the next section, we provide some of our ideas about the required critical international collaboration dimension for resilient smart healthcare.

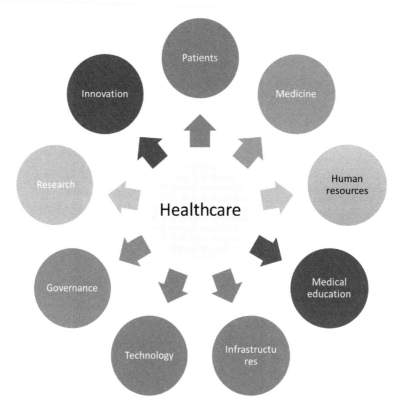

Figure 17.2
Healthcare as a synergetic and collaborative system of systems.

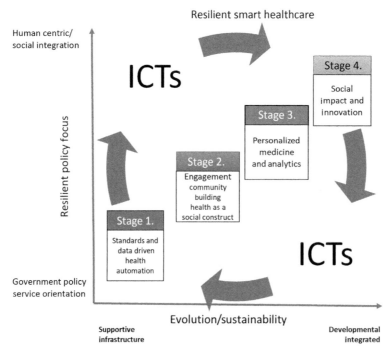

Figure 17.3
An evolutionary process for resilient smart healthcare.

17.3 International collaboration for resilient smart healthcare

Medical innovation and technology-driven-innovation for smart healthcare are extremely complicated systems for analysis. The variety of actors, resources, and technology sophistication as well as the requirement to comply with standards, governmental policies and regulations sets a demanding framework for utilization.

In our book series, we emphasize on research-led medical innovations highlighting the necessity to put together researchers, actors, and medical experts in the same coworking, collaborating team worldwide toward high-impact healthcare services with social impact and value. The current debate on the social impact for example of Big Data research (Spruit & Lytras, 2018) or the latest developments of Artificial Intelligence Research in Healthcare (Chui & Lytras, 2019) pose critical questions: How can we extend the beneficiaries of medical innovations? How countries without the same sophistication and research excellence in medical innovation can also exploit the benefit of resilient healthcare and best practices.

To our understanding within this context, there is fertile ground for joint, collaborative initiatives, and shared services. We can vision a holistic global ecosystem of systems for medical innovations, where different business models with scalable social and economic impact can cooperate. Consider the following example: in a country like Greece, we need a sophisticated Big Data Analytics service for healthcare that exists in United States. The question that arises is the following: Is it possible to deploy the same system that successfully works locally, and which are the requirements for this integration and transition at local context?

In Fig. 17.4, the overall idea is medical innovations as services or applications require efficient, sustainable business model. The launch in to the healthcare market of advanced innovations requires feasibility studies, business plans, and flexible business models. For sure, a very simplistic approach would be to consider local and global business models. For example, consider a Virtual Reality enabled service powered by a company that offers worldwide 3D representations of clinical surgeries. Or an Artificial Intelligence system powered by machine learning algorithms for personalized medicine. The dimension of social economic impact refers to governance and policy making. Various significant goals and objectives for resilient smart healthcare can be included in this dimension. In the simplistic version of Fig. 17.4, we only included four of them namely treatment, prevention, awareness, and global act.

In the next scheduled books, we plan to focus on several of the key technologies of our times and their contribution and impact for resilient smart healthcare (Fig. 17.5).

The constitutional technological parts, of medical innovations, including numerous emerging and streamline technologies as discussed in previous chapters, have significant policy implications. For the sake of the scientific dialog and further research in Table 17.1, we highlight some key ideas.

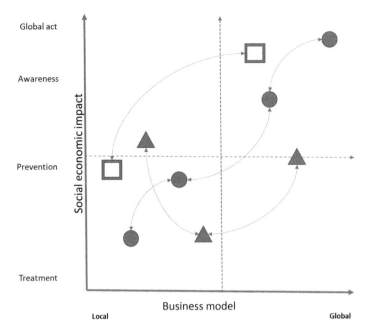

Figure 17.4
A holistic global ecosystem of system of systems for medical innovations.

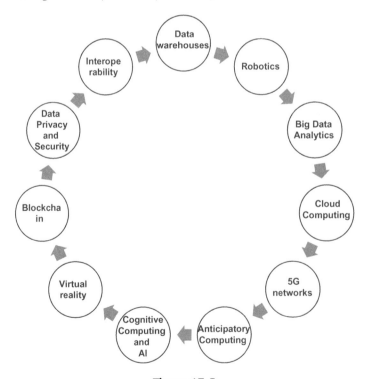

Figure 17.5
Technologies with a great impact on resilient smart healthcare.

Table 17.1 Smart healthcare-related Policy implications based on emerging technologies.

Technologies (ICT)	Policy and technology implications
Data warehouses	Interoperability of patients data worldwide
	Compliance of healthcare systems to General Data Protection Regulation (GDPR)
Robotics	Standardization
	Moral issues related to use of robotics in healthcare
Big Data Analytics	Decision driven medicine regulations
	Design of key performance indicators (KPIs) and analytics for health decision-making
Cloud Computing	Data protection
	Healthcare as a service
	Healthcare as an infrastructure in the cloud
	Policies for distributed healthcare services on the cloud
5G networks	On demand resilient healthcare services
Anticipatory Computing	Opinion mining and sentiment analysis of policy awareness for resilient smart healthcare
Cognitive Computing and AI	Artificial intelligence for personalized medicine
	AI for healthcare budgeting and control
	AI for health recommendation services
Virtual reality	VR for medical education
	VR labs
Blockchain	Trusted healthcare networks for personalized services
	Advanced privacy and security for smart resilient healthcare
Data Privacy and Security	Regulation frameworks
	Interoperability of healthcare records
Interoperability	Interoperability of services, data, applications

It was a great pleasure to work on this inaugural volume in our new book series in Elsevier. The next book on process is entitled *Big Data and Analytics for Smart Healthcare* and it is planned for publication on Spring 2020.

References

Agyeman, A., & Ofori-Asenso, R. (2015). Perspective: Does personalized medicine hold the future for medicine? *Journal of Pharmacy & BioAllied Sciences, 7*(3), 239.

Chui, K., & Lytras, M. (2019). A novel MOGA-SVM multinomial classification for organ inflammation detection. *Applied Sciences, 9*(11), 2284. Available from http://dx.doi.org/10.3390/app9112284.

Meulendijk, M., Spruit, M., Willeboordse, F., Numans, M., Brinkkemper, S., Knol, W., ... Askari, M. (2016). Efficiency of clinical decision support systems improves with experience. *Journal of Medical Systems, 40*(4), 1−7.

Spruit, M., & Lytras, M. (2018). Applied data science in patient-centric healthcare: Adaptive analytic systems for empowering physicians and patients. *Telematics and Informatics, 35*(4), 643−653. Available from https://doi.org/10.1016/j.tele.2018.04.002.

Spruit, M., Vroon, R., & Batenburg, R. (2014). Towards healthcare business intelligence in long-term care: An explorative case study in the Netherlands. *Computers in Human Behavior, 30*, 698−707.

Visvizi, A., & Lytras, M. D. (2018). It's not a fad: Smart cities and smart villages research in European and global contexts. *Sustainability, 2018*(10), 2727. Available from https://doi.org/10.3390/su10082727.

Further reading

Bibri, S. E., & Krogstieb, J. (2017). Smart sustainable cities of the future: An extensive interdisciplinary literature review. *Sustainable Cities and Society*, *31*, 183−212.

Karvonen, A., Federico, C., & Federico, C. (Eds.), (2018). *Inside smart cities: Place, politics and urban innovation*. London & New York, NY: Routledge.

Lützkendorf, T., & Balouktsi, M. (2017). Assessing a sustainable urban development: Typology of indicators and sources of information. *Procedia Environmental Sciences*, *38*, 546−553.

Lytras, M., Raghavan, V., & Damiani, E. (2017). Big Data and data analytics research: From metaphors to value space for collective wisdom in human decision making and smart machines.. *International Journal on Semantic Web and Information Systems*, *13*(1), 1−10.

Lytras, M. D., & Visvizi, A. (2018). Who uses smart city services and what to make of it: Toward interdisciplinary smart cities research. *Sustainability*, *2018*(10), 1998. Available from https://doi.org/10.3390/su10061998.

Lytras, M. D., Visvizi, A., & Sarirete, A. (2019). Clustering smart city services: Perceptions, expectations, responses. *Sustainability*, *11*(6), 1669.

Visvizi, A., & Lytras, M. (2018). Rescaling and refocusing smart cities research: From mega cities to smart villages. *Journal of Science and Technology Policy Management (JSTPM)*. Available from https://doi.org/10.1108/JSTPM-02-2018-0020.

Visvizi, A., Lytras, M. D., & Mudri, G. (Eds.), (2019). *Smart villages in the EU and beyond*. Bingley, UK: Emerald Publishing. ISBN: 9781787698468 (forthcoming June 2019). Retrieved from: <https://books.emeraldinsight.com/page/detail/Smart-Villages-in-the-EU-and-Beyond/?K = 9781787698468>.

Index

Note: Page numbers followed by "*f*" and "*t*" refer to figures and tables, respectively.